The Battling Bucs of 1925

ALSO BY RONALD T. WALDO
AND FROM McFARLAND

Hazen "Kiki" Cuyler: A Baseball Biography (2012)

*Fred Clarke: A Biography of the
Baseball Hall of Fame Player-Manager* (2011)

The Battling Bucs of 1925

*How the Pittsburgh Pirates
Pulled Off the Greatest Comeback
in World Series History*

RONALD T. WALDO

McFarland & Company, Inc., Publishers
Jefferson, North Carolina, and London

LIBRARY OF CONGRESS CATALOGUING-IN-PUBLICATION DATA

Waldo, Ronald T., 1961–
　　The battling Bucs of 1925 : how the Pittsburgh Pirates pulled off the greatest comeback in world series history / Ronald T. Waldo.
　　　　p.　　cm.
　　Includes bibliographical references and index.

　　ISBN 978-0-7864-6459-3
　　softcover : acid free paper ∞

　　1. Pittsburgh Pirates (Baseball team)— History.
2. World Series (Baseball) (1925)　I. Title.
GV875.P5W35　2012
796.357'640974886 — dc23　　　　　　　　　　2011044173

BRITISH LIBRARY CATALOGUING DATA ARE AVAILABLE

© 2012 Ronald T. Waldo. All rights reserved

No part of this book may be reproduced or transmitted in any form or by any means, electronic or mechanical, including photocopying or recording, or by any information storage and retrieval system, without permission in writing from the publisher.

Front cover image: Pirates team photograph, 1925 (National Baseball Hall of Fame Library, Cooperstown, New York); cover design by David K. Landis (Shake It Loose Graphics)

Manufactured in the United States of America

McFarland & Company, Inc., Publishers
　Box 611, Jefferson, North Carolina 28640
　　www.mcfarlandpub.com

To the memories of
my uncle, George Wallace, and my aunt, Irene Waldo,
who both passed away in 2010

Table of Contents

Preface 1

1. Gaining Valuable Experience in a Tight Pennant Race 5
2. Building a Team to End New York's Dynasty 22
3. Spring Training at Paso Robles 38
4. A Sluggish Start 54
5. Booming Bats Lead to a Turnaround 70
6. Battling New York for the Top Spot 86
7. The Pennant Race Tightens 102
8. Putting a Stranglehold on First 117
9. Clinching the National League Pennant 133
10. Game One to Washington, Game Two to Pittsburgh 149
11. Washington Grabs Control 164
12. Pittsburgh Battles Back 179
13. Carey and the Pirates Overcome Johnson and the Weather 196
14. Champions of the World 213
15. The Champions' Troubles in '26 228

Appendix A: 1925 Pittsburgh Pirates Statistics 245
Appendix B: 1925 World Series Box Scores 247
Appendix C: 1925 World Series Statistics 254
Chapter Notes 256
Bibliography 278
Index 279

Preface

The 1920s were a magical era in history when prosperity led to opulence and excessively lavish lifestyles for a new breed of Americans. The Roaring Twenties were a time when people partied, drank, danced and generally celebrated life to the fullest. Prohibition was still in effect, but this did not stop the masses from consuming illegal bootleg liquor. The social role of a woman was turned upside-down by flapper girls who did things that were frowned upon only a few years earlier. During this period of celebration and economic success, baseball changed and grew just as the country did. Baseball fans were devoted to their teams and many who played the game were influenced by the same vices that tempted the average American. During the 1920s, baseball games were important social events, part of the very fabric of the national culture.

Pittsburgh was still the steel capital of the world during the Roaring Twenties. The town was populated by hard-working people who loved to play hard when recreation time rolled around. Police struggled to stay a step ahead of bootleggers. Crime in Pittsburgh may not have been as bad as the days of gunfighters in the Wild West, but it was rampant enough that thieves and burglars were referred to as "bandits" by local newspapers. Pittsburgh's populace, both rich and poor, enjoyed leisure activities, just like the inhabitants of any other major city in America. Baseball was one such satisfying outlet, and the Smoky City's population loved their Pittsburgh Pirates.

The Pirates were a team that underachieved during the first five years of the decade. They came close to winning the National League pennant in 1921 and 1924 but faded as the rival New York Giants grabbed the flag both seasons. Throughout the decade, Pittsburgh's players were criticized for lacking the courage and tenacity to claim the pennant. Even though Pittsburgh's fans were sometimes tougher on their own players than those from opposing teams, they quickly jumped to the aid of their favorite sons when outside forces offered negative opinions about the Pirates. By 1925, Pittsburgh owner Barney Dreyfuss had built a team that enjoyed the respect — and sometimes effusive praise — from baseball lovers across the United States.

Various stories in and out of the world of sports made headlines in 1925. Football coach Walter Camp passed away in March, and by December, controversy would dog the NFL after the league title was awarded to the Chicago Cardinals, who had been beaten badly by another two-loss team, the Pottsville (PA) Maroons. In May, Roald Amundsen and two other men flew two airplanes from Alaska to the North Pole. The famous Scopes trial began in July as John Thomas Scopes was indicted by the State of Tennessee for teaching evolution in a local school. Six days after the trial ended, prosecutor and famous American politician William Jennings Bryan passed away at a house in the hills of Tennessee. While these important events were going on throughout the world, stories were written in Pittsburgh newspapers that covered the local team's magical baseball campaign in 1925. Baseball fans throughout the Smoky City cheered their team as they reached the pinnacle of baseball supremacy, first ending New York's four-year stranglehold on the National League pennant and then defeating the Washington Senators in one of the most exciting World Series in baseball history.

The accomplishments of this championship club seem to be forgotten when Pittsburgh's baseball history is discussed. The 1960 Pirates World Series victory has become iconic, thanks in part to Bill Mazeroski's Game 7 blast. The championship in 1971 is remembered as Roberto Clemente's personal showcase, and Pittsburgh's last World Series victory in 1979 is still on the minds of historians because of Willie Stargell and "We Are Family." Moreover, the 1903 Pittsburgh Pirates pennant winners have received a great deal of attention because they played in the first modern World Series, and the 1909 squad gets its proper due for bringing home the franchise's first championship (and its match-up with the Tigers saw the NL's best player, Honus Wagner, go head to head with Ty Cobb, the AL's best). Even the 1927 World Series appearance receives more attention than that of 1925, since Pittsburgh played the most famous Yankees team of all time, the juggernaut that included Babe Ruth, Lou Gehrig, Tony Lazzeri and the rest of Murderer's Row. These pennant-winning teams all deserve their place in baseball history. But for too long the 1925 Pirates have been crowded out of the conversation about Pittsburgh's greatest, most memorable teams.

I have been enamored of Pittsburgh's baseball teams from the 1920s since I was a small boy, when I talked about that era with my grandfather. The pennant-winning seasons from that decade came alive for me just as I hope this book can bring the magical 1925 season back to life for readers over 85 years later.

In 1951, Branch Rickey and Pittsburgh's management held a special reunion with the 1925 team at Forbes Field as part of a season-long celebration commemorating the National League's 75th anniversary. Players from the 1925 team were honored at two games against the Brooklyn Dodgers, on July 31 and August 1. During an open luncheon at the Hotel Schenley where fans could mingle with these great players, one rooter took it upon himself to get a book that I now own autographed by every player and coach who attended the special banquet. Every living member of the team was there, with the exception of two players who could not make the trip. Men like Barney Dreyfuss, his son, Sammy, and star outfielder Hazen "Kiki" Cuyler were honored posthumously during the two-day event.

By 1951, members of this championship team obviously had moved on to different occupations. Some were still involved in baseball as scouts, executives, coaches, managers and sports commentators. Others left baseball and were employed as farmers, store managers, steamfitters, bat manufacturers, government employees, politicians, electricians, postmen, attorneys and real estate brokers. In 1925, fans throughout the Smoky City fell in love with these ballplayers, some of them affectionately referred to as Kiki, Scoops, Pie, Buckshot and Pooch. Twenty-six years later, the city and franchise gave them a proper tribute. Another 60 years have passed, quietly, since.

A number of daily and weekly papers were consulted during the research and writing of this book, none more than *The Pittsburgh Press* and *The Sporting News*. Reading volumes of old articles from *The Press* in particular helped to bring that era of baseball in Pittsburgh to life for me. I feel that this book will likewise bring the 1925 Pirates season to life for those who wish to read about a golden age in Pittsburgh baseball history.

As I look out my window and watch the snow fall, it seems that the most recent baseball season is a distant memory. Hopefully, this work will in some small way allow readers to feel as if they were present to experience that long-ago 1925 season. I may not get the opportunity to experience as many baseball seasons as my grandfather. I just wish I could have witnessed that one great season in 1925, as he did, when the Pittsburgh Pirates became champions of the baseball world.

1

Gaining Valuable Experience in a Tight Pennant Race

During the first decade of the twentieth century, when baseball saw huge growth in popularity across America, the Pittsburgh Pirates were one of the game's premier teams. They won National League pennants in 1901, 1902, 1903 and 1909. Pittsburgh lost in the first modern World Series, to Boston, in 1903 and then claimed a world championship when it defeated Ty Cobb and the Detroit Tigers in the 1909 Fall Classic. Under the stewardship of field manager Fred Clarke and owner Barney Dreyfuss, the Pirates were able to satisfy Smoky City fans by playing competitive baseball and contending for the pennant each season during that ten-year period.

Dreyfuss's Pittsburgh franchise fell on hard times during the second decade of the twentieth century as he watched every other team in the National League, except for St. Louis, claim a pennant from 1910 to 1919. Clarke's tenure as Pittsburgh's manager ended after the 1915 season. Nondescript skippers such as Jimmy Callahan and famed football coach Hugo Bezdek failed to produce the positive results that Dreyfuss and Pittsburgh fans had grown to expect when first-division finishes were the norm with Clarke at the helm. Prior to the 1920 season, Dreyfuss brought in former catcher George Gibson, a star member of the 1909 championship team, to manage his troops.

The Roaring Twenties were a time when baseball saw its second boom of growth with the advent of the home run and the presence of a major gate attraction like Babe Ruth in New York. Ruth's slugging prowess could not have come at a better time after the throwing of baseball's 1919 World Series by eight Chicago White Sox players came to light. Beginning in 1920, Ruth's power hitting kept the game of baseball breathing when it easily might have been placed on life support as disgusted fans, tired of interference from low-life gamblers, could have walked away. As it turns out, baseball rooters all over the country did not turn their backs on the national pastime. They came in droves to major league ballparks in 11 American cities as a new era of slugging began to slowly replace the thinking man's strategy of small-ball, which previously had been in vogue.

From 1921 through 1923, baseball fans in one of these 11 cities were able to experience the joy of seeing their team play in the World Series. The Big Apple was the place to be each October as the Giants and Yankees played three consecutive Subway Series. Diehard rooters of the other 14 teams in both leagues proudly cheered their favorite players during those three seasons, despite the dominance of the two New York squads. Fans in Cincinnati, St. Louis and Pittsburgh were discouraged that their team had not taken home the bunting, but this did not mean that those patrons were completely dissatisfied with what each team had accomplished.

The Pittsburgh Pirates under George Gibson gave New York a run for its money during the 1921 season. The Pirates held a 7½ game lead over John McGraw's troops on August 23 before Pittsburgh began to falter. Gibson's squad lost five straight games against New York at the Polo Grounds in late August. Two more September defeats against McGraw's squad sealed the Pirates' destiny of a second-place finish behind New York. A slow start by the Pirates in 1922 would cost Gibson his job, as coach Bill McKechnie took control of the reins on July 1 for owner Barney Dreyfuss.

McKechnie was a local boy, born in the Pittsburgh suburb of Wilkinsburg. After a three-game major league debut in 1907, he played for the Pirates from 1910 through 1912 and enjoyed later stints in the Smoky City in 1918 and 1920. McKechnie was able to pull the Pirates from fifth place up to third place with a 53–36 tally for the remainder of the 1922 season. During his first full season at the helm in 1923, McKechnie duplicated that third-place standing as Pittsburgh brought home a first-division finish with an 87–67 record. Pirates owner Barney Dreyfuss was confident that his team was headed in the right direction. As 1924 approached, the Pittsburgh magnate believed that McKechnie was the man who could bring another pennant into his coffer.

Certain conditions that led to Gibson resigning in 1922 still existed on McKechnie's squad as the 1924 season approached. Gibson was criticized by Dreyfuss for not properly enforcing discipline with some of Pittsburgh's free-spirited players during its late-season collapse in 1921. Gibson had his hands full with the "singing quartet" of Walter "Rabbit" Maranville, Charlie Grimm, James "Cotton" Tierney and George "Possum" Whitted. Maranville was the leader of this jovial group, whose shenanigans became a source of constant anger and annoyance for Dreyfuss.[1] Pitcher Chief Yellow Horse, also a constant companion of Maranville in 1921 and 1922, enjoyed the high life a bit too much. Yellow Horse quickly fell into Dreyfuss's doghouse in 1921 during a train ride back to Pittsburgh after a game in Chicago. In the dining car, Yellow Horse and Maranville, both filled with illegal beer they quaffed at an establishment near the train station, put on a show that did not endear themselves to Pittsburgh's owner.²

"Ladies and gentleman," shouted Yellow Horse as he rose from his seat and gestured for everyone to be quiet, "I would like to introduce Rabbit Maranville, that great shortstop of the Pirates, and a sweet little fellow who always minds his own business and has never been known to get into any jams."³

Maranville then rose to his feet, took a few bows, and responded in kind to his friend's ludicrous remarks.

"And now, folks," yelled Maranville, "it gives me great pleasure to introduce Chief Yellow Horse, who not only is a mighty fine pitcher, but the best scrapper in Pittsburgh."⁴

Dreyfuss did not appreciate this sarcastic vaudeville satire being performed by these problem players for his benefit.⁵ Only a few weeks earlier, Dreyfuss had exonerated Yellow Horse when the pitcher confessed to being involved in a brawl on a Pittsburgh street after a night of drinking and carousing. The Pittsburgh owner appreciated his player's forthrightness in admitting the indiscretion before it came to light from another source.⁶ After the incident on the train from Chicago, Dreyfuss's opinion changed. The entire performance did not please Dreyfuss; he told manager Gibson in no uncertain terms that discipline needed to be restored to his team.⁷

By 1924, Maranville and Grimm were the only two men left from the core of troublemaking players who had derailed Gibson's managerial career in Pittsburgh. Smoky City fans loved Maranville's carefree attitude and stellar play on the diamond ever since the diminutive shortstop had been acquired from Boston after the 1920 season. Yet, Pittsburgh management hated Maranville's carousing, playboy lifestyle off the field and reasoned that the shortstop's conduct was detrimental to team unity. McKechnie and Dreyfuss had quietly grimaced throughout some of Maranville's escapades but could not ignore an incident during a trip to Boston in May of 1923. Maranville had finally crossed the line, with the fallout being that he would likely have to play elsewhere in 1924.

The incident occurred while the Pirates made their first Eastern swing in 1923. Boston police pulled over Maranville and cited him for driving while under the influence of alcohol. Yet, Maranville was not actually driving the vehicle at the time; furthermore, he claimed he was not intoxicated. Maranville's friend, who *was* behind the wheel, had definitely consumed too much liquor. Pittsburgh's star shortstop attempted to use his influence with the police officer in an effort to walk away from the situation unscathed. Maranville revealed his identity to the officer, believing the policeman would let him and his friend off because of his status as a ballplayer. This information did not sway the arresting officer, and Maranville was charged with driving an automobile while intoxicated.⁸

Somehow Maranville survived the remainder of the 1923 season in Pittsburgh. Once the campaign was over, Dreyfuss and McKechnie had every intention of trading their shortstop.[9] No deals to Pittsburgh management's liking arose, although rumors abounded throughout the winter that a deal involving Maranville was close to being struck. When Dreyfuss went east in January to meet with president John Heydler about the National League schedule, a meeting with Philadelphia owner William F. Baker was interpreted as a discussion of a deal involving Maranville. Yet, the supposed trade of Maranville for Phillies pitcher Jimmy Ring never reached fruition.[10]

While the off-season scuttlebutt centered around Maranville changing addresses Pittsburgh's shortstop continued to make his winter home in the Smoky City. That winter, Maranville worked for the circulation department of the *Chronicle-Telegraph* newspaper. In spite of his many indiscretions during the past few years, Maranville was still very popular with Pirates fans and continued to be in great demand as a speaker on the banquet circuit. Pittsburgh fans always enjoyed listening to Maranville talk about baseball. He usually devoted his speeches to events that occurred on the diamond, but during this off-season, he always concluded the discussions with his take on trade rumors that included his name.[11] "You've probably noticed that I have been traded this winter to every club in the country from Portland, Maine, to San Diego, California," stated Maranville. "But I'm still here."[12]

Maranville remained a Pittsburgh Pirate on the eve of spring training, but he was no longer considered the starting shortstop. That honor was expected to go to rookie Glenn Wright, a highly touted prospect who came to Pittsburgh from Kansas City of the American Association. Wright was a key piece of the rebuilding process that Bill McKechnie and Barney Dreyfuss planned on instituting in 1924. Pitchers Ray Kremer and Emil Yde, outfielders Hazen "Kiki" Cuyler and Frank Luce, and infielder-outfielder Eddie Moore were other rookies who were expected to join Wright on Pittsburgh's opening day roster in 1924.

McKechnie and Dreyfuss decided that the time was right to give Pittsburgh's team an infusion of youth that would ably complement veteran players like Max Carey, Carson Bigbee and Wilbur Cooper. The Pirates already had given younger men like Harold "Pie" Traynor, Clyde Barnhart and Johnny Gooch an opportunity to show what they could do at the major league level during the past few seasons. Manager McKechnie believed that his team could be a pennant contender for years to come if this mix of players jelled as expected. Owner Dreyfuss liked contending each season, but it was a National League pennant that he craved. The road to October was not always a clear one, however, due to contract holdouts each season.

"I don't know why we should have any," remarked Dreyfuss when asked about possible holdouts from players who had not yet returned signed contracts.

"We always try to satisfy the boys on the matter of salary when we send out the papers. Petty bickering is not to our liking, and we take into consideration, when we decide upon the salary for a season ahead, what has been done by the men during the year just past and reward those who have given their best efforts, if the income from the season justifies it."[13]

Thankfully, Dreyfuss immediately received a signed contract from perennial holdout Walter Schmidt. The veteran catcher never expressed enthusiasm about spring training when the team conducted workouts in Hot Springs, Arkansas, and usually loathed making the trip there. In years past, Schmidt usually attended to business interests and remained at his home out west until the regular season began. The fact that Pittsburgh was preparing for the 1924 season by training at Paso Robles, California, located in Schmidt's backyard, made signing a contract much more appealing for the veteran catcher. It also helped that Dreyfuss supposedly gave Walter a salary increase for 1924.[14]

Pittsburgh's owner was not so lucky in receiving signed contracts from some other key members of the 1924 Pirates. Rookies Glenn Wright and Ray Kremer balked at coming to terms until they were given a portion of the purchase price Dreyfuss paid to obtain them from their minor league teams.[15] Bill McKechnie visited Wright at his winter home in Bartlesville, Oklahoma, and explained to him that the rookie's demand for a piece of the purchase price was something that needed to be negotiated directly with Kansas City. Wright remained adamant that he would not sign, but did acquiesce on the matter of reporting to Paso Robles. Wright decided that it would be unfair to the Pirates not to report after Dreyfuss had paid so much to purchase him.[16]

Wright and Kremer, a rookie pitcher, both showed up for camp at Paso Robles and participated in drills for a few weeks before they signed their contracts. Both players, after a conference with their employer, saw the light regarding their purchases and agreed with management that it was a matter to be taken up with the teams that sold them.[17] Veterans Charlie Grimm and Wilbur Cooper did not immediately join their teammates out west and were labeled as holdouts. Grimm supposedly wanted a raise of 60 percent over his contract from 1923. The Pirates' starting first baseman went to Pittsburgh to discuss matters with Dreyfuss. Brief negotiations occurred before the two men reached a compromise. Grimm signed his 1924 contract, made the trip to Paso Robles and only missed three days of training work.[18]

Cooper remained at his home in Columbus, Ohio, also because his salary demands were not apparently being met by Dreyfuss. Cooper, after hearing that Grimm came to terms, made the trip to Pittsburgh so that he, too, could talk to Dreyfuss. After a long, heated discussion between Cooper and Dreyfuss, the pitcher agreed to a contract and joined his teammates in California. According to local newspapers, Cooper had initially refused to sign a contract because

Dreyfuss was not willing to pay his wife and daughter's expenses for the round trip from Pittsburgh to Paso Robles.[19]

Cooper vehemently denied that this was the case. "I did not insist on the club breaking what I know to be a set rule," said Cooper. "Naturally, I would like to have both Mrs. Cooper and Dorothy with me in the west, but I waived this. My differences with Mr. Dreyfuss was one of money purely, and we settled it amicably."[20]

While these two men were back in Pittsburgh negotiating new deals with their employer, the rest of Pittsburgh's squad began training work in California. The inhabitants of Paso Robles gave the Pirates a big welcome when they arrived. A brass band waiting at the train station escorted the players to their hotel.[21]

Manager McKechnie cautioned his men about the celebration and warned them that this training session was going to be all about hard work. "I don't believe any of you fellows came out here for a joyride," he told them. "If you did, you got off at the wrong station, and the best thing you can do is to pack up and return home. We have a lot of work ahead of us and the only way we are going to accomplish anything is to snap right into it from the start."[22]

McKechnie also let his players know that the automobiles made available at the hotel for transportation to the ballpark that first day would no longer be used. "Enjoy your ride today," shouted McKechnie, as the players entered the vehicles, "for after this we all walk."[23]

McKechnie's players worked very hard throughout the spring training session. This did not mean an absence of bumps along the way for Pittsburgh's manager. Three players took the opportunity during a Sunday break from training to take a joy ride in an airplane. They failed to receive McKechnie's permission to partake in this adventure and only told the manager about it afterwards. Not surprisingly, McKechnie was irate and told them to never repeat this type of behavior while they were under contract to the Pirates. Somehow the players were surprised over McKechnie's reaction. Pittsburgh's manager responded by informing his players they were valuable assets of owner Barney Dreyfuss, who had invested large sums of money in them. It was their obligation to refrain from participating in such dangerous activities, which potentially could bring harm to their bodies.[24]

A second scare occurred for the Pittsburgh contingent when coach Jewel Ens, lieutenant to Bill McKechnie, was quarantined in a hospital with a slight case of scarlet fever. There was concern in the Pirates' camp that this contagious disease could spread to other members of the team. It was initially reported that the entire Pittsburgh team might be quarantined by health officials, but this proved to be nothing more than a sensational story with attention-grabbing headlines. No further action was expected to be taken with any member of the

Pittsburgh organization unless another case of the disease occurred. At the time Ens' illness was diagnosed as scarlet fever, the disease was close to running its course. Jewel almost immediately felt better after being admitted to the hospital. In spite of his improving health, Ens was expected to remain quarantined for a month.[25]

The task of preparing McKechnie's troops for the upcoming season moved into its final stages as March came to an end. As the team concluded its training session, another rumor involving a trade of Maranville decorated the columns of baseball pundits. The latest rumor had Maranville being traded to the Chicago Cubs for pitcher Vic Aldridge. Baseball scribes reasoned that Chicago manager Bill Killefer wanted Maranville to replace the ailing Charlie Hollocher at shortstop.[26] This rumor seemed to lack validity because McKechnie told Maranville prior to spring training he would be Pittsburgh's starting second baseman in 1924.[27]

As camp winded down, many of Pittsburgh's players expressed happiness that their time at Paso Robles was coming to an end. Without question, the town could be categorized as sleepy, with no excitement existing for men who wished to be adventurous during their free time.[28] This proved acceptable for manager McKechnie, who wanted no distractions that would keep his players from the task at hand. "That is exactly the sort of place I was after for training camp," said McKechnie. "This isn't a pleasure jaunt. My men are out here for real work, and I'm not caring about providing evening entertainments for them."[29]

When the opening day roster that would represent the Pirates against Cincinnati on April 15 was announced, it included numerous rookies who were expected to play

Prior to the 1924 season, shortstop Rabbit Maranville was the subject of various trade rumors. Barney Dreyfuss had tired of Maranville's off-field activities and wanted to send his problem player elsewhere. Dreyfuss found no deals to his liking, and Maranville was moved to second base so that rookie Glenn Wright could hold down the shortstop position in 1924 (National Baseball Hall of Fame Library, Cooperstown, New York).

vital roles in 1924. Glenn Wright earned the starting nod at shortstop, and pitchers Ray Kremer and Emil Yde were being counted upon as vital members of Pittsburgh's mound corps. Fellow rookies Hazen "Kiki" Cuyler and Eddie Moore also made the team as reserves. Cuyler was expected to spell starters Max Carey, Carson Bigbee and Clyde Barnhart in the outfield, while Moore could handle work at any position other than catcher and first base.

Pittsburgh's fans were generally excited over the prospects of these five rookie players. Four of the men were mere youngsters, while Kremer was a 31-year-old rookie who had finally made the big leagues after many years of minor league ball. Pirates owner Barney Dreyfuss was equally ecstatic over the immense potential of these rookie players. Dreyfuss publicly gave his opinion about how three of these players would fare during their first season playing in the National League.

> Ray Kremer, whom we secured from Oakland, is a real pitcher, right now. He is smart, knows how to pitch and has all the stuff he needs to get him by. I think he will win a lot of games for us.
>
> We also appear to have unearthed a comer in Emil Yde, who must not be taken for a green rookie, for he possesses a lot of baseball knowledge, and I think he is one of the best prospects we have had in years. He is as cool as can be, has excellent control for a left-hander, and is a remarkable hitter, besides. I figure that he will break into a lot of games this year, besides those in which he is called upon to pitch.[30]

Dreyfuss paused for a moment, and then continued his conversation by assuring Pittsburgh fans that they had no concerns about rookie Glenn Wright starting at shortstop.

"No one need worry about Wright," said he. "Of course, his surroundings are a bit new, but once he gets thoroughly accustomed to his surroundings, he will go great. He has been handicapped by a very sore heel. He is a born ball player, and he can hit. I look for him to drive a lot of balls over our wall this season."[31]

Wright was not the only ailing Pirate as Pittsburgh prepared to open the 1924 season. Outfielder Carson Bigbee, slowed throughout spring training by a cold, was still attempting to regain his strength and add lost weight as opening day approached. Veteran pitcher Charles "Babe" Adams was not expected to help the Pirates much in the early going due to soreness in his pitching arm. Adams left his teammates in California and sojourned to Youngstown, Ohio, to receive treatment from the famous trainer, John "Bonesetter" Reese. Reese told Adams that his arm had suffered no permanent damage, but he added that the veteran pitcher would have to nurse his arm along slowly. Adams rejoined his teammates in time for opening day and proclaimed that treatments were having a positive effect on his lame right arm.[32]

All of the anticipation for the upcoming season was lessened when the

Reds defeated the Pirates, 6–5, on opening day at Redland Field. Pittsburgh watched a one-run lead evaporate when the Reds added single tallies in the eighth and ninth innings to claim victory. Things would not go well for McKechnie's crew during the season's early stages as Pittsburgh stumbled out of the gate and posted a 6–8 record in the month of April. This left Pittsburgh saddled in fifth place in the National League standings.

Pitcher Ray Kremer did well in his first three starts for Pittsburgh. He won two games and tossed a seven-hit shutout against Cincinnati on April 26. Shortstop Glenn Wright showed genuine nervousness while batting and struggled at the plate early on. It was reported that Wright, like so many rookies before him, could not hit a curve ball. Despite Wright's slow start at the plate, he played acrobatically in the field and pulled off plays that brought back memories of Fred "Bones" Ely's fielding prowess.[33]

Pittsburgh's listless performance continued throughout the month of May, as the Pirates posted a 13–12 record and remained mired in fifth place. In a game on May 7 against Chicago at Forbes Field, starting pitcher Wilbur Cooper left for the showers after a little over three innings of unimpressive work. Babe Adams was called on to pitch for the first time that season. The seasoned veteran was unable to continue after having thrown only a few pitches. His pitching arm was still ailing him; numerous trips to Bonesetter Reese had not brought on the desired relief. Adams believed that his arm would respond once the weather became warmer.[34] He would not take his place again on the mound in 1924 until the dog days of August.

Adams' injury was not the only concern on the mind of manager Bill McKechnie. Early in the season, McKechnie accused an umpire of calling him a contemptible name during a heated argument. Pittsburgh's manager readied to fight the arbiter, but was removed from the diamond. As the season progressed, several Pittsburgh players echoed McKechnie's sentiments by complaining that John Heydler's umpires were being unprofessionally abusive.[35] As if overbearing umpires were not a sufficient problem, McKechnie was also dealing with rumors about his imminent dismissal as Pittsburgh's manager. A story was written that claimed that Barney Dreyfuss had approached former ballplayer and minor league manager John C. Calhoun about managing the Pirates. Calhoun also happened to be a Pittsburgh police inspector who had resigned from that post only a week earlier.[36] Dreyfuss quickly killed the rumor, stating that he was happy with McKechnie's work. "I am not hunting for a manager," said Dreyfuss, "and have never even thought of deposing McKechnie."[37]

Not all developments were bad for manager McKechnie as the 1924 season swung into June. After a horrible start at the plate, shortstop Glenn Wright had finally hit his batting stride and slowly raised his average. Wright was particularly proficient at driving home teammates as he led the Pittsburgh squad in RBIs during the early stages of the 1924 season. In the field, he had a powerful throwing arm, whipping the ball to first base with both speed and accuracy, and could make a throw from any position. Wright also received the ultimate praise when writers stated that he covered more ground than any Pirate shortstop since the glory years of Honus Wagner in his prime. Third baseman Pie Traynor felt his job had become so much easier now that Wright was manning the shortstop position.[38] "He only leaves me a small swath to ramble over," remarked Traynor.[39]

Without question, McKechnie's decision to name Wright as the starting shortstop was starting to pay important dividends. If only Pittsburgh's manager had immediately placed *another* rookie in the starting lineup, the Pirates might not have been firmly entrenched in fifth place with a 22–26 record on June 15. Young outfielder Hazen "Kiki" Cuyler was finally given a chance to show his skills when veteran Carson Bigbee was put out of action with an injury.[40] Cuyler did not appear in his first game until May 4. By early June, the rookie outfielder had wrestled the starting job in right field from Bigbee even after the veteran was declared healthy enough to play. Cuyler made up for lost time by hitting fiercely. A free swinger who took healthy cuts at pitches, Cuyler usually connected, and his clutch hitting helped Pittsburgh win several games after his insertion into the starting lineup.[41]

Pittsburgh's manager made another lineup change in which a third rookie player was promoted to regular duty. This switch was difficult, since it involved benching one of the hardest working and most popular members of the Pittsburgh squad. Third baseman Pie Traynor was mired in a horrendous hitting slump that saw his average drop to .239 in June. McKechnie decided to make a change placing young Eddie Moore at third base and sending Traynor to the bench.[42] Given the fact that Pittsburgh' team was hitting well below expectations, McKechnie did not have the luxury of leaving Traynor in the lineup to work his way out of the batting slump. Moore immediately produced when made a starter on June 18.

After Moore went 9-for-21 at the plate in five games, McKechnie was asked if the change at third base was permanent. "I intend using Moore as long as he performs as capably as he has since he was sent to third base," stated McKechnie during the interview. "It would be folly for me to bench him, in view of his fine showing, and send Pie back, for I need all the hitting strength it is possible to muster, and in an offensive as well as defensive way, Eddie is certainly filling the bill. He is good enough for any club in both branches, and in the Pittsburgh lineup he will stay."[43]

McKechnie remained true to his word as Moore remained in the lineup until an unfortunate incident on July 1 in St. Louis forced him from the game. Pitcher Johnny Stuart nailed Moore in the shoulder with a pitched ball that knocked the youngster out of action. Moore tried to downplay the injury, but after the pain in his shoulder became intense, an x-ray examination showed that a bone had been knocked out of alignment. Traynor went back to his position at third base and began playing once again in a manner reminiscent of his 1923 season. The extra rest seemed to revive Traynor, whose struggles earlier in the year could be attributed to a malady he had kept secret.[44]

At the same time McKechnie was playing musical chairs with the third base position, veteran pitcher Babe Adams finally received a definitive diagnosis regarding his injured pitching arm. Adams believed he was afflicted with rheumatism. A physician confirmed this was the case, at least to a certain extent, and concluded that diseased teeth were the cause of his rheumatic condition. Adams then consulted a dentist about having his bad teeth extracted.[45] Adams had the dental work performed and went to his home in Bethany, Missouri, to recuperate. The veteran pitcher's doctor prescribed rest and relaxation, and told Babe not to work his pitching wing for three weeks.[46]

With Adams on the shelf for most of the 1924 season, his absence opened the door for other young pitchers. Southpaw Emil Yde was used as a spot-starter during the first three months of the season before securing a permanent rotation spot in late July. Yde became an instant fan favorite because of his exploits at Forbes Field on June 25. He relieved starter Lee Meadows after the Chicago Cubs scored five runs in the fourth inning. The Danish pitcher stemmed the tide with excellent relief pitching; he also blasted a bases clearing double that tied the game with two outs in the ninth inning. Yde was not quite done putting on a heroic display that day. After Chicago took a one-run lead in the top of the fourteenth inning, Yde's triple in the bottom half of the frame drove home Clyde Barnhart and Johnny Gooch with the game's winning tallies.[47]

Yde, who won his first eight decisions as a big leaguer before suffering a defeat, took it all in stride as he explained his success.

> It may sound funny but I find it easier to pitch winning ball in the National League than in the Western circuit. Of course, I have to face much harder and more consistent hitters up here, but to my mind the superior fielding behind me more than makes up for this. Then the catching helps a lot. In the minors we simply throw anything, in an effort to lay the ball past the batsmen, while here the catchers know everyone's weakness or pet aversion and play up to it. All that this leaves me to do is to look at the signs and try and follow them. My main trouble this year has been wildness, and that to my mind is simply the result of not enough work. You see I seldom get into more than one game a week as a pitcher, and that's hardly enough to put any pitcher at his best.[48]

Yde gave much of the credit for his strong showing to men who played on the field behind him and his team's fine catching corps. Pittsburgh's backstop unit had been thinned by injuries during the summer as Walter Schmidt and Johnny Gooch both missed time. Their absences forced McKechnie to use youngster

Cliff Knox for a few games before veteran Earl Smith was claimed off waivers from Boston on July 14. Smith was a fiery competitor who had argued frequently with manager John McGraw when he played for the New York Giants. The Braves actually tried to pull an unethical stunt by attempting to waive Smith out of the National League. At the same time Pittsburgh put in its claim for Smith, Boston vice president Judge Emil Fuchs announced the catcher's transfer to Los Angeles, a minor league team. Since a major league club's waiver claim always superseded that of a minor league outfit, Smith became a Pirate.[49]

Smith joined his new team just as the Pirates were starting to mesh and make a move in the National League standings. When July concluded, Pittsburgh found itself in third place with a 52–41 record, 7½ games behind league-leading New York. Pittsburgh started a phenomenal Eastern swing on July 25, when McKechnie's boys defeated Boston, 2–1. This win marked the second victory of a seven-game winning streak that was the impetus for a sizzling 15–3 road record against Boston, New York, Brooklyn and Philadelphia. The Pirates continued their stellar play when the Giants came to Forbes Field and were swept by the Corsairs in a four-game series. When the Giants left Pittsburgh on August 16, their lead over the second-place Pirates had been chopped to three games.

Pittsburgh's players were suddenly the darlings of the Smoky City. The names of players such as Cuyler, Wright, Maranaville and Yde were on the lips of devoted rooters who dreamed of Pittsburgh winning the National League pennant. The players, in turn, were happy to give something back to the people who cheered for them each and every day. On July 17, the Pirates' infield lent a hand to the 176th Field Artillery of Pittsburgh. The regiment was having a recruiting party, and the Pittsburgh players assisted Lieutenant W. A. Dunn while he talked to young men who were interested in signing up. Grimm, Maranville, Wright and Traynor stayed on hand at Liberty Avenue and Sixth Street from 11 A.M. until noon to shake hands and present anyone who joined the regiment with an autographed baseball.[50]

This aggregation of players was also doing fine work on the field. The Grimm-Maranville-Wright-Traynor combination received sterling reviews while the Pirates rolled over opponents during their Eastern trip. Maranville had made a seamless switch to the keystone position. He seemed to be playing with more passion in 1924 than in previous seasons. Grimm was hailed as one of the league's finest defenders at first base. Pittsburgh's infield quartet was considered one of the best in the league, and received favorable comparisons to both Connie Mack's "Million-Dollar Infield" and the famed unit of Chance, Evers, Tinker and Steinfeldt that had played for the Chicago Cubs.[51]

While Pittsburgh's infield received praise from Eastern writers, Hazen "Kiki" Cuyler established himself as the team's best player and a particular fan favorite. Handling any type of pitching thrown his way, he had risen to third

1. Gaining Valuable Experience in a Tight Pennant Race

in the hitting race behind Rogers Hornsby and Zack Wheat by early August.[52] Cuyler also played with a strong competitive spirit. During a game against New York on the Eastern road trip, Frankie Frisch was a bit exuberant in tagging Cuyler on the head with the ball at second base. The force from the blow nearly did serious damage. Pittsburgh's newest star had to leave the game, as it took him the remainder of the afternoon to recover his faculties. Cuyler never uttered a word of complaint as his teammates vowed to extract revenge against Frisch.[53]

Cuyler not only hit the ball ferociously, he was also a sensational fielder and a fleet-footed runner. Veteran outfielder Max Carey, one of the best base stealers of his era, acted as the perfect mentor for Cuyler as he taught the youngster the subtleties of becoming an accomplished base thief. Cuyler gladly absorbed the teaching since it became apparent to the rookie that becoming proficient at stealing bases would require thorough knowledge of pitchers' tendencies. Cuyler explained the theory:

> Grabbing a base up here is a lot different from what it is in the minors. Stealing is good baseball, and I like to steal, but the boys in the National League have shown me many things I didn't know. In the minors you seldom find more than one or two smart pitchers on one team, and some have none. Also, minor teams do not carry many pitchers. By constantly studying them, you find who are smart in hiding their intentions about holding up a runner, and you give those wise ones intensive study to learn the tip-off on when they are going to deliver the ball to the plate. The lesser lights usually furnish the tip quite plainly, and you proceed accordingly.[54]

Cuyler's fame may have been growing rapidly throughout the city of Pittsburgh, but this did not mean that the rest of the country was familiar with baseball's newest rising star. After Pittsburgh disposed of New York at Forbes Field, the Pirates went to Warren, Ohio, for an exhibition game on August 17. At 11 o'clock in the morning they left Pittsburgh on the Pennsylvania and Lake Erie train. It was not long before other passengers became aware that Bill McKechnie's team was on board. Throughout the trip to Youngstown, passengers went to the parlor car holding the Pirates, hoping to get a glimpse of their beloved Pittsburgh players. One man took his son back to the Pirates' car, hoping that the lad would see his favorite player, Kiki Cuyler. The little boy was not disappointed and could not suppress his exuberance when father and son returned to their car.[55] "Oh, Mother, I saw Cuyler!" exclaimed the ecstatic boy. "CUYLER? Cuyler?" responded the boy's mother. "Who is he?"[56]

In the meantime, Glenn Wright found out that adulation from the fans could quickly turn into jeers and sneers. Some fans at Forbes Field turned on Wright when he fell into a batting slump and made several bad plays at shortstop. One area of the grandstand began to heckle him vociferously. These patrons were tinhorn gamblers who would sometimes root for the visiting team or boo hometown players because of money they had wagered that day. As lowbrow examples of fans, they had caused many local players grief for over two decades at Forbes Field and Exposition Park. Many of these gamblers had been banned from Forbes Field, but they repeatedly found a way to return and gather in a different section of the ballpark.[57]

Elation over the four-game sweep against New York was tempered a bit when the Brooklyn Robins came into Pittsburgh and returned the favor in late August by sweeping three games. One of the defeats was a 4–3 loss at the hands of Dazzy Vance on August 19. Vance had given the Pirates trouble for years; he seemed to have a personal vendetta against the Corsairs. Brooklyn's star pitcher held no animosity toward Pittsburgh's players, but he did not like club management. He harbored bad feelings against Dreyfuss, who had released Vance in 1915.[58]

After this latest victory, a Pittsburgh fan reminded Vance that he had accumulated a remarkable string of victories against the Pirates. "Well, Dazzy, that's you're tenth straight over the Pirates," remarked the fan. "Yes, and that isn't half enough," was his sarcastic rejoinder, as he went on his way.[59]

The National League pennant race was a three-team affair as the season moved into September. The New York Giants remained in first place with a 75–49 record. Pittsburgh held down the second spot at 73–51, two games behind the Giants. Brooklyn was in third place with a 72–54 record, which left them four games out. All three teams battled gamely as the pennant struggle remained tight through the season's final weeks. For Pittsburgh, the fate of the entire season came down to a three-game series against the Giants, which began at the Polo Grounds on September 23. The Robins and the Giants were in a virtual tie for first place, while Pittsburgh was 1½ games behind the pace setters. A sweep over the Giants would not guarantee that Pittsburgh would win the pennant, but it would greatly improve their chances.

Pittsburgh's prospects looked promising against New York since the Giants had just lost two games against Chicago. John McGraw's squad also was playing without Frankie Frisch and Heinie Groh, two stars who were injured.[60] The hope and expectation that McKechnie's team felt before the series quickly turned to disappointment as Pittsburgh did the unthinkable and lost all three games. On September 23, Hugh McQuillan bested Lee Meadows as New York beat Pittsburgh, 5–1, with Jimmy O'Connell's two-run home run in the fourth inning being the crucial blow. The next day, New York's Virgil Barnes was staked to a 4–0 lead before Pittsburgh scratched out single tallies in the seventh and ninth inning to make the game close. On September 24, the Giants completed the sweep with a 5–4 victory as Pittsburgh's rally fell run short against Art Nehf in the ninth inning.

Pittsburgh went 4–1 during its final five games, but it was not enough to overcome the losses in New York. The Giants claimed their fourth consecutive

National League pennant and opposed the Washington Senators in the 1924 World Series. The Series was a wild affair, which Washington won in seven games. The Senators claimed their first world championship when Muddy Ruel scored in the twelfth inning of the final contest after Earl McNeely smacked a ball toward third baseman Fred Lindstrom. The ball hit a pebble and bounced over his head for a double to left field.

Even though Pittsburgh did not win the pennant, many fans still considered the season a successful one as the Pirates finished in third place with a 90–63 record, only three games behind New York. Although a majority of Pittsburgh's baseball rooters believed their team fought gallantly, there were others who thought the team was filled with spineless players who did not attend to business properly. As the season wound down, rumors abounded that some players had not kept themselves in good physical condition. Specific names were not released, but the belief prevailed that some players were carousing and imbibing to excess. These players seemed to prefer parties and drinking over reaping the benefits of a hefty World Series check, a criticism attached to earlier Pittsburgh teams.[61]

It particularly galled owner Barney Dreyfuss that another pennant had been won by his chief nemesis, John McGraw. Both men maintained a cool relationship toward each other, with ill feelings rooted in Dreyfuss's early years in Pittsburgh when Fred Clarke's teams always battled McGraw's Giants in an unfriendly manner. McGraw was his usual antagonistic self against Dreyfuss and the Pirates in 1924. During an August series in Pittsburgh, McGraw complained to National League president John Heydler that a painted sign in front of the right field bleachers at Forbes Field was interfering with his players' batting efforts. Heydler ordered that the sign, which usually listed upcoming home games, be removed at once.[62]

This incident seemed minor in comparison to two other events involving McGraw and his Giants. The first centered around a postponed game during the late-season series between the two teams in New York. A game scheduled for September 22 was called off by New York management, as per National League rules, due to rainy weather. The decision was made at 11 o'clock in the morning. By noon, the sun had come out and continued to shine throughout the afternoon. Brooklyn was able to play its game at nearby Ebbets Field, but McGraw believed the Polo Grounds' conditions were not suitable for playing a game. Dreyfuss reasoned that McGraw postponed the game so that Frankie Frisch, Heinie Groh and Irish Meusel would have another day to rest their injuries. Dreyfuss became further enraged when McGraw made Pittsburgh stay in New York an extra day to play the postponed game on September 24.[63]

The final incident, and the most egregious in Dreyfuss's eyes, was the dismissal of New York Giants player Jimmy O'Connell and coach Cozy Dolan from Organized Baseball by Commissioner Kenesaw Landis. Philadelphia shortstop Heinie Sand claimed that O'Connell offered him a $500 bribe if the Phillies would "let up" in a game against New York on September 27. Sand brought this information to Landis and John Heydler days later, and baseball's czar immediately banished O'Connell and Dolan. O'Connell quickly implicated Dolan as the instigator. O'Connell also stated that teammates Frankie Frisch, George Kelly and Ross Youngs were privy to the details surrounding the bribe plan. Landis immediately exonerated those three players since he believed there was no evidence that directly implicated them.[64]

Barney Dreyfuss was appalled over the circumstances surrounding the unsavory behavior of these two men. Pittsburgh's owner also had a suspicion that McGraw was involved. Dreyfuss, along with American League president Ban Johnson, believed this incident was so serious that the Robins should have replaced the Giants against Washington, if the World Series was not canceled altogether. Landis had no intention of stopping the Series, and each game was played as scheduled. McGraw quickly rebutted Dreyfuss's and Johnson's comments by saying they were the statements of crackpots. McGraw also intimated that Dreyfuss was still upset because he had built new stands in 1921 and seldom had a chance to use them.[65]

Bill McKechnie's Pittsburgh Pirates came close to capturing the National League pennant in 1924, with much of the credit for the team's success rooted in the play of five rookies. Kiki Cuyler hit .354 in his first big league season. The youngster, learning the nuances of base stealing from master thief Max Carey, swiped 32 bases. Shortstop Glenn Wright hit .287 and led the team with 111 RBIs. Eddie Moore smashed the ball at a .359 clip during limited duty in both the infield and outfield. Rookie pitchers Ray Kremer and Emil Yde supported staff ace and twenty-game winner

Southpaw pitcher Emil Yde had a sensational rookie season for Pittsburgh in 1924. Yde led the National League in winning percentage as he posted a 16–3 record supported by an ERA of 2.83. Yde started out his major league career by winning his first eight decisions. Besides being a solid pitcher, Yde was also an accomplished hitter who batted .239 in 1924 (National Baseball Hall of Fame Library, Cooperstown, New York).

Wilbur Cooper magnificently. Kremer posted an 18–10 record with a 3.19 ERA and Yde led the National League in winning percentage with a mark of 16–3, buttressed by a 2.83 ERA.

Yde, Kremer, Wright and Cuyler had been referred to by a variety of experts as the greatest quartet of rookies to break into the game during the same season in baseball history. The 1924 season would have been a lost cause if not for their efforts.[66] These young Buccaneers had gained valuable experience during a hotly contested pennant race. Hopefully, they would remain vital contributors as Bill McKechnie and Barney Dreyfuss continued to build a team that could end New York's baseball dynasty.

2

Building a Team to End New York's Dynasty

Various rebuilding processes had been undertaken by Pittsburgh owner Barney Dreyfuss after his Pirates team collapsed during the 1910 season. The Dreyfuss squad that beat Detroit in the World Series the previous October stumped all the game's experts by performing well below the Pittsburgh owner's lofty expectations. The early phases of this retooling period yielded mixed results as the Pirates remained competitive during the 1911 and 1912 season. This was quickly followed by the darkest era during Dreyfuss's tenure as owner of the Pittsburgh franchise. A seventh-place finish in 1914 began a string of four consecutive seasons in which Pittsburgh finished in the National League's second division. A three year stretch of fourth-place finishes between 1918 and 1920 showed that improvement might be on the horizon. Nonetheless, these results were certainly unacceptable to an owner like Dreyfuss, whose desire each season was to have his team's name included in the heated discussion of the pennant race.

By 1924, Dreyfuss had built a team that achieved his designated goal of being a first-division club in the National League. Many players who had come and gone during the past 15 years had failed to meet the expectations placed upon them by Dreyfuss. A close call in 1921 had nearly brought the pennant back to Pittsburgh. When his team failed to continue growing in 1922, Dreyfuss made more personnel changes and also replaced George Gibson with Bill McKechnie as the team's pilot. An infusion of youth was a boon to the Pirates' fortunes in 1924, as five rookies played pivotal roles during a tightly contested race that was eventually claimed by the New York Giants, who won their fourth consecutive National League pennant. Dreyfuss and McKechnie both realized that the road to a National League title ran through New York. If they had any intention of re-routing that path through the Smoky City, a squad needed to be built that could derail McGraw's championship aspirations.

The Pirates' team that finished the 1924 season was a mixture of youngsters

2. Building a Team to End New York's Dynasty

and veterans who had been part of Dreyfuss's various rebuilding projects. Pittsburgh's owner built a major portion of the 1924 squad through shrewd purchases of young talent from the minor leagues. Dreyfuss also plugged noticeable holes on the roster through trades with his National League counterparts. The Pirates now consisted of a mix of exciting rookies and veteran players, a few of whom had been with Pittsburgh during its last world's championship 16 years earlier. It was with this aggregation that McKechnie hoped to bring the National League pennant back to Pittsburgh in 1925.

McKechnie himself was part of the original rebuilding process that had occurred during the 1910 season. William Boyd McKechnie was born on August 7, 1886, in Wilkinsburg, Pennsylvania. McKechnie began his career playing in the local county of Butler after he left Washington and Jefferson University in 1903.[1] He saw action for the Pirates in three 1907 games before being farmed out to Canton of the Ohio-Pennsylvania League in 1908. Fred Clarke added McKechnie to the 1910 Pirates roster after the young infielder hit .274 for Wheeling in 132 games during the 1909 season. A scrappy infielder who was a light hitter at the plate, McKechnie could do no better than accrue averages of .217 in 1910 and .227 in 1911.[2] This earned McKechnie another trip back to the minors with St. Paul when Pittsburgh traded him for infielder Art Butler in August of 1912. When Boston drafted McKechnie in 1913, the Braves assigned him to a second stint in the Minnesota city.[3]

After McKechnie left Pittsburgh, he began an odyssey that landed him with various baseball organizations throughout the country. In 1914, he jumped to the Federal League and played for the Indianapolis Hoosiers. When that team moved to Newark in 1915, Bill packed up once again and went east with the team.[4]

McKechnie was given his first opportunity to manage a team when he was named skipper of the Peppers squad on June 19, 1915. He guided Newark's aggregation to a 54–45 record. After the 1915 season, the Federal League folded and McKechnie found himself back in the National League with New York. Bill's stay in the Big Apple was short lived, as he was part of the package that included Edd Roush and Christy Mathewson, who were also sent to Cincinnati during the summer of 1916.

McKechnie made his way back to Pittsburgh in 1918 when the Pirates paid the Reds $20,000 to reacquire the infielder. He played two more seasons for the Pirates before finishing his playing career with Minneapolis in 1921. It was in Minneapolis that McKechnie honed his managerial skills under the guidance of veteran minor league pilot Joe Cantillon. Bill then returned to Pittsburgh as a coach on manager George Gibson's staff for the 1922 season. After an unacceptable 32–33 start by Gibson amid rumors that he had lost control of his undisciplined Pittsburgh squad, McKechnie replaced the former catcher at the helm and managed his first major league game, losing 9–5, against St. Louis on July 1, 1922.

Many of the players who performed for Gibson before he resigned remained on Pittsburgh's payroll through 1924. One of the veterans was a player who actually had a connection with Pittsburgh's last pennant-winning team. Pitcher Babe Adams had broken in with Clarke's championship team in 1909 and starred in the World Series against Detroit that fall. The rookie was used sparingly during the 1909 regular season, but posted an admirable record of 12–3, supported by a 1.11 ERA. Clarke surprised many when he named Adams as his Game One starter against Detroit in the World Series. The young pitcher did not disappoint Pittsburgh's faithful as he tossed three complete game victories against the Tigers, emerging as the star of the Series for the Pirates.

Charles Benjamin Adams was born on May 18, 1882, in Tipton, Indiana. Adams' early opportunities at the major league level did not seem to indicate that he would become the darling of the baseball world in 1909. He failed in late-season trials with St. Louis in 1906 and Pittsburgh in 1907. The Pirates farmed Adams out to Louisville of the American Association for the 1908 season. It was here that Adams was finally able to harness his tantalizing curve ball, as he went 22–12 and fashioned a 2.08 ERA for the Colonels. Adams became the staff ace of the Pirates after he blossomed during the 1909 season. Babe posted records of 18–9 in 1910, 22–12 in 1911 and 21–10 in 1913 with corresponding ERAs of 2.24, 2.33 and 2.15. When Fred Clarke retired following the 1915 season, Adams soon found himself back in the minors; new manager Jimmy Callahan cut Babe loose after a horrible start in 1916.

Adams resurrected his career and returned to Pittsburgh when Kansas City loaned him to the Pirates in July of 1918. This loan became permanent as Babe continued to carve out a successful career as the National League's premier control pitcher. He once again became a prominent member of the Pittsburgh staff and pitched superbly in 1919 (17–10, 1.98 ERA), 1920 (17–13, 2.16 ERA) and 1921 (14–5, 2.64 ERA). By 1924, Adams was a 42-year-old pitcher who added guidance and experience in supporting Bill McKechnie's pitching staff. Yet, most Pittsburgh rooters did not expect Adams to be a major contributor in 1925 given the fact that he missed a majority of the 1924 season with an injured arm.

Babe Adams was the revered, elder statesman of the Pittsburgh Pirates as the 1925 season approached. Following Adams closely in years of major league service was outfielder Maximilian Carnarius, better known as Max Carey to those who followed the Pirates fortunes for the better part of the past decade.[5]

Max George Carey was born on January 11, 1890, in Terre Haute, Indiana. While Carey was enjoying baseball during his impressionable years, the Terre Haute youngster also was being trained to become a Lutheran minister. He studied at Concordia College in Fort Wayne, Indiana, for six years before he continued his academic endeavors at a university with the same name in St. Louis.[6]

2. Building a Team to End New York's Dynasty

While Carey was relaxing at home during the summer of 1909, he and a friend ventured to South Bend in order to watch a Central League game. After the contest, Carey convinced South Bend manager Aggie Grant to give him a tryout at shortstop.[7] Carey appeared in 48 games that summer and hit a less than lustrous .158 at the plate. He resumed ministry classes the following semester and forgot about baseball until he rejoined South Bend in June of 1910, when the school year ended. New manager Eddie Wheeler moved Carey to the outfield, making room for a new shortstop named Alex McCarthy.[8] Appearing in 96 games for South Bend, Carey raised his average to .294. On August 15, 1910, Carey and McCarthy were purchased by the Pittsburgh Pirates.

As a member of South Bend's team, divinity student Maximilian Carnarius played under the alias of Max Carey so that he could maintain his eligibility to play sports at St. Louis' Concordia College. Max decided to keep the Carey moniker as his name when he made his big-league debut at the tail end of the 1910 season. Carey quickly established himself as a speed merchant by winning five stolen base titles during his first eight National League seasons. Carey possessed a baseball philosophy similar to Ty Cobb's, although he did not exhibit the Detroit star's moody or violent behavior.

Max Carey was not as accomplished a hitter as Cobb, but he was more than capable. Carey seemed to improve with age as he enjoyed three consecutive seasons batting over .300 in 1921 (.309), 1922 (.329) and 1923 (.308). Carey also added three more National League stolen base crowns from 1922 through 1924. In addition to being a great player, Carey was also designated the squad's captain. Carey was a consummate team player who was respected by every member of the Pittsburgh Pirates' organization.

Carson Lee Bigbee was one such player. He had spent the past nine seasons playing next to Carey in the outfield at Forbes Field. Bigbee was born on March 21, 1895, in Lebanon, Oregon. A star player at the University of Oregon, he possessed blazing speed, just like Carey.[9] Bigbee joined the Pirates in 1916 after he hit .340 while appearing in 111 games for Tacoma of the Northwestern League. After five seasons of solid play, Bigbee finally burst onto the major league scene when he hit .323 in 1921. Carson followed that up with a career year in 1922, when he hit .350 and drove home 99 runs. Bigbee slipped back to an average of .299 in 1923 because of sinus problems. Still, McKechnie was fond of Bigbee and gave the veteran a chance to remain a starter early in 1924. A .262 average, along with stronger performances from other Pirate outfielders, pushed Bigbee to the bench.

Babe Adams, Max Carey and Carson Bigbee were the venerable members of Bill McKechnie's squad. All three men had experienced Pittsburgh's dark days during the previous decade. They also were responsible for the Pirates fortunes improving during the past few seasons. Of the three, Carey was the only player who was expected to be a major contributor in 1925. Adams and

Bigbee were expected to perform secondary roles and lend veteran support to younger players during the upcoming season.

Barney Dreyfuss's infusion of youth had come in two stages. The first group of building blocks was obtained during the early 1920s; the second batch was purchased during a whirlwind buying spree by Dreyfuss that resulted in five rookies doing excellent work for McKechnie in 1924. The plum of Dreyfuss's first group of minor league whiz kids was third baseman Pie Traynor. When the Pirates purchased Traynor from Portsmouth of the Virginia League for $10,000 in September of 1920, they acquired a player who would become the envy of all other third baseman in the major leagues.

Harold Joseph Traynor was born on November 11, 1898, in Framingham, Massachusetts. Traynor became an accomplished baseball player at Somerville High School. While at Somerville, Traynor also showed his athletic prowess by excelling in football, track, swimming and ice hockey.[10] Traynor made a smooth transition from high school baseball to the professional level when he hit .270 for Portsmouth in 1920. When Traynor joined the Pirates late in the 1920 season, the youngster's energetic and gregarious attitude made an impression on some veteran Pittsburgh players.[11] Unfortunately for Traynor, his attitude had a negative effect on team members who were not used to such displays of enthusiasm. "That will soon wear off," remarked a jaded old-timer who believed Traynor's exuberance would die down quickly.[12]

Harold "Pie" Traynor was purchased by the Pittsburgh Pirates from Portsmouth for $10,000 in September of 1920. Traynor played shortstop exclusively during his time playing for Birmingham in the minor leagues. In 1922, Traynor was chosen as Pittsburgh's starting third baseman. Traynor had a stellar rookie season as he batted .282 and drove home 81 runs (National Baseball Hall of Fame Library, Cooperstown, New York).

After his late season trial in 1920, Traynor was farmed out to Birmingham of the Southern Association for the 1921 season. He hit .336 in 131 games and found himself back on the Pirates roster at the end of the season. In 1922, Traynor was chosen to be Pittsburgh's starting third baseman, even though he had been used exclusively at shortstop during his minor league days.[13] Contrary to the old-time Pirate player's cynical opinion of Traynor in 1920, the young man continued to play with a zest that quickly made him a fan favorite in Pittsburgh. The youngster hit .282 during his rookie season and drove home 81 runs. Traynor followed that up with marks of .338 in 1923 and .294 in 1924.[14] During his first three seasons in Pittsburgh, Traynor consistently made acrobatic plays at third base, unlike any of his predecessors.

Like Traynor, pitcher Johnny Morrison saw his first action in a Pittsburgh uniform late in 1920. John Dewey Morrison was born on October 22, 1895, in Pellville, Kentucky. He bounced between teams at the lower minor league level until he latched on with Birmingham's Southern Association entry in 1919. Morrison struggled during his first season in the Alabama metropolis and won only 12 games. He rebounded nicely in 1920 and recorded a 26–13 record for the Barons. Morrison then posted solid seasons in 1922 and 1923 for Pittsburgh as he went 17–11 and 25–13 while carving out ERAs of 3.43 and 3.49, respectively. Nicknamed "Jughandle Johnny" because of his biting curve ball, Morrison slumped a bit in 1924 and won only 11 games. In spite of Morrison's slump in 1924, the pitcher had improved considerably since his humble beginnings, when Cincinnati Reds outfielder Pat Duncan first observed him playing baseball in the Army.

> Johnny Morrison, the Pirate pitcher is a battery, and a swell battery, too. It's a fact, if you understand the how and why. When I was in the army, a non-com who was a fan told me to go over to the ball ground of another regiment, and look at a remarkable young pitcher named Morrison. I went over, and saw the game — a morning battle between the regiments. But there was no pitcher named Morrison — a boy named Bacon was pitching, and the catcher's name was Morrison! Good catcher, too, as clever a marksman you would wish to see.
>
> They had another game that afternoon, and I went over again. This time, I thought I was crazy, for the battery had switched ends. Bacon, the morning flinger, was behind the bat, and Morrison was on the slab. He won his game handily, and looked so good to me that I got him, as soon as he was out of the army, to join the Birmingham team — the rest of his career is baseball history.
>
> Morrison was a free agent when I met him, for the simple reason that he had never played baseball before he entered the Army. He didn't know what a pitching mound was for, and he didn't know why the umpire didn't bat. Yet he picked up the game so fast that in a few weeks he became one of the best batteries in the army — alternating pitching and catching — and now he is one of the best slab men in the National League.[15]

Morrison did not toil behind the plate in Pittsburgh on days when he wasn't pitching, but Johnny's battery mate from Birmingham during the 1920 season did his fair share of work behind the bat when he pitched. Johnny Gooch worked his way into Pittsburgh's catching rotation during the 1922 season, when he appeared in 105 games and hit a robust .329. John Beverley

Gooch was born on November 9, 1897, in Smyrna, Tennessee. Gooch's baseball career began at the lowest level of the minor leagues when he played for Talladega in 1916. Gooch joined Nashville in 1917 and then made his way to Birmingham, where he spent parts of three seasons there.[16] Gooch started out slowly at the plate in Birmingham and hit only .217 during the 1920 campaign. Johnny improved his hitting stroke the following season and raised his average to .288 while appearing in 136 games. Pittsburgh purchased Gooch from Birmingham late in 1921.[17] Gooch displayed solid defensive work behind the plate and followed up his strong rookie year with averages of .277 (1923) and .290 (1924) in Pittsburgh.

The final player added to Pittsburgh's roster during this first stage of rebuilding was outfielder Clyde Barnhart. Clyde Lee Barnhart was born on December 29, 1895, in Buck Valley, Pennsylvania. Clyde's father was a decent ballplayer, although he never made it at the professional level. Barnhart's father quickly had young Clyde hitting and catching baseballs at a very young age.[18] This training at an early age helped mold Barnhart into a fine player and showed the youngster he had talent that would aid him in pursuit of a professional career.

"No doubt this early training had much to do with any success I have enjoyed since that time," said Barnhart. "I played baseball as far back as I can remember. There never was a time when I didn't hope to be a ball player. And if your life has been molded in such a groove, it's pretty certain, if you have any natural talent at all, that sooner or later it will show itself."[19]

Barnhart tried other occupations before he decided that playing baseball was his true destiny. Barnhart attended the State Normal School where he played while completing his academic obligations. After graduation, Barnhart tried his hand at substitute teaching and found this did not interest him. He then decided to attend manual training school and also began studying to be a pharmacist. He completed half the work required to become a professional mixer of drugs when World War I interrupted his studies. During the war, Barnhart worked for the government and aided the war effort much like many other young men who were not soldiers.[20]

Barnhart played with various independent baseball clubs while he tried to find a niche in society through different school endeavors. This continued dedication to the game while he dabbled in other interests proved to be beneficial for Barnhart when the Pirates signed him as a free agent in 1920 and assigned him to the Birmingham Barons in May. Barnhart played third base for the strong Southern Association club and hit .322 before being recalled by the Pirates in August.[21] Clyde was the first member of the Birmingham Express who made it to Pittsburgh's major league team. Barnhart was converted into an outfielder after Pie Traynor was named Pittsburgh's starting third baseman in 1922. The youngster showed promise at the plate and struck the ball consistently in 1922 (.330), 1923 (.324) and 1924 (.276).

2. Building a Team to End New York's Dynasty

Barney Dreyfuss's second phase of upgrading his team with young talent continued in 1921, just as the cultivation of players like Pie Traynor, Johnny Morrison, Johnny Gooch and Clyde Barnhart was being completed. In September of 1921, the Pirates purchased a fleet-footed outfielder named Hazen Cuyler from Bay City of the Michigan-Ontario League. The youngster had just completed a solid season for the Wolves, hitting .317 in 116 games. Hazen Shirley Cuyler was born on August 30, 1898, in Harrisville, Michigan. As a kid growing up in Bay City, Cuyler first had success in baseball as a pitcher on the local Michigan diamonds.[22]

When Cuyler was 17 years old, he received permission from his parents to enlist in the Army. The young man rapidly rose to the rank of sergeant and was eventually chosen from a group of 50 men to take a West Point examination. Cuyler was one of only two soldiers to pass this test.[23]

When World War I ended, Cuyler returned home to Michigan and worked for an automobile plant in Flint. His exploits on the diamond while playing for the company team in the Detroit Industrial league led Bay City to offer him a contract. After the Pirates purchased Cuyler in 1921, Hazen was farmed out to Charleston in 1922 and then turned over to Nashville in 1923. As a member of the Volunteers, Cuyler was named the Southern Association's Most Valuable Player and awarded an automobile after he hit .340 in 1923.[24]

Cuyler burst on the major league scene during the 1924 season. Pittsburgh manager Bill McKechnie did not immediately warm up to making Cuyler a starter and opted to play veteran Carson Bigbee instead. An injury to Bigbee paved the way for Cuyler to become a regular. The young free-swinger finished the 1924 campaign with a .354 average. Pittsburgh's newest speed demon also scored 94 runs, smacked 27 doubles, smashed 16 triples and stole 32 bases. Cuyler quickly was dubbed "Kiki" by adoring Pittsburgh fans, who usually referred to the star outfielder by his nickname.

Numerous tales spoke of how Cuyler earned this moniker. Some said that it occurred when infielders yelled "Cuy" repeatedly while directing the outfielder to grab fly balls for Nashville. Others reasoned it was due to the false notion Cuyler stuttered as a child and had trouble pronouncing his last name. A third story said Cuyler received the nickname as a child because one of his managers stuttered, usually yelling from the dugout: "C-c-come on. Cuy-cuy-cuy-ler, hit one out."[25] No matter the reason for Cuyler acquiring the nickname, Pittsburgh fans loved the outfielder and proudly chanted "Kiki" at Forbes Field.

Two years after Cuyler was acquired in 1921, Dreyfuss hit the jackpot in player procurement. Prior to the 1924 season, four players, diverse in age and with varying pedigrees, joined Pittsburgh as minor league purchases. Shortstop Glenn Wright, infielder-outfielder Eddie Moore and pitchers Ray Kremer and Emil Yde all debuted for the Pirates in 1924.

Glenn Wright was the jewel of this foursome; he was anointed to replace veteran Rabbit Maranville as Pittsburgh's starting shortstop in 1924, ever before the young man had played a big league game. Forest Glenn Wright was born on February 6, 1901, in Archie, Missouri, a small municipality with a population of about 500 people and local town team. This proved to be an advantage for Wright since his school did not have a baseball team. When Wright finished his studies at the district school, he moved on to the University of Missouri and began taking courses in an effort to earn a business degree.[26]

Wright had been studying at Missouri for two years when he received an offer to play baseball for Kansas City of the American Association. This proffer came as a bit of a surprise to Wright since he had not gained any notoriety while performing in Archie and did not play baseball at Missouri. Glenn accepted Kansas City's offer, and the youngster was shipped to Independence of the Southwestern League for more seasoning. Wright hit .316 in 120 games with Independence and was quickly recalled at the end of the 1921 season.[27] The young shortstop continued his torrid hitting for Kansas City as he hit at a clip of .299 (1922) and .313 (1923) for the Blues. Barney Dreyfuss's scouts quickly turned the owner onto Wright's exploits in the American Association, and the Pirates owner forked over a small fortune to purchase the tall, rangy shortstop.[28]

Wright had a sensational rookie season for the Pirates in 1924. Despite growing pains at the plate, Wright still hit .287 while appearing in all of Pittsburgh's 153 games. Glenn also showed great ability hitting in the pinch as the rookie shortstop led the Corsairs with 111 RBIs. Even though he made 52 errors in the field, Wright was still considered a stellar glove man who handled 963 chances at shortstop. Wright had great range and possessed a capable glove. His greatest asset, however, was a powerful throwing arm that Wright had developed as a child growing up in Archie.

"I always had a good arm," said Wright. "When I was a kid throwing stones, I seemed to have it over the others. It's no particular credit to me. If I make the best of this gift that nature has given me, possibly I might take some credit, but I'm afraid that's still a long ways off."[29]

While Wright polished his skills playing for Kansas City, Eddie Moore was establishing himself as the starting shortstop for the Atlanta Crackers of the Southern Association. Graham Edward Moore was born on January 18, 1899, in Barlow, Kentucky. Moore's baseball experience was minimal when Dreyfuss and McKechnie purchased the young player for the Pittsburgh club. Moore debuted for Omaha in 1921 before being farmed out to a lower minor league team in Dyersburg.[30] After a short stint playing for St. Petersburg in 1922, Moore joined the Crackers during the second half of the year and hit .251 in 87 games. Moore then played a full season for Atlanta in 1923 and batted .268 while appearing in 156 games. The youngster secured a spot on the 1924 Pittsburgh roster out of spring training and surpassed all expectations by batting .359 in 72 games.

The final two minor league prizes that debuted for the Pirates in 1924 were both pitchers who took far different paths to the major leagues. Southpaw twirler Emil Yde joined the Pirates after pitching only three seasons of minor league ball, while right-handed pitcher Ray Kremer toiled for ten years in the bush leagues. When both players finally reached the big leagues for the first time in 1924, Yde was 24 years old and Kremer was a rookie at the age of 31.

Emil Ogden Yde was born on January 28, 1900, in Great Lakes, Illinois. Yde was given a chance to pitch for Cedar Rapids in 1921 but did not win a game while seeing very limited action. The Danish southpaw moved on to Oklahoma City of the Western League and could muster nothing more than a 5–5 record in 1922. Yde emerged from obscurity in 1923 and blossomed into the staff ace of Oklahoma City's squad by posting a 28–12 record in 47 games. This sudden improvement caught the eyes of major league scouts throughout the country. The Pirates were able to fend off other suitors as they made a deal with Oklahoma City in which Barney Dreyfuss purchased Yde for $15,000.[31] The deal was struck on December 1, 1923, with the Pirates also arranging to send a player to be named later along with the cash.

While Yde discovered success at a very young age, Kremer took a circuitous route to the major leagues. Remy Peter Kremer was born on March 23, 1893, in Oakland, California. As a 21-year-old youngster, Kremer began a career that took him through a number of thriving cities on the Pacific slope. Kremer first signed with Sacramento in 1914, and was then sold with

Barney Dreyfuss and Bill McKechnie purchased right-handed twirler Ray Kremer from Oakland of the Pacific Coast League after the 1923 season. As a 31-year-old rookie in 1924, Kremer went 18–10 and posted a 3.19 ERA for the second-place Pittsburgh Pirates (National Baseball Hall of Fame Library, Cooperstown, New York).

the entire franchise to Salt Lake in 1915. That same season, he was shipped to Vancouver. The New York Giants then purchased Kremer in the fall of 1915, but John McGraw sent the young pitcher back to Vancouver early in 1916.[32] Kremer ended up in his home town of Oakland in 1917, pitching for the Oaks during the next seven seasons. He finally emerged in 1922 after several rough years, posting a 20–18 record and an ERA of 2.78. He topped that won-loss record in 1923 by going 25–16, supported by a 3.08 ERA. The Pirates finally purchased Kremer's contract from Oakland in the fall of 1923.[33]

Emil Yde and Ray Kremer both thrived in Pittsburgh during their rookie seasons. Yde topped the National League in winning percentage with a 16–3 mark while Kremer's 18 victories placed him second on the staff behind southpaw Wilbur Cooper's 20 wins. Yde and Kremer seemed capable of someday reaching the 20-victory plateau like staff counterparts Cooper and Johnny Morrison. The fifth member of Bill McKechnie's starting 1924 rotation was a player that Pittsburgh management had not purchased from a minor league team. Lee Meadows arrived via the trade route in order to fill an immediate need on his team. On May 22, 1923, the Pirates received Meadows and second baseman Johnny Rawlings from the Philadelphia Phillies in exchange for pitcher Whitey Glazner, infielder Cotton Tierney and $50,000 in cash.

Meadows was a veteran pitcher of eight major league seasons when he joined the Pirates. Meadows surprised the baseball world when he became the first bespectacled pitcher to reach the big leagues, achieving this feat with St. Louis in 1915. At that time, poor eyesight was seen as a handicap that was too difficult for athletes to overcome. Many observers believed Meadows was foolish to attempt such a bold endeavor since he had used artificial means to improve his eyesight.[34] Meadows defied his critics and carved out a solid major league career with St. Louis and Philadelphia before joining the Pirates in 1923.

Henry Lee Meadows was born in Oxford, North Carolina, on July 12, 1894. Before Meadows defied the odds and debuted with St. Louis in 1915, he plied his trade in the minors for Morristown in 1912 and Durham in 1913 and 1914.[35] Meadows starred for the Bulls, forging consistent seasons in both 1913 (21–14, 1.85 ERA) and 1914 (19–12, 1.86 ERA). At the close of the 1914 North Carolina State League season Durham sold Meadows to the Cardinals.[36] Meadows became a hard luck pitcher in St. Louis and Philadelphia who lost over 20 games in 1916 and 1919. He would post a combined record of 17–13 between Pittsburgh and Philadelphia in 1923. He followed that up with a 13–12 mark in 1924, his first full season with the Pirates.

Johnny Rawlings was another seasoned, veteran player when the Pirates acquired him from Philadelphia in 1923. John William Rawlings was born on August 17, 1892, in Bloomfield, Iowa. When Rawlings was a youngster, his family moved out west to California, where Johnny eventually attended Los Angeles High School. Rawlings' baseball career began out west when he signed with Victoria of the Northwestern League in 1912. After two seasons of playing in British Columbia, Rawlings made his major league debut with Cincinnati in 1914. His stay proved relatively short as he quickly jumped to the upstart Federal League and played there the next season and a half.

After the Federal League disbanded in 1915, Rawlings found himself back in the minor leagues playing for Toledo in 1916. The Boston Braves drafted him in the Rule 5 draft on September 19, 1916. Rawlings remained in the major leagues and played for Boston, Philadelphia and New York from 1917 through 1922. Philadelphia then claimed Rawlings off waivers from New York on May 11, 1923, and included him in the trade with Meadows to Pittsburgh ten days later. Rawlings became Pittsburgh's starting second baseman for the remainder of the 1923 season and hit .284 in 119 games. Rawlings lost his starting job when Rabbit Maranville was moved to second base in 1924. If Rawlings was going to make the 1925 Pittsburgh Pirates roster, it most likely would be as a utility infielder.

When the Pittsburgh roster needed to be tweaked further in 1924, McKechnie saved catcher Earl Smith from a potential trip back to the minors; the Pirates claimed him off waivers from the Boston Braves on July 14, 1924. This move occurred of necessity because both of Pittsburgh's regular catchers were injured with the task of working behind the plate falling to rookie Cliff Knox for a few games. Earl Sutton Smith was a hard-nosed, throwback player who was born on February 14, 1897, in Sheridan, Arkansas. A rough-and-tumble player, he played the game hard and lived life to the fullest. This approach put Smith at repeated odds with John McGraw during his days with the New York Giants.

Smith's career began to prosper when he hit .332 for Fort Smith of the Western Association in 1917. In 1918, he moved on to Rochester of the International League and hit .358 for the Hustlers. Rochester traded Smith to the Giants on January 2, 1919, for a package of players that included Waite Hoyt, Jack Ogden and Billy Kelly. Smith appeared in two World Series with New York before McGraw tired of his antics and packaged him with pitcher Jesse Barnes to Boston for catcher Hank Gowdy and pitcher Mule Watson on July 7, 1923. One year later, Smith became a Pittsburgh Pirate, hitting .369 in 39 late-season games for the Corsairs in 1924.

McKechnie and Dreyfuss did not rest on their laurels while the Pirates battled for the National League pennant in 1924. Team scouts continued to scour the country looking for talent that could improve Pittsburgh's team in 1925. The success of players like Wright, Cuyler, Moore, Yde and Kremer gave Pittsburgh management a high level of confidence in assessing minor league talent. Dreyfuss was willing to continue the rebuilding process through this method largely because the advice of his scouts had been impeccable.

Scout Chick Fraser was responsible for Pittsburgh signing a young phenom pitcher from Oklahoma City named Don Songer.[37] The southpaw was a teammate of Yde in 1923; he became Oklahoma City's staff ace in 1924 after the Danish pitcher left. Donald C. Songer was born on January 31, 1899, in Walnut, Kansas. Songer spent his early career playing for a variety of cities in 1920 and 1921 before he blossomed in 1922 by going 31–4 for the Enid Harvesters of the Western Association. Oklahoma City signed the southpaw and Songer responded by going 18–9 in 1923. In 1924, Songer won 23 games and lost 14 for an Oklahoma City team that failed to win half of its games. Fraser considered Songer the best pitching prospect that he had ever seen.[38]

A Pittsburgh baseball fan echoed that sentiment when Songer's purchase was announced by the club. "Songer is by all means the best pitcher in the Western Association," remarked a former Oklahoma City man who now resided in Pittsburgh.[39]

Songer saw action in four late-season games for the Pirates during the 1924 season and was also credited with a no-decision in his first major league start against the Chicago Cubs on September 26. While Songer was adjusting to the major leagues as Pittsburgh finished the season, Dreyfuss was busy signing two more players who would be given an opportunity to make the Pirates' roster in 1925. The first was a young outfielder named George Haas, who had only two years of minor league baseball under his belt. Roy Spencer was the other player, a catcher who played for Birmingham of the Southern Association in 1924.

George William Haas was born on October 15, 1903, in Montclair, New Jersey. At the age of 20, Haas starred for Williamsport of the New York–Pennsylvania League and swatted at a .342 clip in 114 games. During the 1924 season, Haas split time playing for Pittsfield of the Eastern League and Oklahoma City of the Western League. While in Pittsfield, Haas hit .304, and smacked 15 doubles, eight triples and six home runs. Haas, a left-handed batter who threw right-handed, joined the Pirates in Philadelphia late in 1924 but did not appear in any games.[40]

Roy Hampton Spencer was born on February 22, 1900, in Scranton, North Carolina. Spencer came to Pittsburgh late in 1924 from a Birmingham team that had sent a large number of star performers to the Pirates a few years earlier. Spencer's career began when Detroit signed him from Omaha of the Western League in 1923. Tigers manager Ty Cobb opted to farm out Spencer to Augusta for more seasoning. After a season of playing baseball in the town where Cobb had gained stardom during his minor league days, Spencer was sold to Birmingham, where he hit .307 in 90 games for the Barons in 1924.[41] Spencer was expected to compete with veteran Walter Schmidt for the third-string catching position on Pittsburgh's roster in 1925.

If George "Mule" Haas was to become the next Kiki Cuyler, or Don Songer could pitch as effectively in 1925 as fellow southpaw Emil Yde did in

1924, the Pirates once again would be considered a strong pennant contender for the upcoming season. The nucleus for a team that could be expected to claim Pittsburgh's first championship since 1909 was now in place.

All Bill McKechnie and Barney Dreyfuss needed was one major move that would change the baseball landscape in Pittsburgh. The Pirates were a very competitive team from 1921 through 1924, but Dreyfuss failed to capture the National League pennant which had eluded him for so many years. It would take a bold, aggressive move to reconfigure a Pittsburgh squad that looked like champions, but only on paper, before each season began. Despite the Pirates' success each year, certain players were repeatedly preventing Pittsburgh from taking that next step. Manager McKechnie decided the time was ripe to make a daring move that would hopefully improve Pittsburgh's fortunes in 1925.

On October 27, 1924, McKechnie pulled the trigger on a blockbuster deal that saw pitcher Wilbur Cooper, first baseman Charlie Grimm and second baseman Rabbit Maranville being shipped to the Chicago Cubs. In return for these three veteran players, the Pirates received right-handed pitcher Vic Aldridge, second baseman George Grantham and first base prospect Al Niehaus. The Pirates did not even wait for the annual National League meetings in December to make one of the biggest trades in franchise history. Yet, the initial reaction from Pittsburgh fans was negative. Many Smoky City fans believed that Chicago management had cheated the Pirates in this deal. In contrast, fans in the Windy City were ecstatic. They quickly hailed president Bill Veeck and manager Bill Killefer as brilliant geniuses.[42]

A large faction of the Pittsburgh fandom had always showed devout loyalty to Maranville in spite of his extra-curricular activities. Barney Dreyfuss became thoroughly disgusted with Maranville's escapades during the campaigns of 1922 and 1923. Dreyfuss tried to trade his free-spirited player after the 1923 season but found no takers. Even though Maranville behaved admirably in 1924, his prior conduct made him expendable.[43] Although Grimm was not a troublemaker to the extent of Maranville, Dreyfuss believed the Pittsburgh first baseman did not take his job seriously. Despite being one of the best fielding first basemen in the National League, Grimm was included in the Chicago trade for two specific reasons. He had held out for more money prior to spring training in 1924. He also endured a serious run-in with McKechnie during the summer.[44]

Cooper's inclusion in this transaction was a surprise to some people considering the southpaw was a four-time twenty-game winner for the Pirates. He was not a troublemaker like Maranville and lived a clean-cut life away from the field. Yet, Cooper did have a moody personality that did not endear him to a large section of the Pittsburgh population. While on the mound, when things were not going well, Cooper had a tendency to let his unhappiness affect his pitching. Supporters of Cooper stated that the southpaw was misunderstood and only acted that way because he had a deep, burning desire to win games.[45]

First baseman Al Niehaus seemed to be the key piece of baseball property acquired from Chicago in the blockbuster deal. Albert Bernard Niehaus was born on June 1, 1899, in Cincinnati, Ohio. In 1921, at the age of 21, Niehaus started his career playing for Jacksonville in the Florida State League. Niehaus moved on to Bradenton in 1923 and hit .364. He moved up to Chattanooga in 1924 and continued his torrid hitting, posting a .366 average with 11 home runs. Manager Johnny Dobbs of rival Memphis told McKechnie that Niehaus was the best first baseman ever developed in the Southern Association. Despite the fact that Niehaus had never played a major league game, Barney Dreyfuss was confident his new first baseman would capably fill Grimm's shoes at first base.[46]

The other two players acquired by McKechnie certainly were not afterthoughts. George Grantham was brought in to compete with Clyde Barnhart and Carson Bigbee for a spot in the Pirates' outfield. The winner of that battle would have the privilege of joining Kiki Cuyler and Max Carey in Pittsburgh's outer garden. In the meantime, Emil Yde's breakthrough season in 1924 made fellow southpaw Wilbur Cooper expendable. By acquiring Vic Aldridge, Bill McKechnie was gaining a pitcher who was younger than Cooper.

George Farley Grantham was born on May 20, 1900, in Galena, Kansas. Grantham, a product of Northern Arizona University, started his minor league career playing for Tacoma of the Pacific Coast International League in 1920. Grantham split time between Tacoma and Portland in 1921 and batted .325. The left-handed hitting youngster moved on to Omaha of the Western League, where he hit .359 for the Buffaloes in 1922. Chicago then purchased Grantham from Omaha in September of 1922. He was named Chicago's starting second baseman for the 1923 season and responded by hitting .281 during his rookie campaign. Grantham followed that with another solid season at the plate in 1924. The free-swinging infielder hit .316 in 127 games for Chicago and led the National League in strikeouts for the second consecutive season.

Victor Aldridge was born on October 25, 1893, in Crane, Indiana. In 1915, Indianapolis Indians manager Jack Hendricks saw potential in Aldridge during a tryout and signed him.[47] Hendricks farmed the youngster out to Erie for more seasoning, but he returned to Indianapolis in 1916. Aldridge posted a 16–14 record supported by a 2.40 ERA for the Indians. The Chicago Cubs then purchased Aldridge at the season's conclusion and kept him on their roster for the 1917 and 1918 seasons. After two years of unimpressive pitching in Chicago, Aldridge pitched three seasons of minor league baseball in the Pacific Coast League.[48] The right-hander made his way back to Chicago and remained with the Cubs for three seasons. Aldridge enjoyed solid seasons in 1922 (16–

15, 3.52 ERA), 1923 (16–9, 3.48 ERA) and 1924 (15–12, 3.50) while ably complementing Chicago's staff ace, Pete Alexander.

After the trade between Chicago and Pittsburgh, Rabbit Maranville returned to the Smoky City from a relaxing hunting trip and issued a statement to the local press. Maranville announced that he intended to remain a permanent resident of the city. He would reside in Chicago during the season and be in Pittsburgh when the Cubs played at Forbes Field.[49] Once the season was over, Rabbit would then spend his winters in the Smoky City.

Maranville also gave out a statement regarding his intentions for the 1925 baseball season. "I intend to give Chicago my best services," said the Rabbit, "just as I have always given Pittsburgh my best. I have no intention of removing my home from this city. I am educating my daughter here, and I have a host of friends here, whom I desire to retain. Pittsburgh's baseball club has my best wishes. I hope the Cubs win the 1925 pennant, with the Pirates finishing one notch lower."[50]

By rolling the dice and trading long-standing, proven performers, Bill McKechnie had backed himself into a corner. If the Pirates failed to claim the National League pennant in 1925, the criticism surrounding the blockbuster trade would likely reach a deafening crescendo among disgruntled Pirates fans. McKechnie took a chance making a deal that he believed would improve team chemistry and morale. If McKechnie's team did not claim the NL title, it was highly probable that Pittsburgh's baseball patrons would be calling for a change in the managerial chair.

3

Spring Training at Paso Robles

Pittsburgh manager Bill McKechnie had certainly taken a risk in making the unpopular trade with Chicago after the 1924 season. If Vic Aldridge, George Grantham and Al Niehaus failed in Pittsburgh, McKechnie could expect to be excoriated by both the fans and the local press.

Some Pirates rooters still held McKechnie personally responsible for the team's failure to capture a pennant in 1924. They were quick to point out his mistakes and believed Pittsburgh's manager needed to apply much more rigid discipline upon his players. One such player was pitcher Johnny Morrison, whose production fell off considerably during the 1924 season. Morrison's downfall was blamed on his lack of conditioning. His escapades, along with those of some other veteran players, were well known to Smoky City fans. The local populace reasoned that McKechnie should have handed out punishment to such offenders, no matter how valuable they were to Pittsburgh's baseball club.[1]

Despite all of the criticism, Barney Dreyfuss stated that he was satisfied with the work McKechnie did in 1924 and let it be known that Bill would be back as leader of the Pirates in 1925 if he so desired. McKechnie had no intention of leaving, since he was far from completing the rebuilding process that had begun in Pittsburgh a few seasons ago.[2] It was evident that Dreyfuss and McKechnie had a mutual admiration for each other.

"We have been going through a process of development," said McKechnie, "and it has not yet been completed. If you all know Mr. Dreyfuss as well as I do, you would know that nothing is dearer to him than a winning team. He has co-operated fully with me, and together we are trying to strengthen our forces so that we can give the loyal fans here a real winner next season."[3]

McKechnie exhibited his solidarity with Dreyfuss when the manager joined the owner and made a trip to Washington during the 1924 World Series to meet with Commissioner Kenesaw Mountain Landis. The purpose of the excursion was to bring new information surrounding the O'Connell-Dolan bribery scandal to baseball's czar. Dreyfuss and McKechnie soon found they had wasted their time rushing off to the nation's capital. While all three men were aboard an elevator at the Willard Hotel, Landis refused to talk about the affair with Dreyfuss and verbally berated him about his desire to dig deeper into the scandal. Dreyfuss asked Landis if the matter could be discussed further in his room; the Judge responded by stating that he would not be in. This curt response on Landis' part angered the usually docile McKechnie.[4]

"Why won't you be in?" shouted McKechnie.[5]

Landis quickly turned toward McKechnie and returned fire to Pittsburgh's irate manager. He leaned over until his face nearly touched McKechnie's and yelled another curt, sarcastic response.[6]

"Who are you? I have nothing to do with you," screamed Landis.[7]

Landis then reached his floor and left the elevator before the situation turned uglier. As the Judge departed company from the two disappointed Pirates representatives, McKechnie told Landis that he was a "front runner."[8] The context of Dreyfuss's evidence never became known, but most baseball experts assumed that his information supported the possibility that New York manager John McGraw had full knowledge of Jimmy O'Connell's and Cozy Dolan's role in bribing Heinie Sand. Dolan had angered Dreyfuss one year earlier when the New York coach approached Pirates third baseman Pie Traynor and advised him to hold out for a salary of $15,000 in 1924. Dreyfuss believed that John McGraw had told Dolan to make these recommendations to Traynor in an effort to turn the third baseman into a malcontent. When questioned by Commissioner Landis in 1923, Dolan stated he only suggested to Traynor that he should be paid more money in 1924, and was not ordered to do so by McGraw.[9]

While Dreyfuss and McKechnie were unable to receive an audience with baseball's czar, a member of the Pirates' squad was summoned to the chambers of the game's highest authority. In late October, when McKechnie's return as Pittsburgh's manager for 1925 should have been headline news, a story appearing in a Rockford, Illinois, newspaper trumped other prose written about the Pirates. Pitcher Emil Yde reportedly made statements that indicated that the O'Connell-Dolan bribery scandal was the tip of the iceberg. Yde was quoted as saying that other members of the Philadelphia Phillies besides Sand had been approached about throwing ballgames. When Landis saw the story, he quickly requested Yde's presence in his office. When player and judge met, Yde denied that he had ever made those remarks. After the meeting, Landis demanded a retraction from the editor of the Rockford paper.[10]

"This disposes of another flock of baseless rumors," Landis said after his talk with Yde. "The fans may rest assured that the O'Connell-Dolan affair is still being investigated, but we are fortunate in so quickly scotching this false assertion reflecting on players, who had no connection with such a transaction as O'Connell and Dolan attempted to put over."[11]

Yde also denied two other quotes that were attributed to him in the article. The first rebuff surrounded an alleged statement by Yde in which he said carousing on the part of some Pirates hurt the team's pennant chances during the closing weeks of 1924. Yde's alleged comments concluded with the pitcher contending that some of his teammates went on a wild, drinking spree during a crucial series in Boston.[12]

Yde's second denial revolved around his contract negotiations with Dreyfuss. The article stated that Yde had already signed a three-year deal that would pay him handsomely through 1927.[13] Yde denied that this information had any validity. Ironically, a Pittsburgh newspaper simultaneously released a story stating that Yde had indeed signed a three-year deal that would pay him $8,000 per year.[14] The Rockford newspaper's original story matched the information from Pittsburgh's periodical, including the detail that Dreyfuss paid Yde an extra $1,000 for agreeing not to play basketball during the winter as part of his duties as a YMCA physical director.[15]

Yde's meeting with Landis directly ended any involvement from a Pirates player, manager or owner regarding the O'Connell-Dolan bribery scandal. This did not mean that Dreyfuss and his players might not be affected indirectly from further fallout surrounding this case. When the scandal story initially broke, members of the United States Congress became galvanized and decided that it was time the federal government exerted oversight control over Organized Baseball. After American League president Ban Johnson had declared the 1924 World Series between New York and Washington should be cancelled, Congressman Sol Bloom, a Tammany Hall politician who represented the Manhattan district of New York, declared baseball should be regulated by federal act.[16]

> The nation-wide interest in the World's Series now in progress, combined with the national chagrin that one of the participating teams is involved in a scandal convinces me that the time has come when the Federal Government should take a supervisory interest in baseball.
>
> Baseball is a matter of interstate commerce. The two major leagues and most of the minor leagues, all larger minor leagues, are interstate affairs. Congress has the power to regulate the interstate operation of railroads and the interstate movement of foodstuffs, medicines, etc.
>
> If Congress can do this, it can regulate interstate baseball. The sport is a national pastime and it has taken such a hold on our people that the government should provide some sort of regulation for the good of the sport itself, as well as the protection of the public. Baseball magnates recognized the demand for some sort of super regulation when Judge Landis was chosen as czar, but the game is too big for one man to control. When Congress reconvenes, I shall introduce a regulatory bill, and I believe it will be enacted into law.[17]

Luckily for Dreyfuss and his fellow baseball magnates, the wheels of the government machine moved slowly regarding this matter. A petition was circulated to Congress requesting that the government take control of baseball.[18] The timing of this move seemed intriguing since the game was continuing to peak in both popularity and as a financial boon for baseball's moguls. If the government took control of baseball, it would expect a piece of the monetary pie without taking any of the financial risk of men like Dreyfuss. Even though the proposal for such a bill quickly lost traction and died, Dreyfuss pondered what effect such government control would have on the players moreso than baseball's owners.

"The man who is fostering the movement — Collier, is a Clevelander, editor, I believe, of a small paper there," stated Dreyfuss. "He has been writing me for three years about baseball reforms. I don't think the present movement will get very far. I wonder how the ballplayers would like all drawing the same salary, regardless of ability or accomplishment."[19]

Dreyfuss reasoned that baseball players who excelled on the field would not be willing to accept a government mandated salary system, in which everyone was given equal pay for playing the game. It would be preposterous to expect that a third-string catcher make the same amount of money playing baseball as Ty Cobb or Babe Ruth. Although the present system was not perfect and was skewed in the owners' favor, a player still had a chance at achieving a decent life if he worked hard and excelled on the diamond. If the current system was not in place, players would lack the freedom to make demands for their services.

Prior to sending out contracts for the 1925 season, Dreyfuss received a tip from a Pittsburgh sports writer that some of his players' salary requests would be exorbitant. Dreyfuss quickly responded to this report when it was intimated that he would have difficulty signing some players.[20] "Perhaps I don't want the men referred to," Dreyfuss responded as he thanked the writer for tipping him off.[21]

Dreyfuss believed that he had always treated his charges fairly when it came to salary negotiations. Some players had challenged Dreyfuss in the past, but the owner usually signed his players by opening day. Two of the players who were reported as possible challengers to Dreyfuss during the off-season were youngsters who played well during the 1924 season. One youngster claimed he had played for "peanuts" in 1924 and proclaimed publicly that he intended to "get his" next year, or else he would not play baseball. A second young player who received critical acclaim in 1924 reasoned that he was just beginning his career in baseball. If Dreyfuss did not pay him what he wanted, the player was young enough to give up the game and find another job that would provide better financial security.[22] Dreyfuss needed to walk a fine line in negotiations with such players so that the fan base in Pittsburgh did not become alarmed when some star players were categorized as holdouts.

Two players who had been holdouts prior to the 1924 season were now residing in Chicago. Charlie Grimm and Wilbur Cooper were two members of the Pirates that Dreyfuss had difficulty signing each year. After the 1924 season ended, rumors abounded that Grimm and Cooper were going to make contract demands that would probably rile Dreyfuss.[23] After the season, Cooper boasted that Barney would have to pay him substantially next season if the southpaw were to continue playing baseball.[24] Both of these contract issues became a moot point when McKechnie sent Cooper and Grimm to Chicago. As far as the threats coming from those two Pirate rookies, one of the players signed a contract for 1925 at management's salary without making any complaint.[25]

Team business was placed on the back burner for one evening when a group of Pittsburgh baseball fans held a dinner on October 25, 1924, to commemorate the 25th anniversary of Barney Dreyfuss becoming owner of the team. Dignitaries from across the country attended the banquet in order to honor one of baseball's most influential magnates. Some of the players that Dreyfuss had brought from Louisville to Pittsburgh when the two clubs consolidated prior to 1900 were also in attendance. Included in this group were Fred Clarke, Honus Wagner, Tom McCreery, Deacon Phillippe, along with many others. Most of the speeches given that night emphasized the inherent honesty of baseball and the fact that most Americans loved the game. Each speaker stressed that the presence of one dishonest man in baseball did not mean the game should be condemned, just as the discovery of one thief in business did not prove that all businessmen were corrupt. Curiously, Commissioner Landis was invited to Dreyfuss's testimonial dinner, but could not attend due to a prior commitment.[26]

After one night of merriment Dreyfuss and McKechnie went back to work and continued to tweak Pittsburgh's roster. While most of Pittsburgh prepared to celebrate the Thanksgiving holiday, Bill McKechnie announced that Eddie Moore would be called upon to replace Rabbit Maranville at second base.[27] With Moore being moved to the infield fulltime, this opened another spot in Pittsburgh's outfield, which was expected to be secured by George Grantham. The first base job was rookie Al Niehaus' to lose, while all other starting positions on McKechnie's team belonged to players who held down those spots during the 1924 season. The only situation that McKechnie had not resolved was how playing time at two outfield spots would be split between Kiki Cuyler, Clyde Barnhart, Carson Bigbee and Grantham.

Prior to the December league meetings in New York, Barney Dreyfuss obtained a young infielder as insurance in case Moore failed as Pittsburgh's newly minted keystone player. Dreyfuss purchased second baseman Lafayette Fresco Thompson, Jr., who was the son of a personal friend of Pittsburgh's owner. Dreyfuss shipped pitcher Arnold Stone and an unspecified amount of cash to Omaha of the Western League for Thompson's services. After making the purchase, Dreyfuss claimed he had been trying to acquire Thompson for more than a year.[28]

In 1924, while playing for Omaha, Thompson hit .317 in 168 games. As the top second baseman of the Western League that year, Thompson scored 150 runs and banged out 220 hits, including 36 doubles, 17 triples and seven home runs. His total of 43 stolen bases served notice that the young infielder would fit right in with Pittsburgh's stable of fleet-footed players.[29] When Thompson decided to make baseball his career, the elder Thompson explained to his son that if he did not eventually become a competent big leaguer who earned a worthwhile salary, he could find some other line of employment. The senior Thompson decided that no bush league players would take up residence at his home.[30]

While Dreyfuss was busy acquiring Thompson in order to push Moore during spring training, Jack Onslow was signed to become McKechnie's pitching coach. Onslow was a native of Tarentum, Pennsylvania, who managed the Allegheny Steel independent team a few years earlier. In 1924, Onslow managed Richmond of the Virginia League and led the team to the pennant. Besides his duties handling Pittsburgh's pitchers, Onslow was also expected to take his turn on the coaching lines with manager McKechnie and coach Jewel Ens. Onslow's addition to Pittsburgh's coaching staff meant that Grover Land would not return to the Pirates in 1925.[31]

Bill McKechnie and Barney Dreyfuss's son, Samuel, who acted as Pittsburgh's team treasurer, attended both the minor and major league meetings held in New York.[32] Before the major league festivities began in early December, McKechnie gave an encapsulated view of where the Pirate team stood, as writers asked the manager if he would be involved in any trade discussions.

"I am pretty well satisfied as our roster stands," said the Pirates' boss. "I feel sure we will have a better outfit than last season. Our big trade with Chicago added to the hitting and base running strength of our club, and also deprived our roster of a couple clowns.

"Of course, there may be some more changes before spring time rolls around, but there will be no sensational transfers. Some of the youngsters now on the roster will be let out under optional agreements, but aside from that, I look for nothing big to transpire."[33]

When Barney Dreyfuss was pinned down by a writer to give his assessment of any constructive activity being accomplished at the meetings, he practically echoed McKechnie's sentiment verbatim. "So far as I am concerned," said Dreyfuss, "I will be satisfied to go along with what we have right now. I believe that trade which we made with the Chicago Cubs helped us in more ways than one. It gives us a better hitting team, a better stealing combination, and I believe there will be more harmony, and a greater respect for discipline and the rules.

"We won't have so many clowns on the team, but I imagine we can get along very well without the comedy stuff. Baseball is a serious business, and we have sought to get players who will so take it."[34]

It was difficult to determine whether Dreyfuss and McKechnie's comments were sincere, or if these statements were made so as to conceal trade discussions. It was rumored that the Pirates' leaders were turning their covetous eyes toward St. Louis Cardinals first baseman Jim Bottomley. A deal for Bottomley seemed realistic since St. Louis was interested in acquiring outfielder Carson Bigbee. Besides Bigbee, it was rumored that catcher Walter Schmidt, infielder Johnny Rawlings and an unknown pitcher could be included in any potential package.[35]

Pirates management denied there was any substance to these rumors and expressed confidence that Niehaus would be a capable first baseman. The Bottomley rumors seemed plausible since Pittsburgh had put in a waiver claim with another big league team for veteran first baseman Jake Daubert only weeks before Niehaus was acquired. Cincinnati placed Daubert on waivers so that he could accept a job managing the Reading Internationals. Pittsburgh planned on offering Daubert more money than he would have received as a minor league manager if the first baseman was assigned to Pittsburgh.[36] The Pirates' plan for Daubert became painfully irrelevant when the 40-year-old first baseman died on October 9, 1924, from complications following an appendectomy one week earlier.

The Pirates made no deals at the meetings in New York. This did not mean that Barney Dreyfuss was done making changes to his team's roster. As Pittsburgh's inhabitants prepared to celebrate the Christmas season, Dreyfuss cut loose a veteran player whose salary had eaten up a sizeable chunk of Pittsburgh's payroll the past few seasons. Catcher Walter Schmidt was granted his unconditional release after every major league team had passed on making a waiver claim. It was apparent that no team wanted to pay the $4,000 waiver price to Pittsburgh for a man whose 1924 salary was $12,000. Schmidt was always a difficult man to sign during his time as a Pirate; the catcher's stubborn holdouts each year sealed his fate in Dreyfuss's eyes. The acquisition of Earl Smith made Schmidt expendable and supported McKechnie's philosophy of rebuilding for the future.[37]

"We regret Schmidt's departure," said manager McKechnie, in announcing his release, "but it is in line with our policy to reconstruct. We have plenty of other good backstops, and will not be weakened. Schmidt was given his unconditional freedom, because president Dreyfuss wanted him to be able to pick his own assignment, if he desired to remain in the game."[38]

A second veteran was given his unconditional release and replaced by a much younger arm. Pitcher Jeff Pfeffer, secured from St. Louis through the waiver wire in June of 1924, was shown the door, and Louis Koupal was secured from Omaha. Pittsburgh traded pitching prospect Robert L. Burns and an undisclosed amount of cash to secure Koupal's services from Omaha. The 25-year-old, right-hander won 22 games and lost 10 for the Buffaloes in 1924. Scout Chick Fraser had recommended Koupal's purchase at the same time he submitted a favorable report for pitcher Don Songer, who was acquired months earlier.[39] A host of scouts followed Koupal's exploits late in 1924, but many were turned off by Omaha owner Barney Burch's hefty price tag.[40] It was believed the Pirates paid $40,000 to secure Koupal's services.

The addition of men like Koupal, coupled with veteran players like Schmidt being released, meant that the flavor of Pittsburgh's 1925 roster had turned more youthful. When Charlie Grimm, Wilbur Cooper and Rabbit Maranville were traded to Chicago, the Pirates immediately became one of the National League's youngest clubs in terms of age and major league experience. Manager McKechnie stated that he took full responsibility for every change that had recently been made. He believed that the Chicago trade, along with any other modification made to the Pirates' roster, added to his team's punch and aggressiveness, and improved harmony.[41]

McKechnie also felt excited over the prospect of what rookie first baseman Al Niehaus might accomplish during his first season in Pittsburgh. "There is only one thing about Niehaus that is worrying me," said Wilkinsburg Bill, "and that is, that I have not heard a single word of adverse criticism of him since his acquisition. Scores of men have talked to me about him, and written me letters about him, and in every instance they have ardently boasted him.

"I have heard it said in a round about way that he is not the fastest man in the world. Well, perhaps that is true, but, if so, we will be no worse off than we had been in that position."[42]

While McKechnie talked about the upcoming 1925 season, he also tried to explain the inherent reason why the Pirates had failed to capture a pennant the previous year.

"It was at home plate that we lost the 1924 pennant," said the local manager. "We didn't have the drive that a consistent winner needs. We had the bases filled with two outs many times, and didn't get a run because we didn't have the power to drive in runs under such circumstances. I believe that condition has been remedied, and that we will present a stronger front all-around than last season."[43]

McKechnie seemed to be more at ease giving interviews about the upcoming season than he had been at times during the 1924 campaign. During an earlier November talk with Ralph S. Davis, sports writer for *The Pittsburgh Press*, McKechnie revealed that 1924 was a stressful year due to some personal issues that occupied the manager's mind. McKechnie was not in the best of health during that season. This revelation coupled with the fact that McKechnie also dealt with an undisclosed serious illness to a family member at home, made it difficult for him to give the Pittsburgh team his undivided attention. McKechnie labored under this intense strain, which was exasperated by the fact that Pittsburgh became involved in a red-hot pennant race.[44]

By the winter of 1925, it seemed that all of McKechnie's problems were behind him.[45] McKechnie's health had improved; he was much more jovial and content when he talked about the upcoming season. Pittsburgh rooters were hopeful that McKechnie would be able to manage the 1925 team without being weighed down by the heavy burden of personal problems. Many Smoky City inhabitants could relate to McKechnie's plight, as families of mill workers suffered from part-time closings of Pittsburgh's mills and factories in 1924. In spite of the area's industrial blight, fans still poured into Forbes Field to watch the Pirates.[46]

Pittsburgh management announced the team's 1925 spring training schedule during early January. Once again, camp would be held at Paso Robles, California, with the Pirates leaving for the Pacific Coast on February 24. Three weeks of intense training would be followed by exhibition games against minor league teams in San Francisco, Los Angeles and Vernon. The team would then begin its trek east on April 6, playing additional exhibition games in various stops before the season opener in Chicago.

The exhibition slate consisted of ten games against San Francisco from March 21 to 29, with two Sunday doubleheaders being played. From there the team would move to Vernon for a three-game series in late March and early April. Pittsburgh's training on the coast would conclude in Los Angeles on April 3, 4 and 5. Exhibition games slated for the trip back east were scheduled in Oklahoma City on April 8 and 9, April 10 at Little Rock and two contests in Memphis on April 11 and 12.[47]

Thoughts of spring and rebirth, always prevalent when a new baseball campaign began, dominated the minds of many throughout Pittsburgh. Some diehard fans probably wished that they, too, could make the trip to Paso Robles. A little less than a month before the start of training, winter wreaked havoc across Pittsburgh and Allegheny County. On January 28, 1925, temperatures in Pittsburgh and the surrounding area ranged between -3 and -21 degrees. The bitter temperature recorded in nearby Midway gave it the distinction of being the coldest spot in the United States that day.[48]

Despite the cold weather gripping Pittsburgh, Pirates management decided work would commence to expand the seating capacity of Forbes Field. Late in January, Barney Dreyfuss announced that the Pittsburgh Athletic Company, the corporation that owned Forbes Field, was prepared to award a contract bid for construction at the ballpark. Work would begin immediately and eventually add an additional 10,000 seats to Forbes Field by the end of June. The planned construction called for the double decker tier stands to be extended from the present right terminal of the stadium around to the middle of the field. The current triple decker grandstand would not be affected in any way.[49]

The new improvements at Forbes Field would make it necessary to shorten right field down the foul line by 55 feet. When the new stands reached completion, the right field line would stand an even 300 feet from home plate. The new structure would consist of steel and concrete and would be built on property that the Pittsburgh baseball club already owned. Forbes Field's seating capacity would increase to 40,000 by the time the project was completed in June. This meant that Dreyfuss's baseball palace would rank among the game's largest ballparks in terms of seating capacity. On many occasions during the 1924 season, Forbes Field proved to be too small, as many paying customers wanting to see the Corsairs in action had to be turned away. These improvements and expansions were expected to cost Pittsburgh's owner several thousand dollars.[50]

Shortly after the ballpark announcement was made, Barney Dreyfuss, Sam Dreyfuss and manager Bill McKechnie attended the National League's Golden Jubilee meeting in early February.[51] A meeting on February 2 in New York was held to discuss particulars regarding the National League's yearlong celebration commemorating its rise to existence in 1876. It was determined that there would be a special celebration in each National League city throughout the summer of 1925. Saturday, June 6, was chosen as the day for Pittsburgh's grand remembrance. Before the regular season game against the Philadelphia Phillies that day, a special game was scheduled to be played between the current Pirates squad and members of the 1901 team.[52]

Most members of that elite team were still alive, and every player who was extended an invitation by Dreyfuss had gladly accepted the offer to be in Pittsburgh on June 6. Members of the 1901 team expected to participate in the gala celebration included the following: Fred Clarke, left field; Tommy Leach, third base; Claude Ritchey, second base; Honus Wagner, shortstop; Clarence Beaumont, center field; Kitty Bransfield, first base; Tom McCreery, right field; Chief Zimmer and Jack O'Connor, catchers; and Deacon Phillippe, Jesse Tannehill, Sam Leever and Jack Chesbro, pitchers.[53] Pittsburgh fans were ecstatic that Leever would attend after a local newspaper had earlier reported the death of the Goshen, Ohio, resident. To his credit, Leever took the erroneous report in stride. The former star pitcher actually enjoyed reading his own obituary and appreciated the beautiful words said about him. Leever stated that he was not even "half dead," and said he never felt better in his life.[54]

Like Pittsburgh's fans, Dreyfuss was equally giddy over the prospect of an event celebrating his team's glorious past. "I have written all the old-timers for their measurements, and will provide them with a set of uniforms, exact style and pattern of the uniforms worn in 1901," said President Dreyfuss, commenting upon his plans for the reunion. "We are going to make this a real occasion, that will not soon be forgotten. I believe the fans of Pittsburgh would like to see the old days in action again. Of course, I do not know how long some of them will be able to last in the game, but as they fall by the wayside, we will rush substitutes into their positions."55

The Golden Jubilee celebration dates were officially released after the National League schedule for 1925 was ratified by baseball's powers. For decades, Dreyfuss had been a pivotal member of the scheduling committee. Surprisingly, Dreyfuss was not kind to his own club when he drafted the 1925 schedule. Once the National League season commenced, the Pirates were expected to travel 15,279 miles across the country's railways in order to fulfill their schedule. The spring training trip alone to Paso Robles was expected to cover 6,050 miles of territory. This was the longest journey to be undertaken by any National League club for spring training. Cincinnati was expected to make the second longest odyssey for the season at a total of 12,814 miles. Since Pittsburgh was the only Western city not permitted to play Sunday baseball due to Blue Laws, Dreyfuss's players would be spending more time on trains in 1925.56

The Pirates' Eastern party left Pittsburgh on Tuesday, February 24, and arrived in Chicago the following morning. After picking up some players there, the Pirates' contingent headed straight to Paso Robles. The team was expected to arrive on Saturday, February 28. The first camp workout was scheduled for March 2. When the Pirates' Train Express from Pittsburgh reached its destination, Barney Dreyfuss was there to greet them. After the recent National League meeting, Dreyfuss had started westward with his golf clubs in tow, hoping to spend as much time as possible relaxing by playing a few rounds on the California links. A few Pirates teammates who wintered out west also awaited their brethren who resided east of the Rocky Mountains during the off-season.57

A long cross-country trip such as this, which lasted the better part of five days, could have been considered boring for a group of players who were chomping to hit the playing diamond. The field at Paso Robles, much improved over the past training session in 1924, was expected to offer a great opportunity for McKechnie's troops to partake in quality training.58

The members of Pittsburgh's traveling party experienced an interesting anomaly on February 26 when they ate their trio of meals in three different states. Breakfast was taken at Dodge City, Kansas, lunch at La Junta, Colorado, and dinner at a restaurant in Las Vegas, New Mexico. The train crossed into Arizona that evening and began the final leg of its sojourn toward California.59

When the large delegation of players arrived in Paso Robles on February 28, every player was present except for two. The first was outfielder Clyde Barnhart, whose absence was excused due to an illness in his family. Vic Aldridge was the other player not present. Aldridge's absence was not excused;

3. *Spring Training at Paso Robles* 49

the recently acquired pitcher was considered a holdout. Dreyfuss and McKechnie had expected Aldridge to board the Pirates train in Chicago, but when it arrived there, Vic was nowhere to be found. Aldridge had not yet returned a signed contract, and manager McKechnie stressed that the next move was up to his newest pitcher.[60] "I don't know what ails him," said Mac, "but the matter is entirely up to him. We have gone as far as we will go and that is final. It is his next move."[61]

In 1923, the Chicago Cubs had promised Aldridge a $2,500 bonus if he reached a certain victory total. Aldridge did not reach this goal and was granted only a $500 salary increase by the Cubs in 1924. The salary that Barney Dreyfuss offered to Aldridge was considerably larger than what he was paid in 1924, including the bonus. McKechnie believed Pittsburgh management had negotiated fairly with Aldridge. There was a suspicion among Pirates rooters that Aldridge was holding out in order to avoid the training trip. Whatever the reasons behind Aldridge's holdout, Dreyfuss decided to use the silent treatment, leaving Aldridge to ponder his action without any coaxing on the part of Pittsburgh management.[62]

The remaining group of Pirate players in Paso Robles quickly realized that McKechnie intended to run a much tighter ship in 1925. In the past, McKechnie had never been much of a taskmaster. McKechnie generally believed his players would adhere to rules regarding clean living based on his own actions as a player. In 1924, McKechnie chose not to dole out harsh penalties for those who had abused the rules. During the off-season, McKechnie realized that his further employment as Pittsburgh's manager necessitated a change in policy. Prior to the team's first practice, McKechnie explained his rules of conduct during a meeting. He stated that whiskey drinking and high stakes card games would be prohibited in 1925.[63]

> The drinking of liquor will not be permitted on the club this year. If boozing is discovered among any of you — I care not whether veteran or youngster I found guilty — he will be suspended at once. No matter what the cost may be — if I have to break up my entire club — I am going to see that such a rule is strictly adhered to.
>
> In the past three or four years, our chances have been hurt by such actions on the part of some of the players. During that time I have shielded them. I have never fined nor suspended a player since I became manager of the Pittsburgh club. But I am through covering up the faults of others. It has got me nowhere in the past and I fail to see where it will obtain better results in the future. Therefore the guilty one, even if he is the best player I have on the club, will be dropped immediately.[64]

McKechnie concluded the meeting by telling his troops that each man would have to take a temperance pledge in 1925. The manager also cautioned his players to conduct themselves professionally on the diamond. McKechnie also covered the subject of Philadelphia's Heinie Sand, who had implicated Jimmy O'Connell and Cozy Dolan in the much talked about bribery scandal. McKechnie stated that no Pirate player could be abusive toward Sand because they believed him to be a snitch.

"I believe that Sand did exactly the right thing," explained McKechnie. "I think he should be commended by every player in the league. It is only through such actions that the game can be kept clean, and I intend, as soon as the season opens, to write a letter to that effect to the president of the Philadelphia club.

"And another thing—I want to hear no references to Sand as being yellow. If any such remarks come to my ears, especially while we are playing the Phillies, the maker of them will be promptly suspended. That is to be the rule of this club and I propose to see that it is upheld."[65]

None of McKechnie's players expressed any objection to his rules; each man seemed prepared to concentrate on training. Included in this group were some players who were training despite illness and personal tragedy. Max Carey was in camp, ready to play even though his 14 month old son, Richard, had died from pneumonia at their Los Angeles home in January.[66] Pie Traynor seemed recovered after undergoing a minor postseason operation.[67] Glenn Wright was also available for the first practice of the spring even though he had been weakened by a bout of influenza. Over the winter, Wright's tonsils had been removed, resulting in a string of colds. Wright contracted influenza when his immune system became too weak to stave off the sickness' attack.[68]

The condition of Pittsburgh's shortstop seemed to improve after the Pirates' Train Express to California picked up Wright in Kansas City. Wright participated in the team's morning workout on March 2, but was excused from afternoon activities by McKechnie. As Wright hit the field in the morning, his usually strong frame seemed to be missing about ten pounds of muscle. He appeared exhausted at the end of the practice session. Though Wright did not participate in the afternoon workout, he remained on the field offering encouragement to his teammates.[69]

Wright indulged in only light workouts the first week of training at Paso Robles. Ever cautious, McKechnie let the star shortstop regain his strength before permitting more rigid training.[70] When Wright was finally able to return to the lineup, another veteran player replaced him on the injured list. On the morning of March 12, pitcher Johnny Morrison left practice after complaining of a sharp pain in his side. A physician at Pittsburgh's hotel diagnosed the pain as a light attack of appendicitis and immediately ordered Morrison to remain in bed. When the pain did not subside, the physician examined Morrison a second time and diagnosed him with a hernia accompanied by an inflammation of the appendix.[71]

Morrison suffered through immense pain that evening and the next morning.⁷² The pain that Morrison had originally experienced the previous morning was much different from the agony he felt 24 hours later, causing the doctor to reconsider the diagnosis. The physician expected that Morrison would be confined to bed for a few days, but then advised him to try wearing an elastic truss. After donning the apparatus, Morrison displayed enough pain-free mobility that the doctor allowed him to resume exercising on the field.⁷³

Early reports from Pittsburgh's training sessions showed that the two newest members of the Pirates' infield were progressing nicely. First baseman Al Niehaus was playing as well as expected in filling Charlie Grimm's spot at first base. All of Pittsburgh's baseball correspondents noted Niehaus' serious, professional demeanor. They also praised his powerful swing and tendency to hit line drives. At second base, Eddie Moore was working hard to overcome his shortcomings in replacing Rabbit Maranville. A scrappy individual, Moore worked feverishly on drills in an effort to improve his tendency of over-running ground balls by taking the wrong angle.⁷⁴

As the Pirates prepared to break camp and begin their exhibition schedule, a group of younger players made a push to form a strong rookie class. Pitcher Lou Koupal arrived at training camp in excellent shape and showed a good repertoire of pitches. Southpaw Don Songer served notice that he might also be included in the mix for a spot on the 1925 staff. Bernard Culloton, a Fordham University product, looked good despite not receiving any advance reviews.⁷⁵ Second baseman Fresco Thompson also showed ability when Moore could not play in some exhibition games due to an injury.⁷⁶

During the first leg of the exhibition schedule against San Francisco, Vernon and Los Angeles, Pittsburgh's infield play left Bill McKechnie disappointed. In their defense, Pirates players felt the poor, soft under-footing of the Vernon and Los Angeles infields affected their play.⁷⁷ The last leg of the exhibition schedule presented other issues, as two starting players came down with injuries. Eddie Moore did not accompany the team as he opted to receive treatment for his injured left shoulder in Oklahoma City. The shoulder pain was the latest malady to plague Moore, who had also been troubled by sore arms and legs. An electric vibrator applied by an Oklahoma doctor seemed to help, as it partly adjusted the strained ligament in Moore's shoulder.⁷⁸

Al Niehaus was the second starter knocked out of action due to an injury. In an exhibition game against Little Rock, Niehaus suffered a charley-horse injury that was expected to sideline him for the last two exhibition games and possibly the season opener.⁷⁹

Pittsburgh concluded its exhibition tour on April 11 and 12 in Memphis by splitting the two-game series. The Pirates had played 15 exhibition games garnering an 11–4 record. McKechnie's team enjoyed its biggest success against San Francisco, winning six out of eight games against the Seals.⁸⁰

As Pittsburgh's exhibition season wound down, the distinct possibility existed that Moore and Niehaus would not be ready for the season opener in Chicago on April 14. Other players remained in question. Pitcher Vic Aldridge had not yet signed a contract, missing all of training camp and the entire exhibition season. When asked about Aldridge's status, Barney Dreyfuss responded in a way that characterized his attitude toward holdouts throughout his tenure in Pittsburgh. "Vic Aldridge is back in Terre Haute and Terre Haute is still on the Wabash," said Dreyfuss. "There is no correspondence between us, and there will be none unless the former Cub does the writing."[81]

Bill McKechnie backed his boss' position when he stated that he could survive without Vic Aldridge, and was prepared to formulate his pitching plans without the veteran. As Pittsburgh management continued to preach the company line in public, negotiations were being conducted behind the scenes with Aldridge. This plan was quickly exposed as Pittsburgh correspondents discovered Dreyfuss was attempting to bring his newly acquired pitcher into line. Many fans in the Smoky City reasoned that money was not the issue with Aldridge. They felt that Aldridge had avoided the training trip because he was not fond of participating in what he considered senseless conditioning work.[82]

Aldridge waited until the last moment before signing a contract in 1925. The day before the season opener against Chicago, Dreyfuss announced that Aldridge and the Pirates had come to terms. Dreyfuss declined to release the salary figure Aldridge would receive, but it was believed the ex–Cub would be paid approximately $10,000.[83]

The signing of Vic "Schoolmaster" Aldridge supplied the last piece to Pittsburgh's roster for the 1925 season. Several youngsters remained with the team as Bill McKechnie prepared for the season opener in Chicago. Aldridge joined Lee "Specs" Meadows, Ray "Whiz" Kremer, Emil Yde, Johnny Morrison, Babe Adams, Bernard "Bud" Culloton, Don Songer and Lou Koupal on the pitching staff. The infield con-

Vic Aldridge angered Pirates management by holding out and missing spring training in Paso Robles, California. Aldridge, who was acquired in the big trade with Chicago, signed on the eve of the 1925 season opener at a salary of $10,000 (National Baseball Hall of Fame Library, Cooperstown, New York).

sisted of Al Niehaus, Eddie Moore, Johnny Rawlings, Glenn "Buckshot" Wright and Harold "Pie" Traynor. Pittsburgh's outfield featured a diverse group of individuals that included Max "Scoops" Carey, Carson "Skeeter" Bigbee, Hazen "Kiki" Cuyler, Clyde "Pooch" Barnhart and George "Boots" Grantham. McKechnie's catching corps consisted of Earl "Oil" Smith, Johnny Gooch and rookie Roy Spencer. The final cuts left promising youngsters George "Mule" Haas and Fresco Thompson, off the roster assigned to minor league affiliates to receive more seasoning.

Pittsburgh's roster, the youngest in the National League, included five rookie players. The nucleus of McKechnie's squad included young players like Wright, Traynor and Cuyler, who had experienced immense success during their formative years and appeared capable of further improvement.

Bill McKechnie believed that he had a team that could compete for a pennant. New players had been added with the hope that his team would experience an uplift in morale and attitude. Team cohesiveness was deemed necessary if Pittsburgh planned on dethroning the New York Giants as the top National League club. The time had arrived for McKechnie and his brigade to topple John McGraw's four-year dynasty.

4

A Sluggish Start

Fans across America awoke on the morning of Tuesday, April 14, with a feeling of anticipation and excitement. The 1925 season was slated to begin that afternoon in eight major league cities. Fans from Boston who rooted for perennial tail end teams each season felt just as hopeful for a successful season as their New York counterparts who had enjoyed a recent string of pennants. Opening day represented the season's holy baptism, as imperfections of past seasons were washed away and cleansed in the minds of loyal rooters.

Opening day held special significance for fans in Pittsburgh and Chicago. Baseball's schedule makers arbitrarily made it possible for the two teams involved in one of the winter's most discussed trades to meet during the National League's initial docket of games. Fans in both Pittsburgh and Chicago received the opportunity to immediately critique the blockbuster deal engineered by Bill McKechnie in October of 1924. Yet their assessment would be tempered by the fact that half of the men involved in the trade were not available to play in the opening series. On Pittsburgh's side, Vic Aldridge was out of shape and needed to first participate in team workouts. Al Niehaus remained on the shelf with a nagging charley-horse injury.

In the Cubs' camp, shortstop Rabbit Maranville was out of action due to a broken ankle. Maranville suffered the injury while Chicago had played in Los Angeles during spring training.[1] Despite the fact that Maranville was unable to play, Chicago manager Bill Killefer planned on having his new captain sit in the dugout so that he could be involved in strategic decisions.[2] Given the exclusion of these three men from opening day festivities, only Wilbur Cooper, Charlie Grimm and George Grantham could be evaluated during the Pirates' first series of the season.

On the morning of April 14, hours before Pittsburgh took the field against Chicago, manager McKechnie offered his assessment on how well the Pirates would do in 1925.

> I like the chances of the Pirates very much. Of course, we are not as well conditioned as we have been in other years, but such a failing was caused by bad

weather and came in spite of the fact that all players worked hard at every opportunity. It will be only a week or so if weather conditions are any ways favorable until they will be ready for the hardest sort of opposition.

The pitchers especially suffered because of frequent layoffs. While I have plenty of faith in their ability to come through in the first games of the season, I would be much more optimistic if they had been favored with real training weather the last week of our stay on the Pacific coast.

However, you can bet your boots that the Buccos will finish one, two, three this year. The club, as a whole is a great improvement over that of 1924. Unless I am greatly mistaken, they will hit the ball harder and they will field as well. Besides, on the base paths, they are smarter and faster than the aggregation of last year. The general spirit — in other words, morale — is also higher and that is one item that figures prominently into the makeup of any pennant contender."[3]

McKechnie's enthusiasm surrounding the season opener almost turned to grave concern. During batting practice, Earl Smith took a hefty cut at a pitch, the bat slipping out of his hands. The unexpected projectile flew past the batting cage and grazed Hazen Cuyler's forehead. Luckily for Cuyler, he was struck by the knob of Smith's bat, and not the barrel, leaving only a small contusion.[4] The "Flint Flash" had no intention of letting a small bump on the head prevent him from playing on opening day.

McKechnie chose southpaw Emil Yde as his opening day pitcher, while Chicago skipper Bill Killefer countered with veteran Pete Alexander. Pittsburgh's opening day batting order, as decided upon by McKechnie, appeared as follows: 1. Carson Bigbee (LF), 2. Max Carey (CF), 3. Eddie Moore (2B), 4. Pie Traynor (3B), 5. Kiki Cuyler (RF), 6. George Grantham (1B), 7. Glenn Wright (SS), 8. Earl Smith (C) and 9. Emil Yde (P).

Thirty-seven thousand paying customers jammed their way into Cubs Park to witness the opening day events. The Cubs stretched ropes across the field in order to accommodate an overflow crowd of 5,000 fans. Before the game, Pirates and Cubs players paraded to the flagpole, accompanied by a band and the Lakeview High School cadets. As part of the ceremony, both the American flag and a National League Golden Jubilee pennant were raised. The festivities concluded at home plate, where the Chicago players received baskets of flowers from adoring fans.[5]

Opening day turned out to be a grand event for Chicago fans, as their beloved Cubs plastered the Pirates, 8–2. Pitcher Pete Alexander smacked the first home run of the season for either club when he hit a solo blast off Yde in the third inning. The Cubs secured a victory by bunching their hits, while Alexander kept Pittsburgh's safeties well scattered. The game's decisive blow came in the seventh inning, when catcher Gabby Hartnett launched a three-run homer over the bleacher wall.[6] Yde lasted seven innings for the Pirates, but was charged with eight runs, six of which were unearned because of errors by Eddie Moore, Earl Smith and Emil himself. In terms of positive developments,

Pie Traynor went 2-for-4 and scored both of Pittsburgh's runs. Earl Smith and Kiki Cuyler also recorded two hits apiece as the Flint Flash blasted a double and knocked in one run.

McKechnie's brigade did not waste time extracting revenge against Chicago the following day. Lee Meadows pitched eight-plus innings of sharp ball before being bailed out by Johnny Morrison in the ninth inning, as the Pirates defeated the Cubs, 8–4. Pittsburgh's players were merciless against former teammate Wilbur Cooper, chasing him from the mound after only two innings of work. Pittsburgh's second inning opened with Kiki Cuyler blasting a triple to deep center field. Coach Jewel Ens, playing first base because of Cooper's status as a southpaw, then drilled a home run into the left field seats. Shortstop Glenn Wright made it back-to-back home runs, smashing a Cooper offering into the bleachers.[7] Wright went 3-for-4, while Cuyler was 3-for-5 with two triples and three RBIs.

George Grantham later replaced Ens in the field and handled ten chances flawlessly at first base. Grantham had volunteered to play first when Al Niehaus went down with his injury.

Donning a mitt without any practice at the position, Grantham made several fine plays at first. He surprised his teammates by handling all types of throws to the bag. Bill McKechnie believed that if Grantham was not a fluke at first base, he might prove more valuable than originally expected.[8]

The Cubs bounced back against the Pirates on Thursday, April 16, behind a complete game performance from Sheriff Blake. The Cubs broke a 3–3 tie in the fifth inning when they pushed four runs across the plate. The Pirates' Ray Kremer plunked Chicago's Cliff Heathcote, who was promptly sacrificed to second by Sparky Adams. Gabby Hartnett then made it 5–3 when he lifted Kremer's final pitch of the game into the center field bleach-

George Grantham was acquired on October 27, 1924, from Chicago, along with Vic Aldridge and Al Niehaus. When Niehaus was unable to answer the season's opening bell due to an injury, Grantham volunteered to play first base. Grantham sparkled around the bag even though he had never played the position during his career (National Baseball Hall of Fame Library, Cooperstown, New York).

ers. Veteran Babe Adams came on in relief and retired the next Cubs hitter before uncharacteristically walking three straight batters. Blake then helped his own cause with a single that scored two more runs. The Cubs recorded the game's last run when Hartnett smashed another home run over the left field wall, the sixth inning blow securing Chicago's 8–3 victory.[9]

Pittsburgh's Glenn Wright starred at the plate once again as he went 3-for-3 with a double and a solo home run in the second inning. Eddie Moore went 2-for-3 and scored a run. Rookie pitcher Bernard Culloton saw his first major league action, relieving Adams in the seventh inning and pitching two frames of shutout ball.

Chicago earned a third victory in the final game of this series on Friday, April 17, defeating Pittsburgh 9–6. Pitcher Johnny Morrison continued the Pirates' penchant for serving up homers as Gabby Hartnett and Jigger Statz connected in the third inning. Youngsters Lou Koupal and Don Songer finished the game after Morrison gave up eight runs and nine hits during three and a third innings of work. Carson Bigbee and Eddie Moore were the bright spots for Pittsburgh, as each man went 3-for-4. Bigbee also scored two runs while Moore drove home three of Pittsburgh's markers. Catcher Johnny Gooch made his first start of the season and went 2-for-3 at the plate with a double and three runs scored.

After losing three out of four games against Chicago, Bill McKechnie's squad boarded a train and traveled to Cincinnati on the second leg of the season-opening road trip. Rain greeted the Corsairs when they arrived in Cincinnati on Saturday, April 18. A slight drizzle that hit Pittsburgh's players when they exited the train station turned into a thunderstorm that finally let up just as the Pirates arrived at their hotel. By 10:30 A.M. the rain had ceased, but the game seemed destined to be postponed since the grounds at Redland Field were soggy and wet.[10] Fortunately, the sun broke through the clouds shortly before noon and aided in drying Cincinnati's field. In spite of some sloppy conditions, 8,600 paying customers pushed through the turnstiles for the afternoon affair.[11]

The Pirates might have wished it was still raining, as the Reds crushed the Pirates, 12–2, behind Pete Donohue's complete game. Donohue tormented the Pirates both on the mound and at the plate. In the second inning, Pete blasted a bases loaded triple over Max Carey's head in center field. In the eighth inning, Donohue stroked a double over Carson Bigbee's head in left field before eventually scoring a run.[12] Hughie Critz, Edd Roush and Curt Walker banged out three hits apiece for Cincinnati. Babe Adams, Ray Kremer and Lou Koupal all pitched poorly as the Reds garnered 16 hits on the day.

In the meantime, baseball suffered a major loss. On the morning that Pittsburgh lost its fourth game of the season, longtime Brooklyn owner and president Charles H. Ebbets passed away in a New York hotel. Ebbets had been afflicted with heart trouble for a number of years and was confined to his bed since returning from a trip to Clearwater, Florida. It was reported that Ebbets' health had shown considerable improvement during the past few weeks, but Brooklyn's owner suffered a relapse. His son, Charles H. Ebbets, Jr., and daughter, Genevieve Ebbets, were at their father's bedside when he passed away.[13] With Ebbets' death, Pittsburgh Pirates owner Barney Dreyfuss became the dean of magnates in the National League.[14]

Dreyfuss's players continued to play lackluster ball as the Reds thumped the Pirates once again on Sunday, by a score of 6–2. Eddie Moore and Pie Traynor each went 2-for-4 as Reds pitcher Dolf Luque scattered seven hits during a complete game effort. Moore also knocked in one of Pittsburgh's runs while Traynor smacked a triple and scored a run. Emil Yde dropped his second decision of the season, giving up four runs on five hits during his six and a third innings of work. Luque and Yde were locked in a scoreless pitcher's duel until the Reds busted the game open in the seventh inning. Yde was chased from the hill when Cincinnati parlayed a walk, two singles and two triples into four runs. In the meantime, Pittsburgh's free-swinging batters fell victim to Luque's dominance, as the Cuban pitcher recorded eight strikeouts.[15]

Pittsburgh finally salvaged a game from Cincinnati, beating the Reds on Monday, April 20. Lee Meadows gave a masterful performance as he allowed only two runs on seven hits in nine innings during a 4–2 Pirates victory. Eddie Moore starred at the plate for Pittsburgh by going 3-for-5 with a double and two RBIs. The Pirates scored their first run of the game, in the third inning when new leadoff man Clyde Barnhart walked, stole second and came around to score on Pie Traynor's double. In the fifth, Barnhart smacked a one-out double and crossed home plate when he kept running from second on Eddie Moore's groundout to third baseman Babe Pinelli.[16]

Pittsburgh added two crucial insurance runs in the game's last two innings against southpaw Eppa Rixey to offset a Cincinnati rally in the eighth inning. Kiki Cuyler doubled to right field to open Pittsburgh's half of the eighth, and then scored after consecutive sacrifice bunts by Jewel Ens and Glenn Wright. Barnhart scored Pittsburgh's last run in the ninth inning when he reached first on shortstop Sammy Bohne's error, went to third on Max Carey's single and came home on Moore's double.[17] Barnhart acquitted himself nicely from the top spot after being added to the starting lineup one day earlier as a replacement for Carson Bigbee, who was ill with influenza.[18]

The season-opening road trip was a dismal one for Bill McKechnie and his players. Pittsburgh's combined 2–5 record against Chicago and Cincinnati did not represent the kind of results Pirates fans expected from a pennant contender. Despite his team's horrible start, McKechnie was confident the Pirates would start winning when they met Chicago in the home opener at Forbes Field on April 22.

4. A Sluggish Start

Once the Pittsburgh contingent finally reached the Smoky City after spending almost two months training and playing on the road, Eddie Moore hustled off to Linesville, Pennsylvania, to consult with a physician regarding his injured shoulder and other nagging maladies. After receiving treatment, Moore pronounced that he felt better and promised that he would occupy his position at second base for the home opener.[19]

One important member of Pittsburgh's entourage was unable to engage in opening day festivities at Forbes Field. Barney Dreyfuss had been confined to his apartment for several days due to illness. Dreyfuss's physician advised him not to attend the home opener and run the risk of suffering a setback to his health.[20] Dreyfuss also wanted to attend Charles Ebbets' funeral, but was advised against doing so by his doctor.[21] As a result, the opening day arrangements were ably handled by Barney's son, Sammy, and secretary Sam Watters. Prior to the game, a band concert directed by Danny Nirella, with a quartet of singers adding accompaniment, entertained the Forbes Field crowd. The annual flag raising at the center field flagpole officially commemorated the start of another season in Pittsburgh. The Pirates raised both the American flag and the Golden Jubilee pennant of the National League as part of a rousing ceremony.[22]

Over 30,000 fans packed Forbes Field for the opener against Chicago. The overflow crowd made new ground rules necessary due to the roping off of areas on the field.[23] Johnny Morrison received the opening assignment against Chicago's Tony Kaufmann. Neither team did any damage until the Pirates scored a run in the third inning on back-to-back triples by Morrison and Clyde Barnhart. Chicago tied the game in the fourth when Kaufmann doubled, was sacrificed to third base and then scored on an out. Pittsburgh took the lead for good in the sixth inning, as Pie Traynor opened the frame with a triple. Glenn Wright fouled out, but then Kiki Cuyler, Al Niehaus and Earl Smith slashed consecutive singles, plating two more runs.[24]

Pittsburgh finished the scoring in the eighth inning with three more runs. Cuyler opened the frame with a triple, and Kaufmann walked Smith intentionally. Morrison came through in the clutch and smashed his second triple of the day, driving home both base runners. When Max Carey singled, Morrison came around to score the final run in Pittsburgh's 6–1 victory.[25] Pittsburgh's batters connected for seven triples against Chicago's Kaufmann, with Cuyler, Barnhart, Traynor and Morrison accounting for all of the three-base safeties. Morrison went the route for Pittsburgh, as he allowed one run on five hits, walked one and struck out three.

First baseman Al Niehaus finally made his major league debut in the home opener. Niehaus played coolly in front of a massive crowd. He fielded his position effortlessly and struck a timely single at the plate. Niehaus hit several line drives, continuing his trend from the spring exhibition games.[26]

Pittsburgh's modest two-game winning streak came to an end on Thursday, April 23, during a slugfest at Forbes Field. Chicago prevailed, 10–9, as starting pitcher Ray Kremer did not last the third inning, giving up five runs. Babe Adams, Lou Koupal and Don Songer attempted to right the Pirates, but each man allowed Chicago to score. Earl Smith hit an eighth inning pinch-hit solo homer to tie the score, 8–8, but Songer allowed Chicago to score the winning marker in the top of the ninth inning. Kiki Cuyler starred at the plate by going 3-for-5 with two RBIs. Max Carey went 2-for-4 with two runs scored, Eddie Moore was 2-for-3 with two runs, two RBIs, one double and a triple, and Glenn Wright went 2-for-5 while nearly duplicating Moore's statistical line for the day.

Chicago continued its dominance over Pittsburgh the following day as Pete Alexander shut down the Buccaneers' attack and cruised to an easy 7–2 victory. Carey, Cuyler and Barnhart were the Pirates' only bright spots, as each man banged out two hits. The Cubs murdered Pittsburgh pitching for 15 hits, with six of the safeties going for extra bases. Former Pirate Charlie Grimm swatted a quartet of hits including two triples, a double and a single. The Cubs' Bob Barrett equaled Grimm's hit total by slashing three singles and a double. Every player in the lineup for Chicago, other than Alexander, banged out at least one hit.[27]

Starter Emil Yde was yanked from the game after only one and two-thirds innings of work. Vic Aldridge made his first appearance of the season, relieving Pittsburgh's beleaguered starter. Aldridge's work for the remainder of the game lent proof to the belief that he was still not ready to pitch. Aldridge had difficulty locating the plate as Bruins batters showed patience at the plate. Aldridge was only a slight improvement over Yde, who was bombarded for seven hits in less than two innings of work. Yde's third setback of the campaign equaled his total number of defeats for the entire 1924 season.[28]

Chicago made it three wins in a row over Pittsburgh in a tightly contested game on Saturday, April 25. After some early fireworks by the Cubs, starter Lee Meadows settled down and kept the Pirates in the game by tossing shutout ball over the final seven innings. Unfortunately, Chicago did enough damage in the first two innings to secure a 4–3 victory. In the first inning, Meadows walked Jigger Statz and Cliff Heathcote to start the game. Bob Barrett tried to sacrifice the runners, but popped a foul ball to Earl Smith instead. Gabby Hartnett then continued his assault on Pittsburgh pitching by drilling a Meadows offering over the left field fence. Charlie Grimm followed suit in the second inning, when he was credited with a solo blast on a ball that landed on the foul line and caromed into the bleachers — a bounce home run.[29]

The Pirates finally chipped away at Chicago's 4–0 lead in the sixth inning. Max Carey led off with a single. After Kiki Cuyler struck out, Eddie Moore followed with a single that moved Carey to third. Clyde Barnhart then crushed a double to the right field wall, scoring Carey and sending Moore to third base. Pie Traynor lined a single to center that drove in two more runs. The promising inning ended after Glenn Wright flied out and Traynor was gunned down by Hartnett trying to steal second. Pittsburgh's last rally in the eighth inning expired after Cuyler singled but was left stranded when liners by Moore and Barnhart were snared by Chicago outfielders.[30]

Pittsburgh fans who viewed the standings as the National League season's second week concluded could not be happy with what they saw. As of April 25, the Pirates stood in seventh-place, ahead of only cellar dweller Boston, with a record of 3–8. Pittsburgh's poor showing was underscored by their deficiency in all aspects of the game. Kiki Cuyler (.385) and Eddie Moore (.405) were the only Pirate regulars hitting above .300. Newcomer George Grantham had performed capably in a pinch at first base, but was hitting a pathetic .050 for the season. After four games of action, fellow Cubs acquisition Al Niehaus was only hitting .125. Though light hitting by the Pirates squad was an issue for manager Bill McKechnie, it was not his biggest problem. Pittsburgh's pitching had been ravaged by the opposition. The earned run averages of Babe Adams (12.86) Vic Aldridge (4.91), Ray Kremer (6.75) and Johnny Morrison (5.27) offered compelling testimony that supported the premise that Pittsburgh's hurlers were simply not very good.

Prior to the season opener in Chicago, McKechnie had expressed concern over the possibility that his pitching staff had not received enough work during the training season. His starting pitchers sometimes cruised for a few innings before imploding in the fourth or fifth frame, indicating that they were not well conditioned. Many Pittsburgh rooters blamed Pirates management for the pitching staff being ill prepared. Others who showed more faith believed that time and additional work would eventually cure the ailments of McKechnie's group of hurlers.[31]

While Chicago was in Pittsburgh, some of Rabbit Maranville's closest friends held a testimonial dinner for the former Pirate. Mayor Magee headed a group of local baseball enthusiasts who oversaw the proceedings on the night of April 22. After the dinner, appreciative friends gave speeches in which they told Maranville they were sorry to lose him as a player, but hoped he would remain an inhabitant of Pittsburgh. Maranville responded by saying that he wished his ankle had already healed so that he could do damage to the Pirates in the series. The shortstop's friends also presented Maranville with a $500 Liberty Bond as a token of their appreciation.[32]

The Pirates hoped to improve their fortunes as they boarded a train to St. Louis for a game against the Cardinals on Sunday, April 26. Babe Adams silenced the Smoky City critics who believed Pittsburgh's pitching staff was poor by pitching the kind of gem that was reminiscent of the Fred Clarke era. Adams tossed a complete game and scattered seven hits as Pittsburgh defeated

St. Louis, 6–1. Al Niehaus had his best day in a Pirates uniform by going 3-for-4 with two doubles and a run scored. Clyde Barnhart, Glenn Wright and Adams lent support to Pittsburgh's hitting attack by slashing two hits apiece. Wright blasted a solo home run off Jesse Haines in the fifth inning, and Earl Smith turned the trick again in the eighth inning.

Eddie Moore was a defensive standout for the Pirates, as he single-handedly squelched the Cardinals only chance of coming back. During St. Louis' budding rally, Adams gave up three consecutive singles with one out. The next batter drilled a line drive off Adams' glove; Moore snatched the ball before it bounded into the outfield. Not only did Moore steal a base hit, but he managed to turn a rapid double play that ended the threat.[33]

After an off-day on Monday for both clubs, the series resumed on Tuesday, April 28, with Pittsburgh once again claiming victory, 7–3. Johnny Morrison tossed a complete game, allowed one earned run on 10 hits and one walk. Glenn Wright went 3-for-4 while Pie Traynor and Max Carey recorded two hits apiece for the Corsairs. Flint Rhem took the loss for St. Louis, as Pittsburgh chased the Cardinals' starter with seven runs in four-plus innings of work.

The Pirates struck quickly in the second inning against Rhem, loading the bases on singles by Clyde Barnhart and Glenn Wright and a walk to Al Niehaus. Smith sent all three base runners home by crushing a double to left field. Wright then added to Pittsburgh's lead in the fourth inning when he smacked a solo home run into the right field bleachers. McKechnie's young guns added three more runs in the fifth inning. Max Carey singled and was sacrificed to second by Kiki Cuyler. Eddie Moore drove Carey home with a double, and Pie Traynor knocked home his teammate with another double. Wright drove home Pittsburgh's final run when his base hit allowed Traynor to scamper home.[34]

Just as Bill McKechnie's team began to show a bit a progress by taking two games from St. Louis, bad weather intervened and left the Pirates idle for three straight days. The final game of the Cardinals' series on April 29 was postponed due to rain. When the Pirates returned home from their short trip, they dragged the ominous weather back with them. Cold and rainy conditions prevented every game on the National League schedule from being played on April 30. Another rainy day kept Pittsburgh and Cincinnati indoors, as the second game of that series was scrapped as well.[35]

Pittsburgh and Cincinnati were finally able to meet on Saturday, May 2. Pittsburgh's players seemed unaffected by days of inactivity as they exploded for their largest offensive output of the season, destroying the Reds, 18–3. Kiki Cuyler went 3-for-5 with a double and triple, scoring three runs. Pirates catcher Earl Smith also went 3-for-5, scored two runs, and drove in three. Max Carey and Clyde Barnhart each had two hits. Barnhart drove home four runs and Carey legged out an inside-the-park home run with a runner on in the sixth inning. Pitcher Lee Meadows tossed a complete game and actually produced the biggest hit of the day when he smashed a two-run home run off reliever Rube Benton, this after the Pirates chased starter Pete Donohue in the first inning.

Meadows' home run over the right field wall caused pandemonium on Pittsburgh's bench. While Meadows proudly rounded the bases after his smash, his teammates in the dugout decided they were not going to offer any congratulatory remarks. When Leo stepped into the dugout after his triumphant dash around the bases, he was greeted by absolute silence from his teammates. Meadows was expecting laudatory comments and words of encouragement, but he received only deafening quiet. Meadows could only stand the silent treatment for a few minutes before he cut loose with a response.[36] "What in the devil's the matter here," Meadows shouted. "Did you fellows think that smash was foul!"[37]

This type of good natured ribbing indicated that Pittsburgh's players were bonding despite the Pirates' slow start and added credence to Bill McKechnie's belief that team morale would be much improved in 1925. A three-game winning streak and an 18-run outburst certainly helped to lift the spirits of McKechnie's men.

Roles were reversed in a Sunday matinee in Cincinnati, when the Reds extracted revenge and defeated the Pirates, 5–4. Single runs in each of the first five innings by the Reds chased starter Johnny Morrison, whose performance could only be characterized as shaky. Morrison lasted four innings and gave up four runs on eight hits. Edd Roush stroked three clean safeties for Cincinnati. Dolf Luque held the Pirates scoreless until the eighth inning when they rallied for four runs. Pete Donohue relieved Luque in the ninth with two outs and fanned Emil Yde to strand the tying run at second base.[38]

The Pirates returned home after their Sunday road trip to Cincinnati and enjoyed an off day before beginning a three-game series against St. Louis at Forbes Field. Poor weather, which had cancelled two games at home a week ago, returned again, making it impossible for Pittsburgh and St. Louis to play. The game scheduled for May 5 was postponed due to rain; the next day's battle did not happen because of cold weather.[39] On May 6, the Pirates squeezed in a short workout between rain showers. It was obvious to anyone who watched that the three-day layoff affected McKechnie's players, who struggled to work the kinks from their atrophied muscles.[40]

Pittsburgh's idleness allowed pundits to step back for a moment and assess the contributions of a few members of the Pirates. Second baseman Eddie Moore emerged as Pittsburgh's leading hitter and had scored more runs than any of his teammates. Kiki Cuyler was second on the team in hitting behind Moore and seemed to be serving notice that his 1924 season was not a fluke. Glenn Wright had played phenomenally at shortstop. Wright ranked third on the team in hitting and consistently pulled off eye-opening plays in the field.[41]

The Pirates received a reprieve from the weather and played St. Louis on Thursday, May 7. A three-game series had been reduced to a one-game engagement; it was the last one at Forbes Field for weeks before Pittsburgh embarked on its first Eastern swing of the season. A wild affair resulted in a 10–9 victory for the Cardinals. McKechnie's pitchers were touched up for 20 hits, as starter Emil Yde was pounded for seven runs in seven-plus innings of work. Babe Adams took the loss after relieving Yde in the eighth and allowing St. Louis to add three more tallies during a six-run outburst that gave them the lead for good.

Al Niehaus and Eddie Moore racked up three hits apiece for Pittsburgh; Moore also scored two runs, smashed two doubles and drove home two teammates. Max Carey, Kiki Cuyler and Earl Smith also chipped in with two hits each. Ralph Shinners and Les Bell led the St. Louis attack as Bill Hallahan picked up the victory with two innings of shutout relief work. On a day when a combined 19 runs and 35 hits should have represented the game's main storyline, a rare play that happened in the ninth inning ended up supplying the major headline in sports pages across the country.

The top of the ninth inning started out innocently when Vic Aldridge walked both Jimmy Cooney and Rogers Hornsby to start the inning. This brought heavy hitting first baseman Jim Bottomley to the plate. The hit-and-run sign was flashed, and Cooney and Hornsby set sail as Aldridge started his motion toward home. Bottomley connected and sent a screaming line drive toward second base. Just as it seemed the ball was headed into center field, Pirate shortstop Glenn Wright scooted over and speared the ball in his glove. Wright's natural momentum carried him to the keystone sack, where he was able to step on second and double up Cooney. The play's final phase was achieved when Wright tagged a befuddled Hornsby before he could retrace his steps back to first base. In a flash of seconds, Wright had recorded the sixth unassisted triple play in major league history and the first since Boston's Ernie Padgett turned the trick in 1923.[42]

Wright's unusual triple play happened so quickly that most Pittsburgh fans were not immediately aware of what they had just witnessed. Many of the Forbes Field patrons did not realize they had seen a triple play until after Pittsburgh's players left the field to take their turn at bat in the bottom of the ninth inning. Once the magnitude of this play dawned upon the paying customers, they let loose a loud yell that rocked the Forbes Field grandstand. The fans clapped in appreciation of Glenn Wright making the most significant play in his career as Pittsburgh's shortstop.[43]

Bill McKechnie's men attempted to shake off the effects of their most recent loss against St. Louis as they began their first Eastern invasion in

4. A Sluggish Start

On May 7, 1925, shortstop Glenn Wright turned an unassisted triple play against St. Louis at Forbes Field. Wright's rare feat occurred in the ninth inning. Jim Bottomley smacked a line drive that Wright caught near second base. Wright stepped on the keystone sack to double up Jimmy Cooney and then completed the triple play when he tagged Rogers Hornsby, who was running from first base. Once Pittsburgh fans realized what had happened, they gave Wright a standing ovation (National Baseball Hall of Fame Library, Cooperstown, New York).

Philadelphia. The Pirates' pitching staff continued to struggle as the Phillies teed off against five Pittsburgh hurlers and claimed a 15–7 victory. Staff ace Lee Meadows did not make it out of the first inning as five Philadelphia players crossed home plate. Ray Kremer pitched weakly in relief and served up home runs to both George Harper and Heinie Sand in two innings of work. Don Songer and Lou Koupal were equally horrific before Bud Culloton stopped the bleeding with three innings of shutout relief. Max Carey went 4-for-5, scored three runs, smacked two doubles and stole two bases for Pittsburgh. Earl Smith joined the home run parade by blasting a two-run shot off pitcher Hal Carlson in the fifth inning.

Poor pitching and another humiliating defeat were not McKechnie's lone problems. Injuries were beginning to mount, and the Pirates' cohesiveness was suffering as a result. Eddie Moore's injured shoulder was getting worse due to the everyday strain of performing at second base. In the third inning of the recent game against Philadelphia, the piercing pain became so excruciating that Moore had to leave the game and give way to veteran Johnny Rawlings. First baseman Al Niehaus played the entire game in spite of aggravating his charley-horse in the previous match against St. Louis. Improper bandaging at the point of distress in Niehaus' leg had brought about another strain. Even though the rookie first baseman limped noticeably throughout the debacle against Philadelphia, Niehaus did not plan on sitting out unless his leg gave out completely.[44]

Catcher Earl Smith was the third member of Pittsburgh's walking wounded. Smith sustained his injury in the fifth inning when he was struck by a foul tip. An examination of his left hand showed the knuckle was badly bruised. When Smith awoke on Saturday morning, his knuckle was swollen. Like Niehaus, Smith was determined to play despite the injury.[45] Unfortunately for Smith, when McKechnie announced his starting lineup for that afternoon's game against the Phillies, he stayed on the bench while fellow injured teammates Moore and Niehaus played.

The Pirates rebounded in the series' second game against Philadelphia as they slipped past the Phillies, 6–5. Johnny Morrison picked up his third victory of the season with a pitching line of three earned runs, 11 hits, five walks and two strikeouts in seven innings of work. Lee Meadows earned his first save when he pitched two innings of shutout relief. Glenn Wright and Al Niehaus each went 2-for-4 and Johnny Gooch went 2-for-3 while subbing for the injured Earl Smith. Wright, only two days removed from his magnificent play at Forbes Field, performed with mixed reviews before Philadelphia's patrons. Pittsburgh's shortstop committed two errors in the fifth inning, enabling the Phillies to score two runs. Wright then offset those negative plays in the seventh inning, when he smacked a solo home run into the left field bleachers off southpaw Clarence Mitchell.[46]

Philadelphia placed a two-spot on the board during the bottom half of the frame and took a 5–2 lead into the eighth inning. Persistence on Pittsburgh's part allowed McKechnie's squad to rally for four runs in the eighth and secure an important victory. Gooch started the inning by singling to right field. Carson Bigbee was sent in to run for Gooch as Johnny Rawlings stepped to the plate as a pinch hitter for Morrison. Rawlings slapped a ground ball to second baseman Lew Fonseca, who tossed the ball to shortstop Heinie Sand covering at second. Sand was unable to record a force play since his foot was not touching second base when he received Fonseca's toss. The umpires ruled both Pittsburgh runners safe. McKechnie added more speed to the base paths when he substituted George Grantham as a pinch runner for Rawlings.[47]

Max Carey made the Phillies pay for Sand's mistake when he stroked a double that scored Bigbee and sent Grantham to third. Kiki Cuyler made an out before Eddie Moore was hit by a pitched ball, loading the bases. Clyde Barnhart then drove in Grantham when he singled off Mitchell's glove. Pie Traynor kept the rally going by driving a hit to center that brought Carey home with the tying run. Wright then played hero and goat in the same at-bat, when his drive to the right field fence knocked in Moore with the go-ahead run. Pittsburgh's shortstop did not look to see how the play was developing in front of him and made a direct beeline for second base. When Wright reached the keystone sack, he realized that Traynor was still standing there. Traynor was caught in a rundown between second and third, before Al Niehaus lined to outfielder George Burns for the inning's final out.[48]

Wright's gaffe had no bearing on the game's outcome as Philadelphia failed to score during the last two innings. In spite of the gritty comeback on the part of McKechnie's troops, the official National League standings posted at the completion of Saturday's games showed Pittsburgh holding down the basement with a 7–11 record. Pirate fans certainly did not expect to see their favorite team residing in the league's cellar one month into the National League season. Pittsburgh's hitting had improved during the past few weeks with Barnhart, Cuyler, Gooch, Moore, Smith and Wright now all batting above .300. Yet, McKechnie's main problem continued to be sporadic pitching, which could not be counted on to see the Pirates through tough times.

A Sunday rest day for Pittsburgh and Philadelphia due to Pennsylvania Blue Laws was followed by a second day of idleness, as rain prevented the two teams from playing on Monday, May 11.[49] A steady drizzle gripped the City of Brotherly Love shortly after daybreak and continued throughout the day. With practice out of the question, the Buccaneers spent the day quietly relaxing. A few young players took a tour of the city while a couple of golf matches were hastily thrown together, enabling players to keep busy during yet another idle day.[50]

The Monday afternoon rainout necessitated a doubleheader on Tuesday, May 12, between the Pirates and Phillies. Two days of rest worked wonders for Bill McKechnie's injured players, as the conditions of Eddie Moore, Al Niehaus and Earl Smith had improved greatly since Saturday.[51] Vic Aldridge was chosen by McKechnie to make his first start in a Pirates uniform during the first game of the doubleheader. Aldridge battled gallantly against staff ace Jimmy Ring until the sixth inning, when the Phillies broke a 1–1 tie by putting up seven runs. Heavy slugging, combined with a hit batsman, an error by Pie Traynor and horrendous defense by Niehaus allowed Philadelphia to score often, as they eventually secured an 8–5 victory.[52] The big blows in the frame were struck by Ring, who hit a grand slam with none out, and George Harper, who connected for a three-run blast with one out. Kiki Cuyler was Pittsburgh's top gun, going 3-for-5, while teammates Clyde Barnhart, Glenn Wright and Traynor recorded two hits apiece.

Pittsburgh responded with a 13–8 victory in the nightcap, as the Pirates and Phillies combined for 28 hits. Pittsburgh starter Ray Kremer did not make it out of the first inning and was relieved by Lee Meadows after Philadelphia tied the score at 2–2. Meadows recorded his fourth win of the season as he gutted his way through seven tough innings. Babe Adams recorded his first save of the year with two innings of shutout relief. Barnhart recorded one hit in the second contest when he beat out an infield tap. This, coupled with Barnhart's home run in the first game, meant that the Pittsburgh outfielder had now hit safely in 14 consecutive games.[53]

Glenn Wright and Hazen Cuyler were Pittsburgh's stars for the day. Wright drilled two doubles in the first game and followed that with another two-bagger and two singles in the second game. Cuyler failed to record a hit in the first game, but was practically unstoppable during Pittsburgh's victorious conclusion in Philadelphia. Cuyler collected four hits, smacking two doubles and two singles. He walked once and reached first base when he was plunked by a pitched ball. Cuyler also scored five Pittsburgh runs and drove Phillies pitchers from the mound in both the second and third innings.[54]

After the Corsairs won two out of four games in Philadelphia the Eastern trip continued on to Boston. Despite the fact that Pittsburgh claimed those two games, manager McKechnie was not happy with his team's defense and decided to change the infield's composition. McKechnie benched rookie first baseman Al Niehaus and replaced him with George Grantham. Niehaus was mired in a horrible batting slump that saw his average drop to .212. Making matters worse for the first baseman were his struggles in the field, including a boneheaded play against Philadelphia the previous day. McKechnie concluded that a short rest would do his rookie some good by providing Niehaus a chance to rejuvenate himself on the bench.[55]

When the Pirates arrived in Boston for their first game on Wednesday, May 13, word awaited infielder Johnny Rawlings that his father had passed away suddenly the previous day.[56] Rawlings would not be able to attend the funeral of his 73-year-old father since the travel time to California from Boston made it impossible for him to make it in time.[57] A somber mood in Pittsburgh's dugout was slightly uplifted when the Pirates opened the second leg of their Eastern swing with a 5–4 victory over Boston. Ray Kremer finally secured his first victory of the season after bailing out starter Emil Yde and pitching four innings of one-hit ball. Pittsburgh stroked 13 hits as Pie Traynor led the attack by going 3-for-4. Max Carey, Hazen Cuyler, Clyde Barnhart and Glenn Wright gave able support, as the four players accounted for eight hits, four runs and two RBIs.

McKechnie's decision to place George Grantham at first base seemed to steady Pittsburgh's infield. Pie Traynor and Eddie Moore made several scintillating grabs of hard hit grounders by Boston hitters. Not to be outdone by his infield mates, Cuyler grabbed a short fly ball in the ninth inning and threw a perfect strike to Grantham at first, doubling up the base runner and ending the game.[58]

The Pirates cruised in the series' second game on Thursday, May 14, as Johnny Morrison shut down Boston, 7–1. Morrison pitched a complete game, gave up one run on five hits, struck out seven and walked two. Kiki Cuyler went 2-for-4, scored two runs, smacked a double and drove home a run. Clyde Barnhart copied Cuyler's plate work identically, while also scoring one run and driving home two teammates.

The Pirates defeated the Braves with relative ease, but fireworks erupted in the eighth inning when one of manager Dave Bancroft's ex-players had a confrontation with a Boston fan. Pittsburgh catcher Earl Smith had been brutally heckled by a fan along the first base line throughout the game. In the top of the eighth, after Smith supposedly spiked Boston first baseman Dick Burrus while touching first base, the Pittsburgh player's tormentor became insulting. During the bottom half of the inning, when Smith charged after a foul ball near the first base stands, another round of epithets flew from his antagonist's mouth. Smith decided he had heard enough. Pittsburgh's catcher jumped into the crowd and connected with a healthy punch against his adversary before umpire Cy Rigler dragged Smith into the Pirates' dugout.[59]

Rigler arrived quickly on the scene because he sensed that Smith was close to reaching a breaking point. Once Smith calmed down, Rigler informed Pittsburgh's catcher that he had been expelled from the game. As Smith made his way to the exit leading to the clubhouse, a second Boston fan assumed the role of agitator and tossed a chair that struck Earl's head. Smith attempted to climb the grandstand railing so that he could reach his second assailant, but was prevented from doing so by third base umpire Peter McLaughlin.[60]

Even though Smith allowed his pugnacious attitude to get the best of him, he showed his teammates a sturdy fighting spirit that was required of a pennant winner. After their game on May 14, the Pirates stood in seventh place, six and a half games behind the league-leading New York Giants. Yet, there was still plenty of baseball to be played. Pittsburgh's players realized the time had come to discard the second-division stigma and begin playing like a legitimate pennant contender.

5

Booming Bats Lead to a Turnaround

League jurisprudence was doled out swiftly in the case regarding Pirates catcher Earl Smith. National League president John Heydler wired Bill McKechnie at noon on May 15 to inform him that Smith was suspended indefinitely until a more thorough investigation could be conducted. The possibility also existed that Heydler would levee a fine against Smith. Baseball fans in Pittsburgh speculated that the Pirates' catcher could be given a minimum ban of ten days if Heydler followed precedent in such cases when players attacked fans.[1] Yet, Heydler's justice was the least of Smith's problems as he also faced legal issues in Boston. W.J. Lewis, the Hub fan who Smith hit with his fist, initiated a sworn warrant that charged Pittsburgh's catcher with assault for the incident that occurred in Braves Field's box seat section.[2]

In his affidavit, Mr. Lewis claimed that he was not the spectator who heckled Smith. Lewis also stated that he had a number of witnesses who would back his story. In contrast, some of Smith's teammates claimed unequivocally that he had made no mistake regarding the identity of his antagonist.

Smith's battery case was supposed to be heard at the Brighton police court at nine o'clock in the morning on May 16. The catcher's case ended up being postponed until Pittsburgh made its next trip to Boston in July. On Friday night, Smith developed severe pain in his head due to the injury he suffered when a second Braves fan tossed a chair at him. A physician examined Smith on Saturday morning and concluded that Pittsburgh's fighting catcher was in no condition to make his scheduled court appearance.[3]

While Smith recuperated from his head injury, McKechnie's ball club spent another day sitting idly by as weather wiped out another game on the schedule. The Pittsburgh-Boston game scheduled for Friday, May 15, was cancelled due to rainy weather. An early morning downpour turned into a steady drizzle that made playing the third game of this series an impossibility. It was

5. Booming Bats Lead to a Turnaround

Pittsburgh catcher Earl Smith was suspended after he punched a fan at Braves Field in Boston on May 14, 1925. Smith assaulted W.J. Lewis because the Boston fan relentlessly heckled the Pirates player throughout the game. Smith's hearing before a local court was postponed due to the headaches he experienced as the result of a second Boston fan striking him in the head with a tossed chair (National Baseball Hall of Fame Library, Cooperstown, New York).

expected that the postponed date would be added to the schedule on July 13 so that both teams would play a matinee doubleheader in Boston.[4]

Baseball resumed for the Pirates on May 16 as they captured a wild, ten-inning affair over Boston, 7–5. Veteran Babe Adams pitched eight strong innings for the Pirates and left the game with the score tied at 4–4 after being lifted in the ninth for pinch hitter Carson Bigbee. Emil Yde picked up his first victory of the season when three Pittsburgh runs in the top of the tenth inning offset Boston's one tally during the bottom of the frame. Max Carey starred for the Pirates as he went 3-for-5, scored one run, drove home one and stole a base. Kiki Cuyler, George Grantham and Johnny Gooch gave ample support, as they chipped in two hits each for Pittsburgh. Cuyler and Grantham each drilled a triple and also drove home one run apiece.

Pittsburgh continued its winning ways when the long Eastern trip shifted to Brooklyn on Sunday, May 17. The Pirates drove former nemesis Dazzy Vance from the mound in the sixth inning, defeating the Robins, 8–5. Lee Meadows tossed a complete game for Bill McKechnie's squad and allowed only two earned runs on nine hits. Pie Traynor led a Pirates attack that rapped out 15 hits on the day. Traynor went 3-for-5, stroked a double, scored two runs and swiped two bases. Max Carey, Kiki Cuyler, Clyde Barnhart and George Grantham banged out two hits apiece and scored the remainder of Pittsburgh's six runs. Grantham and Cuyler also connected for long solo shots off Vance in the fourth and seventh innings as each player smacked his first home run of the season.

Horrendous fielding ended Pittsburgh's five-game winning streak and helped Brooklyn bring home a victory the following day. Starter Vic Aldridge was chased from the mound in the fourth inning, as the Pirates suffered a 12–7 defeat. Emil Yde relieved Aldridge but was unable to record an out as Brooklyn built up a 10–3 lead through four innings. Youngsters Don Songer and Lou Koupal did admirable work and only allowed one unearned run apiece in four-plus innings. Cuyler starred at the plate for Pittsburgh by going 3-for-4, smacking a double and scoring two runs. Pittsburgh was ragged in the field, ringing up six errors on the day. Each Pirate infielder was charged with a miscue, while Songer and Johnny Gooch accounted for Pittsburgh's other two errors. In fairness, Grantham's blunder was a bit undeserved as he was charged with an error when Glenn Wright's throw hit the dirt in front of his mitt and caromed away.[5]

Bill McKechnie received some good news on May 19 when he was notified by John Heydler's office that Earl Smith's suspension had ended.[6] Pittsburgh's catcher had been kept off the field for four days for striking a fan in the stands at Boston. Smith's return to action did little to help Pittsburgh's cause, however, as Brooklyn won its second consecutive game by defeating the Pirates, 9–5. Max Carey went a perfect 4-for-4 at the plate as the Corsairs lost the contest despite out-hitting Brooklyn, 14 to 10. Clyde Barnhart, Glenn Wright and George Grantham each chipped in with two hits apiece. In spite of the offensive outburst, the Pirates showed an inability to hit in the clutch. In the second frame, three Pirate runners were left stranded. Two men perished on the paths in the fourth, and one man was left standing idly on a base in every other inning.[7]

Fielding mistakes also figured significantly in handing Pittsburgh another defeat, as McKechnie's players booted four balls. A muff by Carey in center during the second inning contributed to two Brooklyn runs. A dropped foul ball by Earl Smith, and Grantham's errant throw added two more runs to the Robins' tally in the fourth inning. In the fifth inning, a blast that bounced past Carey in center field aided Brooklyn in adding yet another run to its total. Even though Carey was not charged with an error on the play, it was the type of fly ball that Pittsburgh's veteran outfielder usually handled gracefully with relative ease.[8]

While the Pirates were stumbling on their road trip, an Eastern scribe wrote an extensive story that claimed that Pittsburgh's fans were not happy with their team's performance. The writer also stated that Smoky City inhabitants were demanding Barney Dreyfuss's scalp because he had allowed Charlie Grimm, Rabbit Maranville and Wilbur Cooper to be traded to Chicago. This particular story seemed overly sensational given that there had been only minimal complaining on the part of Pirates fans over this trade. Most of the complaints came from a small group of people who were close friends of the three players. They seemed to be the only Pittsburghers who insisted on keeping the deal with Chicago an issue to discuss while the Pirates struggled during the season's early weeks.[9]

If the written words of this Eastern baseball pundit actually carried legitimacy, Pittsburgh fans would have been more justified in calling for the firing of Bill McKechnie. McKechnie was the one who initiated and finalized the trade with Chicago. Since the deal had been consummated the previous fall, McKechnie had assumed total responsibility for any consequences surrounding the transaction. Of course, Dreyfuss agreed with his manager in this respect and stood by McKechnie's decision to trade Grimm, Cooper and Maranville. Since Dreyfuss had the final word in all things involving the Pittsburgh organization, this particular writer felt he was justified in claiming the Pirates' magnate was the deserving object of Smoky City patrons' scorn.

Pittsburgh finished the third leg of its Eastern trip, defeating Brooklyn in convincing fashion on May 20 by a score of 12–3. Baseballs rang off the bats of Pittsburgh's players throughout the afternoon as McKechnie's brigade blasted 22 hits. Clyde Barnhart, Pie Traynor and Glenn Wright had four hits apiece, combined to score six runs and accounted for seven RBIs. Traynor also pulled off the fielding feature of the game when he started a double play in the sixth inning after gobbling up a hot grounder. Traynor also displayed fearlessness on the base paths in the first inning after reaching first base on a single. When Wright followed with a single to left, Traynor bolted from first to third. When Brooklyn outfielder Zack Wheat lobbed the ball to second so that Wright would be held at first base, Traynor moved into high gear and tore into home plate without drawing a throw.[10]

Ray Kremer pitched magnificent ball for the Pirates despite the fact he was feeling ill. Kremer had been suffering from a severe case of tonsillitis since Pittsburgh started its Eastern trip in Philadelphia. The residual effects of the illness did not seem to bother Kremer as he tossed a complete game against Brooklyn and limited the Robins to six hits. Kremer was wild at times as he walked six men and hit another Brooklyn batter but he only allowed one extra base hit and kept Brooklyn's safeties fairly scattered.[11]

The crucial part of Pittsburgh's road trip shifted to the Polo Grounds, as McKechnie's boys began a four-game series against arch nemesis New York on Thursday, May 21. McKechnie's choice of Babe Adams as the first game starter seemed a bit odd since he did not pitch well in ballparks with shorter distances to the outfield fences. For that reason, Adams had not worked a game at Philadelphia's Baker Bowl bandbox the last few seasons.[12] Adams lasted only four innings and gave up four runs on six hits. Pittsburgh's veteran pitcher also allowed Hack Wilson's solo home run in the second inning. Johnny Morrison was tagged with the loss when he gave up an unearned run in the sixth inning that stood as the deciding tally in a 5–4 New York win.

Kiki Cuyler smacked the biggest shot of the day for either team when he crushed a two-run, inside-the-park home run against the Giants' Jack Scott in the fifth inning. Cuyler's mammoth smash traveled to the wide open confines of center field at the Polo Grounds. Only days earlier, Giants first baseman Bill Terry had launched a blast into that area that measured 462 feet. Cuyler's rocket, according to witnesses who were present for both home runs, eclipsed the distance of Terry's clout, as it landed 10 feet closer to the Giants' clubhouse located beyond center field.[13]

Bill McKechnie's squad looked for retribution when the series' second game commenced on Friday, May 22. The Pirates knocked Giants starter Hugh McQuillan from the game with a five-run first inning. After Max Carey started the game with an out, Eddie Moore singled and Kiki Cuyler was plunked by a McQuillan pitch. Moore stole third base as McQuillan held onto the ball and then scored on Clyde Barnhart's single. Pie Traynor followed with a base hit that scored Cuyler from second and allowed Barnhart to scamper into third. Both men trotted home when Glenn Wright drilled his sixth home run of the season into the left field stands' upper tier.[14]

Pittsburgh's fortunes looked good with staff ace Lee Meadows staked to a five-run lead before he even took the mound. But Meadows struggled and

5. Booming Bats Lead to a Turnaround 75

gave up five runs on ten hits in five-plus innings of work. After Hack Wilson's two-run homer tied the game, 5–5, Meadows gave way to Vic Aldridge with one out in the sixth inning. Both Aldridge and Giants reliever Wayland Dean continued to put scoreless innings on the board before Pittsburgh finally broke through with the winning run. In the tenth inning, Traynor's line drive caromed off Dean's shin and bounded toward right field, with Traynor making it to second base before the ball was retrieved. He moved to third on an out by Wright and scored when George Grantham dumped a single into center field.[15] Aldridge then kept the Giants off the board in their half of the tenth and received credit for the victory in Pittsburgh's 6–5 win.

Outfielder Clyde Barnhart went 3-for-5 and ran his hitting streak to 23 consecutive games. During Pittsburgh's five-run first inning, Barnhart strained a leg muscle when he slid into third base. Fortunately, Barnhart felt only slight pain in the injured area when he awoke on Saturday morning. Clyde was hobbled a bit, but the injury did not seem to be serious. Barnhart planned on playing that afternoon in order to test his injured leg. If Barnhart were unable to continue, Carson Bigbee would be called upon to take his place as he had done in the tenth inning the previous day.[16]

Barnhart did start in left field as New York demolished Pittsburgh by a score of 10–1. Clyde's leg troubled him sufficiently during the first few innings that Bigbee replaced him in the fifth inning. Before he left the game, Barnhart smacked a single that extended his hitting streak to 24 games.[17] The Giants roughed up starter Emil Yde to the tune of six runs in the first three innings. Bud Culloton and Lou Koupal attempted to stop the onslaught, but they, too, were battered freely by Giants batters. New York secured the contest with a four-spot in the first inning. Freddie Lindstrom opened with a single off Yde's glove. Ross Youngs forced his teammate at second, but moved to third when Bill Terry drove a single past George Grantham. George Kelly drilled a long single that bounced into the right field stands, scoring Youngs. Irish Meusel's high chopper eluded Grantham, went for two bases and sent Terry across the plate. Hack Wilson followed with a single that drove home Kelly and Meusel with New York's third and fourth runs of the inning.[18]

Official National League standings at the conclusion of Saturday, May 23, showed Pittsburgh in fifth place with a 14–16 record. The Pirates trailed the first-place Giants by nine games. New York's 24–8 record was the best in major league baseball; John McGraw's squad was 6½ games ahead of second-place Brooklyn.

Bill McKechnie had eight Pirates who were hitting above .300, a fact that showed that Pittsburgh's bats were coming to life. McKechnie now needed his pitchers to follow suit if Pittsburgh had any intention of chipping away at New York's lead.

The Pirates were forced to reflect on their humiliating loss a bit longer when their scheduled game against New York on Sunday was postponed. A spring shower that began prior to game time caused the "no game" sign to be posted at the Polo Grounds' box office. After the decision was made to cancel the game, a blistering rain storm broke out throughout the city. The Pirates expected the postponed game to be rescheduled when Pittsburgh made its next trip to New York in July.[19] In the meantime, McKechnie and his squad grabbed the Sunday evening flyer out of New York and headed back to Pittsburgh after having been on the road for 17 days. With the train scheduled to arrive in the Smoky City on Monday morning, McKechnie hoped to squeeze in a practice session before the afternoon engagement against Chicago.[20]

As luck would have it, outside forces again intervened and prevented McKechnie from having a much needed practice. Whereas weather had been the common culprit in circumventing McKechnie's training plans since the season began, it was a four-hour delay arriving home that scuttled his plans this time. Pittsburgh's train did not arrive in Altoona until nine o'clock in the morning, with the delay due to a wreck in Harrisburg between two freight trains the previous night. This setback meant that Pirates players would have to hustle directly from the train to Forbes Field in order to prepare for that afternoon's game against Chicago.[21]

The Pirates returned home after posting an 8–6 record during their first Eastern swing of the season. McKechnie's squad caught fire offensively during their time in Philadelphia, Boston and New York. The Buccaneers were hitting .275 when they embarked east, but they saw that average jump to .313 as the final games were being played against John McGraw's New York Giants. In contrast sub-par pitching and horrendous fielding were holding Pittsburgh back. The Pirates looked like a strong fielding unit on paper, but this did not translate into results on the field. Their fielding average of .944 was well behind the .969 mark of their opponents. Strangely, McKechnie's team had committed numerous defensive gaffes in 27 games, as they made 63 errors, compared to only 33 by their opponents.[22]

With regard to McKechnie's pitching staff, Pirates hurlers were still having trouble completing games. Ray Kremer and Johnny Morrison were starting to win some games, but both pitchers had tossed few complete games and had been hammered freely by opposing batters. Emil Yde and Vic Aldridge had pitched horribly and had not come close to their past levels of performance. Pittsburgh fans blamed Aldridge's miserable performance on his refusal to sign his contract early and missed spring training as a result. In spite of his pitching and defensive shortcomings, McKechnie was confident those facets would improve once the Pirates could practice regularly. Pittsburgh's long home stand, which ran into June, was expected to give McKechnie a chance to conduct morning workouts on a daily basis.[23]

Two thousand diehard Pittsburgh fans braved unseasonably cold weather to watch the Pirates squeak by Chicago, 5–3, in the first game of the crucial home stand.[24] On a day when the weather was more conducive for football or hockey, Johnny Morrison tossed a complete game for Pittsburgh. Morrison allowed three runs on seven hits while striking out two. On offense, Clyde Barnhart, Earl Smith and George Grantham banged out two hits apiece. Barnhart stroked a double, scored one run and drove home another as he extended his hitting streak to 25 games.[25]

Barnhart was quietly having the best season of his career in 1925. Barnhart continued to toil in anonymity, helping his mates win games despite a nagging charley-horse injury. On the field against Chicago, Barnhart showed no ill-effects from the injury as he covered plenty of ground in left field and handled several difficult chances. Clyde did receive some criticism for his mishandling of Ike McAuley's lofty fly ball, which eluded the left fielder and landed for a double.[26] Yet, this complaint seemed trivial given Barnhart's remarkable speed in covering ground in the outfield.

The Pirates continued their winning ways when they shellacked Chicago, 7–2, on Tuesday, May 26. Ray Kremer tossed Pittsburgh's second straight complete game, as he scattered 11 hits and held Chicago to two runs. Clyde Barnhart saw his hitting streak come to an end when he took an 0-for-4 collar at the plate. Kiki Cuyler drilled the longest blast of the day when he connected against Percy Jones in the first inning; he also hit a smash that eluded outfielder Cliff Heathcote and rolled to the fence near the flagpole.[27] Cuyler's two-run, inside-the-park home run gave the Pirates a lead that they never relinquished. The Pirates built on their lead in the third inning when Jones walked three, hit a batter and gave up a double to first baseman Al Niehaus. The Pirates scored their last run in the fourth when Max Carey stole second, third and home in succession. Carey's pilfer of the plate was part of a double steal as Eddie Moore grabbed second base on the play.[28]

McKechnie's brigade made it three wins in a row as Vic Aldridge tossed yet another complete game, and Pittsburgh defeated Chicago, 13–3, on May 27. Aldridge was effective as he allowed two earned runs, seven hits, and six walks, and struck out seven Chicago batters. Aldridge's only major mistake occurred when Tommy Griffith hit a solo home run in the fourth inning. Glenn Wright and Earl Smith starred at the plate as each player went 3-for-5. Smith piled up three doubles and scored two runs. Wright drove home five Pirates and scored two runs. Wright's grand slam blast off pitcher Sheriff Blake helped blow the game open as Pittsburgh scored seven runs in the fourth inning. Max Carey, Eddie Moore and Aldridge provided capable support at the plate by slashing two hits apiece.

The St. Louis Cardinals followed Chicago into town to begin a four-game series on Thursday, May 28. Lee Meadows won his sixth game of the season as Pittsburgh defeated St. Louis, 7–4. Meadows tossed a complete game and allowed no earned runs on eight hits. Errors by Pie Traynor and Glenn Wright led to three unearned runs off Meadows in the second inning.[29] Those three runs proved only a minor inconvenience to Pittsburgh's players as they rapped out 11 hits and chased St. Louis starter Jesse Haines in the seventh inning. Max Carey, Eddie Moore and George Grantham each blasted two hits. All three players drilled a triple apiece, as they accounted for four of Pittsburgh's seven runs.

Pittsburgh ran its winning streak to five games by winning a tightly contested battle over St. Louis on Friday, May 29, by a score of 6–5. Babe Adams was unable to give McKechnie's staff its fifth consecutive complete game, as he allowed St. Louis to tie the score in the ninth inning before giving way to Ray Kremer. The Cardinals took an early lead in the fifth when Rogers Hornsby's two-run home run highlighted a three-run inning. Pittsburgh jumped back on top in the bottom of the eighth, when Pie Traynor smacked a clutch, two-out, inside-the-park homer. Kremer was credited with the victory after Pittsburgh rebounded in the bottom of the ninth inning. St. Louis pitcher Leo Dickerman committed a crucial mistake when he hit Kiki Cuyler with a pitched ball that allowed the deciding run to score after Pittsburgh had loaded the bases.[30]

As Pittsburgh continued to climb in the National League standings, Barney Dreyfuss and Bill McKechnie made two roster moves that indicated they were still looking to reshape their team. The first transaction occurred on May 29, when the Pirates signed veteran first baseman Stuffy McInnis to a contract. McInnis had not played during the spring due to his refusal to accept a salary cut from Boston; he became a free agent after his release from the Braves. McInnis was an aging player but his experience and reputation as a solid fielder at first base were two assets that Dreyfuss and McKechnie believed would benefit Pittsburgh in the long run.[31]

McInnis' addition to the Pirates' roster meant that rookie first baseman Al Niehaus had likely seen his days in Pittsburgh end. The youngster struggled during his National League baptism, hitting only .219 while appearing in 17 games for Pittsburgh. Niehaus' play around first base was also shaky as he committed six errors.

One day after McInnis signed a contract, Niehaus was sent packing in a deal with Cincinnati that saw Pittsburgh acquire pitcher Tom Sheehan.[32] Niehaus' departure left a bad taste in the mouths of some Pittsburgh baseball fans who believed that his exit proved that McKechnie's trade with Chicago was an abject failure. They pondered how the Pirates would be doing if McKechnie had not included Charlie Grimm in the package for Niehaus. The fans did not realize that McKechnie reluctantly traded Grimm only after Chicago manager Bill Killefer threatened to kill the blockbuster deal if Grimm was not included.[33]

5. Booming Bats Lead to a Turnaround

The Pirates ran their winning streak to seven straight games by demolishing St. Louis during a holiday doubleheader on Saturday, May 30. Pittsburgh won the morning game as Emil Yde resurrected his 1924 form in beating St. Louis, 4–1. Yde tossed a complete game, scattered eight hits, walked four and struck out three. McKechnie's team claimed victory in the sixth inning with the score tied, 1–1. George Grantham started the outburst by drilling a two-base hit off the fence in left field. Johnny Gooch then reached first base under unusual circumstances when he tried to sacrifice Grantham to third. Gooch placed a bunt single down the third base line. Several Cardinal players chose not to pick up the ball, hoping it would roll foul, but it did not. Yde's out then moved Gooch to second, and Grantham scored one batter later on Max Carey's single. Gooch followed suit with Pittsburgh's third run when Eddie Moore singled off pitcher Alan Sothoron's glove.[34]

The Memorial Day afternoon matinee at Forbes Field saw the Pirates savagely beat St. Louis, 15–5. Pittsburgh starter Johnny Morrison was shaky during the game's first two innings, as he allowed St. Louis to push four runs across the plate. This did not seem to matter to Pittsburgh's batters as they blasted 19 hits against two Cardinals hurlers. Clyde Barnhart starred at the plate for Pittsburgh as he went 4-for-5 with two triples, scored four runs and knocked in five runs. Pie Traynor and Glenn Wright had three hits apiece, as both players combined to score four runs, while smacking two doubles and two triples, and driving home five Pirates teammates.

Pittsburgh took control of the game in the third inning. With St. Louis clinging to a 4–3 lead, Kiki Cuyler tripled to right field and scored on Clyde Barnhart's single to center. Eddie Dyer was called in from the bullpen to replace starter Pea Ridge Day. Pie Traynor greeted the new St. Louis pitcher with a double to left that moved Barnhart to third. Glenn Wright blasted a two-run triple to deep right field and then scored the Pirates' seventh run when George Grantham legged out a hit on a ground ball to second baseman Rogers Hornsby. The inning came to an end when Earl Smith hit into a double play and Morrison grounded out.[35]

Pittsburgh added four more runs in the fourth inning when Cuyler, Barnhart, Traynor and Grantham all crossed home plate. A two spot in the sixth inning and a solo blast by Smith that struck the second tier of the right field stands gave Pittsburgh a 14–5 lead after seven innings. The Pirates scored their final tally in the eighth, when Barnhart singled and scored on Traynor's triple; it was the third extra base hit for Pittsburgh's third baseman on the day.[36] The two victories pleased the Pittsburgh fans that participated in the holiday festivities at Forbes Field. Their decision to join the Pirates' organization in celebrating Memorial Day also brought a smile to owner Barney Dreyfuss's face as 45,000 people pushed through the turnstiles to watch the two games.[37]

A perfect week catapulted the Pirates to third place. They stood at 21–16 with the conclusion of games on May 30. The Corsairs now trailed first-place New York by only 4½ games.

The Pirates left the cozy confines of Forbes Field for a short, two-game engagement in Chicago against the seventh-place Cubs. The game did not begin well in the Windy City, as Chicago blitzed the Buccaneers during a Sunday afternoon affair, 11–2. Starter Ray Kremer was knocked around freely until giving way to reliever Tom Sheehan in the fifth inning. Sheehan's first appearance as a Pirate received mixed reviews. He hurled three and one-third innings, gave up two earned runs, and seven hits. Gabby Hartnett connected for his sixth home run against Pittsburgh pitching in 1925 when he blasted a two-run shot off Sheehan in the eighth inning. Pittsburgh's Eddie Moore bagged his first homer of the season when he struck a two-run blast against Sheriff Blake in the fifth inning.

The Cubs made it two wins in a row on Monday, June 1, when they defeated McKechnie's brigade, 6–5, despite two hits apiece for Max Carey, Hazen Cuyler, Glenn Wright and Clyde Barnhart. Barnhart's two-run bounce home run off Pete Alexander in the fourth inning aided a Pittsburgh surge that saw the Pirates take a 5–2 lead after five innings. Such support usually would have been enough to guarantee Vic Aldridge a victory, but two of Pittsburgh's most dependable fielders made egregious mistakes in the seventh inning. Pie Traynor and Wright each cut loose with throws that missed their mark. The errors allowed Chicago to score three runs and tie the score. Pittsburgh's sordid fielding became even more harmful when ex–Pirate Charlie Grimm connected for a home run in the eighth inning against Aldridge, securing Chicago's victory.[38]

A two-day break in the National League schedule did not mean that Bill McKechnie's squad would be free from actual game conditions. McKechnie and Barney Dreyfuss scheduled two exhibition contests aimed at keeping the Pirates sharp until they played their next game at Forbes Field on June 4. The Pirates were scheduled to play against the South Bend team in Indiana on June 2, and an Elks team from the Pittsburgh suburb of Beaver Falls on June 3. It was reported that both amateur squads expected to see their largest crowds of the season in these games.[39]

A group of Pittsburgh players, consisting mainly of pitchers, were permitted to miss the contest in South Bend; they returned home to Pittsburgh in preparation for their upcoming three-game series against Philadelphia.[40] When Bill McKechnie brought the remainder of his squad home after the exhibition game in the city that houses Notre Dame University, the Pirates were greeted with some of the hottest temperatures seen in Pittsburgh in many years. On June 2, the mercury reached 91 degrees in the Smoky City, shattering a 30-year record for high temperature. Ninety-three degree heat enveloped the Pittsburgh region on June 3, as the Pirates played their exhibition game in Beaver Falls.[41]

A few hours before the Pirates took the field for their Thursday game against Philadelphia, Pittsburgh's city schools were ordered to close their doors at 1 P.M. due to the intense heat. Eighty thousand pupils in grade schools and high schools throughout the city were dismissed early when U. S. weather forecaster W.S. Brotzman projected the temperature would reach 95 degrees that afternoon. The decision was made following a conference between school superintendent Davidson and physicians from the city health department.[42] As Pittsburgh's inhabitants continued to battle the sweltering heat, players from the 1901 Pirates began making their way into the Smoky City for Barney Dreyfuss's huge "Golden Jubilee Celebration" to be held on Saturday, June 6.

Former Pirate catcher Chief Zimmer arrived in Pittsburgh on June 2 after making the trip from his home in Cleveland. Tommy Leach planned on reaching the city via automobile after a long drive from his lodging in Lake City, Florida.[43] Leach arrived in Pittsburgh on June 3, as did fellow star outfielder Clarence "Ginger" Beaumont.[44] Former player-manager Fred Clarke had arrived in town earlier than all of his ex-teammates and was feverishly working out for several days in anticipation of the big celebration.[45] Dreyfuss planned on having a gala event to celebrate the National League's fiftieth anniversary. Commissioner Landis and National League president John Heydler were expected to be on hand to witness the activities at Forbes Field. Dreyfuss's former players were also scheduled to be the owner's guests of honor at an informal banquet that evening. All of the old-timers were expected to reach Pittsburgh in time to occupy reserved seats at Forbes Field for the June 4th game between the Corsairs and Phillies.[46]

Members of the 1901 Pittsburgh Pirates were treated to a splendid game as Bill McKechnie's Buccaneers torched Philadelphia, 16–3. Lee Meadows tossed a complete game for Pittsburgh and raised his record to 7–2 as he allowed three runs on ten hits and struck out seven Phillies. Kiki Cuyler led the way for Pittsburgh with a 4-for-5 day as he drove home three runs and stole a base. George Grantham and Carson Bigbee also chipped in with three hits apiece and combined to score four Pittsburgh runs. Bigbee was pressed into service since Clyde Barnhart had been called to his home in Hagerstown, Maryland, due to the illness of one of his children.[47]

Cuyler put on a classic performance for the old guard of Pirates players in attendance at Forbes Field. The Pirate outfielder wielded a poisonous bat as he hit for the cycle, added a walk, scored four runs and stole a base. His first-inning solo home run against Philadelphia starter Jack Knight was of the inside-the-park variety. Cuyler played just as phenomenally in the field. The Flint Flash was credited with the defensive gem of the game in the third inning, when he covered significant distance grabbing a fly ball. Philadelphia had two men on base with one out, when a blistering drive by George Harper to the outfield seemed destined to knock in two runs. Cuyler dashed to right center, near the eastern side of the newly constructed stands, and made a leaping one-handed grab of Harper's blast. Cuyler's peg to the keystone sack doubled up Lew Fonseca, who had started home with the crack of the bat.[48]

Philadelphia extracted a small modicum of revenge the next day, defeating the Pirates on Friday, June 5, by a score of 6–5. Ray Kremer was charged with the loss even though he pitched five solid innings of relief after starting pitcher Johnny Morrison had stumbled. Max Carey, Pie Traynor and Stuffy McInnis each went 2-for-5 at the plate and combined to score two runs while driving home three teammates. This was McInnis' first start at first base, as part of McKechnie's plan to use the veteran against southpaw pitchers. Philadelphia won the game in the eleventh inning, when pitcher Clarence Mitchell helped his own cause by driving home Heinie Sand with a single to right field. The Phillies were given an opportunity to push the game past regulation when Russ Wrightstone's three-run drive off Morrison in the sixth inning tied the score at five.[49]

Clyde Barnhart was Pittsburgh's best player during the early stages of the 1925 season. Barnhart hit safely in 25 consecutive games until he was stopped by Chicago on May 26. Barnhart's breakout season was interrupted in June, when he was called to his home in Hagerstown, Maryland, due to the illness of one of his children (National Baseball Hall of Fame Library, Cooperstown, New York).

The blistering heat in Pittsburgh finally broke courtesy of some rain showers, as Barney Dreyfuss took his turn celebrating the National League's fiftieth anniversary on Saturday, June 6. Falling rain did not diminish the excitement and enthusiasm at Forbes Field. Dreyfuss felt that the throng of rooters would have been an overflow crowd if the threatening conditions did not exist.[50] Many of the fans in attendance came to watch the players who were part of the franchise's first National League pennant in 1901 play a short exhibition game against the current aggregation. The contest between the 1901 squad and Bill McKechnie's group of players was scheduled to begin at 2:30 in the afternoon. As soon as that exhibition was completed, the regular game between Pittsburgh and Philadelphia would begin immediately.[51]

Before the game, the 1901 Pirates met at Honus Wagner's sporting goods store on Wood Street in downtown Pittsburgh, so that each player could drive to Forbes Field in an omnibus, the mode of transportation in their playing days. Each player entered the old-time contraption, which featured an aging mustached driver occupying the front seat. Chief Zimmer sat beside the driver and Jimmy Burke took a seat on the roof of the special bus, which was loaned by the J.P. Eichleay Company. Wagner rode in a special phaeton behind the larger omnibus. Once the vehicles reached Forbes Field, the procession was headed by the East Liberty Post American Legion Band. The omnibus made one trip around the field before it stopped in front of the home team's bench. The 1901 players then dismounted from their horse drawn vehicle and posed for photographs.[52]

After photos were taken, the current squads from Pittsburgh and Philadelphia joined the old-timers and began a march to the flagpole. Judge Kenesaw Landis, his secretary Leslie M. O'Connor, National League president John Heydler, Pirates president Barney Dreyfuss, team treasurer Sam Dreyfuss and Harrison Nesbit joined in the procession. Other old-time baseball players such as Ed Abbaticchio, Billy Murray and "Uncle Al" Pratt, who all resided in Pittsburgh, were also invited to march with the band preceding the flag raising ceremony. The American Legion band played "Tessie," the battle anthem of Boston's fans in the inaugural World Series against Pittsburgh in 1903, while leading the group of players and dignitaries. Once the procession reached the outfield flagpole, Old Glory and the National League Golden Jubilee flag were raised while the band performed a stirring rendition of the Star Spangled Banner.[53]

Before McKechnie's squad and the 1901 team took the field, a special ceremony involving Fred Clarke was conducted at home plate. Clarke was given a basket of flowers by members of the East End Republican Club who were deep admirers of the former Pirates player-manager. Clarke choked back tears as Forbes Field's fans cheered the touching gesture. Among the onlookers who expressed their happiness were Clarke's wife, Annette, and his daughters, Muriel and Helen.[54]

The lineup for the 1901 squad read like an all-star team of players from the first decade of the twentieth century. Former batting champion Ginger Beaumont was placed in the leadoff position, with Tommy Leach hitting out of the two hole. Clarke hit third, while the incomparable Honus Wagner batted cleanup. Kitty Bransfield, Claude Ritchey, Tom McCreery and Chief Zimmer rounded out the starting position players for the game that was slated to last three innings. Two World Series heroes were chosen to oppose each other, as Deacon Phillippe took the mound for Clarke's squad and Babe Adams was selected to pitch by McKechnie. The players seemed to enjoy themselves as the 1925 squad prevailed, 5–3. Adams pitched all three innings for the 1925 team, while Jesse Tannehill relieved Phillippe in the second, and former spitball pitcher Jack Chesbro handled mound duties in the third inning. Kiki Cuyler and Glenn Wright picked up two hits apiece for the 1925 squad. The great Honus Wagner gave Pittsburgh's current generation of fans a glimpse into the past when he banged out two safeties for the 1901 aggregation.[55]

Associating with baseball royalty seemed to invigorate McKechnie's players for their regular contest against Philadelphia. The Pirates knocked Phillies starter Hal Carlson from the mound after he walked Max Carey, Eddie Moore, Kiki Cuyler, Carson Bigbee and George Grantham to start the first inning.[56] Pittsburgh scored five runs in the frame and proceeded to breeze to an easy 9–3 victory. Emil Yde tossed a complete game for Pittsburgh, allowing two earned runs on seven hits. Glenn Wright and Pie Traynor rapped out two hits each while Carey, Cuyler and Moore combined to score six of Pittsburgh's runs. Moore contributed the game's most exciting play of the day when he drilled a Jack Knight offering that rolled to the flagpole for a two-run, inside-the-park home run. Cuyler turned in the defensive gems of the game in the fourth and sixth frames, when he speared drives off the bats of Chicken Hawks and Jimmie Wilson.[57]

The Pirates' victory over Philadelphia left them with a 23–19 record, good for third place in the National League standings. They trailed second-place Brooklyn by 1½ games, while the league-leading Giants held a six-game lead over the Corsairs.

As the Pirates awaited the arrival of the Boston Braves for a four-game series at Forbes Field, they made a short trip to Johnstown, Pennsylvania, for a Sunday exhibition game. Pittsburgh was scheduled to play a game against the Mid-Atlantic League's Johnstown Johnnies, who featured Pirates prospects Joe Cronin, Mike Martineck and Eddie Montague.[58] Despite Pennsylvania's Sunday Blue Laws that prohibited baseball games from happening on the Sabbath, the contest went off without a hitch as Pittsburgh claimed a 9–4 victory.

The Pirates resumed the task of competing against National League teams when they opposed Boston on Monday, June 8. Vic Aldridge, a focal point of contempt for almost two months, tossed a complete game and beat Boston, 8–4. Aldridge survived a tough start and allowed only two earned runs on seven hits. Fellow ex–Chicago teammate George Grantham starred at the plate by going 4-for-4 on the day. Grantham also scored a run, smacked a double and drove home a run. Pittsburgh's newest first baseman was playing stellar baseball having raised his average to .351 since replacing Al Niehaus as the starter. Pie Traynor and Kiki Cuyler continued their hot hitting and added support to the cause by smacking two hits apiece.

Boston reversed the tables against Pittsburgh the following day, as the Braves went 11 innings to claim a 7–4 victory. Max Carey led the way for Pittsburgh by going 3-for-5 with a run scored. Third baseman William Marriott topped all Boston batters with four hits. Pirates starter Lee Meadows worked into the 11th inning, even though he was smacked frequently by Boston's hitters. Meadows was charged with seven runs on 15 hits in ten innings of work. The Braves broke a 3–3 deadlock in the 11th, when they scored four runs off Meadows. Pitcher Jesse Barnes supplied the crucial hit by smacking a two-run single with the bases loaded. That prompted Bill McKechnie to replace Meadows with Ray Kremer, who allowed two inherited base runners to cross home plate.[59]

The Braves made it two victories in a row when they defeated Pittsburgh on Wednesday, June 10, by the score of 6–4. Johnny Morrison, lacking his best stuff, lasted only five innings, giving up four runs on eight hits. Babe Adams and Tom Sheehan pitched adequately in relief, but the Pirates were unable to overcome an early 5–0 deficit. George Grantham enjoyed his second consecutive perfect day at the plate as he went 3-for-3 and scored a run. Pie Traynor's three-run, inside-the-park homer proved too little as the Pirates were unable to rally against Braves starter Skinny Graham. Pittsburgh's Eddie Moore went 2-for-2 at the plate, but needed to be replaced by Johnny Rawlings after injuring his leg while running out the second hit.[60]

Pittsburgh gained a split with Boston when McKechnie's marauders destroyed Boston on Thursday, June 11, by a score of 11–3. Rawlings capably replaced Moore at second base by going 3-for-4 with a run scored, a double and two RBIs. Max Carey, Kiki Cuyler and Johnny Gooch each recorded two hits and combined to score five of Pittsburgh's runs. Pitcher Emil Yde picked up his third straight victory and improved his record to 4–4. Besides doing gilt edged work on the mound, Yde also did damage with the bat. In four trips to the plate, Yde banged a single, a double and a triple. Yde's personal hitting clinic allowed him to score three runs and drive home a trio of teammates.[61]

Fans in the Smoky City said goodbye to Boston and prepared to witness a titanic encounter between two rivals, as New York rolled into Pittsburgh for a four-game series. As had been the case so many times during Barney Dreyfuss's ownership tenure in Pittsburgh, the Pirates and Giants were holding down the National League's top two spots. The Giants had won two out of three games at the Polo Grounds less than a month ago, but Bill McKechnie's troops did not seem overly concerned with past results.

6

Battling New York for the Top Spot

Years of experience had taught Barney Dreyfuss that pennants were not won or lost in June. Pittsburgh's upcoming four-game series was crucial, but the outcome would not necessarily determine who would be crowned as National League champion in 1925. Pirates manager Bill McKechnie knew that a four-game sweep by New York would not end his team's season at that moment, but he was aware of the psychological damage such a defeat could inflict on his squad. McKechnie did believe that a strong showing by his club could set the tone for future campaigns between the teams.

Both teams were shorthanded due to injuries and would play without crucial performers in this anticipated series. Eddie Moore was out of Pittsburgh's lineup with a charley-horse. New York also would be without three important members of their entourage. Frankie Frisch was shelved with a broken finger, and Freddie Lindstrom was absent due to a finger injury. Bill Terry was also hurting, but was expected to see action in some of the series' games. The Giants would also play without their esteemed manager John McGraw. Illness had prevented McGraw from sitting in the dugout for much of the 1925 season. Hughie Jennings, who did admirable work during "Little Napoleon's" absence, was expected to manage the Giants against Pittsburgh even though McGraw was well enough to resume his managerial duties.[1]

The Pirates fired a loud salvo at New York on Friday, June 12. Pittsburgh defeated the Giants convincingly, 6–2. Vic Aldridge was masterful on the mound as he tossed a complete game and allowed only two runs on eight hits. Kiki Cuyler went 3-for-4 and Max Carey, Johnny Rawlings, Glenn Wright, Earl Smith and George Grantham chipped in with two hits apiece. Grantham slammed the longest hit of the day when he drilled a two-run home run against Virgil Barnes in the second inning. Though it had no effect on the outcome, the Pirates were the victims of a peculiar triple play in the first inning. A Cuyler grounder to shortstop Travis Jackson led to Carey being caught in a rundown

Max Carey showed the fans at Forbes Field why he was one of the most clever players in baseball. In the third inning of a game against New York on June 12, 1925, Carey scored from third on a shallow fly behind second base. In the fifth inning, he scored from second on Kiki Cuyler's sacrifice fly to left field (National Baseball Hall of Fame Library, Cooperstown, New York).

and Rawlings being tagged out at third. Cuyler fell prey to the third out after he was trapped between first and second.[2]

Even though Grantham's home run gave the Pirates a lead they never relinquished, it was Carey's daring running that stoked the spirits of his teammates. In the third inning, Carey tagged up from third and scored after Giants outfielder Billy Southworth snagged a shallow fly ball behind second base. Southworth, never expecting Carey to run on such a short fly, did not even attempt a throw to the plate. In the fifth inning, Carey led off with a single. Pittsburgh's veteran outfielder moved to second base after a Rawlings sacrifice. Cuyler followed by blasting a deep drive to left field. Carey broke for third base after outfielder Irish Meusel hauled in the long drive. Much to the amazement of New York's players, Carey did not stop at third and kept running toward home. Panic set in among the Giants as Carey crossed home standing up before a peg could ever be made to catcher Hank Gowdy.[3]

Carey's hustling and heady play during the series' first game inspired his teammates. Twenty-eight thousand fans who packed Forbes Field on Saturday, June 13, were sent home happy for a second day in a row as Pittsburgh defeated New York, 6–4. Eddie Moore, back in the lineup after missing only two games, went 2-for-4 and scored two runs. Kiki Cuyler, Clyde Barnhart, Pie Traynor and pitcher Lee Meadows also recorded two hits apiece for Pittsburgh. Meadows pitched a complete game, gave up four runs on nine hits, walked four and struck out three. Meadows' only mistake in the game came when New York's Bill Terry connected against a fifth inning offering for a two-run home run.

The Pirates secured victory against New York starter Hugh McQuillan when they broke a 3–3 tie in the seventh inning and pushed three runs across. Meadows started Pittsburgh's rally when he stretched a liner to center field into a double. Max Carey then smacked a grounder to first baseman Terry that went for an infield single when no one covered the bag. With runners on the corners, Moore then singled to right and drove home Meadows. Following suit from the previous day, Carey tested the New York fielders by attempting to score from first base. The Giants won this round, throwing Carey out at home plate.[4]

Moore scored Pittsburgh's second run of the inning on Cuyler's double. Kiki came around to score when Traynor drilled a triple that bounded past Ross Youngs in right field. Traynor followed the lead of team captain Max Carey when he tried to leg his hit into a four-bagger, but was cut down at the plate by George Kelly's strong throw after Youngs made a perfect peg to the cutoff man.[5] Pittsburgh's daring running did produce one positive result, when Cuyler and Barnhart pulled a double steal in the third inning, with Hazen snagging home on the play.[6]

Pittsburgh's second consecutive victory over New York was not the biggest news on a summer Saturday in the Smoky City. An announcement by Barney Dreyfuss superseded all other events of the day. Dreyfuss announced that former manager Fred Clarke was rejoining the Pirates' organization in the capacity of team vice-president. Clarke was also named as an assistant to manager McKechnie. Within this role, Clarke would be permitted to sit on the bench and travel with the team as he performed an advisory role for McKechnie. The deal was consummated with Clarke purchasing a small interest of stock in the Pittsburgh team.[7] In addition to being an assistant to the manager and club president, Clarke would also be responsible for heading up Pittsburgh's scouting system.[8]

Clarke's appointment was something that had been discussed by Dreyfuss and his former manager for weeks. Negotiations between the two baseball icons began when Clarke came to Pittsburgh in preparation for the old-timer's game that was part of Pittsburgh's Golden Jubilee Celebration one week earlier. Most of the important details were worked out weeks earlier, with the announcement finally made after a few minor issues were ironed out.[9] When Dreyfuss announced Clarke's appointment, Dreyfuss stated that the responsibility of running a baseball organization had become too overwhelming for a man his age. He hoped to ease some of the burden by hiring a man with Clarke's pedigree.[10] Pittsburgh's baseball fans reacted with delight when Dreyfuss made the announcement. They believed Clarke's fiery spirit and thorough knowledge of the game would add beneficial intangibles to Pittsburgh's crusade.[11]

The Pirates played the kind of ball that typified Fred Clarke's past teams once action resumed against New York on Monday, June 15. Bill McKechnie's team won a tightly contested affair, 7–6. The Giants battled gamely as two-run home runs by George Kelly in the third inning and Frank Snyder in the ninth nearly brought them back. Babe Adams picked up the victory in relief for Pittsburgh after he replaced starter Johnny Morrison in the fifth inning. Adams pitched five innings and scattered four hits, with Snyder's blast marking the veteran twirler's only lapse. Max Carey, Eddie Moore, Clyde Barnhart and Pie Traynor each recorded two hits, while accounting for five RBIs.

Clarke's presence on the bench seemed to ignite the Pirates. In the top of the fifth inning, Giants rookie Eddie Farrell had to leave his major league debut when Eddie Moore spiked the University of Pennsylvania recruit in the right arm with an aggressive slide.[12] The Giants attempted to extract revenge for Moore's play in the bottom of the fifth, when Farrell's replacement, Heinie Groh, kept the toe of his shoe on Clyde Barnhart's body for a few seconds after a play at third base. The usually docile Barnhart became enraged, jumping to his feet and prepared to battle Groh. Heated words were exchanged between the two players, but no punches were thrown. An incensed Pittsburgh fan sitting in seats along the third base line showed his displeasure with Groh by tossing a pop bottle onto the diamond.[13]

The final, unscrupulous event of the game occurred in the sixth inning, when New York pitcher Jack Scott drilled George Grantham with a pitch. Pittsburgh's first baseman retaliated by hurling his bat at Scott. The wooden projectile did not connect, but there was no doubt as to Grantham's intent. Both dugouts emptied onto the field as players from each team seemed ready to fight with fists or baseball bats.[14] Cooler heads prevailed as umpires Barry

McCormick and Bill Klem quickly restored order. The arbiters ordered Grantham to leave the field, banishing Pittsburgh's first baseman for tossing his bat in Scott's direction. When National League president John Heydler reviewed the incident after the game, he chose not to suspend Grantham. Heydler took into account the tense conditions that existed, punishing Grantham with only a $50 fine.[15]

It was believed that Heydler also took into account Grantham's genuine anger at having a pitcher throw at his head. During the first few months of the season, it seemed that National League hurlers were indiscriminately using the bean ball more than they had in past years. Two or three Pittsburgh players who liked to hug the plate had been plunked on numerous occasions. Their appeals to league umpires regarding the frequency with which they were being hit by opposing pitchers fell on deaf ears.[16] Some admirers of the sensational Kiki Cuyler believed that there was a conspiracy among National League pitchers to injure the Pirates' outfielder by beaning him.[17]

Civility returned to Forbes Field as Pittsburgh and New York battled in the final game of their four-game series on Tuesday, June 16. Pitchers from both squads were treated rudely as the two teams combined for 37 hits. Billy Southworth, Bill Terry and George Kelly all struck home runs for New York. Pittsburgh's Kiki Cuyler was also credited with a four-base marker when he legged out a solo, inside-the-park home run against pitcher Walt Huntzinger in the fifth inning. Max Carey went a perfect 5-for-5 and Glenn Wright was 4-for-6 with three runs scored and three runs batted in. Wright turned into the game's hero in the tenth inning when his two-run walk off homer against Art Nehf capped a monumental four run rally, as Pittsburgh prevailed, 13–11.[18]

Bill McKechnie's troops had definitely made a strong statement by sweeping the first-place Giants. By winning all four games of the series, the Pirates reduced their deficit to two and a half games behind the Giants, while also serving notice that a fifth consecutive pennant for John McGraw's squad was not guaranteed. While the Pirates squad appeared to be bonding, it seemed that McGraw was facing some of the issues that plagued McKechnie in the past. While in the Smoky City, New York pitcher Virgil Barnes sprained his ankle by supposedly slipping in a bath tub. This story quickly lost its validity when McGraw stated that Barnes injured himself while carousing on a night when the player failed to abide by an 11:30 P.M. curfew. McGraw immediately suspended Barnes for violating team rules and sent the pitcher back to New York.[19]

Brooklyn followed New York into Pittsburgh for a four-game series against the high-flying Pirates. The Pirates made it six wins in a row when they defeated the Robins, 8–3, on June 17 behind Emil Yde's solid pitching. Yde went the distance, as he gave up two runs on nine hits, walked five and struck out two batters. Brooklyn's Burleigh Grimes held the Corsairs hitless through four innings until a light downpour began to fall at Forbes Field. A previous hand injury, coupled with the sudden wet weather, rendered Grimes ineffective. The rain made it difficult for Grimes to harness his famous spitball pitch. His wildness led to two Pittsburgh runs in the fifth inning. Several pitches that Grimes grooved in the sixth frame led to three more runs for the Pirates.[20]

Dazzy Vance ended Pittsburgh's winning streak the following day and handled the Corsairs with relative ease. Brooklyn claimed a 6–2 victory on Thursday, June 18, as Vance out-pitched Ray Kremer. Glenn Wright and Eddie Moore slapped two safeties apiece as Vance held Pittsburgh to seven hits. Pittsburgh returned to the winning track during a Friday affair at Forbes Field, as the Pirates defeated Brooklyn, 9–6, behind Lee Meadows' complete game performance. Pie Traynor went 3-for-4 while Wright, George Grantham and Earl Smith chipped in with two hits each. With the victory, Meadows became the first National League hurler to register ten wins.[21]

Brooklyn actually had Pittsburgh on the ropes early, after Dick Cox smacked a two-run home run off Meadows. The Pirates rallied from a 3–1 deficit when they finally solved starter Rube Ehrhardt in the seventh inning. After Clyde Barnhart opened the inning by making an out, Pie Traynor banged a triple to left field. Glenn Wright's single drove home Traynor, and George Grantham followed with a double that put runners on second and third. Wright and Grantham both scored when Smith drilled a single to left field. Pitcher Lee Meadows helped his own cause by beating out an infield hit. Eddie Moore followed with a single that drove Smith home. Tiny Osborne was called from Brooklyn's bullpen to relieve the beleaguered Ehrhardt, but Kiki Cuyler greeted the Robins' new pitcher by crushing a triple to left that drove home Meadows and Moore with the inning's final tallies.[22]

The Pirates did not need a late-game rally to secure victory during the final game of the Brooklyn series on Saturday, June 20. The Pirates ran roughshod over three Robins twirlers as they slugged their way to a 21–5 victory. Max Carey and Kiki Cuyler led a Pittsburgh attack that smacked 25 hits on the day. Carey hit for the cycle as he went 4-for-6, scored two runs and drove home four teammates. Cuyler went 4-for-5, scored five runs, drove home six and accounted for 12 total bases as he hit two homers, one triple and a single. Glenn Wright drove home five runs and smacked Pittsburgh's other home run of the day, drilling a two-run shot off Brooklyn's Nelson Greene in the fifth inning.

Brooklyn scored a single run against Babe Adams before Pittsburgh returned fire in the home half of the first inning. After Carey popped out, Eddie Moore singled and Cuyler lifted a Jesse Petty pitch over the left field wall for a two-run home run. Clyde Barnhart walked, Pie Traynor made the inning's second out, and Wright delivered a triple to left that scored Barnhart.

Stuffy McInnis followed with a single that scored Wright and sent Petty to the showers. Bill Hubbell came on in relief and gave up a quick single to Earl Smith and a walk to Babe Adams before retiring Carey for the inning's final out.[23]

The Robins scored another run in the second before Pittsburgh retaliated with five of its own. Moore singled and Cuyler was struck by a pitched ball before Barnhart popped up to Milt Stock. Traynor's single scored Moore and moved Cuyler over to third, prompting Brooklyn manager Wilbert Robinson to replace Hubbell with Nelson Greene. Wright's double drove both men home, and Wright trotted across home plate after McInnis slapped a single to center. After Smith forced McInnis at second base, Adams singled and Carey drove home Smith with a double. Wright's big blast against Greene in the fifth sailed over the fence in deep right field, while Cuyler was credited with a grand slam, inside-the-park home run in the sixth when a drive to the fence eluded right fielder Dick Loftus.[24]

Prior to his sparkling day at the plate, Max Carey was bestowed an honor recognizing his off-the-field lifestyle. Before the final game against Brooklyn began, Carey was summoned to home plate and presented with a gold watch and chain courtesy of his Missouri-Lutheran friends in the city of Pittsburgh. Members of the St. Andrews Church in the East End presented their gift in honor of the man who had attended Concordia Missouri Lutheran Seminary before baseball became his way of life.[25]

Pittsburgh's players were given an opportunity to enjoy a Sunday away from the game before beginning a four-game series in St. Louis on June 22. Bill McKechnie's troops relaxed and reflected on a home stand that saw Pittsburgh post an 11–4 record. While some Pittsburgh players recharged their batteries before another round of games, Kiki Cuyler enjoyed watching a game with his son at Forbes Field between the Homestead Grays and Homewood on Saturday evening.[26]

Before the Pirates left for St. Louis, Pittsburgh management announced that pitcher Lou Koupal had been released to Kansas City of the American Association, with a club option that allowed him to be recalled on 48 hours notice. McKechnie and Barney Dreyfuss believed Koupal showed great promise, but they decided to assign him to the Western Double-A team so that he would be able to get regular work.[27] Just days prior to Koupal's release, southpaw pitcher Don Songer was optioned to Oklahoma City for the same reason.[28]

Pirates hitters did heavy damage for the second straight game when they defeated St. Louis, 24–6, during a Monday matinee at Sportsman's Park. Max Carey went 4-for-4 and scored four runs. George Grantham also went 4-for-4, scoring four runs with a double, two home runs and six RBIs. The Pirates clubbed six home runs against Cardinals pitchers Flint Rhem and Johnny Stuart, as Hazen Cuyler, Clyde Barnhart, Pie Traynor and Earl Smith joined

Grantham on the list of long ball hitters. Pittsburgh took control of the game with eight runs in the first inning before Rhem gave way to Stuart. Cuyler's blast over the left field wall with Carey on board gave the Pirates a 2–0 lead. A single and two walks loaded the bases before Grantham cleared them, making it 6–0 when he blasted a drive into the right field stands.[29] Ray Kremer picked up the win in relief for Pittsburgh as he pitched stellar ball in support of Vic Aldridge, who left in the third inning. Kremer pitched seven innings and gave up three runs on seven hits.

Poor weather finally slowed down the Pirates, as their game against St. Louis on Tuesday, June 23, was postponed due to rain.[30] This necessitated a doubleheader being played on Wednesday. Mother Nature allowed Pittsburgh and St. Louis to return to the diamond on June 24 as Bill McKechnie's squad gained a split in the twin bill. After scoring a combined 45 runs during their past two games, the Pirates could only muster three against Jesse Haines in the first game as St. Louis prevailed, 11–3. Starter Emil Yde was shellacked by Cardinals hitters and gave up 10 runs on nine hits in five and a third innings of work. St. Louis second baseman Rogers Hornsby did particularly heavy damage as he connected for a solo home run against Yde in the first, and then followed that up with a three-run shot off the southpaw in the sixth inning.

The Pirates regained their bearings in the doubleheader's second game, as they defeated St. Louis in a tightly contested battle, 7–6. Max Carey, Glenn Wright and Clyde Barnhart recorded three hits apiece for the Pirates. Wright smacked his tenth long hit of the season and Carey also smashed a solo home run off Cardinals starter Bill Sherdel. Johnny Morrison picked up the victory for Pittsburgh before wilting in the ninth inning and giving way to Babe Adams. The Pirates entered the ninth inning leading St. Louis, 7–4, before Rogers Hornsby closed the gap by connecting for a homer against Morrison with Jack Smith on base. A single by Jim Bottomley prompted Manager McKechnie to summon Adams from the bullpen. Adams quickly recorded the inning's second out when he induced Max Flack to hit a pop up to Eddie Moore. George "Specs" Toporcer followed and appeared to hit a game-winning home run when he drove an Adams pitch deep to right field. Fortunately for the Pirates, Toporcer's drive landed foul by about a foot. Torporcer returned to the plate and then grounded out to Stuffy McInnis at first base, as Adams recorded his second save of the season.[31]

The Pirates claimed the fourth game of the series on Thursday, June 25, when McKechnie's men won another squeaker over St. Louis, 4–3. Clyde Barnhart was Pittsburgh's top hitter, as he went 3-for-4 and knocked in two runs. Lee Meadows raised his record to 11–3 by tossing a complete game. Pittsburgh's staff ace gave up two earned runs on seven hits and two walks. The crucial point in the game from Pittsburgh's perspective came in the seventh inning with St. Louis leading, 3–2. After an intentional walk to Earl Smith loaded the bases, McKechnie conferred with Meadows before he opted to let his pitcher bat in lieu of a pinch hitter. Meadows responded by working out a walk that tied the ballgame. After Max Carey fouled out to catcher Bob O'Farrell, St. Louis pitcher Leo Dickerman walked Eddie Moore, and Glenn Wright crossed home plate with the winning run.[32]

After completing their game, McKechnie and his players jumped into taxicabs and sped off for a train station outside of the St. Louis city limits. Once the Pirates arrived there, a "Big Four Express" awaited to transport them to Cleveland. A transfer on Friday morning to the "Erie Lines Express" would cover the remainder of the trip as the Pirates anticipated arriving in the Smoky City around noon.[33] If everything went as planned and there were no delays due to poor weather or train derailments, the Pirates would have a few hours to physically and mentally prepare for that afternoon's game against Cincinnati.

The Pirates made it three victories in a row when they defeated the Reds, 5–3, on June 26 behind pitcher Ray Kremer's complete game. Kremer raised his record to 6–4 as he allowed three earned runs while scattering 12 hits. Eddie Moore, Clyde Barnhart, Pie Traynor and Stuffy McInnis paced the Pirates with two hits apiece on the day. McInnis emerged as the game's star as he made plays around first base that reminded fans of the veteran's glory days playing for Connie Mack's Philadelphia Athletics. In the sixth, Cincinnati's Edd Roush took a healthy cut at one of Kremer's offerings and smashed it on a line toward first base. The ball seemed destined to land in the outfield for extra bases as it screamed down the first base line. McInnis nimbly lunged for the drive, corralled Roush's sizzling smash and ran to the bag ahead of Cincinnati's team captain. Besides excelling in the field, McInnis also smacked a single and an RBI double.[34]

A Saturday doubleheader closed out the short home stand before the Pirates and Reds both hopped a train to resume their battle in Cincinnati. The afternoon twin bill on June 27 marked the first time that Barney Dreyfuss's refurbishment project at Forbes Field would be put to good use by Pittsburgh's baseball fans. The palace's new stands enjoyed a successful initiation as more than 37,500 patrons packed into Forbes Field to watch the Pirates and Reds gain a doubleheader split.[35] Pittsburgh claimed victory in the first game by a score of 3–2 as Babe Adams out-dueled Cincinnati's Dolf Luque. The Reds prevailed in the nightcap, 6–2, as Pete Donohue claimed victory over Vic Aldridge, who needed assistance from Johnny Morrison and Tom Sheehan out of the Pirates' bullpen. Kiki Cuyler starred in the first game for Pittsburgh by going 3-for-3 with a double, a run batted in and a run scored. George Grantham was the Pirates' batting star in the second contest as he went 2-for-4 and scored a run.

While the Pirates were back in Pittsburgh for a few days, a rumor made the rounds that owner Barney Dreyfuss planned on selling the interest in his club to a local syndicate. It was reported that Fred Clarke, Senator John P. Harris and oil man J.C. Trees planned on purchasing the Pittsburgh Pirates from Dreyfuss. This tale was quickly met with much skepticism, as most baseball writers reasoned that the three men tied to this sale could not possibly raise the monetary capital necessary to purchase Dreyfuss's club. All who were connected to this rumor denied that it contained any validity. Dreyfuss did not seem ready to retire from a game that he so deeply and passionately loved. It also was apparent to anyone who closely followed the day-to-day operations of Pittsburgh's club that Barney's son, Samuel, was being groomed to take control of the club whenever the elder Dreyfuss decided it was time to retire.[36]

Dreyfuss had every reason to be enjoying the game as the 1925 season progressed. Standings in the National League after games on Saturday, June 27, showed New York in first-place with a 39–25 record while the Pirates were just one-half game behind at 37–24. Heavy hitting was the main reason behind Pittsburgh's resurgence. The Pirates had ten batters who were hitting above the .300 mark. Clyde Barnhart was leading the team with a .396 average, while Kiki Cuyler (.360), George Grantham (.359), Max Carey (.357), Earl Smith (.343), Pie Traynor (.339), Eddie Moore (.329), Glenn Wright (.329), Stuffy McInnis (.320) and Johnny Rawlings (.316) rounded out Pittsburgh's brigade of heavy swatters.

The Pirates secured another victory on Sunday, June 28, when they defeated Cincinnati, 5–2. Emil Yde tossed a complete game as he allowed two earned runs on nine hits, four walks and three strikeouts. Max Carey went 3-for-5 while Pie Traynor, Stuffy McInnis and Johnny Gooch added capable support by banging out two hits each. Carey's seventh inning home run over the left field fence against Rube Benton was one of the longest blasts ever seen at Redland Field.[37]

The Pirates earned a series sweep over the Reds when they defeated Cincinnati on Monday, June 29, by a score of 8–1. Johnny Morrison raised his record to 8–5 as he tossed a complete game, allowed one run on eight hits, walked three and struck out four.

Glenn Wright led the way at the plate for Pittsburgh as he went 4-for-5, smacked a double and drove home a run. Max Carey, Kiki Cuyler and Clyde Barnhart recorded two hits apiece and accounted for four RBIs. Pittsburgh basically sealed the game in the first inning, as Barnhart's triple drove home both Moore and Cuyler.[38] This victory had added significance as a day off for New York allowed the Corsairs to move into first place. The Pirates led second-place New York by four percentage points as Bill McKechnie's brigade held down the National League's top spot for the first time in 1925.

The Pirates remained on top of the National League in spite of losing a tough game to Chicago on Tuesday, June 30, by a score of 1–0. Lee Meadows and the Cubs' Tony Kaufmann locked up majestically, as both pitchers hurled scoreless ball until Chicago broke through in the eighth inning with the game's only run. Charlie Grimm singled to center and moved to second after Rabbit Maranville laid down a perfect sacrifice bunt. Second baseman Sparky Adams then drilled a double past Barnhart that drove Grimm home with the winning tally.[39]

Pittsburgh rebounded nicely the next day as Ray Kremer held on despite allowing 13 hits and defeated the Cubs, 8–6. Max Carey and Kiki Cuyler each recorded three hits for Pittsburgh. Carey also scored two runs, smacked two doubles and drove home a run, while Cuyler scored a run and knocked in two teammates. Glenn Wright's two-run home run against Pete Alexander was the big blow during a six-run seventh inning that propelled Pittsburgh to victory.

Despite Pittsburgh's convincing victory, New York was able to reclaim first place by virtue of a doubleheader sweep of the Philadelphia Phillies. Following their afternoon conquest against Chicago, the Pirates' squad boarded a flyer for Pittsburgh. The Pirates were expected to reach the Smoky City on Thursday morning to begin their last home series that afternoon before the second Eastern swing of the season.[40] Three Pittsburgh players were nursing a variety of bruises as the Corsairs returned home for four games against Cincinnati. Glenn Wright and Earl Smith had both been spiked on the fingers on successive days by Chicago outfielder Arthur "Butch" Weis. George Grantham's glove hand was swollen as a result of catching throws hurled from the powerful arms of Wright and Pie Traynor. Thankfully, none of the injuries were deemed serious enough to keep any of the Pittsburgh players from being in the lineup against Cincinnati.[41]

The city of Pittsburgh was heartened by the team's recent climb in the National League standings, but fans remained cautious given that such success was always followed by disappointment in past years. On more than one occasion in the 1920s, the Pirates faded in September and allowed the Giants to claim the pennant. Even though Bill McKechnie had done well in running the Pirates' craft, there were many in Pittsburgh who believed another failure meant that the Wilkinsburg native's managerial tenure could end. Some of these fans believed that Fred Clarke was brought back by Dreyfuss so that he could be a calming and steadying influence on Pittsburgh's players.[42] The team's fighting spirit seemed to intensify once Clarke returned to the scene.

The Pirates proved rude hosts as Pittsburgh defeated Cincinnati, 2–1, in the series' first game on Thursday, July 2. Tom Sheehan picked up his first victory in a Pirates uniform after replacing Vic Aldridge in the fifth inning and shutting down his former teammates by pitching three-hit, shutout ball over the final five frames. Dolf Luque suffered the defeat when he allowed two runs in the sixth inning. The crucial victory put the Pirates back in first place as Max Carey walked, Kiki Cuyler tripled and Clyde Barnhart lofted a sacrifice

6. Battling New York for the Top Spot

Pittsburgh manager Bill McKechnie (right) is pictured with Fred Clarke. On June 13, 1925, Barney Dreyfuss announced that Clarke would return to the Pirates' organization as a vice-president and assistant manager to McKechnie on the bench. Many fans in Pittsburgh believed Clarke was brought back so that he could be a steadying influence for the Pirates' young players (National Baseball Hall of Fame Library, Cooperstown, New York).

fly that accounted for Pittsburgh's only two runs on the day.[43] Cincinnati returned the favor on Friday afternoon as Pete Donohue tossed a four-hit shutout and the Reds defeated the Pirates, 8–0. Babe Adams was knocked from the mound in the second inning after Cincinnati scored four runs. Johnny Morrison and Bernard Culloton pulled relief duty, as the Reds rapped 13 hits, with Hughie Critz, Ike Caveney, Bubbles Hargrave and Donohue getting two safeties apiece.

Gorgeous weather prevailed on Saturday, July 4, as 48,000 fans pushed through the turnstiles at Forbes Field to witness a holiday morning-afternoon doubleheader between Pittsburgh and Cincinnati. The morning paid attendance was slightly under 22,000 while the afternoon matinee was witnessed by approximately 26,000 patrons.[44] Smoky City rooters were sent home happy from Forbes Field after watching evening fireworks displays, as the Pirates swept Cincinnati and pushed their lead over second-place New York to two games. Emil Yde raised his record to 7–5 as he bested the Reds, 7–5, in the morning game, while Lee Meadows won his 12th game of the season during the afternoon event that saw Pittsburgh win, 7–1. Max Carey and Eddie Moore each went 2-for-3 in the first game and combined to steal four bases. Moore, Clyde Barnhart and Stuffy McInnis rapped out two hits apiece in the nightcap, and accounted for three runs scored, along with three doubles, a triple and three RBIs.

Carey's base running was one of the highlights of the opening contest, as the National League's top base stealer pilfered three sacks. In the first inning, Carey walked and stole second while pitcher Harry Biemiller held onto the ball. He moved to third base on an out and then swiped home plate when Biemiller's throw to catcher Bubbles Hargrave arrived just as Carey was crossing the dish.[45] The Pirates then secured victory in the eighth inning when they added two crucial runs that proved the difference in the game. Moore and Cuyler opened the frame with back-to-back singles. Barnhart then laid down a sacrifice bunt in the direction of third baseman Babe Pinelli, whose throw to first baseman Rube Bressler was wide of the target. Babe's errant toss allowed Moore to score and left Cuyler perched on third base. Kiki scampered across home plate moments later with the second run after a Cincinnati double play.[46]

There was no suspense whatsoever in the afternoon contest as the Corsairs blitzed Cincinnati starter Eppa Rixey. Pittsburgh did all the necessary damage in the third inning, jumping out to a quick 4–0 lead. Rixey retired Carey and Moore before giving up a walk to Cuyler. Singles by Barnhart and Traynor brought the Flint Flash around the bases with Pittsburgh's first run. Glenn Wright followed by placing a drive in the left-center field gap that bounced to the Forbes Field scoreboard. Wright's two teammates preceded him across the plate as Pittsburgh's shortstop completed the circuit, credited with an inside-the-park home run. McInnis' seventh-inning triple was another crucial blast, as it came with two men on base and helped pad Pittsburgh's lead.[47]

Before the Pirates embarked on their second Eastern swing of the season, Bill McKechnie's squad had a single Sunday game, to be followed by an exhibition game at Forbes Field against the Washington Senators on Monday, July 6. Pittsburgh took care of business in Chicago, defeating the Cubs, 3–2. Pie

Traynor and Ray Kremer emerged as heroes of the day, with the victory allowing the Pirates to remain two games in front of second-place New York. Traynor was a perfect 4-for-4 at the plate, including two doubles, and made spectacular plays at third base throughout the game. Kremer did not allow Chicago a hit until the eighth inning when Art Jahn singled. Kremer lost the shutout one batter later when Gabby Hartnett blasted an RBI double. Outfielder Cliff Heathcote's solo home run in the ninth inning brought home Chicago's other tally for the day.[48]

The Pirates returned home to Forbes Field for one day to oppose Washington in an exhibition game. Rookie pitcher Bernard "Bud" Culloton was chosen by McKechnie to oppose a Senators lineup that consisted of players who helped defeat the New York Giants in last year's World Series. Culloton showed great form as Pittsburgh defeated Washington, 5–4. Clyde Barnhart slammed a home run over the left field fence, putting the Pirates ahead. In the top of the ninth, Washington put the tying run on base before Culloton buckled down and retired the side.[49] After the game, the Pirates boarded a train once again and began a trip to New York for a four-game engagement against the Giants. Pirates fans who wanted to follow their team on the road congregated on Penn Avenue in downtown Pittsburgh at the Moose Temple Auditorium. The 3:30 P.M. game scheduled for July 7 and the 1:30 double header the following day would be reproduced on the auditorium's huge electric scoreboard. A direct wire would report all the exploits at the Polo Grounds, with real time updates given to the large crowds expected to gather at the Moose Temple.[50]

Fans who viewed the auditorium's electric scoreboard on Tuesday, July 7, became excited in the first inning, when Eddie Moore and Kiki Cuyler connected for back-to-back solo home runs against New York starter Kent Greenfield. This represented only a moment of cheerful news on Penn Avenue, as New York took a 5–3 lead and chased Vic Aldridge from the mound in the fifth inning. Reliever Tom Sheehan was hammered for two more markers before he unexpectedly dropped to the ground in pain while pitching the eighth inning.[51] It was evident that Sheehan had experienced an injury as Bill McKechnie and Pie Traynor escorted him from the diamond to Pittsburgh's clubhouse.[52] A preliminary examination by a physician showed that Sheehan had pulled a muscle in his side.[53]

While Babe Adams slowly strolled to the mound from Pittsburgh's bullpen, several of his teammates could be seen lying on the field taking a much needed rest. The Pirates seemed to be showing signs of exhaustion after spending three consecutive nights traveling in Pullman berths throughout the United States. This, coupled with the fact that McKechnie's squad had played games on successive afternoons in three different cities, seemed to reduce his players' stamina for the first New York game. Most of Pittsburgh's players stayed in their hotel rooms rather than check out New York's nightlife their first evening in the city, providing further evidence that McKechnie's players were fatigued.[54]

Pittsburgh's players were afforded an opportunity to gain an extra day of rest when their July 8 doubleheader against New York was postponed because of rain. A light sprinkle one hour before game time was followed by steady showers that prompted Giants management to reschedule the twin bill for Thursday, July 9. The extra day away from the field was also expected to rejuvenate a group of New York players who were suffering from various bumps and bruises. While the Pirates enjoyed a day of rest and relaxation, a closer examination by a physician revealed that pitcher Tom Sheehan would be sidelined for a week or more due to a muscle being torn loose from his ribcage.[55]

The extra day of rest worked wonders for Bill McKechnie's brigade as Pittsburgh crushed New York by a score of 12–3 in the doubleheader's first game. Emil Yde went the route for the Pirates, as he gave up two earned runs on eight hits and one walk. Pittsburgh's batters feasted on four different New York pitchers, rapping out 16 hits in the game. Clyde Barnhart led the way by going 4-for-5. He also scored three runs, smacked a double and drove home two runs. Glenn Wright went 3-for-5, scored a run and drove home three Pirate teammates. Eddie Moore, Pie Traynor, George Grantham and Johnny Gooch aided Pittsburgh's cause by drilling two hits apiece. Traynor and Gooch also accounted for half of Pittsburgh's RBIs in the game.

The Giants gained a doubleheader split in the nightcap, as they rallied from a 4–3 deficit and defeated the Pirates, 7–5. Pitcher Johnny Morrison appeared to be headed for a victory until New York's George Kelly ruined Pittsburgh's party by crushing a three-run home run in the seventh inning. Morrison deserved a better fate on the hill; two errors by Max Carey and a miscue by Eddie Moore led to New York scoring three unearned runs. Still, Pittsburgh's right-handed pitcher was in line to gain his ninth victory despite giving up 15 hits in the game. Carey and Moore also garnered two hits each. Moore connected for a meaningless solo homer in the ninth inning that brought home Pittsburgh's fifth and final marker.

Round three between the National League titans seemed to be going the Giants' way as they won two of the first three games against first-place Pittsburgh. Standings at the close of play on Thursday, July 9, showed that Pittsburgh stood atop the National League with a record of 45–28. New York held down the second-place spot, one game behind with a 46–31 mark. Powerful hitting on the part of Pittsburgh's players had helped launch the team into first place while the pitching staff was still finding their way.

Batting averages, in general, had risen anywhere from 40 to 60 points higher than the team averages of major league clubs over a decade ago.[56] A livelier ball was believed to be the reason that hitting had improved dramatically in both the National and American leagues during the Roaring Twenties. The ball being used in 1925 seemed to be even more energetic than its predecessors. Players who did not usually hit for high average were joining the elite hitters in the game. Yet some magnates believed the lively ball was hurting baseball because it was eliminating strategy from the game. A faction of owners wanted to force manufacturers to change the ball's construction so that most of the liveliness would be eliminated for the remainder of that season.[57]

One baseball writer authored a tongue-in-cheek article in which he compared the new ball to the unpredictable flapper women who became prominent during that era. During the 1920s, flapper women were known for rebelling against the establishment's belief of how females should behave. The flapper girls usually dressed provocatively, smoked and drank, and drove in fast cars. In making the comparison between these women and the livelier baseball, the writer stated that the ball used in 1925 had the true flapper characteristic of hardness, sprightliness and ingratitude.[58] As part of the article, Pirates pitcher Babe Adams was asked to give his opinion about the current ball resembling a flapper woman. Adams remained on point and discussed the lively ball only from the viewpoint of a baseball player.

> I first began to notice it about three years ago but since then it has grown absolutely wild until it is almost a golf ball.
> The manufacturers may say there is no change, but I know that it has been changed even though they may not realize it.
> It's ruining the game. You never see a sacrifice any more. The pitcher cannot show his stuff. It is easier for the batter to hit, harder for the pitcher to pitch and more difficult for the fielders to handle.[59]

This lively, "flapper" baseball certainly had a hand in affecting the performance of Pirates pitchers and fielders. Bill McKechnie's staff now seemed to be making the necessary adjustments required to cope with the golf-ball like tendencies of the ball. The lively ball was also partly responsible for the strong showing of Pittsburgh's hitters during the season. McKechnie's hitters were free swinging, heavy hitters who thrived as a result of the ball being used in 1925. Pittsburgh's slugging had served the team well. It would need to continue if the Pirates planned on remaining in first place.

7

The Pennant Race Tightens

On July 10, a torrential downpour in Pittsburgh caused gridlock on the city streets; over one and a quarter inches of rain fell in a 55-minute span between 6:25 and 7:20 A.M. Gravel was washed away from railroad tracks, live wires were blown to the ground by high winds, and trees fell on wires, starting various fires. Numerous Pittsburgh fire stations were summoned to put out blazes throughout the city. Garbage and trash floated onto downtown streets, causing traffic to stop dead. Street cars were jumping their rails as the cascading water overwhelmed Pittsburgh's streets. Flooding occurred in low lying streets when storm sewers were unable to handle the heavy stream of water. Automobiles that navigated such streets became stranded in the high water, their engines unwillingly stalled.[1]

The Pirates did not experience weather like that in New York City, but it rained sufficiently in the Big Apple so that Friday's game between the Pirates and Giants was called off. An idle afternoon gave the Pirates' players a chance to assess the bizarre news that was announced only a few days earlier. On July 7, Chicago Cubs president William Veeck announced that Rabbit Maranville was assuming the managerial reins in place of deposed skipper Bill Killefer.[2] This seemed like an odd choice to those who wondered how an unmanageable player could be expected to instill discipline as the team's manager. With Maranville prominently in the news again, Smoky City fans reflected upon the monumental deal that had sent Rabbit from Pittsburgh to Chicago.

The early negative returns regarding Bill McKechnie's trade with Chicago had now turned to praise and admiration for the manager. After labeling the deal a disaster for many months, Pittsburgh's rooters shifted gears and claimed that McKechnie pulled off a remarkable deal by stealing Vic Aldridge and George Grantham from Chicago. Aldridge was pitching better than Wilbur Cooper, and one veteran Pirates fan claimed Grantham alone was worth all of the players McKechnie sent to Chicago. The trade not only improved McKechnie's aggregation on the field, but it also ushered in a new era of harmony where team rules and regulations were actually followed.[3]

In a bit of an ironic twist, Chicago happened to be in New York at the same time as the Pirates, who had their game cancelled against Brooklyn on July 10. Chicago's newest manager showed his undisciplined side when he was involved in a fracas with a New York cab driver during the Cubs' day off. Three Chicago players were arrested when they caused a disturbance at Forty-Second and Broadway. Maranville, Clark Pittenger and Herbert Brett became involved in a fight with taxi driver George Warner after a dispute over the players' cab bill. Warner supposedly called the three players "cheapskates" for not tipping him. One of the Cubs' players punched Warner in the jaw, and other taxi chauffeurs quickly came to the aid of their fellow driver. To make matters worse, the incident happened during rush hour and tied up traffic for several minutes. The charges were eventually dropped when Warner declined to prosecute and the involved traffic cop freely admitted he did not know how the trouble had started.[4]

Pitcher Lee Meadows was the Pittsburgh Pirates' staff ace throughout the 1925 season. On June 19, Meadows defeated Boston, 9–6, and became the first National League hurler to record his 10th victory. On July 11 in a game against Brooklyn, Meadows blew a five-run lead by giving up six runs in the eighth inning. Meadows still recorded his 13th win of the season when his teammates rallied for two runs in the ninth (National Baseball Hall of Fame Library, Cooperstown, New York).

Pittsburgh returned to action on Saturday, July 11, and defeated Brooklyn, 7–6. Pie Traynor, Johnny Gooch and Lee Meadows rapped out two hits apiece for the Buccaneers. Meadows cruised along pitching shutout ball until the eighth inning, when Brooklyn scored six runs and took the lead. Zack Wheat's bases loaded triple made it 5–4 before Brooklyn grabbed a one-run lead on Jack Fournier's two-run home run. Pittsburgh then rallied in the ninth inning and claimed victory when Clyde Barnhart and Pie Traynor smacked back-to-back triples. Ever aggressive, Traynor tried to stretch his hit into a four-bagger and scored the decisive tally when catcher Zack Taylor muffed Hod Ford's relay throw to home plate.[5]

Taylor went from goat to hero in one day when his ninth-inning bounce home run against pitcher Ray Kremer gave Brooklyn a 4–3 victory over Pittsburgh on Sunday, July 12. Kremer dropped to 8–5 on the season, as the long ball stained an otherwise solid start. Wheat smacked a two-run homer in the fifth inning that turned a one-run Pirates lead into a deficit. Kiki Cuyler starred at the plate by going 4-for-5. The Flint Flash also scored two runs, smacked a triple and blasted his tenth home run of the season against Brooklyn starter Tiny Osborne.

Pittsburgh returned to the winners circle the following day when Vic Aldridge tossed a complete game and scattered seven hits en route to a 4–2 Pirate victory. Aldridge's only glaring mistake on the mound against Brooklyn occurred when Fournier took him downtown in the sixth inning and increased the Robins' lead to 2–0. Pie Traynor and Clyde Barnhart led a Pirates attack that banged out nine hits against Bill Hubbell. Traynor went 3-for-4, scored a run, hit a triple and drove home a run while Barnhart went 2-for-4, scored two runs and knocked in a teammate. Pittsburgh claimed victory in the ninth inning, overcoming a 2–1 deficit. Kiki Cuyler reached second base when infielder Milt Stock threw wildly to first after fielding a ground ball. Barnhart followed with a sharp single that brought Cuyler home with the tying run. Traynor moved Barnhart to third with a single, and Glenn Wright drove him home with a long sacrifice fly. George Grantham's single pushed Traynor to third; Pie eventually scored Pittsburgh's fourth run on Johnny Gooch's sacrifice fly to left field.[6]

An interesting twist was added to Pittsburgh's final series game against Brooklyn on Tuesday, July 14. Southpaw Emil Yde took the hill against staff ace Dazzy Vance, who was riding a six-game winning streak. During the first three games of this series, Vance's mouth had worked overtime as he ridiculed Pittsburgh's players. Dazzy also cautioned the Pirates to make sure they were careful when his turn in the rotation came. Most of Vance's taunting fell on deaf ears as the Pirates ignored his rants.

One remark that did not go unnoticed occurred when Fred Clarke appeared in the Pirates' dugout during one of the games and Vance directed a statement toward the entire Pittsburgh bench.[7] "That's the stuff, Fred," Vance yelled, "get ready — these bums'll need you by the time September rolls around. They'll flop again."[8]

The Pittsburgh players' verbal response was best summed up by Pie Traynor, who assessed Vance's deriding comment as a "dirty crack."[9] McKechnie's brigade otherwise kept quiet when Vance took the mound for a Tuesday matinee at Ebbets Field. Vance lasted only four innings and left the game with Pittsburgh holding a five-run lead. Emil Yde tossed a complete game as the Pirates defeated Brooklyn, 8–5. Yde allowed one earned run on 11 hits, while walking five and striking out four. Max Carey led the way for Pittsburgh by going 4-for-5 at the plate. The Pirates' captain also scored three runs, smacked a triple and stole two bases. Eddie Moore, Clyde Barnhart and Yde banged out two hits apiece, scored three runs and accounted for five RBIs.

Pittsburgh's Eastern swing continued on to Boston as the Pirates played the Braves in the first contest of a five-game series on July 15. As Pittsburgh's players prepared to do battle with the last-place Braves, Pirates catcher Earl Smith prepared to go to court on July 16. Smith planned on telling his side of the story to a judge, assuming that the man whom Earl had punched in Boston in May actually showed up at the proceeding to press assault charges.[10] As a result, Smith was not in McKechnie's starting lineup for the first game as Boston prevailed against Pittsburgh, 4–3.

Starter Johnny Morrison gave up four runs on ten hits in six innings of work. Pittsburgh collected only six hits against Boston starter Larry Benton, as Pie Traynor and Johnny Gooch rapped out two safeties apiece. Early in the contest, the Pirates seemed disinterested, as if they had little regard for their lowly opponent. The Pirates seemed to be playing down to the level of their competition, even though McKechnie had cautioned his men against such a habit.[11]

Boston's hold over the Pirates continued the next day when the Braves defeated McKechnie's squad, 9–8, in an extra-inning affair. Lee Meadows pitched poorly, as Boston blitzed him for five runs in five-plus innings of work. Ray Kremer did not fare much better as he gave up four runs on seven hits in four and a third innings and was charged with the loss. On offense, Eddie Moore was Pittsburgh's supreme hitter as he went 4-for-5, scored two runs, and drove home two teammates. Kiki Cuyler was credited with his 11th home run of the season when he smacked a drive off pitcher Rosy Ryan to the flagpole in right-center field. Cuyler scampered around the bases with an inside-the-park homer, scoring Moore ahead of him. But Boston won the ballgame in the tenth inning when Abie Hood's single drove home Joe Genewich with the deciding run.[12]

Pittsburgh's second consecutive defeat at Boston's hands dropped the Pirates to second place, one game behind New York. On Friday, July 17, Pittsburgh finally won a game against its New England hosts, claiming a ten-inning, 7–3 victory. Vic Aldridge pitched effectively, lasting eight innings and giving up two runs on seven hits. Babe Adams raised his record to 5–3 for the season by tossing two innings of hitless relief. Kiki Cuyler continued his hot hitting by going 3-for-5. Pie Traynor and Glenn Wright smacked two hits apiece, with Pittsburgh's third baseman also scoring two runs and driving home four teammates.

The Pirates wound up the third leg of their Eastern swing with a doubleheader in Boston on Saturday, July 18. Pittsburgh won the first game by a score of 9–8; Boston gained a victory in the nightcap, winning a tightly contested 2–1 game in 11 innings. In the first game, Emil Yde was credited with the victory even though Boston assaulted him for eight runs on 17 hits in a little over eight innings of work. In the second game, Johnny Morrison lost despite giving up only two runs and nine hits in ten innings of mound work. Max Carey, Kiki Cuyler and Emil Yde each banged out three hits in the first game, accounting for five runs scored and five RBIs. In the second contest, Cuyler went 2-for-5 with two triples and Carson Bigbee went 2-for-4 at the plate. Bigbee replaced the slumping Clyde Barnhart in Pittsburgh's lineup after the Corsairs outfielder complained of severe pains in a leg muscle he strained on Friday during practice.[13]

A five-run second inning, aided by Boston mistakes, acted as a springboard to Pittsburgh's victory in the first game. Glenn Wright led off the inning with a single to center. Stuffy McInnis hit a comebacker to pitcher Johnny Cooney, whose throw to second base was dropped by Dave Bancroft. Johnny Gooch followed with a double to right field, scoring Wright and moving McInnis to third base. Emil Yde drove both base runners home when he drilled a double down the left field line. Yde was caught in a rundown between second and third on Max Carey's infield grounder, but Pittsburgh's pitcher made it to third when Doc Gautreau's toss hit him in the back. Carey stole second, and when catcher Oscar Siemer's throw bounced into center field, Yde scored, with Carey moving to third. Pittsburgh scored its fifth run of the inning when Carey and Moore maneuvered a perfect squeeze play.[14]

Precise bunting allowed Boston to score the winning run in the tenth inning of the second game. Jimmy Welsh beat out a slow, rolling bunt along the first base line to start the final frame. Dick Burrus then laid down a beautiful bunt to the right of pitcher Johnny Morrison, who threw late to first base. Gus Felix followed with a sharp single to left field that drove Welsh home with the winning tally.[15]

On the morning of the doubleheader, Pittsburgh catcher Earl Smith had his day in court postponed for the fourth time since charges were filed against him in May. Smith's hearing was delayed on three different occasions during the team's current stay in Boston because the man making the charges was allegedly ill. On Saturday morning, a magistrate at the Brighton Police Court decided that the hearing would occur on August 26. Many fans now believed that Smith's case would eventually be thrown out since the constant court delays had given the entire affair a comical tone.[16]

Before moving on to Philadelphia for the home stretch of their Eastern swing, the Pirates traveled to Baltimore for a Sunday afternoon exhibition game against Jack Dunn's Orioles. Rookie pitcher Bud Culloton took the hill against Baltimore and gave the regular pitchers a day off. Culloton pitched a solid game, as Pittsburgh prevailed, 9–8.[17]

Before Pittsburgh began its series in Philadelphia, manager McKechnie once again impressed upon his players the importance of playing hard against every National League opponent. McKechnie's meeting prior to the Boston series had not seemed to resonate with his players as Boston won three out of five games.[18]

McKechnie's talk had little effect, as the Pirates fell to sixth-place Philadelphia, 6–3, on Monday, July 20. The Phillies' Jimmy Ring out-pitched Lee Meadows, who dropped to 13–5 for the season. Eddie Moore, George Grantham and Clyde Barnhart smacked two hits each and Barnhart drove home two Pittsburgh runs. A balk and a wild pitch by Meadows lent a hand to the Phillies putting two of their six runs on the board.[19] In the eighth inning, Philadelphia third baseman Clarence Huber greeted relief pitcher Babe Adams by hitting a solo home run that added the final tally for the day.

As Pittsburgh's players made preparations to oppose Philadelphia once again on Tuesday, July 21, comments attributed to Washington Senators manager Bucky Harris in *The Pittsburgh Press* raised a few eyebrows within the Pirates' organization. Harris' team currently was locked in a tight battle for American League supremacy with Connie Mack's Philadelphia Athletics. Despite the fact that both teams were currently in a virtual tie for the league's top spot, Harris expressed supreme confidence that his team would prevail and claim their second consecutive American League pennant. Some American League followers believed Harris was being overconfident, since they expected Philadelphia to hold down the league's summit position at season's end.[20]

One comment in particular that Harris made aroused the emotions of Pittsburgh's players. It centered around his prediction regarding the 1925 World Series. "I'd like to see the Pirates in the next World's Series," Harris was quoted as saying. "We'd beat them sure! But the Giants will give them a hard fight."[21]

Former National League president Harry C. Pulliam once said: "Take nothing for granted in baseball."[22] Many Pirates players believed that Harris should follow this advice and keep his mouth shut. Bill McKechnie and Barney Dreyfuss had no intention of looking past their championship race in the National League and thinking about the 1925 World Series. McKechnie wanted his players to focus on the task at hand and ignore Harris' comments.

When the Pirates took the field against Philadelphia, they certainly did not look like a team that was concentrating on the task before them. The Phillies gained their second consecutive victory against the Corsairs, as pitcher Clarence Mitchell limited Pittsburgh's batters to four hits. George Harper started the Phillies rolling in the second inning when he smashed a solo home run against Ray Kremer. Philadelphia prevailed by a score of 4–2, making Eddie Moore's fifth homer of the season in the seventh rather inconsequential.

The Pirates seemed to be regrouping the following day as they blitzed their way to a 7–3 lead after four-and-a-half innings of play. But rain started to fall while the Phillies took their turn at bat in the bottom of the fifth. Umpires Charlie Moran and Bob Hart stopped the game and declared the game unofficial since Philadelphia had not completed its turn at the plate in the inning.[23] The Pirates quickly changed into street clothes in the Baker Bowl's visitors clubhouse and hustled to the train station while rain continued to fall throughout the City of Brotherly Love. The Pirates had spent 18 days on the road and complied a mediocre 6–8 record during their second Eastern swing of the season. The Pirates did well against Brooklyn and New York, but flopped miserably against two National League bottom feeders. The Pirates returned home in second place, one-half game behind league-leading New York.

The Pirates put a stop to their three-game losing streak when they defeated St. Louis by a score of 3–2 on Thursday, July 23. Emil Yde pushed his record to 11–5 after becoming locked in a monumental struggle against St. Louis pitcher Jesse Haines. Yde pitched a complete game, allowing two earned runs on eight hits and three walks. Pittsburgh's Danish southpaw seemed to be headed for a loss until the Pirates rallied in the ninth inning to steal a victory. With the score in favor of St. Louis 2–1, Kiki Cuyler started the ninth-inning rally by tripling to the temporary fence in front of Forbes Field's right field stands. Manager Rogers Hornsby instructed his infielders to play in to prevent Pie Traynor from executing a squeeze play. This strategy backfired when Traynor swung away and hit a blooper behind first base that eluded Cardinals fielders for a double and allowed Cuyler to score. Glenn Wright sent fans home happy when he scorched a single to center that pushed Traynor home with the game's winning run.[24]

Four runs in the first three innings by Pittsburgh on July 24 proved enough for pitcher Johnny Morrison, as the Corsairs made it two victories in a row, downing St. Louis, 5–3. Max Carey was Pittsburgh's top hitter as he went 3-for-4, scored two runs and stole a base. Pie Traynor also swatted two hits and recorded three putouts and an assist at third in support of Morrison, whose tantalizing curve ball resulted in numerous Cardinals players hitting groundballs throughout the game. Morrison tossed a complete game and raised his record to 9–8 as he allowed two runs on ten hits. "Jughandle Johnny" had still failed to compile a creditable winning percentage in 1925, but his repertoire of pitches seemed as strong as ever. As was the case with many pitchers who relied on a devastating curve ball, Morrison was highly effective when his curve was breaking properly.[25]

St. Louis' Duster Mails shut down Pittsburgh's vaunted attack during the series' third game on Saturday, July 25. Mails held the Pirates to three hits as St. Louis cruised to an easy 7–2 victory. Rogers Hornsby started the Cardinals nicely in the first inning, when he blasted a two-run home run against Pittsburgh starter Babe Adams. The Pirates scored two runs in the fourth to tie the game as Kiki Cuyler stole second and third before pilfering home as part of a double steal involving Pie Traynor. Adams weakened in the seventh, when St. Louis added four runs to their total on a walk, a single and three doubles. After Roy Spencer pinch hit for Adams during the bottom of the seventh, Tommy Sheehan saw his first action since being injured weeks earlier and allowed one run on four hits during the final two stanzas.[26]

The National League standings on Saturday evening showed that Pittsburgh was clinging to first place over New York by five percentage points. Pittsburgh's hitters were still cutting a swath of devastation against opponents' pitching staffs as nine Pirates continued to bat over .300. Clyde Barnhart was leading the way with a .359 average, while Hazen Cuyler (.347) and Max Carey (.336) ranked close behind. Pittsburgh's pitching staff was also rounding into shape, as Lee Meadows, with his 13–5 record supported by a 4.16 ERA, remained one of the league's best. Fellow hurlers Emil Yde (11–5, 4.09 ERA) and Johnny Morrison (9–8, 3.85 ERA) had finally hit their stride.

Despite a .335 batting average, George Grantham had been missing from Bill McKechnie's lineup since the Pirates played St. Louis in their first game after returning home. Grantham contracted a cold in Philadelphia and McKechnie thought it best to give his starting first baseman a few days off.[27]

The Pirates made a trip to the Windy City for a Sunday game on July 26. The Buccaneers defeated Rabbit Maranville's squad, 6–4. Vic Aldridge hurled a complete game for Pittsburgh as he allowed four runs on seven hits, three walks and five strikeouts. Max Carey and Pie Traynor both went 4-for-5 and accounted for half of Pittsburgh's runs. Light hitting Sparky Adams gave Chicago a short-lived lead in the first inning when he smacked a solo home run. Pittsburgh took the lead for good in the fourth when Glenn Wright blasted his thirteenth homer of the year, a two-run shot off pitcher Tony Kaufmann.

Bill McKechnie's troops jumped on a train back to Pittsburgh after spending a day in Chicago and returned home to begin a four-game series against Boston. Some of Pittsburgh's players still felt badly regarding the team's performance when the two teams had clashed in Beantown. The Pirates' players knew they would have to play harder against last-place Boston this time around. McKechnie felt confident that his players had learned a lesson and would respond with a more intense effort. What Pittsburgh's manager did not foresee was how this fighting spirit was about to spill over among his own players.

The Braves chased starting pitcher Ray Kremer and took a 4–0 lead into the seventh inning. Pittsburgh responded with three runs in the seventh and a solo marker in the eighth inning to tie the score at 4–4. Despite another strong day by Kiki Cuyler, the game went into extra innings after neither team was able to score in the ninth inning.

Cuyler had added another triple to his league leading total earlier in the game. The Flint Flash was having a phenomenal sophomore season as he continued to duplicate his 1924 performance. Cuyler was the first National League player to score 100 runs and was also among the league leaders in outfield assists. Always businesslike, Cuyler was not temperamental, but he did possess a fighting spirit that bubbled over in the tenth inning of the game against Boston.[28]

Boston grabbed the lead in the tenth frame when a Johnny Morrison alley ball was launched into Forbes Field's right field stands by Dave Harris. As the Pirate players made their way to the dugout after Morrison retired the side, Cuyler rushed over to catcher Johnny Gooch and began criticizing his teammate for signaling that type of pitch in such a crucial situation. Gooch did not take kindly to his roommate's suggestion that he had committed a mental gaffe. Within a few seconds after reaching the dugout, Gooch and Cuyler angrily exchanged punches. Bill McKechnie, Fred Clarke and a few Pirate players separated the two combatants before any serious physical damage could be inflicted.[29]

The Pittsburgh players regrouped and struck down the Braves for a 6–5 victory, as they scored two runs in the bottom of the tenth inning. Eddie Moore walked and moved over to third base on Cuyler's double. Clyde Barnhart successfully sacrificed Moore home, tying the game. Boston pitcher Jesse Barnes then proceeded to load the bases by walking Pie Traynor and Glenn Wright. Cuyler then tore home with the winning run on Stuffy McInnis' sacrifice.[30] After Cuyler crossed home plate and headed for the dugout, McKechnie brought him and Gooch together. The two men shook hands and expressed their regrets, ending the incident.[31]

Lee Meadows twirled the Pirates to their second consec-

Catcher Johnny Gooch did not appreciate being criticized by roommate Hazen "Kiki" Cuyler after Boston's Dave Harris smacked a 10th-inning home run at Forbes Field on July 27, 1925. Cuyler questioned Gooch's pitch selection, and a short fight ensued. Pittsburgh eventually won the game when Cuyler scored the winning run in the bottom of the 10th (National Baseball Hall of Fame Library, Cooperstown, New York).

utive victory over Boston on Tuesday, July 28, when Pittsburgh grabbed a 5–1 victory. Meadows tossed a complete game, giving up one run on seven hits and two walks. Pie Traynor starred at the plate by going 3-for-4 while Max Carey slapped two hits, smacked a double, scored two runs and stole a base. Boston starting pitcher Larry Benton gave the Pirates headaches until the fifth inning when they scored three runs. Carey opened the inning with a single and was sacrificed to second by Eddie Moore before stealing third base. Kiki Cuyler drew a walk and moved to second when Clyde Barnhart tapped to catcher Oscar Siemer. Traynor's single scored Carey, and Pie moved to second base on an ill-advised throw to home plate. Glenn Wright's single drove Cuyler and Traynor home with the inning's last runs.[32]

Boston fought back gallantly after Pittsburgh took an eight-run lead in the series' third game on Wednesday but still fell to the Corsairs, 8–6. Emil Yde improved his record to 12–5 as he gutted out eight tough innings, giving up six runs on 15 hits. Johnny Morrison earned his third save of the season when he pitched an inning of shutout relief. Stuffy McInnis led the way offensively against his former team by going 3-for-3 at the plate, with two runs scored and a run batted in. Kiki Cuyler and Johnny Gooch supported the cause with two hits apiece. One of the game's highlights occurred when Max Carey connected for a solo home run against Johnny Cooney in the fifth inning.

A four-game sweep over the Braves was circumvented when Boston defeated Pittsburgh, 5–1, during the series finale on Thursday, July 30. Vic Aldridge was victimized by a Boston attack, surrendering five runs on nine hits in just over six innings of work. First baseman Dick Burrus connected for a huge two-run homer against Aldridge in the fifth inning, giving Boston a three run lead. Tom Sheehan relieved Aldridge with a man on third in the seventh inning and did fine work in pitching two and two-thirds innings of shutout ball. Sheehan continued to do an admirable job pitching out of the bullpen since being acquired from Cincinnati for Al Niehaus in May. Some Pittsburgh fans believed Sheehan should be rewarded by receiving a start from manager Bill McKechnie.[33]

Philadelphia and Pittsburgh were afforded an opportunity to relax on Friday, July 31, as rain postponed the game that afternoon at Forbes Field.[34] Both teams were back on the field for a Saturday afternoon doubleheader, as 19,000 fans poured into Pittsburgh's palace and watched Philadelphia pull off a sweep that dropped Bill McKechnie's team back into second place.[35] Philadelphia won the first game by a score of 3–2 and then claimed victory in the late afternoon contest, 4–2. Cheers that rang from the Forbes Field patrons after the first contest began to turn to jeers during the day's second battle. Horrible defensive play by the Corsairs indicated that Pirates players were not as attentive to their work as they should have been.[36]

Pittsburgh received solid hitting from Johnny Gooch, Glenn Wright and

Stuffy McInnis during the first game. Gooch led the way by going 3-for-4 as he smacked a double and drove home one run. Wright and McInnis combined for four hits, two runs, one double and a triple. Philadelphia's Art Decatur locked horns and bested Ray Kremer by tossing a complete game and scattering nine hits. Kremer was not as proficient for the Pirates. After seeing his pitcher give up three sizzling hits that allowed Philadelphia to tie the game in the fourth inning, Bill McKechnie decided to relieve Kremer with Johnny Morrison. Pittsburgh's relief pitcher only allowed four hits over the next five innings, but one of them was a solo home run over Forbes Field's left field wall. The eighth-inning blast by catcher Butch Henline proved to be the game winning tally.[37]

Lee Meadows pitched a strong game during the afternoon twin bill's second act, but suffered defeat when shoddy fielding by his teammates allowed Philadelphia to score two unearned runs. Phillies starter Jimmy Ring proved masterful on the hill as he allowed five hits. Eddie Moore was the only Pirate who had multiple hits, as he went 2-for-2 at the plate. In the seventh inning with the score tied, 2–2, Philadelphia failed to push across a run even though Moore, Glenn Wright and Earl Smith committed errors during the frame.[38]

Bad fielding finally caught up with the Pirates in the eighth as Philadelphia scored two runs to take the lead. After retiring the first Phillies batter, Meadows walked Jimmie Wilson. Clarence Huber followed with a single that sent Wilson to third base. After Meadows retired Lew Fonseca for the second out, Bernie Friberg walked. With the bases loaded and two men out, Meadows induced Ring to hit a soft fly ball to Max Carey. While the inning seemed over in the minds of thousands of Pirates fans, Carey dropped Ring's easy fly ball and allowed Philadelphia to claim victory.[39]

Sunday Blue Laws prevented Pittsburgh and Philadelphia from playing on August 2. Rather than give his team a day of rest, Bill McKechnie took the players to Akron, Ohio, for an exhibition game against a semi-pro team. The decision on the part of McKechnie and Barney Dreyfuss nearly had devastating repercussions when Pie Traynor was spiked by a player who gashed his leg sliding into third base. When the injury initially happened, there was grave concern that Traynor could miss extended time away from the game.[40]

Besides possibly having to replace Traynor, McKechnie was also considering other changes in an effort to awaken his troops from their funk that featured three straight losses to second-division teams. McKechnie contemplated placing George Grantham in left field for the slumping Clyde Barnhart. Pittsburgh's starting left fielder was playing hurt; numerous maladies seemed to be contributing to Barnhart's horrendous batting slump. On Saturday, Carson Bigbee had replaced Barnhart in the second game of the doubleheader against Philadelphia. Bigbee's play did little to instill much confidence in manager McKechnie wanting to use him again.[41]

When the Pirates took the field for their first game of another doubleheader against Philadelphia on Monday, August 3, Grantham was at first, Traynor at third base and Barnhart in his customary position in left field. The Pirates won the first game when they defeated the Phillies, 3–2. Emil Yde picked up the victory for Pittsburgh as he went six and a third innings and gave up two runs on eight hits. Babe Adams earned his third save of the season by pitching two and two-thirds innings of shutout baseball. Vic Aldridge went the route in a nightcap that lasted 11 innings and was won by Pittsburgh by the same score of 3–2. Grantham starred at the plate in the first game by going 2-for-3 with two runs scored and two runs driven home. Earl Smith topped McKechnie's hitters during the second contest when he went 3-for-4.

George Grantham's hitting directly contributed to Pittsburgh winning the afternoon's first contest. His third-inning home run against Hal Carlson scored Pie Traynor ahead of him and gave Pittsburgh a 2–0 lead. Grantham scored what became the game's deciding run in the fifth when he singled and eventually crossed home plate when Emil Yde made an out. Vic Aldridge and Philadelphia's Johnny Couch locked up in a hearty pitchers' duel in the second game, in which the Pirates' hurler held Philadelphia to nine scattered hits while he struck out seven batters. In the bottom of the seventh inning, Earl Smith tied the game for Pittsburgh when he drilled a two-out, solo homer against Couch. Pittsburgh won the game in the eleventh, when Aldridge's two-out single drove home Traynor with the deciding marker.[42]

The mood of Pittsburgh's rooters turned from ecstatic to sour once again as Philadelphia scorched Pirates pitching during the series finale on Tuesday, August 4. Philadelphia exploded for 14 hits against three Pirates pitchers and cruised to an easy 8–4 victory. Heinie Sand, Freddie Leach, Russ Wrightstone, Lew Fonseca, Butch Henline and Bernie Friberg collected two hits apiece for Philadelphia. Pittsburgh starter Johnny Morrison did not retire a Phillies batter and was charged with four runs on five hits. Tom Sheehan did an admirable job in long relief as he gave up four runs in eight stanzas of work before being relieved by rookie Bud Culloton. By the time Pittsburgh reached Philadelphia's Clarence Mitchell in the late innings, it was too late. Stuffy McInnis and Clyde Barnhart each recorded two hits and drove home a run apiece for Pittsburgh.

Throughout Barney Dreyfuss's tenure as owner of the Pirates, Pittsburgh's fans had always exhibited a fickle side; they cheered local players when things went well and jeered when times got tough. Even legendary players like Honus Wagner and Fred Clarke had been booed and heckled on occasion when their performances did not measure up to past standards. During the recent five-game series against Philadelphia, many Forbes Field fans had been vocal in voicing their displeasure of the Pirates' play in general and manager Bill McKechnie's work specifically. The fans booed throughout the Philadelphia series despite the fact that Pittsburgh was still holding a slim lead over second-place New York in the National League pennant race.

One fan who described himself as Pittsburgh's most enthusiastic rooter wrote a letter to the editor of a local newspaper telling his tale regarding the contempt he felt for disloyal patrons. This particular fan gave McKechnie the largest share of credit for developing the current Pirates' aggregation. Pittsburgh's most enthusiastic fan, who missed few games at Forbes Field, became angered as he sat in the stands and listened to scurrilous comments around him. Many fans expressed derision toward McKechnie. In his letter to *The Pittsburgh Press*, this fan commented that he could not understand how such jeers were being directed at a manager whose team was in first place.[43]

> There are occupants of certain seats at Forbes Field who never miss an opportunity to criticize the management of the club. No matter what goes wrong, McKechnie is blamed for it. When some bit of good baseball is pulled off, he is not given credit for it, but when the slightest mistake is made, or even when a well-planned play fails to produce the desired results, the knockers raise their voices and lament the folly of McKechnie remaining in his position.
>
> I believe we should be fair to all men, and I think fairness to McKechnie demands that he be loyally supported as he and his men strive to bring us the first pennant since 1909. We fans can help along by boosting all the time.[44]

Loyal Pittsburgh baseball rooters at Forbes Field did not receive a chance to silence their contentious counterparts on Wednesday, August 5, as the first contest of a four-game series against Brooklyn was postponed by rain. The game remained part of the current series when it was determined the postponement would be made up as part of a doubleheader on Saturday. A day of rest was welcomed by many Pirate players who were nursing nagging injuries. Bill McKechnie also believed his squad would benefit from some free time since continuous competition the past few weeks had proved stressful during a tight pennant race. Yet, his players did not receive a full day off, as McKechnie put his charges through a crisp workout as the falling raindrops ceased for a brief period of time.[45]

The Pirates returned to the field on Thursday, August 6, and defeated Dazzy Vance for the second game in a row since Brooklyn's star pitcher had taunted the Pittsburgh squad. Ray Kremer was sensational on the mound as he raised his record to 9–7 and defeated Brooklyn, 5–1. Kremer tossed a complete game, allowed one run on nine hits and struck out three batters. Max Carey was Pittsburgh's offensive star as he went 2-for-4 and stole a base. Neither team pushed a run across home plate until Pittsburgh turned the trick twice in the fifth inning. Eddie Moore led off the frame with a double and came around to score when Earl Smith laced a single to right field. Kremer sacrificed Smith over to second and Pittsburgh's catcher ran ferociously when he scored all the way from second base on Vance's wild pitch. Kremer's only blemish occurred in the sixth when a hit batsman, a double and a sacrifice fly produced Brooklyn's only run.[46]

Pittsburgh showed its spirit once again on Friday, August 7, as McKechnie's men made it two wins in a row, defeating Brooklyn, 10–9. Max Carey, Pie Traynor and Kiki Cuyler each went 3-for-4 at the plate and accounted for six runs, hitting three doubles and driving home three Pirate teammates. George Grantham and Glenn Wright also added two hits apiece as Pittsburgh totaled 18 safeties on the day. Johnny Morrison picked up the victory in relief when he tossed a shutout inning in the ninth. Brooklyn pitcher Rube Ehrhardt seemed to have the game in hand as the Pirates came to bat in the bottom of the ninth, trailing by two runs. Pittsburgh rallied to win the game by scoring three runs, as rookie Roy Spencer's single drove home Traynor with the deciding tally.[47]

An ugly incident in the game's seventh inning proved that emotions could boil over as a by-product of fierce competition. A fist fight broke out between Brooklyn pitcher Burleigh Grimes and Pittsburgh's Max Carey. The scuffle occurred when Carey, trapped in a rundown between second and third, did his best to avoid being tagged by Brooklyn's infielders. During the rundown, Grimes stepped in Carey's path and dared Pittsburgh's fleet footed player to take him on. Carey ran straight at Grimes and was greeted by a punch from Brooklyn's pitcher. Carey quickly defended himself, wailing away at Grimes with several punches of his own. Members from both teams ran onto the field and separated the two combatants. Grimes, not known as a passive player when such incidents arose, was ordered from the field immediately. After umpires Cy Pfirman, Peter McLaughlin and Bob Hart conferred for a few minutes, they awarded third base to Carey and promptly told Pittsburgh's outfielder that he, too, had been ejected.[48]

When the umpires' report reached John Heydler's eyes following the game, he fined and suspended Grimes. Carey received no punishment as the National League president concluded that Pittsburgh's captain had not instigated the fight and was only defending himself after being attacked by Grimes.[49]

Fans who attended the doubleheader between the two teams on Saturday, August 8, wondered if more fisticuffs would ensue. The only fireworks that occurred at Forbes Field involved Bill McKechnie's offense. The Pirates convincingly swept the Robins by scores of 12–8 and 5–4. Relief pitchers claimed victories for Pittsburgh in both games, as Johnny Morrison pushed his record to 12–10 with a win in the first game and Babe Adams upped his season's mark to 6–4 by pitching three innings of shutout ball during the nightcap.

Pittsburgh's batters drilled Brooklyn's pitching for 13 hits in each game. Kiki Cuyler and Glenn Wright were the pacesetters during the first game as they each went 3-for-4 and combined to score four runs, while driving home four more runs. George Grantham and Eddie Moore banged out two hits apiece and played a role in four of Pittsburgh's 12 runs. In the meantime, Emil Yde was shaky on the mound for Pittsburgh. He was relieved by Tom Sheehan in the fifth inning, after the southpaw pitcher allowed six runs and eight hits. Sheehan and Morrison gave up only one more run during the final four innings as Pittsburgh rallied to win the game with five runs in the eighth inning.

The Pirates showed resilience once again in the second game of the doubleheader; Pittsburgh came back from a four-run deficit to claim victory. Brooklyn held a 4–0 lead until Pittsburgh scored three runs in the sixth inning and two more in the seventh. George Grantham and Kiki Cuyler starred for Pittsburgh as each player rapped out three hits. Cuyler also scored one run, smacked a double, drove home a teammate and stole a base. Pie Traynor and Eddie Moore gave capable support to the Corsairs' cause by banging two hits apiece. Earl Smith's crucial two-run double helped cap Pittsburgh's second magnificent comeback of the day. Adams entered the fray for Pittsburgh after Vic Aldridge stumbled in allowing Brooklyn to score four runs on nine hits in six innings of work.

Pittsburgh's four-game sweep of Brooklyn, coupled with New York losing six straight games against St. Louis and Cincinnati, allowed the Pirates to build their largest margin of the season over their nearest rival. National League standings at the end of Saturday, August 8, showed Pittsburgh in first place with a 62–39 record, while second-place New York trailed by five games at 58–45. The Pirates had constructed their largest cushion of the season over the Giants despite struggling at times on the home stand against National League cellar dwellers like Boston and Philadelphia. The Pirates' heavy slugging continued to be the main story as Hazen Cuyler (.350), Clyde Barnhart (.342) and Max Carey (.336) led a group of ten Corsairs players who were still hitting over .300.

Sunday supplied an off day for the Pirates, as Bill McKechnie and Barney Dreyfuss decided not to schedule any exhibition games and give the team some rest. With one more Eastern team still scheduled to make the trip to Forbes Field during this home stand, McKechnie and Dreyfuss wanted to be sure Pittsburgh's players were focused and ready to play. New York was coming to town for a four-game series, with the outcome possibly reshaping the National League's landscape. Round four between the Pirates and Giants was scheduled to begin on Monday, August 10. John McGraw's men needed to win decisively if they hoped to keep pace with the league-leading Pirates.

8

Putting a Stranglehold on First

The Giants ended their six-game losing streak by rallying to defeat Cincinnati, 5–4, on Sunday, August 9. While John McGraw's troops finally cleansed the stench of defeat, Pittsburgh's players sat at home and rested fully. Anticipation in the Smoky City ran high as the train carrying the Corsairs' most hated rival pulled into Pittsburgh's Union Station. Bill McKechnie's Pirates appeared to be at full strength, while the Giants continued to be crippled by nagging injuries. New York's Travis Jackson, a star shortstop, was not sure if he would be able to play because of a bad knee.

The weather provided more thrills and excitement than the Pirates did during the series' first game on Monday, August 10. Patrons at Forbes Field were treated to an electrical show courtesy of a powerful thunderstorm that superseded any fireworks on the field, as New York defeated Pittsburgh, 2–1. The storm, which hit in the fourth inning with New York leading 1–0, suspended play for an hour-and-a-half. Much to the surprise of many in the large crowd, the contest resumed at about 6:00 P.M. Some claimed Barney Dreyfuss had forced the umpires to continue play long enough so that rain checks would be worthless. This belief turned out to be inaccurate since the game's umpires alone had the final say in whether a game was suspended or postponed after a delay lasting more than 30 minutes. Umpires Ernie Quigley, Hank O'Day and Charlie Moran agreed that such an important game needed to continue. After the rain subsided, they ordered Pittsburgh and New York to resume playing in the sloppy, muddy conditions.[1]

New York pitcher Jack Scott was brilliant as he scattered eight hits. Scott also was saved from a dire fate when outfielder Billy Southworth made a sensational first-inning catch.[2] Pittsburgh's Lee Meadows, who pitched well enough to win, dropped to 14–7 on the season after his teammates could push only one run across the plate against Scott. New York struck first in the top frame when Ross Youngs singled, stole second and scored on Irish Meusel's single to left. The Giants recorded the deciding tally during the game's extended fourth inning. Youngs reached second base after third baseman Pie Traynor fielded Ross' ground ball and threw wildly over the head of first baseman George Grantham. The torrential rains then came and suspended play into the evening. When play resumed almost two hours later, Youngs moved to third on Bill Terry's infield out and then scored when Meadows uncorked a wild pitch that eluded catcher Earl Smith. The Pirates scored their only run of the game in the sixth inning when Kiki Cuyler and Clyde Barnhart smoked back-to-back doubles.[3]

With their lead over second-place New York now reduced to three and a half games, Bill McKechnie and Barney Dreyfuss acted swiftly in making a move intended to add depth to their pitching staff. While the Giants were winning Monday's mud bowl, Pittsburgh management announced the signing of southpaw pitcher John "Red" Oldham from Des Moines of the Western League. McKechnie and Dreyfuss both realized the need for another left-hander on the staff to complement Emil Yde. Oldham was a major league veteran who had spent four years pitching for Detroit before he was suspended for failing to report to Ty Cobb's Tigers in 1924.[4] McKechnie hoped the 31-year-old pitcher would add needed stability to his pitching staff. The time certainly seemed ripe to bring the veteran back to the big leagues since Oldham had won six consecutive games for Des Moines.[5]

Twenty-two thousand Pittsburgh rooters pushed through Forbes Field's turnstiles to watch the second game of the pivotal series on Tuesday, August 11.[6] The Pirate faithful felt disappointed as New York carried a 4–2 lead into the eighth inning. Pittsburgh had been unable to dent New York starter Wayland Dean other than the second inning, when Glenn Wright crushed his 14th homer of the year into Forbes Field's right field stands. Ray Kremer started for the Pirates and was touched up for four runs before being lifted for a pinch hitter in the seventh inning. Johnny Morrison came in from the bullpen and gained his 13th victory of the season when Pittsburgh rallied for five runs in the eighth inning to claim a 7–4 victory. For Morrison, who pitched two innings of shutout ball, it was his third victory in relief in the past week.[7]

Pittsburgh's game winning rally in the eighth inning began when Max Carey opened with a double to center field. Carey moved up to third base after George Grantham was retired on a fly ball. Wayland Dean walked Kiki Cuyler, who then followed Carey across home plate after Clyde Barnhart blasted a double to left, tying the game. The Pirates received a break when second baseman George Kelly fumbled Pie Traynor's routine grounder. Traynor was safe at first and Barnhart moved to third. Barnhart scored when Wright made what should have been the third out of the inning. Eddie Moore then lashed a two-out double that brought Traynor around with Pittsburgh's sixth run. Johnny Gooch followed with a walk and Morrison helped his own cause with a single that scored Moore with the inning's last marker.[8]

Johnny Morrison was a solid starter and Bill McKechnie's top reliever during the 1925 season. From August 7 through August 11, Morrison won three games for the Pirates coming out of the bullpen. Morrison led all National League pitchers by appearing in 44 games during the 1925 season. Eighteen of those appearances came as a reliever as Morrison topped all hurlers with four saves (National Baseball Hall of Fame Library, Cooperstown, New York).

Poor weather conditions came into play for the National League's top two teams, who played a Wednesday matinee on Forbes Field's rain-soaked diamond.[9] The Pirates jumped out to an early five-run lead and held off the Giants as they claimed a 5–3 victory. Kiki Cuyler, Pie Traynor and Glenn Wright smacked two hits apiece for the victorious Corsairs. Emil Yde tossed a complete game and raised his record to 14–5 as he allowed three runs on 12 hits. Travis Jackson returned to the lineup for New York and swatted a solo home run off Yde in the sixth inning. Giants starter Virgil Barnes lasted four innings before being relieved by rookie hurler Freddie Fitzsimmons. The young twirler, who was making his first major league appearance, held Pittsburgh scoreless throughout the remainder of the game.[10]

A bases-loaded, three-run double by Glenn Wright started Pittsburgh off quickly against Barnes in the first inning, giving the Pirates an early 3–0 lead. The Pirates added to their lead in the third as two hits, two walks and a sacrifice fly brought home two more runs. The Giants did their scoring when Ross Youngs doubled home two teammates in the fifth inning and Jackson dropped a ball over the left field wall one inning later.[11] The Giants blew a golden opportunity to add more runs in the fourth, when bad base running ruined a big inning. Irish Meusel and George Kelly occupied first and second after each player singled against Yde. Bill Terry followed with another single that appeared to load the bases. Meusel was held at third, but Kelly kept running, only to find his teammate occupying third base. A mix-up followed, as Pittsburgh pulled off a double play when Kelly ran Meusel off the third base bag.[12]

During all of the confusion, Kelly and Pie Traynor became embroiled in a fight on the field.[13] As Kelly ran to third base during the ill-fated play, New York's second baseman deliberately knocked the ball out of Traynor's hand. Traynor immediately jumped on Kelly, and both players wrestled while attempting to land punches against their counterpart. Umpire Hank O'Day stepped in and prevented any fists from connecting. Kelly was declared out as O'Day ruled that he intentionally interfered with Traynor.[14] Since neither player landed a punch or inflicted any damage, both men were permitted to remain in the game.[15]

The Giants were able to gain a split in the four-game series when they defeated Pittsburgh, 4–1, on Thursday, August 13. Kent Greenfield was masterful on the hill for New York as he allowed only one run on five hits. Vic Aldridge took the loss for Pittsburgh, giving up two earned runs during six innings of work. Babe Adams and Tom Sheehan combined to pitch three innings of shutout relief, but Pittsburgh was unable to wrest an early lead away from New York. Frankie Frisch belted out four hits for the Giants while Max Carey went 2-for-4 for Pittsburgh. Shortstop Travis Jackson was forced to leave the game when he re-injured his lame knee. Rain figured in the day's events once again as a brief shower delayed play for 20 minutes during the sixth inning.[16]

New York avoided a monumental disaster by gaining a four-game split with the Pirates. The Giants were still trailing the Corsairs by four and a half games, but they held out hope that they could make up ground when both teams met at the Polo Grounds in late August. Many overly enthusiastic fans in Pittsburgh reacted as if the pennant was now guaranteed. Fans began sending orders for World Series tickets to the Pirates' offices. President Barney Dreyfuss quickly took steps to stop the flow of mail that asked for reservations at Forbes Field for the Fall Classic in two months.[17] Dreyfuss cautioned Pittsburgh's excited baseball fans that it was premature to claim a pennant at this time.

"We have won no pennant, and we are not taking any orders for World's Series tickets," declared Dreyfuss. "When we win, if we do, we will accept all orders that are made, but until we are sure of the flag in our own league, we do not want the fans to request reservations, for they will not be made."[18]

Fans continued to believe that the National League pennant was virtually clinched after Cincinnati became Pittsburgh's latest victim during the first of a two-game set at Forbes Field. On Friday, August 14, the Pirates chased Reds starter Dolf Luque from the hill in the second inning and cruised to an easy 14–6 victory. Lee Meadows tossed a complete game for Pittsburgh and was credited with a victory even though he did not have his best stuff. Meadows gave up six runs on thirteen hits, walking three and striking out two. Stuffy McInnis led the way for Pittsburgh by going 3-for-5 with four runs scored and three runs batted in. Eddie Moore followed suit by rapping out three hits, as he smacked a double and a triple, and scored two runs. Max Carey, Kiki Cuyler and Clyde Barnhart drilled two hits apiece, scoring five Pittsburgh runs and driving home six.

Cincinnati gained revenge against Pittsburgh the following day as the Reds crushed four Buccaneer pitchers during an 8–1 victory. Pete Donohue continued his 1925 hex over Bill McKechnie's team as the star right-hander pitched a complete game and picked up his 18th victory of the season. Ray Kremer pitched horribly for Pittsburgh and did not make it out of the first inning as Cincinnati touched him for four runs. Kremer was forced from the mound by a brutal attack that included home runs by Edd Roush and Hughie Critz. Red Oldham made his first appearance since being obtained from Des Moines and pitched well except for the sixth inning, when he gave up three runs.[19] As if losing the game was not enough for McKechnie's men, the Corsairs did not walk away from the game unscathed as far as injuries. Johnny Gooch was spiked in the third inning and Max Carey injured his ankle while sliding into second base. Outfielder George "Mule" Haas replaced Carey in the outfield and saw his first major league action since being recalled from Birmingham a few days earlier.[20]

Both teams boarded a train and moved on to Cincinnati for a Sunday afternoon game on August 16. The Reds won their second consecutive contest as Eppa Rixey mesmerized the Corsairs and claimed his 16th victory of the season by a score of 6–1. Rixey scattered 11 hits as he kept the Pirates off balance throughout the day. Stuffy McInnis and Kiki Cuyler each went 3-for-4 and Johnny Rawlings banged out two hits. Rawlings saw action at second base after Bill McKechnie was forced to make lineup changes due to Max Carey's ankle injury. Eddie Moore was shifted to right field, with Cuyler assuming Carey's position in center. Johnny Morrison fell one game closer to the .500 mark as he gave up five runs during seven innings of work and saw his record drop to 13–11.

Pittsburgh returned home for an exhibition game against the Philadelphia Athletics on Monday, August 17, before the team embarked on its final swing through the east. The meaningless exhibition game between the Corsairs and Athletics gave Pittsburgh fans a chance to witness what possibly could be a prelude to the 1925 World Series. The Pirates currently stood on top of the National League standings, three and a half games ahead of second-place New York, while Philadelphia held a two-game lead over the defending American League champion Washington Senators. The 3:00 P.M. contest afforded Smoky City rooters an opportunity to do their own scouting in case Pittsburgh met Connie Mack's Athletics in an all–Pennsylvania World Series.[21]

Regular league action resumed on Tuesday, August 18, at Ebbets Field as Pittsburgh opposed Brooklyn. The Pirates started off their Eastern swing well by demolishing the Robins, 11–4. Vic Aldridge picked up the victory after he was called upon to relieve Pittsburgh starter Emil Yde. Aldridge pitched six and a third innings and allowed no runs on four hits. Pie Traynor went 3-for-4 and scored three runs. Kiki Cuyler and George Grantham collected two hits each, combined to score three runs and accounted for six RBIs. Grantham also drilled a three-run, bounce home run against Brooklyn pitcher Bill Hubbell during Pittsburgh's eight-run, third inning.

Despite the fact that Pittsburgh had slaughtered the Robins, all was not well for Bill McKechnie's club. Max Carey's absence from the lineup left a void in the outfield. Uncertainty was evident as Carson Bigbee, Kiki Cuyler and Clyde Barnhart looked shaky against Brooklyn. McKechnie also made a change to his infield unit when he played Johnny Rawlings at second base in place of Eddie Moore. Evidently, a lame leg was the reason for Moore's benching, even though McKechnie indicated that Moore would play the outfield in future games when the Pirates faced a left-handed pitcher.[22]

Those who looked beyond Moore's supposed injury realized McKechnie was benching his second baseman because he was making poor mental decisions and slumping defensively in recent games. The skeptics also believed Moore was being given an opportunity to sit in the dugout so that he could reflect upon the need to approach the game with a more serious attitude.[23] One Pittsburgh fan who wrote a letter to *The Pittsburgh Press* completely agreed with McKechnie's decision to bench Moore. William Burton of 4933 Friendship Avenue alleged that Moore's biggest weakness was his brain.[24]

> I notice the various comments on the ability of Eddie Moore and I wish to go on record that he is the weakest member of the Pittsburgh team. He is weak on any kind of a ground ball, because he lets the ball play him.
>
> When the ball goes to either side of him, he gives a good imitation of a deep-sea diver instead of a ball player. The weakest part of this player is from the neck up. His foolish, playful actions and his inability to think are disgusting the fans. Last year when he was breaking in, he did wonderful work subbing for Traynor, and he did his best in the outfield later. Since he is classed as a regular, he does not take his work seriously. I am looking forward to next year, when surely we will have someone else on second base. If Eddie could read some comments like this, it might make a better ball player of him.[25]

Pittsburgh's restructured lineup did not have as much success against Brooklyn on Wednesday, August 19, when the Robins prevailed in a slugfest by the score of 8–7. Clyde Barnhart was a perfect 4-for-4, smacking a triple and driving home five teammates. Johnny Rawlings and Johnny Gooch also chipped in with two hits apiece. But the Pirates were unable to secure a victory even though they scored seven runs and notched 11 hits off longtime nemesis Dazzy Vance. Brooklyn secured victory in the seventh inning when ex–Pirate Cotton Tierney drilled a triple that cleared the bases of three Robins teammates. Vance's mound work may have been shabby, but the pitching of Lee Meadows and Red Oldham was even more wretched as Pittsburgh's two hurlers allowed 13 hits.[26]

Prior to the start of Pittsburgh's final game of the series against Brooklyn on Thursday, August 20, Pirates management announced that infielder Lafayette Fresco Thompson had been recalled from Kansas City. The young second baseman was expected to report to Brooklyn and would be kept on the roster in the role of utility infielder for the remainder of the season.[27] Thompson watched a compelling game from his front row set on the bench as Pittsburgh won a tight contest, 2–1. Ray Kremer out-pitched Burleigh Grimes and pushed his record to 10–8 with a solid performance. Kremer allowed one run on six hits, gave up three walks and struck out two batters.

Kiki Cuyler was Pittsburgh's star of the day, both at the plate and in the outfield. In the sixth inning with the game tied, 1–1, Cuyler hit a bizarre home run that ended up being the decisive hit of the game. Cuyler smashed what appeared to be an ordinary single off Grimes, but the ball bounced over the head of center field Eddie Brown and rolled to an Ebbets Field exit gate. The speedy Cuyler easily navigated all four bases as he legged out his 12th home run of the season. One inning before hitting his inside-the-park homer, Cuyler victimized Brown when he robbed the Robin of an extra-base hit by making a spectacular, glove-hand catch with the bases loaded. Brooklyn's only tally of the game came when Zack Wheat smacked a home run in the first inning.[28]

Pittsburgh's victory over Brooklyn bumped its record to 67–44. The New York Giants held down the National League's second spot, three games behind the league-leading Pirates, with a 67–50 mark. The Pirates had six games in hand on their bitter rival, making it almost imperative that New York win at least four of the five upcoming games against the Pirates. It came as a surprise to nobody that rain was falling as Pittsburgh and New York prepared to square off for the first game of their crucial series on Friday, August 21. Hours of inclement weather forced the postponement of the game. Fans who came from Pittsburgh to watch their beloved Pirates knock New York out of contention impatiently waited out the poor weather. Before Friday's game was cancelled, New York management gave word that all reserved seats for the series had been sold out with capacity crowds being expected each afternoon.[29]

Giants manager John McGraw believed that the five-game series would act as a catalyst in allowing his players to capture another National League pennant. In newspapers throughout the Big Apple, McGraw was quoted as saying he hoped to thoroughly rout Bill McKechnie's troops. McGraw also chastised Pittsburgh's players by saying that they would follow their usual course of choking like they had in the past. McGraw believed his Giants would run roughshod over the Pirates.[30]

John McGraw severely underestimated the resolve of McKechnie's squad. A crowd of over 50,000 people jammed into the Polo Grounds on August 22 to watch the afternoon doubleheader that opened the pivotal series. New York's fans must have been sickened by the course of events that transpired, as the Pirates responded to McGraw's rhetoric by pulling off an afternoon sweep over the Giants. Pittsburgh obliterated New York in the first contest, 8–1, and then won a squeaker during the nightcap when the Giants succumbed by a score of 2–1. Lee Meadows pushed his record to 16–8 by pitching a gem in the first game, tossing a complete game and allowing only one run on six hits. Vic Aldridge showed Pittsburgh fans why McKechnie traded for him last fall when he, too, pitched a complete game and allowed only one run on nine hits in the second game.

Kiki Cuyler starred at the plate in the first game by going 3-for-5 with two runs scored and three runs batted in. Clyde Barnhart, Pie Traynor, Johnny Gooch and Johnny Rawlings added two hits apiece. Rawlings continued to ably man the keystone position as Bill McKechnie allowed Eddie Moore to remain on the bench for disciplinary reasons.

In the first inning, after Carson Bigbee and Rawlings were retired by Virgil Barnes, Cuyler lined a home run against the Polo Grounds' upper right field tier, giving Pittsburgh a 1-to-0 lead. The Pirates padded their lead in the fourth inning when they pushed across two more runs, which proved to be the deciding tallies of the contest. Barnhart opened the inning with a single to center and moved to third when Traynor's pop fly eluded Frankie Frisch for a single. Glenn Wright's single scored Barnhart and moved Traynor to third. Barnes then struck out George Grantham before Gooch's base hit over short scored Traynor.[31]

Runs were a precious commodity during the afternoon's second game, as Jack Scott and Vic Aldridge matched zeroes throughout the game. Ross Youngs and Grover Hartley slammed two hits apiece for New York, while Pie Traynor and Glenn Wright turned the trick for Pittsburgh. It looked as if Scott's solid pitching might be enough to gain a doubleheader split as New York took a 1–0 lead into the seventh inning. After holding the Pirates hitless in the fourth, fifth and sixth innings, Scott made a mistake in the seventh that ruined a potential New York celebration. Traynor led off the inning with a single and came around to score when Wright blasted his 15th home run of the season into the left-center field stands.[32]

New York averted disaster the following day as 55,000 fans crammed into the Polo Grounds hoping to see the Giants' fortunes improve. Thousands of patrons had to be turned away as the grandstand sold out an hour before game time. The crowd was so dense that police halted traffic blocks from the stadium.[33]

It was not a perfect day for the populace of New York, but the outcome could have been much worse. New York claimed the opening game by a score of 7–4, while Pittsburgh prevailed in the nightcap, bringing home a 3–2 victory. Babe Adams started the first contest for Pittsburgh and once again struggled in a ballpark with a short porch; he allowed five runs on six hits during two and two thirds innings of work. Johnny Morrison pushed his record to 14–11 by gaining a victory, with help from reliever Red Oldham, in the second game.

Kent Greenfield was masterful for New York in the first game, not allowing a Pirates runner to reach base until Kiki Cuyler scratched out a single in the seventh inning. In the eighth inning, with New York holding down a 7–0 lead, the Corsairs finally reached Greenfield by scoring four runs on six consecutive hits before Jack Scott extinguished the fire. In the afternoon's second game, New York dreamed of a sweep until Pittsburgh erased a one-run deficit and struck for two runs against starter Fred Fitzsimmons in the seventh. Singles by George Grantham and pinch hitter Stuffy McInnis tied the game before Johnny Rawlings followed with a double that brought pinch runner Carson Bigbee home with the eventual winning run. Oldham relieved Morrison and held the Giants in check, though McGraw's men threatened on several occasions but could not score.[34]

Stuffy McInnis continued to do a wonderful job of spelling George Grantham at first base since he signed with the Pirates in May. In addition to offering valuable experience to the young Pirates, he had chipped in with a .339 average. During Pittsburgh's last Eastern swing of the season, McInnis had confided to a friend that if the Buccaneers won the National League pennant, the country would be given a chance to watch one of the most wonderful clubs in the game. McInnis was not known as someone who gave his opinion very often. His comment, along with another remark McInnis made in which he stated that Pittsburgh's players had not realized their full potential, was more significant given Stuffy's usual dignified silence on such matters.[35]

The Pirates thrust a dagger into the hopes of New York Giants fans when they defeated John McGraw's men during the series' last game on Monday, August 24, by a score of 9–2. Ray Kremer tossed a complete game for the Pirates and raised his record to 11–8 by giving up two runs on seven hits. Eddie Moore, back in the Pirates' lineup for the second consecutive day as their right fielder, went 2-for-5 and scored two runs. Clyde Barnhart, Johnny Rawlings and Kremer himself rapped out two hits apiece and scored a total of five runs. Rawlings' two-run, inside-the-park home run against reliever Jack Wisner in the sixth inning gave Pittsburgh an insurmountable 9–1 lead. The game had been close until the fifth inning when Giants starter Wayland Dean tired and Frankie Frisch's miscue contributed to Pittsburgh scoring six runs. The crushing defeat left the Giants six games behind the Pirates in the National League standings, with many experts believing that the task of overtaking the Pirates had become hopeless for McGraw and his troops.[36]

Boston was Pittsburgh's next challenger on its Eastern swing, as Smoky City fans dreamed of a pennant flag flying at Forbes Field for the first time in 16 years. The state of euphoria was tempered a bit when the Braves defeated Pittsburgh on Tuesday, August 25, by a score of 2–1. Starter Emil Yde pitched well in defeat, giving up only two earned runs on seven hits in eight innings. Yde's performance was quite remarkable considering he had lost considerable weight on this road trip because of a stomach ailment.[37]

Les Mann of the Braves was almost single-handedly responsible for Boston's win over Yde. After Jimmy Welsh singled in the first inning, Mann tripled to the scoreboard and drove his teammate home. In the sixth inning, Doc Gautreau's single, Welsh's sacrifice and Mann's base hit gave Boston the deciding run. Pie Traynor scored Pittsburgh's only run in the second inning when he tripled and scored on Johnny Gooch's double. Fans from Traynor's hometown of Somerville had turned out in huge numbers at Braves Field to pay homage to their favorite son. President Barney Dreyfuss made the trip to Boston to participate in the pre-game ceremonies that honored Traynor.[38] Pittsburgh's star third baseman was presented with numerous gifts, including diamond studded cuff links and a scarf pin.[39]

Strong pitching was the story line for a second consecutive day, as Lee Meadows and Boston's Bob Smith locked up in a pitchers' duel that saw Pittsburgh prevail, 2–0. Meadows tossed a complete game and shut out the Braves on nine hits. He received the only support he needed when the Pirates scored a solo marker in the first stanza. Eddie Moore led off the game with a walk and moved up to second on Johnny Rawlings' infield hit. Kiki Cuyler reached first after Smith failed to force Moore at third on a bunt by the Flint Flash. Moore scored from third moments later on Clyde Barnhart's sacrifice fly. The Pirates added an insurance run in the ninth inning when Rawlings legged out an inside-the-park homer after his drive to right-center field eluded Jimmy Welsh and Gus Felix.[40]

The Braves continued to play as if they were battling the Pirates for the National League pennant rather than New York. During the series finale between the two teams on Thursday, August 27, Pittsburgh gained its second shutout in as many days when Vic Aldridge stifled Boston's offense and walked away with a 1–0 victory. Aldridge raised his record to 10–6, scattering four hits and striking out three Boston batters. Braves hurler Larry Benton matched Aldridge pitch for pitch in every inning but one. In the third inning, Pittsburgh loaded the bases when Eddie Moore walked, Johnny Rawlings reached first on a scratch single and Clyde Barnhart worked out another walk. With two men out, Benton walked his third batter of the inning, with Pie Traynor's free pass bringing Moore home with the game's winning run.[41]

Bill McKechnie's squad changed venues from spacious Braves Field in Boston to the bandbox of the Baker Bowl for a five-game series against the Philadelphia Phillies. During the first game of the series on Friday, August 28, Philadelphia's ballpark lived up to its reputation as a hitters' paradise. The Pirates and Phillies combined for 31 hits, with Pittsburgh holding on and defeating Philadelphia, 10–9. Kiki Cuyler led the way for Pittsburgh as he went 4-for-6 and scored three runs. Cuyler also swatted his 14th and 15th homers of the season when he legged out solo four-baggers in the first and eighth innings. Eddie Moore and Clyde Barnhart also chipped in with three hits apiece. A five-run rally by Philadelphia fell one tally short in the ninth inning, as the Phillies hammered Babe Adams and Tom Sheehan for seven hits. Ray Kremer was summoned from the bullpen and saved the game when he retired Philadelphia's final batter with the tying run on second base.[42]

The Pirates continued their hitting rampage during a Baker Bowl doubleheader on Saturday, August 29. Pittsburgh won the first game, 11–2, as Emil Yde upped his record to 15–6 on the season by pitching a complete game. The Pirates had an even easier time during the second game as they slugged 17 hits against three Philadelphia pitchers and won, 13–1. Ray Kremer was the beneficiary of Pittsburgh's heavy hitting as he tossed a complete game, allowed one run on five hits, and struck out six. Kiki Cuyler, Clyde Barnhart and Glenn Wright banged three hits apiece in the first game. Wright also drove home five runs and drilled a two-run homer against Art Decatur in the fourth inning. In the second contest, George Grantham was a perfect 4-for-4 and Pie Traynor chipped in with three hits, three runs and four runs batted in.

In the first game, Pittsburgh took control of the game in the fifth inning with assistance from Philadelphia's fielders, as six runs crossed home plate. Earl Smith flied out to start the inning before Emil Yde ripped a single to center. Eddie Moore popped up for the second out, but Johnny Rawlings beat out a grounder to shortstop Wally Kimmick. Kiki Cuyler followed with a single to left. Clyde Barnhart's single to right drove home Yde and Moore, and sent Cuyler to third. Pie Traynor followed with a single to center that was muffed by Freddy Leach. Cuyler scored, Barnhart moved to third and Traynor advanced to second. Glenn Wright followed by topping a weak roller to third baseman Clarence Huber. Barnhart and Traynor both scored when Huber made a desperate attempt to throw out Wright at first and heaved the ball against the grandstand. Credited with a hit, Wright moved up to second on Huber's error. George Grantham's single to center drove Wright home with the inning's final run before Smith made the last out by grounding to first baseman Lew Fonseca.[43]

The first frame turned out to be Pittsburgh's big inning in the second game; the Pirates scored six runs and drove starting pitcher Johnny Couch from the mound. Traynor was Pittsburgh's heavy hitter, smacking a third-inning solo home run into the left field stands against Skinny O'Neal and swatting a two-run blast against Ray Pierce in the sixth frame.[44]

Bill McKechnie's players received a chance to reflect on their recent success as both teams rested due to Sunday Blue Laws in Pennsylvania. While the Pirates loafed and waited to play the last two games of their series, catcher Johnny Gooch traveled back to Pittsburgh so that he could be with his wife, who had just given birth to a baby boy. When Johnny reached the Smoky City, he found Mrs. Gooch and baby doing just fine. Gooch became acquainted with the newest member of his family and quickly shuffled back to Philadelphia to be with his teammates.[45]

Pittsburgh continued its assault against Phillies pitching on Monday, August 31, as the Corsairs pounded 13 hits and defeated Philadelphia, 10–3. Lee Meadows secured his 18th victory of the season by tossing a complete game and allowing only three runs on eight hits. Eddie Moore and Glenn Wright spearheaded Pittsburgh's attack by smacking three hits each, while scoring four runs and driving home three teammates. Kiki Cuyler and Earl Smith added two hits each, with Pittsburgh's catcher also hitting a double, scoring two runs and driving home two teammates. Meadows only mistake occurred when George Harper smacked a solo home run in the ninth inning.

Bill McKechnie's Pirates won their seventh consecutive game on Tuesday, September 1, as they defeated Philadelphia, 10–3. The Pirates pulled off a five-game sweep over the Phillies by outscoring their cross state rival, 54–18, during the final series of the Eastern swing. Vic Aldridge tossed a complete game and gave up three runs on 11 hits, walked four and struck out nine. Pie Traynor led the way offensively by going 4-for-5 and scoring two runs. Earl Smith and Aldridge each smacked three hits and accounted for a total of six RBIs. Aldridge also hit the first home run of his major league career; it came against Hal Carlson in the fourth inning. Eddie Moore later joined his teammate in the home run club when he smacked a solo, bounce home run against Ray Pierce in the eighth inning. In the meantime, Aldridge's only pitching indiscretion occurred in the first inning, when Russ Wrightstone smacked a two-out, solo homer against Pittsburgh's right-hander.

Fans in Pittsburgh hailed the conquering heroes when the Pirates arrived home from their last Eastern swing of the season. A combined record of 13–3 against Brooklyn, New York, Boston and Philadelphia allowed Pittsburgh to pad its lead in the National League to eight games over second-place New York. Pittsburgh stood on top with a 78–46 record, while New York was clinging to the edge of contention with a mark of 73–57.

Barney Dreyfuss still remained unwilling to claim a pennant for his team, but the Pittsburgh owner was quietly confident that the Pirates would prevail. Dreyfuss initiated plans to begin construction on temporary seating at Forbes Field for the World Series. Pittsburgh's owner planned on constructing an additional 10,000 seats that would push Forbes Field's capacity close to 45,000 for the Fall Classic.[46]

The Pirates acted as rude hosts and ran their winning streak to eight games when they defeated Cincinnati at Forbes Field on Wednesday, September 2, by a score of 8–2. The Pirates prevented staff ace Pete Donohue from winning his 20th game, chasing the Reds' starter in the sixth inning. George Grantham led the way for Pittsburgh by going a perfect 4-for-4. Grantham smacked two doubles, a triple and drove home two runs. Eddie Moore recorded three hits and Glenn Wright added two, with the two players accounting for three runs scored and four RBIs. Johnny Morrison pushed his record to 15–11, tossing a complete game, while giving up two runs on 12 hits, walking two and striking out two batters.

St. Louis now rolled into Pittsburgh to begin a three-game series against Bill McKechnie's Corsairs. The Pirates made it nine victories in a row on Thursday, September 3, when they defeated St. Louis, 5–2. Ray Kremer won his fourth consecutive game and ran his record to 13–8 for the season as he tossed a complete game and allowed two runs on 12 hits. Glenn Wright starred at the plate for Pittsburgh as he went 3-for-4 and drove home two runs. Kiki Cuyler and Pie Traynor chipped in with two hits apiece and Bill Sherdel was the latest victim to feel the Pirates' wrath as Bill McKechnie's Pirates continued their dominance against southpaw pitchers.

The Cardinals became the first team to defeat Pittsburgh in over a week when they ended the Corsairs winning streak on Friday, September 4, with a 9–3 shellacking. Pittsburgh's hitters rapped out 11 hits against St. Louis starter

Art Reinhart, but were unable to produce hits in the clutch. Stuffy McInnis went 3-for-4 for Pittsburgh while Pie Traynor and Emil Yde contributed two hits apiece. Yde started for Pittsburgh and lasted into the ninth inning, when he loaded the bases and gave way to Babe Adams. The Cardinals pounded Adams for four hits, including a double, which brought home five St. Louis runs. Rogers Hornsby struck the game's big hit when he drilled his thirty-fifth homer into the right field stands in the eighth inning.[47] One bright spot for the Pirates was Max Carey, who saw his first action in three weeks and drew a walk as a pinch hitter.

Pittsburgh bounced back nicely against St. Louis on Saturday, September 5, and put another game in the win column, defeating the Cardinals, 6–5. Johnny Morrison picked up the victory for Pittsburgh in relief, tossing three shutout innings after Lee Meadows and Tom Sheehan faltered. Stuffy McInnis led the way for Pittsburgh as he went 3-for-3 and scored a run. Johnny Rawlings also smacked three hits with a run scored. Carson Bigbee went 2-for-4 and scored three runs after replacing Eddie Moore in right field during the first inning. Bigbee was pressed into service when Moore pulled a tendon in his leg while making a play in the outfield.[48]

The victory became even more costly from an injury standpoint as Pittsburgh lost the services of second baseman Johnny Rawlings, who broke his ankle sliding into second base during the sixth inning.[49] Specifically, Rawlings broke the fibula in his left ankle as he started to slide into the bag. Rawlings was taken to St. John's Hospital in McKeesport, where his ankle was x-rayed and placed in a plaster cast. Pittsburgh's team physician announced that Rawlings would be out for about a month. "Lucky Johnny," as Rawlings was called by players and scribes, was crying when his teammates gathered around him in the clubhouse after Pittsburgh's victory, distraught over his inability to play in the upcoming World Series, assuming that Pittsburgh made it to the Fall Classic. Rawlings' teammates were also noticeably depressed, since they realized his play at second base was a key reason why the team had surged in recent weeks.[50] Rookie Fresco Thompson replaced Rawlings at second base and smacked a single in his first major league at-bat.

Prior to the final game of the St. Louis series, catcher Johnny Gooch, who recently became the father of a baby boy, was presented with a baby carriage from adoring fans of the Smoky City. Gooch showed his good nature when he acquiesced to the demands of his teammates and gave the carriage a trial run. Gooch grabbed the carriage and took it around the bases as if he were attempting to leg out a long blast to the farthest reaches of Forbes Field. Gooch's teammates laughed at his preview of how he would look as a father pushing precious cargo.[51]

The Pirates hopped a train for a single Sunday date against the Chicago Cubs on September 6. Vic Aldridge held his former teammates in check as

Pittsburgh prevailed, 9–2. Aldridge won his fifth consecutive game and improved his record to 12–6. He tossed a complete game and allowed only two runs on four hits. Pie Traynor and Stuffy McInnis smacked two hits each, while accounting for three runs and two RBIs. Timely hitting, combined with horrendous fielding by Chicago that was influenced by strong winds, permitted Pittsburgh to build an early lead. The Pirates did not seem to miss Johnny Rawlings and Eddie Moore, as young Fresco Thompson played efficiently at second base and recorded a hit.[52]

The Sunday game in the Windy City marked the first time Pittsburgh had played Chicago since former Corsairs skipper George Gibson replaced Rabbit Maranville in early September. According to writers in Chicago, conditions on the club had become appalling during Maranville's tenure; the team was forced to run itself while Rabbit enjoyed the night life with his endless drinking and carousing. While Chicago was playing in Boston, Maranville was evicted from the team hotel because of disorderly conduct.[53] It was this type of behavior that motivated McKechnie to make the blockbuster deal with Chicago that was now being praised throughout Pittsburgh because of the solid play of George Grantham and Vic Aldridge.

After playing one game in Chicago, Pittsburgh returned to Forbes Field for a four-game series against George Gibson's Cubs. The first two games were played as part of a morning-afternoon Labor Day doubleheader on September 7. Pittsburgh gained a split when Red Oldham claimed victory in his first start as a Pirate, winning 8–5. The Cubs gained a split by winning a ten-inning afternoon affair, 9–8.

Pittsburgh's Eddie Moore saw his season turn into a roller coaster ride in August. Manager Bill McKechnie benched Moore on August 18 due to mental lapses that came about since he did not take his work seriously. Veteran Johnny Rawlings replaced Moore at second base. Moore eventually returned to the starting lineup because of an injury to Max Carey. He reclaimed his spot at second when Rawlings broke his ankle in September (National Baseball Hall of Fame Library, Cooperstown, New York).

The Pirates battered former teammate Wilbur Cooper, chasing the Chicago starter after he allowed six runs in five innings during the early game. Kiki Cuyler went 4-for-5 and scored a run while legging out a double and a triple. Stuffy McInnis recorded three hits and scored two runs. Young Fresco Thompson made his first start at Forbes Field, went 2-for-5, and drove home two runs. Oldham repeatedly dodged rallies throughout the game as he allowed 15 hits. Red went the route and avoided major problems until Mandy Brooks hit a three-run homer in the ninth inning.

One of the first game highlights involved Max Carey's return to the starting lineup after being sidelined for almost a month with an ankle injury. Carey played the entire game in center field, went 1-for-4 and stole his 31st base of the season. Carey was permitted to rest during the afternoon matinee, as Pittsburgh lost despite connecting for 12 hits against Chicago starter Guy Bush. Carson Bigbee led the Pirate hitting attack as he went 3-for-6 and scored two runs. Fresco Thompson, Kiki Cuyler and Glenn Wright recorded two hits apiece and combined to drive home five runs. Wright also recorded his 17th home run of the season when he legged out a two-run, four-bagger in the sixth inning.

Ray Kremer started the second game for Pittsburgh but was pulled before he could record an out as Chicago assaulted him for four runs. Pittsburgh then chipped away at Chicago's advantage and eventually took a 7–6 lead in the eighth inning. But Lee Meadows could not hold the lead as Chicago responded with a single tally in the ninth and then gained victory by scoring two runs in the tenth inning. After Bush tired in the tenth and allowed the Pirates to cut Chicago's lead to one run, Tony Kaufmann came in from the bullpen and recorded the game's last out.[54] Meadows saw his record drop to 18–9 in allowing Chicago to score three runs on 12 hits during ten innings of work.

Standings at the end of Labor Day showed Pittsburgh on top of the National League with an 83–48 record, while second-place New York stood eight and a half games behind at 76–58. In the American League, the defending champion Washington Senators had finally put distance between themselves and the league runner-up, Philadelphia, which now trailed by nine games. Historically, Labor Day was considered a crucial marker in that teams that held large leads on the holiday usually ended up playing in the World Series. If Bill McKechnie and his players were able to fend off challengers, the Pittsburgh Pirates would finally be participating in their first Fall Classic in 16 years.

9

Clinching the National League Pennant

The only occurrence that could possibly derail Pittsburgh's hopes of finally claiming the National League pennant after so many close finishes was a protracted losing streak. Fans in the Smoky City hoped that such a poor run was not looming after Chicago made it two victories in a row by defeating Pittsburgh on Tuesday, September 8, by a score of 3–2. The Cubs scored all the runs they needed in the first inning before starter Emil Yde settled down and began to battle Chicago's Pete Alexander. Chicago scored their three runs when Sparky Adams and Howard Freigau singled, Art Jahn tripled and Mandy Brooks delivered a sacrifice fly.[1] George Grantham went 3-for-4 for Pittsburgh, while Max Carey, Glenn Wright and Carson Bigbee added two hits apiece, but it was not enough to complete the rally.

Bigbee played left field for Bill McKechnie when he decided to bench slumping outfielder Clyde Barnhart for a couple of games. This decision was met with strong criticism from some fans who felt it was disgraceful to subject Barnhart to the humiliation of being benched after all he had done throughout the season. Barnhart did his best work of the campaign when he helped lift Pittsburgh out of the second-division and into the National League pennant race.[2] While Barnhart hoped to re-energize his game with a few days off, Pittsburgh catcher Earl Smith was informed that his legal troubles in Boston had ended. The assault charge made by Walter J. Lewis against Smith in May was dismissed after Lewis appeared in court one week earlier. Lewis asked that the charges be dropped after numerous hearings had been postponed during Pittsburgh's three trips to Boston in 1925.[3]

The Pirates wrapped up their season series with Chicago the same way they started it on opening day, by again losing to the Cubs. On Wednesday, September 9, the Cubs defeated the Pirates during an 11-inning affair, 9–7. Max Carey led the way by going 3-for-4 with a double and a stolen base. Hazen Cuyler, Glenn Wright and Pie Traynor also rapped out two hits apiece.

Ray Kremer pitched seven strong innings and allowed only three earned runs and nine hits. Johnny Morrison also pitched three solid innings of relief, but took the loss after poor fielding on the part of his teammates allowed Chicago to score three unearned runs in the 11th inning. In the bottom of the 11th, Pittsburgh mounted a small comeback when Cuyler tripled and scored on Traynor's single. Tony Kaufmann, who had exhibited wildness throughout the game, settled down and snuffed Pittsburgh's rally.[4]

McKechnie's troops left the friendly confines of Forbes Field and moved on to St. Louis, where they played the Cardinals for the last time during the 1925 campaign. As Pittsburgh prepared to open a five-game series in the Mound City, McKechnie hoped his team could put their three consecutive losses to Chicago behind them. The Pirates returned to their winning ways when they defeated St. Louis, 9–5, during the series' first game on Thursday, September 10. Returning to the starting lineup, Clyde Barnhart responded by going 3-for-5 with two doubles and three runs batted in. Glenn Wright went 2-for-4 and blasted his 18th home run of the season, victimizing pitcher Leo Dickerman in the sixth inning.

Vic Aldridge pitched sensational ball for Pittsburgh as he held St. Louis hitless through six innings.[5] Aldridge allowed four hits and seven walks in a little over eight innings of work as he improved his record to 13–6. Aldridge weakened in the ninth when St. Louis filled the sacks and Jim Bottomley crushed a grand slam. Tom Sheehan relieved Aldridge and earned his first save for the Pirates when he prevented St. Louis from doing further damage.[6]

Pittsburgh fell back into a losing rut on Friday, September 11, as St. Louis defeated the Buccaneers, 5–3. Red Oldham dropped to 2–1 after he gave up five runs on seven hits during eight innings. Max Carey and Pie Traynor led the way for Pittsburgh as each player went 2-for-4 at the plate.

A Saturday doubleheader between Pittsburgh and St. Louis was reduced to one game when rain prevented the morning contest from being played.[7] After the rain ceased, the grounds crew at Sportsman's Park tended to the field so that the second match-up could proceed as scheduled. St. Louis made it two victories in a row over the league-leading Pirates when Jesse Haines tossed a shutout and won, 4–0. Glenn Wright went 3-for-4 and Max Carey chipped in with two hits. Lee Meadows' record dropped to 18–10, as he lasted only five innings and gave up three runs on five hits. National League standings at the end of the day on September 12 showed that Pittsburgh's lead over second-place New York had been reduced to seven games. Pittsburgh's hitting had fallen off just a bit; the Pirates now had only eight players hitting over .300, with Stuffy McInnis (.369), Hazen Cuyler (.354) and Max Carey (.342) leading the way.

Pittsburgh and St. Louis played a doubleheader on Sunday, September 13, to make up for the postponed game. The Cardinals pulled off a sweep as Pittsburgh's losing streak reached four games. St. Louis won the opening game by a score of 8–4 as Duster Mails tossed a complete game and allowed three earned runs on nine hits. The Cardinals claimed the five-inning, nightcap, 6–2, after an agreement was reached between the two clubs that allowed the game to be stopped at 5:00 P.M. so that the Corsairs could catch an early train back to Pittsburgh.[8]

Errors did in Pirates starter Emil Yde during the first game, as he was charged with five unearned runs in just under two innings of work. Babe Adams was not very effective in relief, but Tom Sheehan pitched five strong innings and gave up only one run on three hits. Kiki Cuyler smacked his 16th homer of the season when he connected for a two-run blast in the third inning against Mails. In the shortened second contest, Johnny Morrison, Ray Kremer and Yde entered the fray, but could not keep St. Louis at bay. Les Bell and Bill Warwick blasted back-to-back home runs off Morrison in the second inning, and St. Louis starter Art Reinhart held Pittsburgh to four hits during his five innings of work. Clyde Barnhart was the only Pirate who solved Reinhart, as the left fielder went 2-for-2 with a double.

Although Pittsburgh was swept during the afternoon doubleheader, the day held special significance for shortstop Glenn Wright. One thousand friends from Kansas City and Archie were on hand to cheer on their fellow citizen.[9] The Missouri Pacific Railroad ran the "Glenn Wright Special" from Kansas City to St. Louis. Several hundred fans were already on the express when it stopped off at Wright's hometown of Archie and picked up about 130 additional fans. After members of Wright's entourage presented their favorite son with gifts and watched the doubleheader loss, they boarded the express so it could make its way back to Kansas City.[10]

After only two seasons, Wright had developed into the National League's best shortstop. He was a heavy hitter at the plate, and covered more ground than any player who manned the position. Wright's success at shortstop was aided by a powerful throwing arm that allowed him to position himself much deeper on the infield.

"I play a deep field," said Wright, "because I can get more chances there, I can cover more ground and the ball will not so easily go through me. I play as deep as I figure I can and still get the runner. I have always gone on the theory that if I could get my hands on the ball, I could get the runner, and that is true, provided I don't fumble or throw wild."[11]

Wright and his teammates boarded a train of their own and made the trip back to Pittsburgh for their final home stand at Forbes Field in 1925. The four Eastern teams were making their final trip to the Smoky City, with Brooklyn, Boston, Philadelphia and New York strolling into town one last time. During the first game of the Brooklyn series on Monday, September 14, the Pirates ended their four-game losing skid and defeated the Robins, 9–4. Glenn Wright and George Grantham each went 3-for-4, accounted for a total of three runs and combined to drive home three teammates. The Pirates drove Brooklyn starter Guy Cantrell from the mound after two innings and Rube Ehrhardt replaced Cantrell, but his wildness allowed Pittsburgh to score two runs in the fifth; five consecutive hits in the eighth added three more Pirate tallies. Vic Aldridge tossed a complete game and won his seventh consecutive game as the former Cub raised his record to 14–6.[12]

Rainy weather prevented Pittsburgh and Brooklyn from playing their scheduled game on Tuesday, September 15.[13] This necessitated a doubleheader the following day at Forbes Field. The Pirates finished off Brooklyn in splendid fashion, sweeping the afternoon twin bill. Lee Meadows finally won his nineteenth game during the first contest, as Pittsburgh prevailed over Brooklyn, 5–3. Red Oldham tossed a complete game in the nightcap as the Pirates won, 6–2. Meadows and Stuffy McInnis led the way for Pittsburgh during the initial game as each player recorded two hits. George Grantham was Pittsburgh's hitting star in the second game, going 3-for-3 and scoring three runs. Grantham had two singles and a walk, and slammed a second-inning home run against Tiny Osborne that struck a guard rail on the second tier of Forbes Field's new right field stands.[14]

Dave Bancroft's Boston Braves became the next team to succumb at the hands of Bill McKechnie's Pirates, as Pittsburgh opened a three-game series against its stubborn New England opponent with an 11–2 win on Thursday, September 17. Ray Kremer continued his dazzling work during the stretch drive by tossing a complete game and scattering seven Boston hits. Kremer won his fifth consecutive game, raising his record to 14–8 for the season. Earl Smith led Pittsburgh's hitting attack by going 3-for-4 with two singles and a home run into the right field stands. Second baseman Eddie Moore enjoyed a perfect day at the plate as he walked twice and rapped three singles. George Grantham scored three runs and produced a single and a triple.[15] Clyde Barnhart and Pie Traynor also lashed two hits apiece and combined to drive home four Pittsburgh runners.

The National League standings at the end of the day on September 17 showed Pittsburgh with a seven-game lead over the second-place New York Giants. Bill McKechnie's brigade had recovered from a recent slump against Chicago and St. Louis by putting together a four-game winning streak. Pittsburgh still had a substantial lead over New York because John McGraw's team had failed to gain traction while the Corsairs faltered. Still, McKechnie was not satisfied with the prospect of backing into the National League title; he wanted his team to play like a formidable champion. For this to happen, McKechnie needed at least one hero to step forward.

Hazen Shirley "Kiki" Cuyler had been one of Pittsburgh's most consistent performers during the 1925 season. He had a batting average of .348, was hitting for power, had scored a ton of runs and was a lethal threat as a base stealer. He was also one of the few Pirate players who had appeared in every game. Cuyler had an engaging personality that endeared him to Pittsburgh's faithful. He was a quiet, humble young man who did not like to discuss his accomplishments during his first two seasons in the National League.[16] Even though Cuyler was modest to a fault, he willingly talked about the game with teammates, just as stars like Fred Clarke and Honus Wagner had done before him.

> Right hand batters need longer bats than left-handers. There is a reason for this. A right handed pitcher's curved ball naturally breaks away from a right handed batter. There are four times as many right handed pitchers as there are left-handers. Hence, a right handed batter has to reach further for many balls than a left hander. On the other hand, the right-handed pitcher's curves naturally break in for a left-handed batter so he does not need so long a bat.
>
> I believe it is a decided advantage to stand deep in the box at bat. I can watch a curved ball much better from that position. There are batters who claim that you can hit curved pitching to better advantage by standing well up front and meeting the same curves before they break. That sounds logical, but it does not work in my case. I like my full allotment of time to watch the ball, even if the curve breaks wide before it reaches me. You know what it's going to do and can meet it. But if you stand well up toward the front of the box and swing just as it breaks, its liable to fool you. That's my opinion, but I'm not attempting to lay down any general rules for I realize very well that what helps one batter is poison to another.[17]

Cuyler was poison to the Boston Braves when the series' second game commenced on Friday, September 18. Pittsburgh scored early and often in a 9–7 victory that was hallmarked by Cuyler. Cuyler was a perfect 4-for-4, scored two runs and drove home two runs. Max Carey, Clyde Barnhart, Pie Traynor and Glenn Wright each chipped in with two hits and combined to score six runs. Earl Smith equaled Cuyler's mark by going 4-for-4 with two doubles and two runs batted in. Smith's problems in games against his former teammates also continued when he became involved in an eighth inning altercation.[18]

Boston loaded the bases before catcher Mickey O'Neil lofted a fly ball to right that looked deep enough to score Gus Felix from third base. Cuyler snagged the drive and earned an assist when he threw an accurate toss to the plate that Smith snagged cleanly. Felix tore into home plate and bowled over Smith. As Felix crashed into Smith, he spiked Pittsburgh's aggressive catcher. Smith immediately jumped on Felix as he lay on the ground; he began punching the Boston player. Umpire Charlie Moran quickly separated both combatants and expelled them from the game. After the game, an examination showed that Smith had spike wounds on his arm and side. The doctor's early prognosis stated that the injuries were severe enough to keep Smith out of action until the World Series.[19]

Bill McKechnie's Pirates moved one step closer to being the league's representative in the Fall Classic by winning their final game of the season with Boston on Saturday, September 19. The 2–1 victory, coupled with a New York loss against Chicago, pushed Pittsburgh's lead over the second-place Giants to eight games. The Pirates and Braves combined for 23 hits but accounted only for three runs as hurlers Vic Aldridge and Jesse Barnes pitched magnificently in the clutch. Kiki Cuyler was perfect at the plate for the second consecutive day as he went 4-for-4. Pie Traynor supplied capable assistance as he went 3-for-4, hit a double, knocked home a run and stole a base.

The Pirates finally found a way to beat Barnes when they drove home the game's winning tally in the ninth inning. Eddie Moore opened with a single to left and moved to second base on Max Carey's successful sacrifice bunt. Barnes, not wanting to have anything to do with the blazing Cuyler, intentionally walked the Flint Flash. After Carson Bigbee made the inning's second out, Pie Traynor walked to load the bases. Glenn Wright drove home Moore with the deciding run when he drilled a laser into center. Wright had finally become the day's hero after donning goat horns throughout the afternoon. In the first frame, Wright struck out with the bases loaded. In the fifth inning, he stranded two more runners when he lifted a weak fly ball to right that was snagged by Jimmy Welsh. In the eighth inning, Wright left runners standing at second and third when he fouled out to the catcher.[20]

While the Pirates relaxed at home on Sunday, September 20, and awaited the arrival of the Philadelphia Phillies for a four-game series, the Giants stayed alive in the National League race as they defeated Chicago, 6–2. While the Giants were idle the following day, the Pirates reduced their magic number by one game as they defeated Philadelphia during a Monday matinee, 9–7. Kiki Cuyler singled twice during his first two trips to the plate, equaling a National League record by connecting for ten consecutive hits. On Cuyler's 11th try, he fouled out and settled for a tie of the record.[21] The fact that Cuyler achieved the batting record as his team was desperately trying to clinch a pennant made his accomplishment more impressive.

Cuyler's teammates followed the lead of the star outfielder and battered four Philadelphia pitchers for 12 hits. Eddie Moore, Max Carey and Pie Traynor joined Cuyler aboard the hit parade, as all three players banged out two hits apiece. The four linchpins of Pittsburgh's attack combined to score six runs and record five RBIs. Lee Meadows failed in an attempt to gain his 20th victory, lasting only one inning. Johnny Morrison pushed his record to 17–13 after he pitched five and two-thirds innings of gilt-edged relief and allowed only one run on five hits.

The Pirates moved one step closer to clinching the National League pennant while New York was idle. The Pirates won their eighth consecutive game on Tuesday, September 22, defeating Philadelphia, 14–4. Ray Kremer was victorious once again and improved his record to 15–8 as he tossed a complete game. Kiki Cuyler continued his sizzling hitting by going a perfect 4-for-4 for the third time in four games and driving home three Pittsburgh runs. Cuyler also smacked a solo homer against Jimmy Ring and a two-run shot against Jack Knight that pushed his total to 18 four-base hits. Pie Traynor and Glenn Wright each went 4-for-5 and combined to score five runs.

Veteran outfielder Max Carey showed why he was still regarded as the master of base runners in the National League. In the third inning, Carey grounded a single into center field. Cuyler followed with a single to left field that moved Carey to second base. Carey touched the keystone sack and started for third while George Harper fielded the ball. Harper prepared to

During three games in late September against Boston and Philadelphia, Hazen "Kiki" Cuyler tied a National League record by collecting ten consecutive hits. Cuyler achieved this remarkable feat during the heat of the pennant race as Pittsburgh attempted to clinch the National League title (National Baseball Hall of Fame Library, Cooperstown, New York).

fire the ball to the hot corner, but changed his mind after he saw Carey hung up between second and third. When Harper attempted to alter his toss, the ball slipped out of his hand and rolled to right field. Before Harper could make a recovery, the cagy Carey had scored, with Cuyler perched on second. Carey's guile had paid off once again, as he forced an opposing fielder into a hurried mistake.[22]

A special air of anticipation hit Pittsburgh as the Pirates prepared to finish their series against Philadelphia on Wednesday, September 23. A Pittsburgh victory and a New York defeat in one of their doubleheader games against St. Louis meant that the Pirates would clinch a tie for the National League pennant. Strong pitching prevailed on this day, after a summer in which major league hitters had enjoyed the effects of a livelier baseball. Pittsburgh won a tight contest by the score of 2–1. Emil Yde improved his record to 17–9, as he allowed one run on seven hits during eight innings. Tom Sheehan was credited with his second save when he came on in the ninth inning after Philadelphia loaded the bases against Yde. After one run scored, Philadelphia's rally was crushed by Glenn Wright, who started a brilliant double play, the fifth that Pittsburgh turned in the game, to retire the side.[23]

After the Giants were swept in their doubleheader, the Pittsburgh Pirates were crowned champions of the National League for 1925. Congratulatory messages immediately poured in for owner Barney Dreyfuss and members of his pennant-winning team.[24] After some shaky play during early September, McKechnie's Pirates realized that backing into the World Series was not a viable option. They did some of their best work of the campaign in the areas of pitching, hitting and fielding. McKechnie's squad responded by winning nine consecutive games and seizing a title that rightfully belonged to them.

An impromptu celebration took place in Pittsburgh's clubhouse after word reached the players that they had indeed become champions of the National League. Manager McKechnie gave a short speech in which he thanked his players for what they had accomplished. His players likewise assured their skipper that they had deep admiration for him and his managing style. National League president John A. Heydler, who witnessed the clinching game, made his way to the Pirates' clubhouse to offer congratulations to McKechnie and his men. Heydler expressed confidence that Pittsburgh would uphold the honor of the league in the upcoming World Series, but he warned the Pirates not to try to play over their heads against the American League champion Washington Senators.[25] "The same form, the same spirit which you have shown in your own league will carry you through to balldom's pinnacle," said Heydler. "Simply play your game, don't let the opposition over-awe you, and don't try to be supermen."[26]

Heydler was a bit premature in christening Washington as the American League champions since the Senators had not officially clinched the pennant. Washington made this a formality the following day when it swept a doubleheader against Cleveland and Philadelphia lost to St. Louis, sealing a berth in the World Series. The Senators were a confident team loaded with star players. Sam Rice, Goose Goslin, Roger Peckinpaugh, Ossie Bluege, Joe Judge and Muddy Ruel headed a group of hitters regarded as one of the best in the American League. Washington's staff was anchored by the great Walter Johnson, who received adequate support from the likes of Stan Coveleski, Dutch Ruether and Tom Zachary. Fred "Firpo" Marberry was baseball's first true closer. "Boy Wonder" manager Bucky Harris led Washington's charges while playing second base for the Senators. All in all, Washington figured to be a formidable foe for the Corsairs.

Congratulatory messages came from all parts of America as former Pittsburghers and other Pirates fans wished the team luck in the upcoming series against Washington.[27] Mail order sales for World Series tickets at Forbes Field had been taken beginning on September 14 after Commissioner Landis met with officials of the Pirates, Giants, Athletics and Senators. The league set prices at $6.50 for a box seat and $5.50 for reserved seats in the grandstand. Tickets had to be purchased in a three-game block, forcing patrons to shell out between $16.50 and $19.50 for tickets to a trio of Forbes Field World Series games. Even though Landis was principally responsible for setting the prices, some Pittsburgh fans howled that Dreyfuss was being greedy by raising ticket prices from the level that they sold for in the regular season.[28] These complaining fans must not have been aware of Dreyfuss's charitable side. Dreyfuss' plan, in which a dollar was donated to charity each time a ball batted into the stands was returned to the club, had netted $236 in 1925.[29]

Dreyfuss informed his patrons that the Pirates' organization would only accept certified checks for World Series ticket orders. Despite protests from many patrons, the orders came in furiously; Dreyfuss believed that Forbes Field would be filled to capacity during the Fall Classic.[30] Within a week, reserved seats for the ballparks in Pittsburgh and Washington were sold out.

Landis also announced the dates for these games while adding a price of $3.30 for general admission tickets and $1.10 for bleacher seats at both ballparks. The first and second games were scheduled for Wednesday, October 7, and Thursday, October 8, at Forbes Field. Games Three through Five would shift to Washington's Griffith Stadium on October 9, 10 and 11, before the sixth and seventh games would be played; if necessary, in Pittsburgh.[31]

As the dates for these games were announced, presidents John Heydler and Ban Johnson revealed the list of eligible players for the World Series who would represent each pennant winning team from their respective league. Washington's eligible players included Walter Johnson, Stan Coveleski, Dutch Ruether, Tom Zachary, Alex Ferguson, Fred Marberry, Win Ballou, Allen Russell, Muddy Ruel, Hank Severeid, Bennie Tate, Joe Judge, Bucky Harris, Joe Harris, Roger Peckinpaugh, Ossie Bluege, Spencer Adams, Everett Scott, Buddy Myer, Sam Rice, Goose Goslin, Earl McNeely, Tex Jeanes, Bobby Veach and Nemo Leibold. Players participating for Pittsburgh included Babe Adams, Vic Aldridge, Bernard Culloton, Ray Kremer, Lee Meadows, Johnny Morrison, Red Oldham, Tom Sheehan, Emil Yde, Johnny Gooch, Earl Smith, Roy Spencer, George Grantham, Johnny Rawlings, Eddie Moore, Glenn Wright, Pie Traynor, Jewel Ens, Stuffy McInnis, Fresco Thompson, Clyde Barnhart, Carson Bigbee, Max Carey, Hazen Cuyler and George Haas.[32]

Local honors and accolades were quickly bestowed upon Barney Dreyfuss's team. The Pittsburgh Chamber of Commerce immediately arranged a luncheon to honor the pennant-winning Corsairs. It was scheduled to take place at 12 noon in the chamber building on Thursday, October 1. Members of the chamber planned on sending a fleet of automobiles to Forbes Field at 11:00 A.M. in order to escort Pittsburgh's players to the chamber's main dining room. The route was expected to be revealed to the public so that Pittsburgh baseball fans could catch a glimpse of their favorite players. Six hundred and fifty tickets were put on sale for chamber members and their guests. A number of speeches would take place after the luncheon, with the hope that some members of the Pirates would say a few words.[33]

One member of the Pirates' entourage, manager Bill McKechnie, was expected to give a stirring speech. Fans and scribes had proclaimed McKechnie a hero for leading his troops to first place. Those who knew McKechnie from his hometown of Wilkinsburg viewed Bill as a simple man who was active in the community and church affairs and loved to talk about baseball as long as the conversation did not center around him. To his wife, McKechnie remained a modest home-loving man who was quiet and unassuming. During the winter, he enjoyed hunting and hanging around the local fire station.

During an interview with a Pittsburgh newspaper, Mrs. Beryl McKechnie discussed her husband's relationship with their three children.[34]

> Little Billy, I guess, makes up for any lack of enthusiasm that Beatrice or Jimmy may show.
> Billy, you see, is just 12. He is a mascot for the Pirates and the most ardent rooter for his dad.
> He tries to explain to Jimmy how "Pie" or "Max" or "Kiki" stand at the plate or run the bases; but Jimmy is only a year old so he can't appreciate the explanation.
> And Beatrice baffles him with her lack of interest in baseball. He can't quite see why a seven-year-old girl prefers dolls to baseball.
> So it's up to his dad to talk baseball with him. Ever since he made the trip with the team on their last eastern invasion — well, its baseball all the time.[36]

William McKechnie, Jr. was not the only passionate baseball fan in the Wilkinsburg home. Mrs. McKechnie was a keen student of the game who followed it very closely. She attended games at Forbes Field whenever the opportunity presented itself. She had not made any road trips with the team, but those plans were going to change for the World Series. Mrs. McKechnie planned on seeing every game and believed Pittsburgh would prevail over Washington.[37]

Her husband still had some business to attend to before the games against Washington began. The honorable McKechnie, a man who sang on the choir and was a board member of the Mifflin Street Methodist Episcopal Church, still had to manage his team through the regular season's final week.[38]

Pittsburgh closed out its regular season at Forbes Field with a three-game series against the New York Giants. A few months ago, when the National League race was still tight, followers of both teams circled this series as crucial in deciding the National League pennant race. Those expectations were rendered moot since Pittsburgh had already clinched the title. Yet, this series was not meaningless from Pittsburgh's standpoint since the games still allowed McKechnie's squad to sharpen its skills before the start of the World Series. Pirates players still needed to get in their work, while McKechnie needed to be cautious about his players' health.

McKechnie used his regular lineup in a 4–0 loss to New York on Thursday, September 24.[39] Red Oldham and Babe Adams split the pitching duties, as New York's Jack Scott tossed a complete game shutout and allowed only eight hits. Max Carey connected for three safeties against the right-handed twirler.

Cool weather prevented the series' second contest from being played the following day as Pittsburgh management re-scheduled the game as part of a doubleheader on Saturday, September 26.[40] The Giants extracted some hollow revenge against their most bitter rival when they swept both games of the twin bill. McKechnie gave starting third baseman Pie Traynor the day off because of an abscess. Traynor decided to have it lanced with the hope that he would be able to return to the lineup in a few days.[41]

New York took the first contest by a score of 4–3 as Vic Aldridge saw his record drop to 15–7 despite tossing a complete game. Clyde Barnhart and Earl Smith rapped out two hits apiece for the Pirates. New York's Freddie Fitzsimmons gained a shutout in the nightcap as he held Pittsburgh to four hits; his teammates pushed three runs home against Pirates starter Johnny Morrison. In one positive development, catcher Earl Smith saw his first action behind the plate in the first game after missing a week since the spiking against Boston.

Even though the Pirates finished their home schedule at Forbes Field on a sour note, they had still compiled an impressive 52–25 record at the Bellefield ballpark. The Pirates packed their grips and boarded a train for Cincinnati, where the final series of the regular season would be played. The Pirates claimed the first contest of the four-game set on Sunday, September 27, defeating the Reds, 4–3. Max Carey led the way by going 2-for-3 as he scored one run, drove home a teammate and stole a base. Ray Kremer raised his record to 16–8, as the right-handed hurler won his seventh straight game. Two runs in both the fourth and fifth innings turned a three-run deficit into a one run lead that stood up for Pittsburgh before rain brought an end to the game in the top of the sixth inning.[42]

A quirk in the National League schedule gave Pittsburgh four days off until its series with Cincinnati resumed on Friday, October 2. The Pirates returned home to the Smoky City so that McKechnie could hold light workouts for his squad. Pittsburgh's manager planned on holding early practice sessions that would begin at 11:30 or 12 o'clock each day. McKechnie planned to alter this schedule on Thursday so that members of the Pirates' organization could attend the Chamber of Commerce luncheon.[43]

The Pirates had a few other social engagements on their calendar during

Pittsburgh manager Bill McKechnie was hailed as a hero in some baseball circles after he guided the Pittsburgh Pirates to the National League pennant in 1925. On September 29, the Wilkinsburg Elks Club honored its hometown hero during a banquet. In this photo, McKechnie is flanked by 12-year-old son William Jr., who served honorably as the Pirates' mascot (National Baseball Hall of Fame Library, Cooperstown, New York).

the break in the schedule. On Monday night, the entire group of Pirates were guests of the Duncan Sisters at the Nixon Theater in Pittsburgh.[44] Viviana and Rosetta Duncan of Los Angeles, who performed in vaudeville and on Broadway, were at the Nixon performing their famous musical comedy, *Topsy and Eva*, which had been adapted from Harriett Beecher Stowe's *Uncle Tom's Cabin*.

The Pirates were given an opportunity to relax for the evening and watch the Duncans' show, which was currently in the midst of a cross-country tour.

On Tuesday evening, the Pirates' entourage attended a banquet arranged by the Wilkinsburg Elks Club in honor of Bill McKechnie.[45] Some fans who attended noticed that McKechnie had lost weight and looked worn down from the long, grueling pennant race. A thousand people were on hand to honor their favorite citizen, who made a short speech in which he gave all of the credit for Pittsburgh's pennant to his players.[46] Team vice-president Fred Clarke also spoke at the celebration honoring McKechnie.[47]

The former Pirate great offered his opinion about the current team which he had been a part of since being named as an assistant to McKechnie in June.

> This is the best ball team with which I have ever been connected. We had good teams when we won pennants back in 1901, 1902 and 1903, and then again in 1909, but we never had a team like the present aggregation.
>
> These boys know how to do everything well.
>
> If they play their normal game against Washington — and I believe they will — they will certainly make worlds of trouble for the Senators. They not only can hit, but they are the fastest combination in the majors today. There isn't a real slow-foot in the lot. And they have brains, too, gobs of them, which they insist on using.
>
> I never was connected with a club on which there was such splendid spirit. The will to win is ever present, and there is perfect harmony. The players all like their manager, and always carry out his orders to the best of their ability. It is hard to beat an outfit like the present Pirates.[48]

Fred Clarke was rarely someone who could be pinned down to give pennant and World Series predictions when he managed the Pirates from 1900 through 1915. Clarke did not offer any insight into the eventual winner of the upcoming World Series when *Baseball Magazine* interviewed him. He did respond, however, when the interviewer asked Clarke to compare the 1925 squad to his 1909 world champions. Clarke stated that the 1925 pitching staff was better than its 1909 counterpart. Fred also raised a few eyebrows when he claimed that Glenn Wright played shortstop as well as Honus Wagner. Clarke did concede that Wagner was a superior player on the bases and at the plate. The former Pirates manager also claimed that Pie Traynor was as good as Boston's great third baseman, Jimmy Collins.[49]

Clarke saved some of his most effusive praise for two member's of Pittsburgh's outer garden corps.

> Cuyler is a wonder, one of those all round players that you don't see very often. He can field and hit and run bases. He is fast as a flash and has a great throwing arm. He'll also improve, settle down, be surer of himself, develop into a steadier hitter. Cuyler might well become a second Cobb. Time will tell. In any case, he's the best young outfielder who has broken into baseball for many years.

But our club is not all young. There are veterans that deserve notice. Max Carey has worn a Pittsburgh uniform for fifteen years. He's an outfielder without a weakness. The chances that he gets year after year prove that Carey is also a good hitter, a much better hitter than he's given credit for being. And as a base runner, he has no equal. But there is one thing in particular about Carey they seldom mention, but its important. It's his disposition; his high character. Carey would be a credit to any profession. He would have a great influence on any ball club.[50]

While the Pirates team relaxed at home for a few days, final preparations for the first World Series game at Forbes Field were being finalized. Pittsburgh writer John H. Gruber and fellow journalists Louis Dougher of Washington, and St. Louis' Jim Gould were named the official scorers for the Series by Commissioner Landis. Meanwhile, Pittsburgh management finished filling ticket orders for the three-game packages and returned money to patrons who had sent their orders in too late. The fast dispersal of reserved seats guaranteed that at least 38,000 fans would attend each World Series game at Forbes Field.[51]

A large contingent of fans from out-of-town was also expected to be on hand for games at Forbes Field. These patrons were having a difficult time securing reservations at Pittsburgh hotels, even though some of these inns had doubled their usual price of seven or eight dollars a day for a room. The lodging situation became so dire that the Washington Senators were told they could not stay at the Schenley Hotel as all National League visitors did during the regular season. The hotel could only accommodate regular patrons, so the Senators were forced to make reservations at the Morrowfield, a large apartment hotel located outside the city limits.[52]

After four days of social events and practices that kept the Pirates fine-tuned, Bill McKechnie's players made their way to Cincinnati in order to resume their final series of the season. The game scheduled for Friday, October 2, was postponed due to a cool autumn rain that fell over the city. Even though conditions at Redland Field prevented McKechnie's men from practicing, Lee Meadows worked out his arm by throwing lightly to coach Jack Onslow. While Meadows worked his arm with Pittsburgh's pitching coach, the remainder of the squad made a trip to the Latonia Racetrack, located six miles from Cincinnati across the Kentucky border, in order to play the horses.[53]

A solid day of rain soaked the grounds at Redland Field to the point that Saturday's game fell into question as well. Cincinnati management exhibited an obliging nature by leaving the decision as to whether to play the game up to Pittsburgh manager Bill McKechnie. If the Pirates' skipper decided to call off the game, the Pirates would be permitted to hold a practice session at Redland Field instead of playing the scheduled game against Cincinnati. McKechnie decided to accept the plan; the Reds announced that the ballgame had been cancelled.[54]

9. Clinching the National League Pennant

A three-game series was shortened to a two-game set when the Pirates finally hit the field for the first time in a week on Sunday, October 4. Pittsburgh won the doubleheader's first game by a score of 4–2 as Ray Kremer raised his record to 17–8 and Johnny Morrison pitched four innings of relief for his fourth save. Cincinnati gained a 4–1 victory in the nightcap as rookie pitcher Bernard Culloton made his first start of the season. Pittsburgh finished the 1925 season with a 95–58 record. New York came home second at 86–66, eight and a half games behind the pennant-winning Pirates. Cincinnati held down the National League's third spot, 15 games behind Pittsburgh, with a record of 80–73.

Heavy hitting was Pittsburgh's largest asset during its pennant winning campaign. Stuffy McInnis (.368), Hazen Cuyler (.357), Max Carey (.343), George Grantham (.326), Clyde Barnhart (.325), Pie Traynor (.320), Earl Smith (.313) and Glenn Wright (.308) all hit over .300, while Johnny Gooch (.298) and Eddie Moore (.298) batted close to the heralded mark. Cuyler (144), Traynor (114), Carey (109) and Moore (106) topped the 100-run mark. Wright (121), Barnhart (114), Traynor (106) and Cuyler (102) each drove home more than 100 runs. Cuyler's total of 369 total bases represented a franchise record that still stands today, an impressive feat for a team that has had such home run champions as Ralph Kiner and Willie Stargell. Pitchers Lee Meadows (19–10, 3.67 ERA), Ray Kremer (17–8, 3.69 ERA), Emil Yde (17–9, 4.13 ERA), Johnny Morrison (17–14, 3.88 ERA) and Vic Aldridge (15–7, 3.63 ERA) did fine work during the regular season; they were expected to receive the bulk of the workload against Washington.

The Washington Senators finished the 1925 season with a 96–55 record as they, too, finished eight and a half games ahead of the second-place Philadelphia Athletics. Washington featured the best pitching staff in the American League, with Walter Johnson (20–7, 3.07 ERA), Stan Coveleski (20–5, 2.84 ERA), Dutch Ruether (18–7, 3.87 ERA), Tom Zachary (12–15, 3.85 ERA) and Firpo Marberry (9–5, 3.47 ERA, 15 saves) leading the way for Bucky Harris' crew. Even though Pittsburgh was a much better hitting team than Washington, the Senators still featured capable hitters. Sam Rice (.350), Goose Goslin (.334), Joe Harris (.323), Joe Judge (.314) and Muddy Ruel (.310) all batted over .300 for the Senators. Goslin (116) and Rice (111) scored over 100 runs, while Goslin drove home 113 teammates. Shortstop Roger Peckinpaugh, who batted .294 for Washington, was voted the American League's top player when he was named the most valuable player.[55]

Baseball writers and prognosticators across America seemed to be split over who would prevail in the 1925 World Series. Joe Ward (*Pittsburgh Chronicle-Telegraph*), W.F. Eaton (*Boston Telegram*), W.H. Becker (*Chicago Daily News*), Harry C. Robert (*Philadelphia Evening Bulletin*), Regis M. Welsh (*Pittsburgh Post*), Joe Vila (*New York Sun*), James M. Gould (*St. Louis Star*), Tom Swope (*Cincinnati Post*) and J. Roy Stockton (*St. Louis Post*) cast their votes for Pittsburgh. Thomas Holmes (*Brooklyn Daily Eagle*), Frank H. Young (*Washington Post*), Dan Hake (*Philadelphia Record*), Warren W. Brown (*Chicago Herald and Examiner*), Gordon Mackey (*Philadelphia Inquirer*), Henry P. Edwards (*Cleveland Plain-Dealer*), Paul W. Eaton (Washington Correspondent of *The Sporting News*) and Sam Greene (*Detroit News*) believed Washington would be crowned World Series champions.[56]

Ralph S. Davis covered the Pirates extensively writing articles for both *The Pittsburgh Press* and *The Sporting News*. Not surprisingly, Davis believed Pittsburgh would win the 1925 World Series. Davis felt the Pirates would prevail because of the team's youth and its ability to outlast their much older combatants.

> Picking the winner of any baseball series is a hazardous undertaking and especially is this true of a World's Series, where the issue is usually decided within a week.
>
> A series between Pittsburgh and Washington is one between an old team and a young one. The Senators will have the advantage of experience and the poise gained through having competed in last year's classic. The Pirates will be under World's Series fire for the first time. But I have a feeling that their youthful enthusiasm, plus their wonderful all-around batting and base running ability, will carry them through. They have been death to left-handers all season, and doubtless will face more or less southpaw pitching in the big games. Pittsburgh's pitching staff as a whole also looks much better to me than does Washington's. I figure a hard-fought series, with the Buccaneers finally emerging on top.[57]

Many of Davis' fellow journalists agreed with the Pittsburgh writer regarding the competitiveness of the Series. Almost all who gave their expert analysis believed that it would be a close, tight battle. The Pirates wanted to show that they were at least a little bit better.

10

Game One to Washington, Game Two to Pittsburgh

Rooters across Western Pennsylvania anxiously awaited the start of the 1925 World Series. The city of Pittsburgh put on a festive face as fans from around the country arrived at the home of the National League champions on the eve of the Series' first game. A genuine party atmosphere existed throughout the city, which greeted its first appearance on baseball's grand stage in 16 years. The federal government in Washington took special steps to insure that Pittsburgh would remain alcohol free throughout the World Series. The top prohibition officers in the eastern section of the United States were sent to Pittsburgh, where they would work under the supervision of Frederick C. Baird, the divisional administrator. Baird and his men had been authorized to combat the flood of illegal liquor that was expected to pour into Pittsburgh.[1]

Members of both the Pirates and Senators engaged in a celebration of their own that did not include bootleg liquor. On the eve of the Series, Bill McKechnie and Bucky Harris were extended invitations to be guests of general manager Harry Davis of the Davis Theater for "Baseball Night" on Tuesday, October 6. Private boxes on the orchestra and balcony floors were reserved for both teams. McKechnie, Harris, Barney Dreyfuss and Fred Clarke, along with players from both squads, spent an evening watching the theater show. Keeping with the spirit of the moment, the Davis Theater also planned to provide updates of the World Series games with the use of radios on stage. During the Series, baseball play-by-play would be announced during breaks in between vaudeville acts.[2]

While both teams enjoyed a quiet, comfortable evening in the warm theater, thousands of rabid fans braved the cold, wet weather to stand outside of Forbes Field's gates hoping to purchase bleacher seat tickets for Wednesday's game.[3] The fans huddled around bonfires, stayed warm by wrapping themselves in blankets, played cards and even sang in order to pass the time. The large crowd cheered a coal man as he drove by, believing his presence was an omen that warmer weather was on the horizon.[4]

Ralph Arkle of 910 East Diamond Street in Pittsburgh was able to secure his spot at the head of the ticket line by winning a mad dash at two o'clock on Tuesday afternoon. Robert Kline of Denver, Colorado, was second in line, right behind Arkle, waiting for the gates to open at 8:30 A.M. the following morning. A 65-year-old man from Connecticut, who claimed to have seen every World Series since 1903, was also on line. In front of another general admission gate, two men from Columbus, Ohio, built a lean-to shelter that kept the cold rain from hitting their bodies.[5]

These hardy fans wanted to purchase some of the 14,000 tickets that would be sold each day of the Series at Forbes Field. These tickets, available for those patrons who had not been able to purchase reserved seating, included 3,400 seats in the permanent field bleachers at $3.30 each, 6,500 seats in the temporary center field bleachers at $1.10 each, and 4,000 tickets for standing room only in the grandstand area at $3.30 apiece.[6] Ticket scalpers who used area hotels as their base of operations were procuring anywhere from $15 to $25 for tickets.[7] Even though only a total of 40,000 customers could be accommodated for the first Series game on October 7, Pittsburgh management estimated that 75,000 people hoped to push through Forbes Field's turnstiles for that event.[8]

The cold night, which saw the mercury dip to 44 degrees at 7:00 A.M. on game day, seemed to give way to a comfortable autumn day. The sun warmed Forbes Field's glistening diamond. W. S. Brotzman of the Pittsburgh weather bureau predicted that the temperature would reach 60 degrees by 2:00 P.M., when the first World Series contest was slated to begin.[9] By 11:30 that morning, those people who had braved the previous night's cold weather and had purchased tickets had already filled Forbes Field's temporary bleacher section. Ballplayers began arriving at the ballpark at about 11:45. Johnny Rawlings was the first Pirate player who came into sight, as the injured second baseman hobbled on crutches to his box seat.[10]

At about 11:50, Pittsburgh captain Max Carey navigated his way to the press box. Carey stopped and chatted for a moment with some pundits before making his way into the Pirates' clubhouse to shed his street clothes and dress for the game. By 12:30, Forbes Field's grandstand had begun to fill slightly. At 12:35, Pittsburgh's batboy wheeled the famous Corsair cudgels out of the clubhouse and arranged them neatly on the dugout steps. Players from both teams began to appear on the field as Bill McKechnie's and Bucky Harris' squads prepared to take batting practice.[11]

Tom Sheehan took the mound and pitched batting practice to his teammates, who wore new white uniforms. Photographers dotted the field taking pictures to commemorate the start of the Series. An excited Billy McKechnie Jr. posed for a photo with the Washington Senators mascot. Stuffy McInnis walked up to former American League nemesis Walter Johnson and grabbed his hand. A moment later, Game One starters Johnson and Lee Meadows grasped each others' hand as shutterbugs took a multitude of photos.[12]

By now, Forbes Field was nearly filled to capacity. Early arriving fans who had been entertained for hours by the comedy skits of Nick Altrock and Al Schacht were now ready for the game to begin. Danny Nirella's band, the same musical group that supplied entertainment at Forbes Field during the 1909 World Series, ably supported the Clown Princes of Baseball during their performance.[13]

The list of dignitaries occupying box seats at Forbes Field included Pennsylvania Governor Gifford Pinchot, Judge Landis, Ban Johnson, Garry Herrmann, John Heydler and a host of celebrities from the boxing and entertainment industry.[14] Actress Rosetta Duncan, who had invited Pittsburgh's players to be her personal guests at the Nixon Theater over a week ago, presented Bill McKechnie and Bucky Harris with large flower bouquets. Kiki Cuyler received a golden ball and bat from adoring fans. Vic Aldridge was presented with a mahogany clock by his friends, and Washington's Joe Harris, a Franklin, Pennsylvania native, received a diamond ring from admirers.[15]

Forbes Field's press box was filled with prominent writers from across the country. Mixed in among the usual scribes were players and managers such as John McGraw, Ty Cobb, Babe Ruth and Honus Wagner, who were writing syndicated columns during the Fall Classic.

Prior to the game's start, team vice-president and assistant manager Fred Clarke could be seen talking to over-anxious members of the Pittsburgh team in an effort to calm their nerves. In the meantime, Governor Pinchot tossed out the ceremonial first pitch of the game. His speed and control were impeccable as he heaved ball to home plate without a bounce.[16] The pomp and circumstance finally ended when home plate umpire Cy Rigler yelled, "Play Ball."

Joining Rigler's crew as umpires for the 1925 World Series were fellow National League arbiter Barry McCormick and American League umpires Brick Owens and George Moriarty. Managers Bill McKechnie and Bucky Harris presented lineups that had produced excellent results throughout the season. Washington's batting order read as follows: 1. Sam Rice (CF), 2. Bucky Harris (2B), 3. Goose Goslin (LF), 4. Joe Judge (1B), 5. Joe Harris (RF), 6. Ossie Bluege (3B), 7. Roger Peckinpaugh (SS), 8. Muddy Ruel (C) and 9. Walter Johnson (P). McKechnie countered with the following lineup: 1. Eddie Moore (2B), 2. Max Carey (CF), 3. Hazen Cuyler (RF), 4. Clyde Barnhart (LF), 5. Pie Traynor (3B), 6. Glenn Wright (SS), 7. George Grantham (1B), 8. Earl Smith (C) and 9. Lee Meadows (P).

Washington leadoff man Sam Rice wasted little time in starting the 1925 World Series. Rice swung at Lee Meadows' first pitch and grounded out to shortstop Glenn Wright. Meadows then induced Bucky Harris to hit another grounder, this time to Pie Traynor, who easily made the throw to George

Grantham for the second out. Leon "Goose" Goslin then lined to Grantham for the final out of the inning.

During the bottom of the first, Walter Johnson was aided by a superb play from Rice, who snagged Eddie Moore's short fly behind second base for the first out. Max Carey then became the game's first runner when a Johnson offering caught him on the right arm. After a short delay in which Pittsburgh's trainer rubbed Carey's bruise, Max broke for second but was thrown out on an attempted steal by catcher Muddy Ruel. Kiki Cuyler then became Johnson's first strikeout victim when Pittsburgh's star player ended the inning by fanning.[17]

First baseman George Grantham made a marvelous play to start off the second inning. Joe Judge hit a sharp grounder to Wright that Pittsburgh's shortstop almost turned into an error when he threw wildly to first base. Grantham retired Judge by making a one-handed grab of Wright's errant throw and keeping his foot on first base.[18] The play took on further significance when Joe Harris followed Judge and launched a home run that struck the top of a gate between the temporary stands in right field.[19] Umpires initially held up Harris at second base with a double, but after a short conference, the arbiters allowed Harris to cross the plate with a home run, giving Washington a 1-0 lead. Ossie Bluege followed Harris' theatrics by swinging at strike three, and Meadows ended the inning when Roger Peckinpaugh's fly ball was caught by Max Carey in center field.[20]

Johnson continued his mastery over Pittsburgh in the second inning. The Washington ace retired Clyde Barnhart for the first out when Rice hauled in his long drive to center. Pie Traynor recorded Pittsburgh's first hit of the Series when he singled to right field. Traynor was then forced at second after Glenn Wright's hard grounder to first was gobbled up by Joe Judge, who then tossed to Roger Peckinpaugh for the out. Johnson then ended the inning by fanning George Grantham.

In the top of the third frame, fans at Forbes Field were treated to a spectacular play by Traynor, who made a diving catch over the bag to retire Muddy Ruel for the first out. Johnson was unable to help his own cause as Meadows easily retired his counterpart on a groundout to Wright. Rice tried to ignite a two-out rally by hitting a single to right field, but the top of the third inning came to an end when Rice became careless and was picked off first base by Meadows.[21]

Earl Smith led off the bottom of the third by flying out to Joe Harris in right field. Lee Meadows followed by drawing a one-out walk against Johnson. Pittsburgh's inning quickly died when Eddie Moore slapped a ground ball to Peckinpaugh, starting a 6-3 double play.[22] Washington manager Bucky Harris had pulled the first strategic maneuver of the game when he ordered Johnson to walk Meadows. Harris reasoned that if Meadows spent time running the bases, it might adversely affect his pitching at some point during the game.²³

Solid pitching continued to be the dominant theme as Meadows easily handled the Senators in the fourth inning. Bucky Harris led off by reaching first base when Meadows plunked him with the inning's first pitch. But Harris was erased when he became trapped between first and second, as George Grantham speared Goose Goslin's line drive and stepped on first base to double up the confused runner. Joe Judge then ended the inning when he grounded out to second baseman Eddie Moore.

Max Carey became Johnson's third strikeout victim on the day when he fanned to start the fourth inning. Kiki Cuyler followed with a single over the second base bag that brought a round of cheers from the Forbes Field crowd. Yet, those cheers turned to groans when Cuyler was picked off first base. Pittsburgh's speedy outfielder was able to maintain a lengthy rundown before Bucky Harris tagged him out. Clyde Barnhart then made the inning's final out when he whiffed against Johnson.²⁴

Washington finally broke through with a big inning in the fifth, as Lee Meadows labored to keep his opponent at bay. Joe Harris led off with an infield single when he beat Glenn Wright's throw to first base. Ossie Bluege then followed with a single to left that moved Harris to second. Bill McKechnie, who became concerned that Meadows was tiring, now had Babe Adams warming up in the Pirates bullpen. Roger Peckinpaugh recorded Washington's third consecutive hit when he blooped a Texas Leaguer over short, loading the bases. Meadows temporarily stemmed the tide when he fanned Muddy Ruel.

A slight delay occurred as Pittsburgh's players complained to the umpires about overflow fans being on the field. When play resumed, Meadows recorded the second out by fanning Walter Johnson. Just when it appeared that Meadows might wiggle out of trouble, Sam Rice stroked a single over second base, scoring Joe Harris and Bluege. The inning finally ended when Bucky Harris grounded out to Pie Traynor.²⁵

Pittsburgh fans found hope when Traynor led off the bottom of the fifth by driving a Johnson offering into the temporary stands in right field; the home run made the score, 3–1, in Washington's favor. Yet hopes of a forthcoming rally were squelched when Glenn Wright looked at a called third strike. George Grantham reached base when shortstop Roger Peckinpaugh threw wildly to Joe Judge but Earl Smith made the inning's second out by flying out to Joe Harris in right field. Grantham promptly stole second but died on the base paths when Lee Meadows struck out.²⁶

Meadows seemed to regroup after Traynor's home run cut Washington's lead to two runs. Goose Goslin led off the top of the sixth inning by fouling out to Earl Smith. Meadows recorded the second out when he induced Joe

Judge to hit a fly ball to Max Carey. Joe Harris then followed suit with a fly ball to Carey.

Johnson matched Meadows' pitching during Pittsburgh's turn at bat as he set the Corsairs down in order. Eddie Moore made the first out when he hit a grounder to Ossie Bluege. Carey became Johnson's second victim when Judge easily handled his groundball and ran to first base. Kiki Cuyler continued to struggle at the plate, as he lofted a routine fly to Joe Harris in right field.[27]

Meadows made quick work of the Senators in the seventh inning. Bluege led off by striking out. Roger Peckinpaugh was retired on a routine groundball to Pie Traynor before Muddy Ruel made the third out by bunting a grounder to Meadows, who threw to George Grantham at first.[28]

Walter Johnson continued to match Meadows pitch-for-pitch during Pittsburgh's turn at the plate. Clyde Barnhart led off by striking out. Traynor brought the Pittsburgh crowd to its feet when he cracked a Johnson offering to deep center field, but Sam Rice shattered hopes when he hauled in the long fly. Johnson finished off Pittsburgh in the seventh, recording his eighth strikeout of the day by fanning Glenn Wright.[29]

Wright extracted a bit of revenge against Johnson when he robbed the Senators' ace by making a spectacular catch of his drive to deep short. Sam Rice made the second out when he grounded to Wright, who also became involved in the third out when he stabbed Bucky Harris' grounder behind second base and made a strong throw to George Grantham.

Grantham began Pittsburgh's half of the eighth inning by flying out to Joe Harris in right field. Earl Smith then drove a ball into center field for a single. Bill McKechnie sent Stuffy McInnis to the plate as a pinch hitter for Meadows.[30] McInnis' appearance in the game proved very brief as Johnson fanned his former American League counterpart on three pitches. McInnis took healthy cuts at three fastballs but came up empty each time.[31] With two out, McKechnie decided to add a little more speed to the bases, putting Carson Bigbee in to pinch run for Smith. Bigbee promptly moved into scoring position by stealing second base. That is where Bigbee remained as Eddie Moore grounded out to Ossie Bluege to end the inning.[32]

Pittsburgh now featured a new battery in the game. Johnny Morrison replaced Meadows on the mound and Johnny Gooch took Smith's spot behind home plate for the ninth inning. Goose Goslin greeted Morrison by lining a single down the line in right field. Joe Judge laid down a perfect sacrifice that moved Goslin to second, as George Grantham handled the bunt and tossed to Eddie Moore, who covered first base. Morrison then recorded the inning's second out when he struck out Joe Harris. Ossie Bluege ended Pittsburgh's hopes of a scoreless inning when he banged an RBI single to center field. Goslin came around to score Washington's fourth run of the day, while Bluege went to second on Max Carey's throw to the plate. Morrison finally retired the Senators

10. Game One to Washington, Game Two to Pittsburgh 155

when he fielded Roger Peckinpaugh's grounder and threw to first for the final out.[33]

In the ninth inning, manager Bucky Harris brought Earl McNeely into the game for defensive purposes, placed him in center while Sam Rice moved to right field and Joe Harris retired to the bench. Walter Johnson started out the final inning by hitting Max Carey with a pitch for the second time in the game.[34] Carey stood and smiled as the ball smacked him in his left elbow. In the first inning when Johnson drilled Carey on the right elbow, Max had dropped to the ground in pain. The fact that Carey felt little distress on this occasion indicated that Johnson was losing speed on his fastball. Cuyler did not test this theory during his trip to the plate, as he watched three strikes glide by without lifting the bat off his shoulder.[35] Clyde Barnhart followed with a single to left, placing runners at first and second with one out. Unfortunately, dreams of a rally were quickly extinguished as Pie Traynor flew out to center fielder Earl McNeely and Glenn Wright fouled out to Joe Judge.[36]

Walter Johnson had pitched phenomenally during Washington's 4–1 victory in Game One. He tossed a complete game, allowed five hits and struck out ten. Lee Meadows deserved a better fate as he allowed three runs on six hits during eight innings of work. Sam Rice, Joe Harris and Ossie Bluege banged out two hits each and combined to score three of Washington's runs. Pie Traynor was the only Pirates player who solved Johnson's delivery; the Pittsburgh's third baseman went 2-for-4 and drilled a solo home run.

Despite the fact that his team lost the game, Pittsburgh owner Barney Dreyfuss was happy with the game's financial results. A crowd of 41,723 fans shoe-horned its way into Forbes Field, accounting for a total gate receipt of over $180,000.[37]

Prior to the first game of the Series, Dreyfuss revealed that he had received about five times as many orders for World Series tickets at Forbes Field as he had actual seats. Some speculated that Dreyfuss should have shown better foresight and moved the games from Forbes Field to the new facility at the University of Pittsburgh, which accommodated football in the autumn and college baseball in the spring. The stadium's huge bowl seated 70,000 people, which would have permitted more ticket orders to be filled for World Series games. Yet, such an undertaking was impossible in 1925. Pitt Stadium's first football event only had occurred a few weeks before the World Series started, and the coliseum's baseball diamond had yet to be constructed.[38]

Proceedings for the World Series' second game on Thursday, October 8, at Forbes Field followed a similar pattern to the first day's events. Fans stood in line hoping to secure tickets for the various bleacher sections. Entrances to Forbes Field's bleacher sections were opened at 9:00 in the morning, while the remaining gates to Barney Dreyfuss's baseball palace gave fans access two hours later. Once again, patrons who held reserved tickets arrived late in making an

Third baseman Pie Traynor starred for Pittsburgh during the 1925 season. He batted .320 and knocked in 106 runs while playing his usual phenomenal defense at third base. In Game One of the World Series on October 7 at Forbes Field, Traynor was the only Pittsburgh Pirates' player to solve the immortal Walter Johnson. Pie singled in the second and homered in the fifth inning (National Baseball Hall of Fame Library, Cooperstown, New York).

10. Game One to Washington, Game Two to Pittsburgh

appearance at Forbes Field. In contrast, there were very few vacant seats in the $1.10 bleacher section by 11:00 A.M.

Those who arrived at the stadium early seemed to be more lively than the previous day, perhaps because they realized the scope of the game's importance. Nick Altrock and Al Schacht once again entertained the early arrivals with their comedy antics. The weather was expected to be slightly warmer than the previous day, as fans quickly abandoned their overcoats due to the sun's warming rays.[39]

Rookie Bernard Culloton was assigned the task of pitching batting practice against his Pirates teammates. One batter after another drove Culloton's pitches into sections of Forbes Field's stands. As first game starter Lee Meadows warmed up leisurely on the sidelines, he declared that his arm felt good.[40] Prior to the start of the second game, the United States flag was lowered to half mast while players from both teams wore black arm bands on their uniforms and stood in silence. Members of the Pirates and Senators paid tribute to former pitching great Christy Mathewson, who had passed away the previous day.[41]

Christy Mathewson's death came rather unexpectedly on the evening of October 7, 1925, even as the health of the 45-year-old president of the Boston Braves had seemed to be improving. Mathewson had once again gone to a resort at Saranac Lake, New York, in order to fight a relapse of tuberculosis which he originally contracted while stationed in France during World War I. While in Europe, Mathewson inhaled a large quantity of lethal gas, resulting from a department of warfare experiment that went horribly wrong. This occurrence, along with the fact that Mathewson contracted influenza shortly after the failed training exercise, resulted in an affliction with tuberculosis years later. It seemed that Christy was winning his health battle, but Dr. N. Packard, Mathewson's personal physician, stated that pneumonia had developed, contributing to his death.[42]

Mathewson had originally hoped to be present for the World Series games between Pittsburgh and Washington.[43] It seemed somewhat fitting that on the last day of Christy Mathewson's life, Walter Johnson pitched the kind of gem that Matty was known for throughout his career. Mathewson and Johnson, along with Cy Young, had been the game's top pitchers since 1900. Johnson's exceptional performance against Pittsburgh in the first game brought back memories from 20 years ago, when Mathewson dominated Connie Mack's Philadelphia Athletics during the 1905 World Series. A fierce competitor and a respected gentleman, Mathewson was a beloved figure throughout the game. His death figured to cast a pall over the remaining games of the 1925 World Series.[44]

Pirates manager Bill McKechnie chose Vic Aldridge to oppose 20-game winner Stan Coveleski in the second game of the Series. McKechnie was pinning Pittsburgh's hopes on a pitcher who was one of baseball's best during the season's final months. Coveleski was the second right-handed hurler sent to the mound by Bucky Harris, who continued to let star southpaw Dutch Ruether sit in the wings. Harris knew that Pittsburgh had tortured National League lefty pitchers throughout the 1925 season. Like McKechnie, Harris made no changes to his regular batting order for the crucial second game.

Aldridge enjoyed a solid start by retiring the Senators in order during the first inning. Sam Rice was Vic's first victim; the Washington center fielder grounded out to Glenn Wright. Aldridge then struck out Bucky Harris. Goose Goslin connected for a long drive against Aldridge, but it brought only cheers from Pittsburgh's fans as Max Carey hauled in the drive for the third out.

Stan Coveleski made quick work of his Pirates counterparts during the home half of the first frame. Eddie Moore hit a ball to shortstop Roger Peckinpaugh, who gobbled up the slow grounder and threw a perfect strike to first baseman Joe Judge. Carey then struck out as Coveleski threw three perfect spitters near the Pirates' outfielder's knees. Kiki Cuyler made the final out of the inning when he grounded harmlessly to second baseman Bucky Harris.[45]

For the second day in a row, Washington struck first scoring a run after Aldridge argued with an umpire. Washington's Joe Judge slammed an Aldridge curve ball into Forbes Field's right field stands to give the Senators a 1–0 lead. Judge's homer came after home plate umpire Brick Owens called a ball that Aldridge believed was a strike. The questionable call seemed to frazzle Aldridge, as Joe Harris followed Judge by ripping a single to left past Glenn Wright. Harris was then erased on a stolen base attempt, as Earl Smith fired the ball to Eddie Moore to cut down the runner. Manager McKechnie instructed Emil Yde to begin warming up in the bullpen in case Aldridge continued to struggle. Aldridge settled down and retired Ossie Bluege with a second out on a fly ball to left fielder Clyde Barnhart. George Grantham then saved the day for Aldridge when he deftly handled Pie Traynor's wide throw to first on a Roger Peckinpaugh ground ball.[46]

Pittsburgh went quietly during their half of the second inning as Stan Coveleski continued to assert his dominance. Barnhart began the inning by flying out to Sam Rice in center field. As Traynor stepped to the plate, he received a hearty round of cheers for his performance the previous day. Traynor tagged one of Coveleski's offerings down the third base line. Bluege made a sensational play at the hot corner, snagging Pie's drive and throwing to Judge for the second out. Glenn Wright smacked his first safety of the World Series when he drilled a two-out single to right field. He moved up to second base when catcher Muddy Ruel mishandled a Coveleski pitch for a passed ball. Wright then remained at second base when Grantham grounded out to Bucky Harris.[47]

Ruel started out the third inning by striking out on a beautiful drop pitch

Shortstop Glenn Wright solidified his position as one of baseball's youngest stars after only two seasons in the National League. Wright hit .308 in 1925 and led the Pittsburgh Pirates in RBIs with 121. In Game Two of the World Series on October 8 at Forbes Field, Wright hit a critical two-out, solo home run against Stan Coveleski that put Pittsburgh on the board against Washington (National Baseball Hall of Fame Library, Cooperstown, New York).

from Aldridge. The Pittsburgh pitcher also fanned Coveleski. Sam Rice made contact for Washington by lining a two-out single to center field. Rice's speed at first so unnerved Aldridge that the pitcher balked, moving Rice to second base. No further damage was done as Bucky Harris recorded the final out of the stanza by grounding out to Glenn Wright at short.[48]

Earl Smith tried to charge the Pittsburgh crowd by leading off the bottom of the third with a line single to left. Smith was forced at second base on Aldridge's tapper to Coveleski. The Senators should have recorded a double play, but Bucky Harris dropped Coveleski's throw and salvaged only one out when he scrambled to tag Smith. Eddie Moore then struck out by swinging at a Coveleski spitball that bounced in the dirt in front of home plate. Max Carey was able to deliver a two-out hit when his single to right field moved Aldridge into scoring position at second. But no further damage was done. Coveleski retired Carey for the third out after Kiki Cuyler hit a groundball that resulted in a Peckinpaugh-to-Harris forceout.[49]

Vic Aldridge averted potential disaster in the fourth inning when his teammates turned in some of the game's best defensive plays. Wright made a spectacular play on Goose Goslin's seething drive as he handled the hot shot and threw to George Grantham for the inning's first out.[50] Before Goslin was retired, he became involved in an argument when he accused catcher Earl Smith of tipping his bat.[51] Clyde Barnhart then robbed Joe Judge of a hit by making a fine running catch in left field. Pie Traynor nearly pulled off a sensational play the equal of his two teammates when he leapt in the air and barely missed catching Joe Harris' blistering line drive, which glanced off his glove for a single. Kiki Cuyler continued the fine fielding work of McKechnie's Pirates when he hauled in Ossie Bluege's long fly ball to right for the final out.[52]

The Pirates' stellar defensive play during the top half of the fourth seemed to rejuvenate a Pittsburgh crowd that began to clap in unison calling for a Pirates rally. Barnhart led off the inning by hitting a long fly to Rice in center field. Traynor could do little with Coveleski's pitches, as he delivered a groundball to Roger Peckinpaugh. Glenn Wright then stepped to the plate and tied the score at 1–1 when he drove a Coveleski offering into the left field stands, just in front of the scoreboard. The revived crowd continued to cheer as George Grantham made the third out, as catcher Muddy Ruel snatched a foul ball off the hat of a spectator.[53]

Vic Aldridge did not seem strengthened by the Wright home run. Roger Peckinpaugh led off the fifth inning with a single over Wright's head. Ruel followed with a single to center that moved Peckinpaugh to second and prompted Bill McKechnie to start warming up Emil Yde, in the Pirates' bullpen.[54] Aldridge became visibly shaken as he made a bone-headed play on a Coveleski bunt. Aldridge threw to third base even though he had no chance to retire Peckinpaugh.[55] Washington now had the bases loaded with no one out, as Red

Oldham joined Yde in the bullpen. McKechnie's decision to bring his infield in paid dividends when Peckinpaugh was forced at home plate on Sam Rice's ground ball to Aldridge. Ruel was forced for the second out on a Bucky Harris grounder to Wright, who tossed home to Smith. Remarkably, Aldridge worked out of the jam completely when George Grantham made an unassisted play at first base on a Goose Goslin ground ball.[56]

The Senators seemed unfazed by their missed opportunity to break the game wide open. Coveleski recorded the inning's first out when Smith looked at a called third strike. Aldridge was greeted with cheers from Pittsburgh's crowd as he came to plate, but he became easy prey as he was retired on a slow roller to Peckinpaugh at short. Coveleski finished the easy one-two-three inning by retiring Eddie Moore on another ground ball to Peckinpaugh.[57] The score stood at 1–1, as Washington came to bat in the sixth.

Joe Judge nearly gave the Senators a 2–1 lead when he drove an Aldridge pitch just foul into the right field stands. After Judge returned to the batter's box, he smacked a ball that did not have as much distance but was caught by Max Carey. Aldridge induced Joe Harris to lift a fly ball to Carey in center field. Ossie Bluege stepped to the plate but was promptly sent to the ground writhing in pain when an Aldridge fastball smacked the Washington third baseman in the back of his head. Bluege held the injured area tightly with his hands as a doctor rushed onto the field to examine him. After a few minutes, an unsteady Bluege was helped to his feet by teammates and ushered to Washington's clubhouse. Buddy Myer pinch ran for Bluege and was promptly tossed out trying to steal second.[58]

Myer assumed Bluege's position at third base when Washington took the field in the bottom of the sixth inning. Max Carey immediately tested the rookie by dragging a bunt to third, which caught Myer by surprise and allowed Pittsburgh's center fielder to reach first. Kiki Cuyler sacrificed Carey to second, as Coveleski fielded the bunt and retired the Flint Flash by throwing to Bucky Harris covering at first base. Carey moved to third base when Clyde Barnhart was retired on a grounder to Roger Peckinpaugh. Pie Traynor then reached first by working out a walk against Coveleski. Pittsburgh's hopeful inning ended when Traynor was forced at second on Glenn Wright's groundball to Peckinpaugh.[59]

Before Aldridge threw the first pitch of the seventh inning, writers in the press box were informed that Ossie Bluege was not seriously hurt, but was suffering from dizzy spells. In another development, reliever extraordinaire Fred "Firpo" Marberry began warming up in the bullpen as Washington came to bat. Aldridge had a relatively easy inning as he retired Peckinpaugh on a hard groundball smash to Wright, watched Clyde Barnhart chase down Muddy Ruel's line drive for the second out, and induced Coveleski to hit an easy grounder to Pie Traynor.

Coveleski kept the game even at one run apiece when he retired the Pirates without incident in their half of the seventh. Grantham became the first victim after Bucky Harris made quick work of his slow roller. Joe Judge then scooped up Earl Smith's grounder and beat the Pirates' catcher to the bag for the second out. The inning ended when Aldridge popped up to Peckinpaugh at short.[60]

Sam Rice started off the Washington eighth with a leadoff single over second. Bucky Harris pulled off a successful sacrifice when his bunt moved Rice to second, as Grantham threw to Eddie Moore covering first base. After Aldridge broke Goose Goslin's bat on a foul ball, he recorded the second out by handling an easy tapper to the mound. With Rice now perched on third base, Aldridge brought the inning to an end as Joe Judge popped up to second baseman Eddie Moore.[61]

Pittsburgh received a gift from Washington in the bottom of the eighth inning, when Moore was called safe at first base after Roger Peckinpaugh fumbled his groundball.[62] Peckinpaugh was likely unable to handle the ball due to the liberal dose of saliva that pitcher Stan Coveleski had been using.[63] Moore then moved into scoring position when Max Carey grounded out to Bucky Harris at second base. This brought the heavy hitting Kiki Cuyler to the plate. The Pirates' star had been kept under wraps in the Series, with only a harmless single to his credit. Cuyler finally showed the Senators what other National Leaguers had witnessed throughout the season when he crushed a Coveleski offering into the right field stands and gave Pittsburgh a 3–1 lead. The Forbes Field crowd broke into euphoria as Cuyler rounded the bases after his prodigious two-run blast.[64]

The cheers increased when Clyde Barnhart followed Cuyler by banging a single to center field. Peckinpaugh then juggled Pie Traynor's grounder and could not make a play at any base. Coveleski then stiffened, recording the inning's second out when Glenn Wright fouled out to Buddy Myer at third base. Coveleski prevented further damage by retiring George Grantham on a foul out to catcher Muddy Ruel.[65]

The Senators immediately began to work on Aldridge in an attempt to come back. Joe Harris led off the ninth inning with a walk. Bucky Harris, wanting to put more speed on the base paths, brought in Earl McNeely to pinch run for his right fielder. Buddy Myer followed with a single to left field, moving McNeely to second base. Pittsburgh's fans moaned when Aldridge walked Peckinpaugh to load the bases. Harris' decision to pinch hit Bobby Veach for Ruel paid off when the former Detroit Tigers' star lifted a fly ball to Max Carey that brought McNeely home with Washington's second run. Harris then allowed Dutch Ruether, a solid hitting pitcher, to bat for fellow hurler Stan Coveleski. In what could only be described as the most crucial one-on-one battle of the World Series for Pittsburgh, Aldridge struck Ruether out.

Aldridge then stopped Washington's rally, and ended the game, when Sam Rice grounded out to Eddie Moore.[66]

As happy fans filtered out of Forbes Field after Pittsburgh's 3–2 victory, they might have reflected upon the many heroic performances of that sunny afternoon. Vic Aldridge gave a gritty effort as he worked out of numerous jams throughout the game. Aldridge tossed a complete game and allowed only two runs on eight hits. Glenn Wright and Kiki Cuyler were the batting stars, as each man hit crucial homers against Stan Coveleski. Max Carey also chipped in with two hits at the plate and handled numerous chances in center field flawlessly. For Washington, Sam Rice and Joe Harris rapped out two hits apiece.

Pittsburgh owner Barney Dreyfuss once again enjoyed a great day financially as Forbes Field's paid attendance for the second game totaled 43,346, and the gate receipts for the contest topped $185,000.[67] Dreyfuss was certainly ecstatic that the World Series' first two games had resulted in financial success. Yet, he remained an ardent fan who planned on following his beloved Pirates during the World Series.[68] "I love the game," said Dreyfuss. "I like to sit in the grandstand and cheer with the rest; forget all business interests in the club and just yell my head off.

"It seems that all my life I have been a howling fan. Even before I knew what the game was all about there must have been some subconscious spirit that guided me to baseball."[69]

Dreyfuss had joined over 80,000 boisterous fans at Forbes Field during the first two games of the World Series. Citizens of Pittsburgh who normally would have been unable to see the games had benefited from Dreyfuss's decision to expand his ballpark's capacity with both permanent and temporary seating sections. Pittsburgh's fans may have appreciated the additional seating at Forbes Field, but players from both teams were displeased with the stadium layout due to the additional bleachers on the field. Washington's players let it be known emphatically that they did not like Pittsburgh's ballpark. Even Pirates players complained that they were thrown off their game by the new pine bleachers constructed in centerfield.[70]

Forbes Field's layout might have impacted the World Series' first two games, but its influence was minimal compared to what would happen in Washington. Players from the Pirates and Senators would soon discover that the nuances of Washington's Griffith Stadium would affect the game in a most profound way.

11

Washington Grabs Control

The mood in Washington was noticeably different from the atmosphere in Pittsburgh during the first two games of the World Series. One neutral observer from the press corps characterized Pittsburgh's fans as behaving like college freshman during the first two games. As the Pirates and Senators arrived in the Nation's Capital for games Three, Four and Five of the World Series, the atmosphere in Washington seemed more tempered and sedate.[1] Baseball fever was prevalent when Washington and New York played during the 1924 Fall Classic, but the novelty seemed to have worn off for District of Columbia fans.[2] Some of these rooters, who did not know much about Bill McKechnie's Pirates, firmly believed the Washington Senators would win the 1925 World Series without much resistance.

Foul weather put fans throughout Washington in a depressed mood as rain began to fall steadily at about 7:45 A.M. in the morning, just hours before Game Three of the World Series was scheduled to begin. With no letup to the steady drizzle as afternoon approached, Commissioner Kenesaw Mountain Landis walked down to the field at Griffith Stadium to confer with officials of both clubs about game conditions. The umpires advised Landis to postpone the contest since they believed the playing surface would still be in poor shape even if the rain ceased by game time. Landis concurred and made the official announcement at about 1:30 P.M. that the game was cancelled. It was determined that each game in Washington would be pushed back one day, weather permitting.[3]

Many experts believed that the day of idleness would benefit Washington more than Pittsburgh. It gave the Senators' Ossie Bluege another day to recover after being hit in the head by a pitch 24 hours earlier. Pundits also reasoned that an extra day of rest would help veteran pitchers like Walter Johnson and Stan Coveleski.

Pittsburgh manager Bill McKechnie did not agree with the theory that Washington's players alone would benefit from the break in the schedule.[4] He believed a day of rest would rejuvenate his squad, both physically and mentally. "The postponement is just as useful to us, however," said McKechnie. "It gives Vic Aldridge another day and I guess Vic showed about as good pitching yesterday as anybody could want."[5]

Sportswriter Ralph S. Davis of *The Pittsburgh Press* encountered both McKechnie and Max Carey in the lobby of Washington's Wardman Park Hotel, which acted as Pittsburgh's headquarters during their stay in the Capital. McKechnie remained silent when Davis posed the question of which club got the break due to Friday's rain.[6] "It's an even break," interjected Carey. "We will get as much out of the rest as the Senators will."

"Don't you think Washington benefits most because Walter Johnson and Stanley Coveleski are both getting a day of rest they were not counting on?" asked Davis. "And, besides, Bluege will have an extra day in which to recover from that blow on the head."

"I don't think an extra day of rest is going to prevent us from hitting their pitchers in any of the remaining games," Carey retorted.[7]

An idle Friday also gave scribes the opportunity to sit back and reflect on the first two games of the 1925 World Series. One pundit wrote an article in which he stated that first baseman George Grantham represented the weak link of an otherwise sensational Pirates infield. This particular writer had ignored one aspect of Grantham's play. Grantham's hitting may have been weak to date in the Series, but his fielding was absolutely astounding. He had prevented numerous wild throws from becoming errors. Even though Grantham had not played at first base until 1925, he was doing exceptional work during the most important games of the season.[8]

McKechnie's players enjoyed the day off by partaking in various activities. Some of them spent the afternoon watching horse racing at the Laurel Track. Others walked about the city and enjoyed Washington's amenities; others just loafed at the hotel. A number of Pirates who brought their wives on this trip enjoyed a day of sightseeing with their spouses.

Glenn Wright might have been happier than any of his teammates that Friday's game was postponed. An injury might have kept Wright out of the starting lineup if Game Three had been played as scheduled. During a play in which Vic Aldridge balked the previous day, his throw to Wright at second base landed in his glove awkwardly. The ball bent back the middle finger on Wright's left hand to the point that it was severely bruised. A Pittsburgh surgeon lanced the bruised area before the Pirates left for Washington. By Friday, the finger was still stiff, swollen, sore and discolored. Wright expected to play on Saturday and did not believe the injury would affect his batting or fielding since it had occurred to his catching hand.[9]

Even though the weather was not ideal once the sun rose on Saturday, October 10, it had improved sufficiently to the point that Game Three of the

World Series would be played that afternoon. Although the sun was shining, the weather was cold thanks to a blistering wind blowing across the diamond.

Gates for bleacher seats opened at 9:00 A.M. This section, which seated only a few hundred people, was filled almost instantly after the ballpark opened. By 11:00, the crowd had not increased substantially, as cold weather kept Washington's fans from arriving early. By noon, there was little excitement being exhibited outside of the ballpark as idle ushers waited to show customers to their seats. It was evident that the park would not be filled until right before game-time due to the frigid weather.[10]

While the early arrivals at Griffith Stadium sat shivering in their seats, the Pirates' players squeezed in a special appearance before their crucial game against Washington that afternoon. The Pirates were personal guests of President Calvin Coolidge. The Pittsburgh aggregation was driven to the White House at noon in special automobiles; the players met Coolidge at his office in the rear of the executive mansion. Wives and other female relatives who joined the Pirates' players and management on the road trip were not permitted to meet the President. They were forced to wait outside because of rules in place that forbade them from accompanying Pittsburgh's players.[11]

President Coolidge officially received president Barney Dreyfuss, vice-president Fred Clarke, secretary Sam Watters, treasurer Sam Dreyfuss, manager Bill McKechnie, his son Billy, Jr. and all of the players and Pittsburgh newspaper correspondents. Former Pennsylvania Congressman James F. Burke introduced Dreyfuss and McKechnie. In turn, Pittsburgh's manager introduced each of the Pirates players one by one. President Coolidge then chatted for a few moments with the leaders of Pittsburgh's entourage.[12] Mr. Coolidge was an avid baseball fan who attended many games at Griffith Stadium in person. When the meeting ended, Dreyfuss and his charges hustled off to Washington's ballpark so that they could prepare for Game Three of the World Series. President Coolidge and his wife would also attend the game, in addition to throwing out the game's ceremonial first pitch.[13]

As soon as President Coolidge and his wife arrived, a band played the "Star Spangled Banner." When the band finished, a bugler appeared behind home plate and played "Taps" in memory of Christy Mathewson. The flag was then lowered to half mast, as the band played "Nearer, My God, to Thee."[14] During pre-game festivities, the house band played "Tessie" in honor of the Pirates. This tune had been the fight song of the Boston Americans during the first World Series in 1903. A group known as the Royal Rooters sang the song in both Pittsburgh and Boston. Hearing the song again may have distracted former Pirates manager Fred Clarke, who remembered how the tune helped derail his team's concentration during the 1903 Fall Classic.[15]

Home plate umpire Barry McCormick prepared to catch the ceremonial first pitch from President Calvin Coolidge. Hundreds of cameras were fixated on McCormick as Mr. Coolidge did his best imitation of Walter Johnson. The umpire was ready to catch the ball, but a fan ran out in front of him, snagged the baseball, and ran away with the prized possession.[16]

Bill McKechnie decided to put his faith in Ray Kremer as Pittsburgh's Game Three pitcher. Bucky Harris countered with Alex Ferguson, who had done fine work for Washington since being acquired from the New York Yankees in August. The only change made to either lineup was the addition of Buddy Myer as a replacement for Ossie Bluege, who was still feeling the effects of a bean ball from two days earlier.

Ferguson exhibited wildness in the first inning, when he walked Eddie Moore on four straight pitches. Ferguson had a two-ball, two-strike count on Max Carey before he plunked the outfielder in the ribs with a pitch. Kiki Cuyler recorded the inning's first out when his fly ball to left was corralled by Goose Goslin, although gale-force wind nearly blew it over his head. Ferguson worked out of the jam when he induced Clyde Barnhart to hit a ground ball to shortstop that was turned into a Peckinpaugh-to-Harris-to-Judge double play.[17]

Ray Kremer wasted no time retiring Washington's first batter as Sam Rice swung at the first pitch and grounded out to Pie Traynor. Bucky Harris also took a swing at Kremer's first offering and hit a foul ball. Harris then fouled off four more pitches before he flied out to Carey in center field. Goose Goslin then became the Senators' first base runner of the game, hustling all the way to second base when Pirates catcher Earl Smith mishandled strike three and allowed the ball to roll to the grandstand. Smith argued with Umpire Barry McCormick, claiming that Goslin fouled off the pitch. Smith lost his argument and Joe Judge was ordered to take his turn at bat. After Kremer tossed a ball and a strike to Judge, the other umpires notified McCormick that he had erred in allowing Goslin to take second base on Smith's passed ball. Goslin returned to first, and Judge became Washington's third out when he popped up to first baseman George Grantham.[18]

Pittsburgh received a break in the top of the second inning when Pie Traynor led off with a triple after outfielder Joe Harris just missed making a shoestring catch of his drive to right field. The Pirates grabbed an early 1–0 lead when Glenn Wright drove Traynor across home plate with a sacrifice fly to Goslin. Roger Peckinpaugh made a great play to record the second out, racing to the foul line and snagging Grantham's fly. Ferguson ended the inning with a Smith pop-up to Peckinpaugh.

Kremer worked out of a slight jam in the second as Washington stranded two runners. Joe Harris led off by striking out. Buddy Myer's liner deflected off Kremer and bounded to Eddie Moore, whose throw to first nipped the Washington third baseman. Peckinpaugh reached second base when Max Carey muffed Roger's routine fly ball to center field. Washington's two-out lightning continued when Muddy Ruel worked out a walk, but the inning came to an end when Kremer struck out his mound nemesis, Alex Ferguson.[19]

Ferguson made quick work of the Pirates in the third inning. Ray Kremer led off the frame by striking out, Eddie Moore fouled out to Ruel and Carey made the third out when he bunted to Ruel, who tossed to Joe Judge.

Sam Rice started off Washington's half of the third by lining a two-ball, one-strike pitch to center field for a single. Bucky Harris successfully sacrificed Rice to second, as his bunt was handled by Kremer, who then tossed to Moore covering first.[20]

With a runner on second and one out, Bill McKechnie called for Red Oldham to begin warming up in Pittsburgh's bullpen. Kremer settled down and recorded the second out as Goose Goslin's fly ball to Kiki Cuyler in right field moved Rice to third base. Washington tied the contest on Judge's double to right field, which scored Rice. Joe Harris followed Judge's double by smacking a groundball to Glenn Wright, whose throw to first pulled George Grantham off the base. Grantham kept his composure as Judge tore around third base toward home plate; he made an accurate throw to Earl Smith, who tagged Judge for the stanza's final out.[21]

Pittsburgh struck back quickly against Alex Ferguson in the fourth inning. Kiki Cuyler drove Ferguson's third pitch into center field for a double. Clyde Barnhart lined Ferguson's first offering to left field for a single, scoring Cuyler and giving Pittsburgh a 2–1 lead, with Barnhart taking second base on Goslin's throw to home plate. Firpo Marberry began warming up in Washington's bullpen in case Ferguson continued to falter. Ferguson's struggles persisted when Pie Traynor worked out a walk against the right-hander. Both runners moved up a base when Glenn Wright hit a grounder to shortstop Roger Peckinpaugh. Grantham then popped up to Joe Judge for the second out. Ferguson loaded the bases by intentionally walking Smith before ending Pittsburgh's threat when he fanned Ray Kremer.[22]

Washington immediately went to work during the home half of the fourth. Buddy Myer began the inning by working out a walk against Kremer. Wright then made a sensational play when he went to the grass at deep short, picked Peckinpaugh's sharp grounder, and threw to second base to force Myer. Peckinpaugh quickly became Washington's second out when he was cut down by Smith attempting to steal second. Muddy Ruel then worked the count to three balls and two strikes before he hit a fly ball to Clyde Barnhart for the final out.[23]

Eddie Moore started out the top of the fifth inning by striking out. Max Carey followed with a clean hit over second base.[24] When Carey reached first, he noticed that center fielder Sam Rice momentarily held on to the ball as no one covered second. Carey continued running toward second and reached safety when Rice's eventual throw to second came in late.[25] Buddy Myer made a sensational stop of Kiki Cuyler's smash down the third base line and tossed to Joe Judge for the second out. Carey moved to third base on Cuyler's out and remained there when Clyde Barnhart fouled out to Judge.[26]

Washington failed to do anything against Ray Kremer in the bottom of the fifth inning. Alex Ferguson fanned for Washington's first out. Rice reached first base on a single by beating out a slow tapper to Pie Traynor at third base. Rice became the second half of a nifty Pittsburgh double play when Bucky Harris hit a liner to Eddie Moore, who doubled the runner off first.[27]

Rice kept Pittsburgh's lead at one run in the sixth, making a spectacular catch on Traynor's deep drive to center field by reaching over the low fence and grabbing the smash. Glenn Wright reached first base on an error by Roger Peckinpaugh, as Joe Judge could not handle the shortstop's low throw. Ferguson then recorded the second out by fanning George Grantham. Earl Smith kept the inning alive when his single to right field moved Wright over to third. Ray Kremer hit a seemingly harmless grounder that took an odd bounce past Bucky Harris; the run-scoring single gave Pittsburgh a 3–1 lead and sent Smith to second base. Eddie Moore's walk loaded the bases, as Firpo Marberry once again began warming up in Washington's bullpen. Ferguson was able to work out of a potentially disastrous jam when he struck out Max Carey to end the inning, with Judge getting the putout after Ruel mishandled the pitch.[28]

Washington immediately retrieved that run in their half of the sixth inning. Goose Goslin led off the frame by smashing one of Kremer's offerings on a line into center, the ball bouncing into the bleachers for a home run. As Senators fans throughout Griffith Stadium continued to cheer Goslin's blast, Carey hauled in Judge's long drive by lunging at the last minute after initially misjudging the smash due to the swirling winds.[29] The wind had wreaked havoc throughout the day as outfielders from both teams struggled on fly balls. Carey had already dropped an easy fly ball and Goslin had fallen over while snagging a wind-blown ball.[30]

Joe Harris became the third consecutive Washington player to hit Kremer hard when he drilled a single to center field. Bill McKechnie quickly sent Red Oldham and Tom Sheehan to the Pirates' bullpen to begin loosening up. Kremer then settled down and struck out Buddy Myer. Roger Peckinpaugh followed with a blistering single to left that moved Harris to second. Kremer finally brought the inning to an end when Muddy Ruel grounded to Pie Traynor, who forced Harris at third base for the frame's final out.[31]

The blustery wind and chilly conditions continued as Game Three entered the seventh inning, with Pittsburgh leading by a score of 3–2. On the field, base umpires Cy Rigler and Brick Owens kept warm because their positioning allowed them to stand where the sun was shining. First base umpire George Moriarty was not so lucky, as chilly winds from the grandstand shade whipped down on him. Home plate umpire Barry McCormick tried to stay warm throughout the afternoon by arguing balls and strikes with Pittsburgh catcher Earl Smith.[32]

Alex Ferguson retired Pittsburgh in order in the seventh inning. Kiki Cuyler was retired on a grounder to Peckinpaugh, Goslin made a sensational running catch of Clyde Barnhart's long fly to left and Pie Traynor popped out to second baseman Bucky Harris.[33]

Nemo Leibold made his first appearance in the 1925 World Series when he batted for Ferguson in the bottom of the seventh. Leibold showed great patience, drawing a walk against Ray Kremer. Bucky Harris brought in Earl McNeely to pinch run for Leibold. Kremer then recorded the first out when Sam Rice's long drive was snagged by Clyde Barnhart near the foul line. Earl Smith made an egregious mistake with Bucky Harris at the plate. He grabbed the Washington second baseman's slow roller along the third base line even though the ball appeared to be rolling foul. Harris easily beat Smith's throw to first as McNeely moved down to second.[34] Goose Goslin took a healthy cut at a Kremer curve ball near his neck and drove a long foul into the left field upper deck; this prompted the Pittsburgh infielders to play deep against Goslin. The Washington star then surprised everyone on the Pirates when he laid down a bunt and motored to first base uncontested. Bucky Harris' heady decision allowed Washington to load the bases with one out.[35]

Washington tied the game at three runs apiece when Joe Judge hit a sacrifice fly to Max Carey, scoring McNeely. With runners now at first and second with two out, Joe Harris followed with a single to left field that brought Bucky Harris home from second base, giving Washington a 4–3 lead. The Senators' rally finally ended when Buddy Myer topped a ball near home plate that hit him in fair territory outside of the batter's box.

Firpo Marberry took the mound for Washington in the eighth inning as McNeely stayed in the game to play center field and Rice moved over to right. Marberry showed why he was the American League's top fireman by striking out Glenn Wright and George Grantham to start the inning.[36]

Pittsburgh catcher Earl Smith stepped to the plate with two outs. After watching his two teammates come up empty against Marberry's offerings, Smith realized that he needed to make a conscientious effort to put the ball in play. Marberry delivered a pitch to Smith's liking, and Pittsburgh's catcher drove the ball to deep right-center field. Right fielder Sam Rice immediately turned with the crack of the bat and chased Smith's prodigious drive. When Rice leaped into the temporary stands in an effort to catch what seemed to be a game-tying home run for Pittsburgh, he forever linked himself with Smith in the annals of baseball history. Rice tumbled into the crowd and disappeared for a brief moment; everyone in the stadium wondered if he caught the ball. Rice eventually emerged from the crowd with the ball in his glove. Bill McKechnie and his players immediately protested to the umpires that Rice had not made the catch and that Smith should be awarded a home run. Second base umpire Cy Rigler ruled that Rice had indeed made the catch, thereby ending the eighth inning.[37]

Pittsburgh's arguments over Rice's alleged catch fell on deaf ears as Washington came to bat in the eighth. Roger Peckinpaugh was retired on a groundball to Pie Traynor at third. Muddy Ruel then followed by lining a single to left field. Marberry came to the plate and executed a perfect sacrifice bunt to Kremer, which moved Ruel to second.[38] Marberry's play was well executed, with the exception of one detail. It was not his turn to bat. McNeely had stayed in the game after pinch running in the seventh and was now listed in the batting order as the ninth hitter, while Marberry had been placed in the lineup's fifth spot. So rattled over the decision regarding Rice's catch of Smith's fly ball the Pirates failed to notice Marberry batting out of turn. If Bill McKechnie or Fred Clarke were paying attention, Marberry would have been retired for batting out of order with Ruel being forced to return to first base. Frantic Pittsburgh writers in the press box tried to call McKechnie's attention to the oversight, but they were unable to reach him until after Rice grounded to Wright for the final out.[39]

On October 10, Washington Senators outfielder Sam Rice made a controversial catch during the eighth inning in Game Three of the 1925 World Series at Griffith Stadium. Pittsburgh's Earl Smith hit a drive that Rice allegedly caught as he tumbled into temporary bleacher seats. Umpire Cy Rigler ruled the catch was legitimate. Bill McKechnie argued the blast should have been ruled a home run since he believed Rice did not catch the ball cleanly (National Baseball Hall of Fame Library, Cooperstown, New York).

Pittsburgh battled gallantly against Marberry. Carson Bigbee batted for Kremer and flied out to McNeely in center field. Eddie Moore followed Bigbee's out with a sharp single to center field. The game was then delayed for a few minutes when fans jumped over a low outfield fence onto the field. When play resumed after the fans were forced to return to their seats, Max Carey slammed a Marberry offering to right that sent Moore scampering to third. Marberry showed signs of imploding when he struck Kiki Cuyler with a pitch, loading the bases for Pittsburgh. Marberry then toughened, retiring Clyde Barnhart on a pop-up out to Ruel. Pie Traynor seemed destined to receive a game-tying walk when he watched Marberry's first three pitches glide by for balls, but he then took two quick strikes before lofting a fly ball to McNeely in center field that ended the game.[40]

Firpo Marberry pitched two courageous innings of relief and earned the save in Washington's tight 4–3 victory. Bucky Harris had not been certain if he would be able to count on his star relief pitcher due to an arm injury he suffered against Chicago on August 30. Initially, Marberry was slow to respond to treatment. A session with Bonesetter Reese of Youngstown, Ohio, worked wonders for Marberry's ailing arm and allowed him to make three late-season relief appearances.[41]

Joining Marberry as stars of the game were Sam Rice, Goose Goslin and Joe Harris, who each connected for two hits against Ray Kremer. Rice was the game's defensive standout based on his controversial catch of Earl Smith's potential home run. Max Carey was the only Pirate who did much damage against Washington pitching, as he went 2-for-4. Despite the cold weather, 36,495 fans attended the game at Griffith Stadium as Game Three netted gate receipts totaling over $146,000.[42]

Shortly after the game ended, Pittsburgh manager Bill McKechnie hunted down Commissioner Landis in order to consult with the czar about the procedure for filing a protest.[43] McKechnie believed that umpire Cy Rigler had erred in calling Earl Smith out in the eighth inning of the third game. Landis told the Pirates' manager that no protest could be lodged without the facts of the case being presented. McKechnie believed the testimony of two Pittsburgh fans who were sitting in the bleacher section would back his claim. R. J. Asham of Altoona, Pennsylvania, and Sergeant Ralph Lewis, a former Pittsburgh resident who now was an engineering sergeant attached to the United States Army barracks in Washington, backed McKechnie's story. Both men testified that Rice failed to catch the ball, and that a small boy who was sitting in the bleachers actually handed the baseball to him.[44]

McKechnie also believed that Rigler could not positively determine if Rice had made the catch since the outfielder's back was turned toward the field, blocking the umpire's view of what happened.[45] Rice made two statements to the press regarding his catch of Smith's fly ball. After the ballgame, Rice said that Rigler was correct in calling Smith out because he had fairly caught the baseball. Later on that evening, Rice altered his story a bit by claiming he held the ball momentarily before a fan grabbed it out of his glove. The ball was only returned to Rice after he begged the fan for several moments to give it back. Pirates fans who believed Smith was cheated out of a home run were not buying this explanation. They believed if Rice had made such a sensational catch, his first reaction would have been to raise his arm, holding the ball to show the umpires he had caught the baseball. Instead, Rice climbed out of the crowd slowly and threw the ball in disgust to Earl McNeely.[46]

These same diehard Pirates rooters also felt that Rice was aided by partisan Washington patrons who handed him the ball. If Rice had made such a spectacular circus catch, why didn't the fans jump to their feet and scream their approval over such a breathtaking play?[47] After the game ended it seemed McKechnie had a very plausible case if he filed a protest, but the manager had a change of heart and decided to withdraw his complaint. McKechnie thought the matter over and decided not to pursue the issue any further.[48] "We lost the game by not hitting in the pinches," said the Buccaneers' boss, "so we will take our medicine."[49]

McKechnie's decision to drop the matter was surprising given that he was devoted to filing this protest only hours earlier. Many people close to the Pittsburgh situation believed McKechnie had sufficient evidence to support his contention that Sam Rice did not catch the fly ball. Shortly after McKechnie announced that he decided not to pursue this matter, it was reported that Pittsburgh owner Barney Dreyfuss had vetoed his manager's plan to protest the third game of the World Series.[50] Dreyfuss believed that not pursuing this potential protest was the honorable thing to do. "We will take our medicine like men," the Pittsburgh owner told his manager.[51]

Barney Dreyfuss's words certainly rang true as his Pirates team prepared to play Washington in Game Four of the World Series on Sunday, October 11. Due to the fact that rain had postponed Friday's game, Pittsburgh would be facing Walter Johnson during the engagement on the Sabbath. Bucky Harris, looking to gain a huge advantage in the Series, was now able to pitch Johnson in the fourth game thanks to weather interrupting the proceedings two days earlier. Bill McKechnie decided to use his fourth different pitcher of the Series when he chose southpaw Emil Yde to oppose Johnson. The Pirates' manager also made one other change to his lineup, plugging Johnny Gooch in place of Earl Smith behind the plate.

Harris reconstructed Washington's lineup a bit since his squad was facing a southpaw hurler for the first time during the World Series. Harris' new batting order went as follows: 1. Sam Rice (CF), 2. Bucky Harris (2B), 3. Goose Goslin (LF), 4. Joe Harris (RF), 5. Joe Judge (1B), 6. Roger Peckinpaugh (SS), 7. Muddy Ruel (C), 8. Buddy Myer (3B) and 9. Walter Johnson (P). Senators star third baseman Ossie Bluege was shelved for the second consecutive game due to being hit in the head with a pitched ball in Game Two. Bluege planned on watching the game from Washington's dugout in street clothes. Even though Ossie was progressing rather nicely, physicians chose to be cautious with his injury since they feared he might have a slight concussion.[52]

The Washington crowd cheered loudly as Walter Johnson threw his warm-up tosses before the game. When Eddie Moore stepped in to lead off the first inning, Johnson got right to work and retired Pittsburgh's second baseman on a fly out to Sam Rice in center field. Max Carey had better luck against the "Big Train," working out a walk. Pittsburgh seemed to have something going when Kiki Cuyler connected against a Johnson offering and sent a drive toward second baseman Bucky Harris. The Washington second baseman robbed Cuyler of a single, snagging the Flint Flash's hot smash and throwing to first baseman Joe Judge while Carey moved to second. But the inning ended when Johnson struck out Clyde Barnhart.[53]

Emil Yde enjoyed a good start when he retired Rice on a groundball to Glenn Wright. After Yde issued back-to-back walks to Bucky Harris and Goose Goslin, Bill McKechnie became concerned and sent Johnny Morrison to the bullpen to warm up. Yde's early problems ended quickly when Joe Harris grounded into a double play.

Traynor quickly jumped up to the plate in the second frame and recorded Pittsburgh's first hit when third baseman Buddy Myer could not handle Pie's hot smash. Glenn Wright then forced Traynor at second for the first out on a grounder to Roger Peckinpaugh. Grantham moved Wright to second when he beat out a hard, high bounding ball to third for an infield hit. Both runners moved up a base when Peckinpaugh easily handled Johnny Gooch's grounder for the second out. Walter Johnson averted any further issues when Bucky Harris handled Yde's groundball and threw to Judge for the final out.[54]

Judge was easy prey for Yde in the bottom of the second, as the Washington first baseman led off by hitting a weak pop-up to Wright at short. Traynor made a terrific play on Peckinpaugh's difficult roller to third and whipped a throw that narrowly beat the runner to first base. Muddy Ruel prevented a routine inning for Yde when he drilled a single past Wright into the outfield. Despite Ruel's two-out hit, Yde seemed to be settling down and had gained command of his curve ball after a shaky first inning. Yde ended the frame when he fanned Buddy Myer on a called third strike.

Johnson matched Yde's efficiency when he retired the Pirates in order in the third inning. Goose Goslin ran gracefully as he snatched Moore's liner to left for the first out. Max Carey followed by lifting a fly ball to Joe Harris for the second out. Bucky Harris once again robbed Kiki Cuyler of a hit when he fell over while handling the Flint Flash's hot smash and recovered just in time to nip him at first.[55]

Johnson tried to help his own cause during the bottom of the third inning when he led off with a long drive to left that dropped for a hit. But Johnson mistakenly attempted to stretch his blast into a double and was thrown out at second, Barnhart to Wright.[56] As Johnson paused for a moment at second base before hustling off the field, most of the fans were not aware that Johnson had aggravated a previous injury to his thigh and would need to have the area heavily taped so that he could continue pitching.[57] Sam Rice followed by reaching first base on a single when Eddie Moore knocked down his hot smash but could not make a throw to first. The Pirates blew an easy chance to record an out when Wright dropped George Grantham's throw after he fielded Bucky Harris' grounder.[58] Wright's gaffe left runners on first and second with only one out.

Goose Goslin wasted no time giving the local fans something to cheer about, as he drove a Yde offering deep to left field that grazed Clyde Barnhart's fingertips before bounding into the left field stands for a three-run homer. Goslin's clout not only gave Washington its first lead of the game, but it also propelled him to the top of the list for career World Series home runs with five. Goslin slipped past Babe Ruth, who had hit four during three World Series, by crushing his fifth round tripper in two Fall Classics. Things worsened for Yde as Joe Harris followed Goslin's homer by blasting a four-bagger of his own into the same left field stands.[59] In response, Johnny Morrison hurriedly tried to get loose in Pittsburgh's bullpen for the second time in three innings. Visibly shaken, Yde walked Joe Judge and nearly hit the Washington first baseman with ball four. After receiving instructions from McKechnie, Pie Traynor went to the mound to inform Yde his day was over, with Morrison coming in from the bullpen.[60]

Morrison received a break when Judge was thrown out trying to steal, Gooch to Moore. Roger Peckinpaugh then greeted Morrison by singling past Traynor to left. Washington's shortstop had better luck than Judge, as he promptly pilfered second base on a delayed steal. Muddy Ruel walked before Morrison finally ended the inning when Washington's catcher was forced at second on a grounder by Buddy Myer. The Senators now held a 4–0 lead, having sent every man to the plate in the third inning.

Walter Johnson took the hill in the fourth and used his change of pace to retire Pittsburgh in order. Clyde Barnhart clubbed a towering foul ball that Ruel handled with relative ease. Johnson snagged Traynor's bunt and threw him out for the second out. Johnson retired the side when Bucky Harris snatched Glenn Wright's slow roller and tossed to Judge at first base.[61]

Johnny Morrison showed Bill McKechnie that he could subdue Washington. Johnson made the first out when he looked at a called third strike. Sam Rice recorded his second hit of the game when he reached first base after Traynor knocked down his blistering drive. Bucky Harris came to the plate and signaled to Rice that a hit-and-run play was on. As Rice took off for second, Harris swung under one of Morrison's offerings and flied out to left fielder Clyde Barnhart. As Barnhart hauled in Harris' drive, Rice scampered back to first base. Morrison quickly brought Washington's inning to an end when he caught Goslin looking on a strikeout.[62]

Grantham started off the fifth inning by fouling out to Ruel, who hardly needed to move as he snagged George's pop-up. Walter Johnson made quick work of Johnny Gooch, retiring him on a fly ball to Goslin. Morrison made it a quick inning when he was retired on a short fly to Rice in center field.

Morrison showed why he was more proficient on the mound than at the plate when he struck out Joe Harris to start Washington's half of the fifth inning. Gooch, who could not cleanly handle Morrison's strike three pitch, grabbed the ball and threw to Grantham to retire Harris. Pittsburgh's pitcher became directly involved in recording the second out when he handled Joe Judge's hot smash to the mound and threw to first. Morrison kept up his stellar work when he fanned Roger Peckinpaugh. Morrison was pitching effectively by keeping the Senators off stride, mixing in his devastating curve with his fastball.[63]

Walter Johnson continued his masterful performance against the Pirates in the sixth inning. Eddie Moore led off by flying out to Goslin in left field. Max Carey came to the plate and placed a perfect bunt in the direction of first baseman Joe Judge, who could not beat him to the bag. Carey then stole second as Kiki Cuyler looked at a called third strike. Clyde Barnhart continued his struggles, hitting a towering pop-up that catcher Muddy Ruel chased down near the third base bag.

Ruel then came to the plate to lead off Washington's half of the sixth and promptly singled sharply over Pie Traynor's head. Buddy Myer attempted to bunt Ruel over to second, but failed when he popped up to Grantham. Gooch then handled Johnson's roller, but was late getting Ruel at second. Glenn Wright, making a heady play, fired a throw to first that beat the slow-footed Johnson. Rice made the inning's final out when he was retired on a grounder to second baseman Eddie Moore.[64]

Pie Traynor started the top of the seventh by ripping a sizzling single past second baseman Bucky Harris, recording his second hit of the game. Wright followed with another sharp line drive that seemed destined to land safely in the outfield until Harris jumped in the air and snared the smash. Harris then whirled around and threw to Joe Judge at first base to double up Traynor.[65] Instead of having two runners on base, the Pirates were now one out away from the end of the inning. Harris' play became more significant when George Grantham followed Wright by reaching on an infield hit off Judge's glove. The potential rally then ended when Gooch popped up to Harris.[66]

Harris continued to torment the Pirates as he led off Washington's half of the seventh by rapping a single to left field. Goose Goslin followed by lifting a "Texas Leaguer" in back of second base, putting runners at first and second. Joe Harris then crushed a Morrison offering that appeared headed for the bleacher fence. At the last moment, Barnhart leapt in the air and caught the drive before it left the park. Judge then hit a grounder to Grantham that forced Goslin at second, as Bucky Harris moved to third. The Senators decided to maneuver a double steal with two outs and Roger Peckinpaugh at the plate.

Johnny Morrison threw behind Judge at first base as he took off for second. Grantham then fired the ball to catcher Johnny Gooch, who tagged Bucky Harris attempting to score.[67] Umpire George Moriarty called Harris out even though many in the press box believed that he easily beat the throw. The crowd jeered Moriarty for several minutes while Bucky Harris argued with the arbiter, but the call stood, ending the inning.[68]

Regardless of the call, the Senators realized that four runs were likely sufficient support for Walter Johnson on this day.[69] The "Big Train" continued his dominance when he retired Carson Bigbee, who pinch hit for Morrison. Bigbee could muster nothing more than a weak pop-up to Harris at second. Eddie Moore followed by looping a single to center field, but he remained at first base as Max Carey was retired on another pop-up to Bucky Harris, and Kiki Cuyler flied out to Joe Harris in right field.[70]

Washington's Walter Johnson won his second game of the 1925 World Series when he defeated the Pittsburgh Pirates by a score of 4–0 in Game Four at Griffith Stadium on October 11. Johnson's victory pushed the Senators within one game of clinching their second consecutive world championship, as the Series now stood, 3–1, in favor of Washington (National Baseball Hall of Fame Library, Cooperstown, New York).

A big cheer cascaded from the Washington crowd as veteran hurler and 1909 World Series hero Babe Adams took the mound to pitch the bottom of the eighth inning.[71] Adams quickly retired the first batter when Roger Peckinpaugh's roller to third was gobbled up by Pie Traynor. Muddy Ruel then followed with a double down the left field line, his third hit of the game. Ruel moved over to third base after Buddy Myer beat out a slow bouncer to George Grantham, who could not make a throw to first because Adams failed to cover the bag.[72] Bucky Harris decided to play the percentages and put the squeeze play on, mostly because he believed Walter Johnson was a prime candidate to hit into a double play. This idea was foiled when Johnson bunted the ball too softly; Gooch picked up the ball and waited for Ruel to come barreling into the plate. Not satisfied with a mere tag, Gooch smacked Ruel with the ball as he tore toward the plate.[73] Myer moved to third on the play while Johnson occupied first. The inning ended when Johnson was forced at second on Sam Rice's groundball to shortstop Glenn Wright.[74]

The Pirates offered no resistance against Walter Johnson in the ninth. Clyde Barnhart led off by drawing a walk against the Washington star. Barnhart was quickly eliminated on the base paths when the Senators pulled off their second double play of the day. Bucky Harris snatched Pie Traynor's sharp groundball, tagged Barnhart as he was running to second base, and completed the play by making a perfect throw to Joe Judge. Glenn Wright then made the final out of the game when he was retired on an easy grounder to Harris.[75]

Washington's four-run third inning was all that Walter Johnson needed as he tossed a complete game shutout and put the Senators one win away from a world championship. Although Johnson was not as overpowering as he had been in Game One, he still found a way to keep Pittsburgh off balance throughout the Senators' 4–0 victory. Thus far, Johnson had allowed only one Pittsburgh runner to cross home plate during the 1925 World Series.

Washington's Muddy Ruel, Sam Rice and Goose Goslin emerged as the batting stars of the day. Ruel went 3-for-3 while Rice and Goslin rapped out two hits apiece. Goslin's three-run home run in the third inning proved to be the game's decisive blow. For the Pirates, Pie Traynor and George Grantham recorded two harmless singles apiece against Johnson. While Johnson was the game's pitching star, Washington's Bucky Harris won top honors on the field for his stellar play around the keystone. Harris handled 13 chances and tied a World Series fielding record originally set by Pittsburgh's Claude Ritchey during the 1903 Fall Classic against the Boston Americans. Harris accepted six putouts and recorded seven assists, with two of his chances starting double plays for the Senators.[76]

Pittsburgh faced a major roadblock as Washington celebrated its 3–1 lead in the World Series. Because previous Pirates teams had been accused of crumbling under pennant pressure, some observers believed Bill McKechnie's brigade was following the same pattern. With the Pittsburgh franchise's reputation at stake, the Pirates needed some heroes of their own to step forward and completely reverse Series fortunes.

12

Pittsburgh Battles Back

The Pirates faced daunting work as they prepared to play Game Five of the 1925 World Series. No team had ever come back from a three-games-to-one deficit since the Fall Classic was instituted in 1903. Throughout America, most fans believed Washington would repeat as world champions. Washington merely had to win one out of three games. Even if the Pirates were able to rally and tie the Series, they were still looking at the prospect of facing Walter Johnson in a seventh game.

Bill McKechnie's players were not ready to concede the Series. McKechnie's players seemed confident that they would win three consecutive games and capture the 1925 World's Series.[1] "We've done it before," said Pie Traynor on the morning of the fifth game, "and we can do it again."[2]

One hour after Washington defeated Pittsburgh on Sunday, Fred Clarke went to work trying to maintain the spirits of Pirate players.[3] The former Pirates manager had served capably throughout the Series in his role as an assistant to McKechnie. Clarke served as strategist, cheerleader and morale officer. Clarke told the Pirates they were bound to start hitting in Game Five. He reasoned that such a powerful hitting aggregation could not be throttled much longer.[4] "Our fault so far has been that we haven't done any consecutive hitting," said Clarke. "If three or four of our fellows in a row get to delivering with the willow, I have an idea that we'll make trouble yet."[5]

Aside from the Pirates' hitting deficiencies, Pittsburgh's pitchers had done solid work and might have been rewarded for their efforts if only McKechnie's players had hit with their regular season efficiency. The only Pittsburgh hurler who had not pitched well was southpaw Emil Yde. The list of Pirates' offenders at the plate was much longer. Max Carey, Pie Traynor and Earl Smith were the only Pirates who were striking the ball with characteristic authority. Pittsburgh's young players seemed out of sync; Eddie Moore (2-for-15), Hazen Cuyler (3-for-15), Clyde Barnhart (3-for-16), Glenn Wright (2-for-15) and George Grantham (2-for-14) had all struggled with the bat during the 1925 World Series.

For Pittsburgh to have any chance in Game Five, Bill McKechnie needed these cogs to start producing. McKechnie certainly did not need a distraction that could have an adverse effect on his squad's preparation for Game Five. Yet, that's what McKechnie and his Pirates faced because of a New York newspaper correspondent. The writer in question circulated a story stating that veteran outfielder Max Carey would be traded to Chicago during the winter so that he could become the Cubs' new manager. The tale was pure folly, but factuality did not matter if the story interfered with Carey's mindset.

Max quickly put an end to the rumor as he struck down the story's validity.[6] "I know absolutely nothing about it," said Carey. "I have never been approached with any proposition to manage the Cubs, and naturally have never given the idea a moment's thought. I am entirely satisfied where I am, and have no intention of changing my relations with the Pittsburgh club, unless a change is forced upon me."[7]

The Pirates were not the only entity connected to far-fetched rumors, as writers throughout the country continued to promote news making rumors. The Senators also became involved in an odd rumor that contended Goose Goslin and Roger Peckinpaugh would be sold to the Boston Red Sox for $225,000. On the day that his Senators took a 3-to-1 lead in the Series, owner Clark Griffith denied that the story contained any truth whatsoever.[8] "The whole story is ridiculous to the extreme," said Griffith. "There isn't a chance for the players mentioned to play anywhere but in Washington. I am becoming tired of rumors. Whoever is starting them must be crazy."[9]

Writers sometimes made up such stories so that they would look like privileged members of a team's inner circle. Action on the diamond usually remedied these baseless tales. Unfortunately, the weather was gloomy as Senators fans poured into Griffith Stadium for the last time in 1925. Low clouds indicated rain, giving the day a drab and dreary feel. Still, Game Five, scheduled for Monday, October 12, was expected to be a festive affair, with the ballpark filled by people who had a holiday from work due to Columbus Day.[10]

Griffith Stadium was packed with important government officials who took the afternoon off in the hopes of watching the Washington Senators claim their second consecutive world championship. Several cabinet members also sat in boxes near the field. Secretary of Labor James J. Davis and his wife, both natives of Pittsburgh, were part of the cabinet contingent in attendance. President Calvin Coolidge once again was on hand, sitting in his presidential box behind the Senators' dugout. Pennsylvania Congressman Guy Campbell also occupied a box seat nearby. When the Pirates came on the field at 1:00 P.M. for batting practice, the band entertaining early arrivals at Griffith Stadium struck up "Tessie" once again. After Pittsburgh took the field for practice, New York Giants manager John McGraw strolled over to the Pirates' bench in order to have an intense conversation with Bill McKechnie.[11]

12. Pittsburgh Battles Back   181

The reasons for McGraw's presence in Pittsburgh's dugout was two-fold. As an emissary who represented the National League, McGraw wanted Pittsburgh to defeat Washington and protect the league's good name. He gave encouragement to Pittsburgh's players.[12] McGraw also made a suggestion regarding the Pittsburgh lineup that involved a player whom he had competed against in the Fall Classics of 1911 and 1913. McGraw urged Bill McKechnie to make a change that would solidify his infield unit.

"Why don't you get that Grantham out of there?" advised McGraw. "He's not doing you any good. Why not play Stuffy McInnis on first? He's been in a lot of World's Series, and knows what this is all about."[13]

Surprisingly, McKechnie heeded McGraw's advice and placed Stuffy McInnis in the Game Five starting lineup. McInnis replaced George Grantham at first base and took over the seventh spot of the batting order. Earl Smith also returned to McKechnie's lineup after a one-game hiatus. In the meantime, Washington manager Bucky Harris made one change to his starting lineup. He penciled in Ossie Bluege to bat eighth and resume his duties at third base after missing two games due to a bean ball incident.

The pitching match up from Game Two would be repeated, as McKechnie chose Vic Aldridge to start the fifth game while Harris countered with spit ball pitcher Stan Coveleski. Since the right-handed Aldridge was pitching for Pittsburgh, Harris also made a small change to his batting order from the previous day. Joe Judge batted clean-up, as Joe Harris slid back down into the lineup's fifth spot.

Eddie Moore led off the game against Coveleski and fouled out to Roger Peckinpaugh near the stands. Max Carey followed Moore's out by lining a single to left field. Pittsburgh quickly put two runners on base when Kiki Cuyler smacked a "Texas Leaguer" that dropped in front of Goose Goslin in left field. Clyde Barnhart then blasted a Coveleski offering to the outfield. Unfortunately, Barnhart's smash was hit right to left fielder Goose Goslin, who snatched the ball for the second out. Pie Traynor then showed off his solid batting eye and drew a walk, loading the bases for Pittsburgh. But the Pirates' hopes were quickly dashed when Glenn Wright's grounder caromed off Coveleski toward Bucky Harris, who threw out the shortstop.[14]

Washington quickly brought the Griffith Stadium fans to their feet during the bottom of the first inning. Sam Rice continued his dominance by leading off with a single to right field. Bucky Harris then executed a perfect sacrifice; he moved Rice to second when his bunt was picked by Stuffy McInnis, who fired to Moore covering at first. Goose Goslin then gave Washington a 1–0 lead when he lofted a fly ball to left that eluded Barnhart. Washington's rooters hollered their approval as Goslin's double drove home Rice.[15] Goslin, usually regarded as a dead pull hitter, upset Pittsburgh's strategy by dumping a fly ball down the left field line, while Barnhart was positioned in left-center.[16] Vic

Aldridge maintained his composure and recorded the second out by fanning Judge. Joe Harris followed by working out a walk that put two men on with two out. Aldridge then ended the first inning when Goslin was forced at third after Peckinpaugh grounded to Traynor.[17]

In the top of the second, Goslin continued his fine fielding in left when he robbed McInnis of a potential home run. Goose speared McInnis' drive for the first out after making a long run in the outer garden.[18] Earl Smith hit safely in his fourth straight game, banging a one-out single to Sam Rice in center, but was quickly erased on a double play as Aldridge grounded into a Bluege-to-Harris-to-Judge twin killing.[19]

Washington went down in relatively easy fashion against Aldridge in the bottom of the second inning. Muddy Ruel popped up to Eddie Moore at second.[20] Bluege then received a standing ovation; it was his first at bat since Game Two. Bluege seemed a bit tentative as Aldridge struck him out on three pitches.[21] Stan Coveleski attempted to start a two-out rally by drawing a walk, but the inning came to an end when McInnis handled Rice's high chopper and touched first base.[22]

Moore started out Pittsburgh's half of the third by grounding out to Bluege at third. Max Carey followed with a walk. He took off for second and beat Muddy Ruel's throw to Bucky Harris for a stolen base. As Carey arrived at second, he collided violently with Harris. After taking a few moments to gather his faculties, Carey took his place on second base. Kiki Cuyler then strolled to first base after working out a walk against Coveleski. Clyde Barnhart finally broke out of his slump, smacking a single to left that scored Carey and moved Cuyler to third. The Pirates then attempted a double steal, with Barnhart securing second base and Cuyler scampering back to third after he dashed part of the way to home. Cuyler scored Pittsburgh's second run when Pie Traynor lifted a sacrifice fly to Rice in center. Wasting little time, Bucky Harris motioned to the Washington dugout to have Firpo Marberry and Tom Zachary begin warming in the bullpen, but Glenn Wright ended the inning by grounding out to Peckinpaugh at short.[23]

Vic Aldridge took the mound with renewed confidence now that Pittsburgh held a 2–1 edge in Game Five. Bucky Harris tried to bunt his way on, but failed when Aldridge handled his tapper and threw to McInnis for the first out. Goslin then chased the first pitch and grounded innocently to Eddie Moore for the second out. Aldridge made it a routine inning when he induced Joe Judge to loft a fly ball into the waiting glove of Kiki Cuyler.[24]

Coveleski handled Pittsburgh in similar fashion during the top of the fourth inning. McInnis led off by hitting a bad hop grounder that Peckinpaugh handled at short. Earl Smith followed with his second hit of the day, drilling a Coveleski pitch into center field. Aldridge made the second out when he flied to Goose Goslin in left field. Moore then executed Bill McKechnie's call for a hit-and-run play beautifully by singling to right field and moving Smith over to third. Bucky Harris once again called for Marberry and Zachary to begin warming up in Washington's bullpen, but Coveleski wiggled out of the tough situation when Judge snagged Max Carey's hot smash and touched first base to rob him of an apparent hit.[25] Judge skillfully knocked down Carey's line drive, which seemed destined to be a two-run double, and recovered in time to beat him to first.[26]

Joe Harris brought the Griffith Stadium fans to their feet during the top of the fourth inning when he led off by blasting his third home run of the Series into the left field stands. Harris received a smile and applause from Mrs. Coolidge as he trotted by her toward the Washington dugout.[27] Aldridge then proceeded to make quick work of Peckinpaugh, striking out the Washington shortstop. Muddy Ruel followed by singling over Glenn Wright at short. Ossie Bluege then smacked a shot to left field that eluded Clyde Barnhart for a double and moved Ruel to third base.[28] As Stan Coveleski strode to the plate, Bucky Harris held an impromptu conference with his players, while the crowd clamored for someone — Nemo Leibold, Bobby Veach or Dutch Ruether — to pinch hit. After a short timeout, Harris allowed his pitcher to bat.[29] Aldridge recorded the crucial second out when Coveleski looked at a called third strike. The inning ended when Stuffy McInnis handled Sam Rice's grounder and touched first for the final out.[30]

The Pirates were retired in order by Coveleski in the fifth inning. Rice easily handled Kiki Cuyler's long fly to center. Roger Peckinpaugh barely moved on Barnhart's pop-up to short. Joe Harris then made a fine running catch of Pie Traynor's low liner to right field.

Aldridge took the mound in Washington's half of the fifth and mowed down the Senators without difficulty. Eddie Moore threw out Bucky Harris after Washington's player-manager hit an easy grounder to second base. Cuyler handled Goose Goslin's lofty fly ball to right for the second out. Judge became Aldridge's final victim of the inning when he popped up to Pittsburgh shortstop Glenn Wright.[31]

Wright started out Pittsburgh's sixth inning by flying out to Goose Goslin in left field. Stuffy McInnis reached first when Peckinpaugh fumbled his grounder and made a terrible throw to first base. The error was quickly erased when Earl Smith hit into an inning-ending double play that went Coveleski-to-Peckinpaugh-to-Bucky Harris covering at first base.

Joe Harris began Washington's half of the sixth by cracking a single over Pie Traynor's head at third. Peckinpaugh moved Harris to second with a perfect sacrifice bunt, the play going from McInnis to Moore. Muddy Ruel kept the Senators' inning going by drawing a one-out walk, but Vic Aldridge bore down and struck out Ossie Bluege. After catching strike three, Smith whipped a throw to Traynor at the hot corner that caught Joe Harris stealing for the third out.[32]

During Pittsburgh's half of the seventh inning, assistant manager Fred Clarke's premonition regarding the Pirates' hitting prowess finally came true. The inning started out innocently when Coveleski retired Vic Aldridge on a grounder to Bluege at third. Eddie Moore followed by working out a walk. Carey then moved Moore to second base when he singled to left. Moore came around to score and Carey took third after Kiki Cuyler reached first base by drilling a single off Bluege's glove into left. Clyde Barnhart made it a 4–2 lead when he followed Cuyler's hit with a single of his own to right field. Carey scored on Barnhart's drive, while Cuyler took third. Having seen enough of Coveleski, Bucky Harris brought in young right-hander Win Ballou to pitch. Ballou ended the inning without any further damage by striking out Traynor on three pitches and then watching Cuyler get caught in a rundown at third during a double steal.[33]

Ballou's stint was brief since he was scheduled to lead off the bottom of the seventh for Washington. Nemo Leibold pinch hit for Ballou and doubled to right field. Sam Rice followed with a single through the box that bounced into center field. Rice's hit brought Leibold home from second and cut Pittsburgh's lead to one run. Bucky Harris moved Rice up to second with a sacrifice bunt, which was fielded by catcher Earl Smith, who tossed to McInnis at first base for the first out. Rice then scampered to third base when Kiki Cuyler hauled in Goose Goslin's fly to right field. Rice died at third base when Joe Judge followed suit and flied out to Cuyler for the last out.[34]

Southpaw Tom Zachary was brought in by Bucky Harris to assume the pitching responsibilities for Washington in the eighth inning. Glenn Wright exhibited how Pittsburgh feasted on left-handed pitchers by opening the frame with a solid double to left field. Wright then came around to score, pushing the Pittsburgh lead to 5–3 on Stuffy McInnis' single to right field. Smith walked to the plate and proceeded to move McInnis to second base with a sacrifice bunt that was handled by Zachary, who tossed to Judge at first base. Vic Aldridge took a healthy cut at a Zachary offering and slammed a grounder to Bucky Harris at second. McInnis became caught in a rundown between second and third, and was tagged out for the second out, Harris-to-Bluege-to-Peckinpaugh. Zachary ended the frame without further damage as Moore lined out to Rice in center field.[35]

Aldridge handled Washington with relative ease in the bottom half of the eighth inning. Peckinpaugh grounded out to shortstop Glenn Wright, who was then credited with his second assist of the inning when he handled Muddy Ruel's grounder and tossed to McInnis at first base. McInnis then made a beautiful play, chasing Ossie Bluege's foul pop-up and snagging it right in front of Washington's dugout.[36]

Switch hitter Max Carey jumped to the right side for the first time in the Series as he led off against Tom Zachary in the ninth inning. Carey hit a slow tapper back to Zachary, who tossed to Judge for the first out. Zachary made it two quick outs in the inning when he retired Kiki Cuyler on a ground ball to Judge. Clyde Barnhart then drew a two-out walk against Zachary, and Pie Traynor kept the inning alive when he singled past Peckinpaugh, moving Barnhart to second. Bucky Harris, deciding that Zachary was done, summoned Firpo Marberry from the bullpen. Wright greeted the Senators' premier reliever by slashing a single past Bluege at third, scoring Barnhart and giving Pittsburgh a 6–3 lead. The inning finally came to an end when Stuffy McInnis flied out to Goose Goslin in left field.[37]

Vic Aldridge took the mound in the ninth inning holding a comfortable three-run lead. Spencer Adams batted for Marberry and struck a grounder to Aldridge, who tossed to McInnis at first. Sam Rice was retired for the second out when he hit an Aldridge offering to Glenn Wright at short. Aldridge then completed the victory for Bill McKechnie by inducing Bucky Harris to hit a lazy fly to left that was caught easily by Clyde Barnhart.[38] Aldridge gained credit for his second victory of the Series, as Pittsburgh prevailed over Washington, 6–3, in Game Five. In tossing a complete game, Aldridge scattered eight Washington hits while he walked four and struck out five.

After struggling at the plate through the first four games of the Series, Kiki Cuyler, Clyde Barnhart and Glenn Wright recorded two hits apiece and combined to score three runs and drive home four Pirate teammates. Max Carey and Earl Smith also rapped out two hits each while Pittsburgh's center fielder also scored two runs. Clarke's prediction regarding the Pirates hitting returning to form proved accurate as Pittsburgh totaled 13 hits on the day.

On the morning of Game Five, Cuyler had echoed Clarke's sentiment when a writer talked to him at the Wardham Park Hotel as he was leaving for the ballpark.[39] "There ought to be a lot of base hits in our bats today," said Cuyler. "We hit about .308 during the National League season, and we've hit about .150 in the first four games of this series. There's going to be a break, and it's got to come today."[40]

Though the Pirates' offense had returned, Washington manager Bucky Harris was not concerned that Pittsburgh had sliced into his team's World Series lead. Stan Coveleski had been anxious to avenge his defeat at the hands of the Pirates in Game Two. The task was too great for the veteran pitcher, who may have returned to the mound without enough rest between games. Coveleski looked like a tired, aging pitcher as Pittsburgh's batters smacked his off-speed curves and junkball tosses.[41]

Pittsburgh fans who made the trip to Washington for the three games at Griffith Stadium finally had something to cheer about as the Series shifted back to the Smoky City. Some of the ardent fans celebrated their team's victory as if it were the clinching game of the World Series. Pirate rooters who were making their way to the train station for a trip back to Pittsburgh organized a

Vic Aldridge pitched brilliantly during Game Five of the 1925 World Series, when Pittsburgh faced elimination. Aldridge tossed a complete game and won his second game of the Series as Pittsburgh defeated Washington, 6–3, on October 12 at Griffith Stadium (National Baseball Hall of Fame Library, Cooperstown, New York).

"snake dance" down Pennsylvania Avenue to the railroad yard. These enthusiastic fans were still dancing when the train pulled out of the railroad station.

If there were no delays on their trip back to Pittsburgh, Bill McKechnie and his men would arrive in the Smoky City around midnight. A good night's sleep for McKechnie and his players was crucial since the World Series was scheduled to resume that afternoon at Forbes Field.[42]

Much of the baseball talk in the Smoky City centered around the sudden eruption of Pittsburgh's batters in Game Five. Fans engaged in passionate discussions regarding who had been the best player to date in the 1925 World Series. Names such as Cuyler, Traynor, Aldridge, Rice, Johnson, Goslin and both Harrises on the Senators were given consideration.

Newspapermen from across the country reached their own conclusions regarding this particular topic. While the Series was still being played in Washington, pundits sat down one evening at the Raleigh Hotel to ponder this subject. Men like Damon Runyan, Billy Evans and a host of others concluded that Pittsburgh's Glenn Wright deserved recognition as the best player on either World Series team. Some of these experts believed that Wright was one of the best players to ever break into the big leagues. Wright feared no pitcher, was exceedingly quick on the bases, and was a defensive whiz who also showed a keen ability to analyze plays in front of him. Wright's success was even more impressive given that he had played only two seasons in the major leagues.[43]

While Wright was crowned the best player in the World Series by national writers, veteran first baseman Stuffy McInnis received much of the credit for steadying the Pirates during Game Five. Whenever Vic Aldridge ran into problems on the mound, McInnis strode to the hill and offered advice to his teammate. After Joe Harris homered in the fourth inning, Aldridge looked dejected. McInnis quickly called time and whispered into Aldridge's ear. When play resumed, Aldridge struck out Roger Peckinpaugh. After two more men reached base that inning, McInnis once again gave Aldridge wise counsel, and no further damage was done. In addition, McInnis positioned his fellow infielders so perfectly that they always seemed to be in the proper spot for each Washington batter.[44]

Pirates players were pleased that they had returned to the familiar environs of Pittsburgh. Bill McKechnie's team was kept busy for three consecutive days when games were played in Washington. Before Game Three began, the Pittsburgh aggregation squeezed in an appearance at the White House to meet President Calvin Coolidge. When the team took the field for pre-game practice before Game Five, Pirates players were swamped with autograph requests from adoring fans. Many of these rooters were women, a fact that came as no surprise to Pirate observers.[45] The Pirates' roster was loaded with handsome gentlemen like Pie Traynor, Glenn Wright and Kiki Cuyler who were particularly popular with female fans. As a result, Pittsburgh players signed baseballs, souvenir programs and books amidst a swarm of enthusiasts.[46]

Pittsburgh's rooting populace was also thrilled that their favorite team had returned home to play another day. On the morning of Tuesday, October 13, 500 people lined up to purchase bleacher seat tickets for Game Six of the World Series. Many of these fans who stood at the head of the line were girls and women that had been permitted to occupy prime real estate due to the generosity of men who graciously offered up their spots.

A bright sun, which almost immediately dried away the previous evening's rain, began to peer through the morning fog. The gates for Forbes Field's center field bleacher section opened at 9:00 A.M.[47] Forbes Field's groundskeepers emerged at 11:30 to roll the base paths and the skinned portion of the field in an effort to ready it for play. The diamond looked to be in perfect condition even though a recent mixture of rain and snow had left the pathways from the player's bench to home plate muddy.

By noon, the concrete bleachers in left field were only filled to one-third of capacity and there were still several empty areas in the center field bleachers. Nick Altrock and Al Schacht once again entertained the early arriving faithful with their comedy stunts.[48] As game time drew nearer, the grand old ballpark finally began to show signs of life. By then, the level of enthusiasm seemed to be greater than during the first two games at Forbes Field.

Overcoats and blankets were the norm for many customers who sat down in their Forbes Field seats. Even though the sun was bright and warm, an autumn chill gripped Pittsburgh as players from both teams arrived on the field for practice.[49]

Unfortunately, batting practice did not go well for one member of Pittsburgh's squad. Eddie Moore injured his hand while taking swings in the batting cage. He immediately left the playing field and hustled off to the clubhouse to receive treatment. Before Pittsburgh's trainer could look at Moore's injury, the young second baseman was seen crying under the grandstand while holding his hand, which was throbbing in pain.

Honus Wagner happened to meet Moore while he was wailing disconsolately. Pittsburgh's ex-player-turned correspondent, walked up to the youngster to ask him about the injury.[50] "Does it hurt so much?" asked Wagner as he approached Pittsburgh's second baseman.

"I'm not crying because of any pain," replied Moore, "but I'm afraid I won't be able to bat at my best, and I want to help the boys win today."[51]

Wagner offered encouragement to the young second baseman.[52] When Bill McKechnie revealed his starting lineup for the game, Eddie Moore was listed as the team's second baseman and leadoff hitter. In fact, McKechnie's lineup was the same one he had used during the fifth game of the Series in Washington.

12. Pittsburgh Battles Back

Bucky Harris made one change to his starting lineup. Hank Severeid replaced Muddy Ruel behind the plate for the Senators. Harris altered the batting order a bit, bumping Ossie Bluege to the sixth spot on the lineup card, with Roger Peckinpaugh and Severeid batting seventh and eighth. Joe Harris and Joe Judge also swapped spots in the lineup. In terms of pitching, the two men who hurled against each other in Game Three took the mound for a rematch at Forbes Field on Tuesday, October 13. Ray Kremer was chosen by Bill McKechnie to keep Pittsburgh's hopes alive, while Bucky Harris countered with Alex Ferguson.

Fred Clarke stood next to Kremer and chatted with Pittsburgh's pitcher as he warmed up before the game.[53] Clarke was conversing casually in an effort to keep Kremer's nerves in check. Once the game began, Eddie Moore became involved immediately when Sam Rice rapped a groundball to Pittsburgh's second baseman. Moore juggled the hot smash, but his throw to Stuffy McInnis still beat Rice to the bag. Kremer recorded the second out when Bucky Harris hit a roller in front of home plate that Earl Smith snatched and tossed to first. Suddenly, the Pirates' fans at Forbes Field grew silent when Goose Goslin drilled a two-out homer into the left field stands to give Washington as early 1–0 lead. Joe Harris made the final out with a grounder to Kremer who made the clean toss to McInnis at first.[54]

When the Senators took the field in the bottom of the first, Sam Rice was greeted by a chorus of jeers as he took his position in center field. Rice was subjected to a series of vile comments from angry Pittsburgh fans who believed he had unfairly prevented Earl Smith from being credited with a crucial, home run in Game Three.[55] The fans' treatment seemed a bit odd since it was umpire Cy Rigler who made the unpopular call that possibly cost Pittsburgh the game.

Washington manager Bucky Harris pulled an interesting stunt when he had southpaw Dutch Ruether warm up in right field before the bottom of the first inning.[56] But when the inning started, Alex Ferguson took his spot on the mound. Eddie Moore came to the plate and stood nonchalantly as he always did. Ferguson attempted to get Moore to bite at a curve ball, but the strategy failed as Moore launched Ferguson's first pitch past Ossie Bluege into left field for a base hit.[57] Max Carey stepped in and sacrificed Moore to second, with Bluege throwing to Joe Judge at first for the out. Kiki Cuyler left Moore standing at second as he hit a routine fly ball to Rice in center. Ferguson then escaped the first inning unscathed when Bluege handled Clyde Barnhart's smash down the third base line and threw to first to end Pittsburgh's hopes of scoring.[58]

The mood turned somber at Forbes Field after Washington added another run in the second inning to take a 2–0 lead. Judge opened the frame by stroking a single to right field. Bluege came to the plate and attempted to sacrifice his teammate to second. The strategy failed as his bunt was fielded by Kremer, who made a clean throw to Wright at second. Bucky Harris then called for the hit-and-run play as Roger Peckinpaugh strolled to the plate. Peckinpaugh delivered a soaring double past Cuyler in right that brought Bluege home from first. While Kremer was facing Washington's Hank Severeid, he whirled around and attempted to pick Peckinpaugh off second base, but a wild throw allowed him to move over to third base. Severeid recorded the inning's second out by hitting a short fly to Barnhart in left. Ferguson then hit a fly ball that was snagged by Cuyler in right field, ending the inning.[59]

Pie Traynor brought Pittsburgh's rooters to their feet when he led off the bottom of the second inning with a sharp single over the head of second baseman Bucky Harris. Traynor was quickly erased on a force play at second when Glenn Wright grounded meekly to Peckinpaugh. Ferguson then fanned Stuffy McInnis for the second out. The hopes of Forbes Field's fans were buoyed a bit when Earl Smith followed with a single over second that moved Wright to third, but Ferguson settled down and fanned Ray Kremer on three pitches as the Pirates' hurler looked helplessly at a called third strike.[60]

Sam Rice opened the third inning by lining a bullet at Kremer. The pitcher closed his eyes, ducked, stuck out his glove, and snagged the blistering drive for an out.[61] Pie Traynor then grabbed Bucky Harris' bouncer and threw a perfect strike to Stuffy McInnis at first base. Goose Goslin made the final out for Washington when his high pop-up was easily handled by Glenn Wright.[62]

Eddie Moore led off Pittsburgh's half of the third by working out a walk against Alex Ferguson. Max Carey followed by striking a grounder over the mound toward Washington shortstop Roger Peckinpaugh, who grabbed the ball and raced to second base in an attempt to beat Moore to the bag.[63] Peckinpaugh touched the bag and believed he had executed a force play, but second base umpire George Moriarty declared Moore safe. Moriarty claimed that Peckinpaugh had missed the bag with his foot. The Washington shortstop vehemently disagreed as he showed Moriarty the chalk on his shoe. Other Senators players joined in the discussion to support their teammate, but Moriarty could not be swayed.[64]

Moriarty's decision had immediate implications on Pittsburgh's half of the third inning. Kiki Cuyler stepped to the plate and sacrificed Moore and Carey up one base; the beautiful bunt was handled by Bluege, who tossed to Bucky Harris covering first base. Moore crossed home plate and Carey moved up to third when Clyde Barnhart grounded to Bluege at third for the second out. Pie Traynor then brought Carey home from third with the tying run by banging a single over second base. With Glenn Wright at bat, Traynor decided to challenge catcher Hank Severeid's throwing arm by taking off for second base. Traynor easily made it to second and then moved over to third when Severeid's throw sailed into center field. He remained stranded, as Wright ended the inning by grounding out to Bluege at third.[65]

The questionable call by Moriarty was crucial in allowing Pittsburgh to score two runs and tie the ballgame. Its hard to know what strategy Bill McKechnie might have used with Cuyler at the plate if a runner had been on first with one out. If Cuyler had been retired, Barnhart's groundout would have ended the inning without Pittsburgh scoring any runs. But Bucky Harris' squad could not dwell on the adverse decision. They were now involved in a tight game that was tied, 2–2.

Ray Kremer seemed invigorated now that Washington no longer led by two runs. Joe Harris began the fourth inning by swinging wildly at a ball that he missed by nearly a foot for strike three. Joe Judge then became Kremer's second strikeout victim of the inning when he swung hard at an inside pitch and came up empty. Ossie Bluege finally connected against a Kremer offering and drove a single over Glenn Wright's head. But Bluege was quickly erased on a pickoff play at first that saw him involved in a rundown that went from Kremer to McInnis to Moore back to Kremer.[66]

Stuffy McInnis started off Pittsburgh's half of the fourth inning by driving a long fly to Sam Rice, who made the catch in center field. Alex Ferguson then fanned both Earl Smith and Ray Kremer to conclude an easy one, two, three inning.

Kremer took the mound in the fifth inning and continued to mow down Washington batters. Roger Peckinpaugh became the inning's first out when Pie Traynor raced to the pitcher's mound and snagged the Washington shortstop's pop-up. Hank Severeid then grounded out to Wright at short. Kremer brought the Senators' inning to an abrupt end when he fanned Ferguson on a called third strike that cut the corner of home plate.[67]

Eddie Moore stepped to the plate in the bottom of the fifth inning, leading off a frame for the third time in the game. Alex Ferguson started off Moore with a low pitch that he let go by for ball one. Ferguson then countered with a curve ball, shoulder high, that Moore met squarely with his bat. Moore's shot soared to deep left field. Bedlam reigned throughout Forbes Field as Moore's blast soared over the barrier in front of the left field scoreboard for a home run. Fans must have wondered if Eddie's hand was still bothering him as he delivered the big hit that put Pittsburgh in front, 3–2. As Moore scampered across home plate, his teammates grabbed him and began shaking his hand. Moore's fellow Pirates then hoisted the young second baseman on their shoulders.[68]

Max Carey followed Moore's heroic endeavor by lining out to right fielder Joe Harris. Ferguson settled down and recorded the second out when he retired Kiki Cuyler on a ground ball to Roger Peckinpaugh. Clyde Barnhart almost duplicated Moore's effort when he crushed a Ferguson offering to deep left field. Barnhart ended up with a double when the ball struck the left field fence, but the inning came to an end when Goose Goslin hauled in Pie Traynor's long drive to left.

Kremer made quick work of the Senators in the top of the sixth inning. He retired Sam Rice when Traynor grabbed his grounder behind third base and gunned a perfect throw to Stuffy McInnis. Glenn Wright then made a nice pickup of Bucky Harris' grounder and tossed a quick underhand throw that nipped Washington's manager at first. Kremer unexpectedly showed a touch of wildness as he walked Goslin on four straight pitches, but he ended the inning when Joe Harris grounded out to Eddie Moore.[69]

Fans were treated to some unintended humor when Washington pitcher Alex Ferguson accidentally threw the ball into the grandstand while warming up on the mound. He regained his control and fanned Glenn Wright looking on a nifty curve ball. Stuffy McInnis tried to ignite a rally by drilling a one-out single over second base. Earl Smith followed by hitting a deep, towering drive that was hauled in by right fielder Joe Harris. Ferguson ended the inning when he struck out Kremer for the third time that afternoon.

Kremer continued to keep Washington's batters off balance in the seventh inning. Joe Judge was retired for the first out when he lofted a deep drive to Kiki Cuyler in right field. Ossie Bluege followed by slapping an easy grounder to Pie Traynor; Bluege was called out at first when McInnis picked Traynor's low throw out of the dirt. Roger Peckinpaugh then lifted a lazy fly to left, which Clyde Barnhart hauled in for the final out.[70]

When Judge batted in the top half of the seventh inning and launched a drive to right, first base umpire Brick Owens noticed something wrong with the right field grandstand railing. Owens was concerned that overzealous fans could fall onto the field due to the grandstand's faulty barrier.[71] Owens held up play prior to Pittsburgh's half of the seventh as carpenters worked on the broken field box. When play finally resumed, Eddie Moore reached first base on Roger Peckinpaugh's throwing error. Max Carey came to the plate and moved Moore over to second with a sacrifice bunt to Ferguson. Kiki Cuyler registered the inning's second out when he hit a fly ball to Goose Goslin in right field. Clyde Barnhart kept the inning alive when he drew a two-out walk that put runners on first and second, but the Pirates' stanza ended when Barnhart was forced at second base on Pie Traynor's hard smash to Roger Peckinpaugh.[72]

Catcher Hank Severeid attempted to ignite the Senators in the top of the eighth inning by drilling a long single to left field. Bucky Harris replaced the slow-footed Severeid on the base paths with pinch runner Earl McNeely. Harris also brought in Nemo Leibold to pinch hit for Alex Ferguson. McNeely wasted no time trying to reach scoring position as he stole second base on Kremer's first pitch to Leibold. Kremer kept his focus with the tying run at second, inducing Leibold to hit a pop-up to Eddie Moore at second. Pittsburgh recorded the second out when Sam Rice's grounder was handled by Stuffy McInnis, who made an unassisted play at first as McNeely moved over to third base. Bucky Harris opted to remove himself for pinch hitter Bobby Veach, but Kremer was able to work out of the jam courtesy of a grounder to Moore at second.[73]

Harris sent Muddy Ruel and Win Ballou into the game as Washington's new battery, while Spencer Adams took Bucky's position at second base.[74] Adams was placed in the eighth spot of the batting order, Ruel assumed the ninth position, and Ballou slid into the second spot. Ballou looked wild when Pittsburgh's half of the eighth began. Glenn Wright trotted down to first after he drew a walk against Ballou. But Wright did not remain on base very long as Stuffy McInnis followed by hitting into an unusual double play. On the play, Joe Judge handled McInnis' pop fly and doubled up Wright when he raced to first and touched the bag before the Pittsburgh's shortstop did. Ballou finished off Pittsburgh as Earl Smith grounded out to Ossie Bluege at third base.[75]

Three more Washington outs stood between Ray Kremer and a complete game victory that would guarantee a seventh game to be played on Wednesday afternoon. Kremer quickly recorded the first out on Goose Goslin's pop-up to Eddie Moore.[76] Joe Harris followed Goslin to the plate. Pirates fans throughout Forbes Field gasped when Harris hit what appeared to be the most prodigious blast of the 1925 World Series. Harris sent the ball to the deepest region of Forbes Field. Center fielder Max Carey frantically chased Harris' long drive. The ball soared over Carey's head and struck the screen in front of the outfield bleachers. Making a fine play, Carey grabbed the ball and held Harris to a double by making a quick throw toward the infield. Since Harris' drive was to dead center, the ball made it only to the bleacher screen, rather than landing among Forbes Field's spectators.[77]

Instead of the game being tied at three, Washington had a runner on second with one out. Joe Judge followed Harris to the plate and hit a pop-up to shortstop Glenn Wright.[78] The game, and Pittsburgh's fortunes in the World Series, were now riding on a battle between Ray Kremer and Ossie Bluege. Bluege hit a weak grounder to Pittsburgh third baseman Pie Traynor, who handled the chopper and threw across to Stuffy McInnis for the game's final out.[79] The 1925 World Series would now go to a seventh game thanks to the Pirates' 3–2 win over Washington.

Bill McKechnie's brigade had accomplished the improbable by winning two consecutive games while facing elimination. Barney Dreyfuss's players had been maligned on past occasions when they played poorly under pressure. This group of Pirates had turned in a different result.

Ray Kremer was a big reason why Pittsburgh had tied the Series at three games apiece. Kremer tossed a complete game and snuffed out a number of Washington rallies throughout the afternoon. Kremer scattered six hits, while walking one batter and striking out three.

Pittsburgh second baseman Eddie Moore shows off his nonchalant batting stance for the cameras. Moore was the Game Six hero of the 1925 World Series. His solo home run against Alex Ferguson in the fifth inning secured Pittsburgh's 3–2 victory on October 13 at Forbes Field. Prior to the game, Moore was seen crying under the grandstand after he injured his hand during batting practice (National Baseball Hall of Fame Library, Cooperstown, New York).

While Kremer's pitching was a key factor in Pittsburgh's Game Six victory, it was Eddie Moore's clutch hit that allowed Pittsburgh to extend its season by one more game. It was only two months ago that Moore was in Bill McKechnie's doghouse. Eddie was a temperamental young man who wore his emotions too visibly. Hours before the sixth game of the 1925 World Series, Moore was crying in despair because he feared an injury would result in poor performance. In a few short hours, Eddie Moore went from such depths to becoming Pittsburgh's new darling. Moore's play had been the impetus behind Pittsburgh's Series-tying victory. The Pirates were one victory away from their second world championship in team history, as McKechnie's players braced for a third meeting against Washington's Walter Johnson.

13

Carey and the Pirates Overcome Johnson and the Weather

Washington's Walter Johnson had undoubtedly been the star of the 1925 World Series. Johnson, who was considered the greatest pitcher of his era, won Games One and Four with relative ease. The veteran hurler had allowed only one Pirates player to cross home plate in 18 innings of work on the hill. Pittsburgh's batters had been unable to mount any kind of attack against Johnson in games started by hurlers Lee Meadows and Emil Yde. It was unclear who Bill McKechnie would call upon to assume the responsibility of opposing Johnson for Game Seven on Wednesday, October 14. Pittsburgh's baseball fans might have scratched their heads when reports indicated that McKechnie had told reporters upon arrival at the clubhouse before Game Six that Red Oldham would start a potential seventh game. McKechnie explained that he had Johnny Morrison in reserve if Oldham faltered. Pittsburgh's manager also eliminated Lee Meadows as a possible Game Seven starter due to the pitcher's arm failing to respond after throwing a steady diet of curve balls in Game One of the Series.[1]

Many Pittsburgh fans were hoping that McKechnie would turn to Vic Aldridge for the seventh game of the World Series. This choice was illogical since Aldridge would be pitching with only one day of rest if he were asked to start the Wednesday afternoon game. On the other hand, Aldridge had been Pittsburgh's star player in this Fall Classic.

Max Carey's hitting and the fielding of both Glenn Wright and Pie Traynor represented other Series highlights for Pittsburgh. For Washington, Bucky Harris' fielding and the heavy hitting of Goose Goslin and Joe Harris had contributed to the Senators' strong showing in the series to date. Many heroes had performed admirably during the 1925 World Series, but American League MVP Roger Peckinpaugh's name did not enter the conversation. Peckinpaugh had struggled in the field and committed six errors, many of which occurred when he seemed to be rushing on plays involving speedy Pittsburgh players.

13. Carey and the Pirates Overcome Johnson and the Weather 197

Peckinpaugh's fielding woes were not the only problem that confronted Washington's shortstop on the eve of Game Seven. Peckinpaugh incurred the wrath of Commissioner Landis when he criticized George Moriarty's crucial Game Six umpiring decision through the press. On the play in question, Peckinpaugh handled a Max Carey chopper that bounded over the head of pitcher Alex Ferguson. Peckinpaugh snagged the ball behind the mound and rushed to second in an attempt to force Eddie Moore. Moriarty called Moore safe when he determined Peckinpaugh did not touch the bag with his foot. That evening, Moriarty picked up an early edition of a morning newspaper and read Peckinpaugh's scathing comments in print. Washington's shortstop laid the blame for the defeat on the hands of Moriarty.[2]

Writer Harry Nelly of *The Chicago American* reported that Moriarty immediately headed for Landis' apartment after reading the malicious comments. Moriarty awoke Landis from bed at 11:30 P.M. and threatened to cease working as an umpire in the World Series. A former player-turned-umpire, Moriarty was seething with anger over the comments that Peckinpaugh made. Landis quickly calmed Moriarty down and urged him to change his mind about walking away from a World Series obligation. After a few moments of pleading on Landis' part, Moriarty abandoned his one-man strike.[3]

Washington catcher Muddy Ruel also made some comments in print that were unfavorable to Moriarty. In response, Landis called Peckinpaugh and Ruel to his room and demanded public apologies from both players. Written statements of apology and regret on the part of both Senators appeared in newspapers throughout America the following day.[4]

The public apologies were not the only baseball story creating a stir on Wednesday afternoon as fans awaited the start of Game Seven at Forbes Field. Pittsburgh treasurer Sam Dreyfuss confirmed a story that had initially appeared in the early Tuesday edition of a Pittsburgh newspaper. Dreyfuss announced that Pittsburgh had purchased the contracts of infielder Harold Rhyne and outfielder Paul Waner from the San Francisco club of the Pacific Coast League. Dreyfuss did not divulge any financial terms surrounding the purchase, but one reliable source close to the situation claimed the Pirates paid $100,000 to purchase Rhyne and Waner. San Francisco team secretary George A. Putnam traveled east to watch the World Series and finalize the deal with Pirates officials. Pacific coast scout Joe Devine recommended the purchase, which was considered one of the biggest between a major and minor league team in many years.[5]

While Pirates management was making personnel decisions with an eye toward the 1926 season, rabid fans throughout the Smoky City prepared to root for their beloved Corsairs during the deciding game of the World Series. Since no tickets had been pre-sold for this game, admission passes were sold through Tuesday night at 15 Forbes Field ticket windows and downtown agencies. At 8:15 on Wednesday morning, two windows at Forbes Field were opened to sell the final 1,000 reserve tickets. Three hundred enthusiasts were standing in line when the ticket windows opened. The lines at the windows where bleacher seats were being sold for $1.10 and $3.30 seemed much larger than the lines for Game One a week earlier.[6]

Pirates management had extra policemen on hand to prevent a sudden rush that could destroy fragile fencing that separated the spectators in temporary bleacher sections from the diamond. Danny Nirella's band again supplied entertainment as patrons began taking their bleacher seats before noon. Al Schacht ran out and took Nirella's baton from his hand and proceeded to march in perfect time leading the band. Nick Altrock joined in and did a comic dance of his own that did not seem to be coordinated to the music.

Bill McKechnie was not available when a writer pressed coach Jewel Ens to verify or deny the notion that Red Oldham would oppose Walter Johnson on the mound that afternoon. Ens responded to the scribe by telling him that McKechnie had informed him a half-hour earlier that Oldham would indeed be starting Game Seven.[7]

By noon, the wooden and concrete bleacher sections at Forbes Field were completely filled. One witness stated that the line of people hoping to purchase tickets for those sections had stretched from the ballpark's ticket windows to Carnegie Library. As the crowd continued to pour into the stadium two hours before game time, it looked as if rain would begin to fall at any moment, as the skies became laden with heavy, thick clouds. Nonetheless, the Pirates players took the field at 12:40 P.M. and headed to the cage for batting practice, where they began swatting balls into Forbes Field's bleacher sections. Bucky Harris' Washington Senators arrived on the diamond at 1:00 P.M. The Senators did not seem to be exhibiting the same confidence they had shown when they led the World Series, three games to one. Harris' players looked subdued and showed little pep as they went through their practice session.[8]

The skies became very dark when Washington's players hit the diamond. Fans who had already arrived at their seats looked skyward with the expectation of a massive downpour. Potentially poor weather was the main reason why Pittsburgh owner Barney Dreyfuss chose not to attend the game at Forbes Field. Dreyfuss had come down with a severe cold while the Pirates were playing in Washington. His physician ordered him to remain in his apartment for a short period of recuperation. Dreyfuss planned on listening to the crucial game's play-by-play over a radio in his dwelling.[9]

As it turned out, Dreyfuss's radio would be rendered useless unless he wanted to listen to music or news reports. Rain began falling steadily throughout Pittsburgh and showed no signs of letting up as game time approached at Forbes Field. The 2:00 P.M. start time came and went without any official determination regarding the game. When newspaper scribes approached Commissioner Landis in the press box to ask him about the situation, the Judge responded by telling the pundits to sit tight for awhile. After the rain fell for an hour, Landis finally decided to postpone the contest. Some in attendance at Forbes Field wondered why baseball's czar took so long to cancel the game. It was apparent to those present, as early as 1:50 P.M., that there was no possible way a game could be played that afternoon. The fans were forced to sit on rain soaked seats for 40 minutes before Landis called off Wednesday's contest.[10]

Game Seven of the 1925 World Series was pushed back one day to Thursday, October 15. The extra day of rest was expected to work wonders for both teams. Pittsburgh's batters could expect Walter Johnson to be that much tougher since he would now be pitching on three days' rest. The rainout also meant that Bill McKechnie could choose to come back with Vic Aldridge if he so desired. McKechnie had led the press to believe that Red Oldham would pitch Game Seven if it had been played Wednesday afternoon. When Oldham took his turn during batting practice, the choice looked like a certainty. The situation changed when McKechnie sent Johnny Morrison out to take some batting practice after the rain began to fall. McKechnie then announced that Morrison would take the mound if the game was able to be played despite the rain.[11]

A stroke of luck and poor weather made it possible for Aldridge to enter the fray once again in search of his third victory in the 1925 World Series. If Aldridge won, he would join Deacon Phillippe and teammate Babe Adams, who had turned the trick during the Fall Classics of 1903 and 1909, respectively.

In a strange side note to the Series, a group of fans that gathered in a Pittsburgh radio shop to listen to World Series games had become fear stricken when a black cat entered the premises just as Game Five began. Some of the men wanted the cat to be shown the door, but employee Charley Pollard rescued the feline and permitted his new pet to remain for the game. After the Pirates won the game, other employees from the shop bestowed the moniker of "Tom" on the black cat. On Tuesday afternoon, Tom strolled into the shop as the game began, and the Pirates won once again. The cat was present for Wednesday's game, as well. When it started to rain outside, Tom strolled out of the building and started for home. A Game Seven win by Pittsburgh guaranteed that Tom would be dubbed the most popular cat in Butler County.[12]

Pittsburgh weather forecaster W.S. Brotzman predicted that the temperature would rise to 55 degrees on the afternoon of October 15. Brotzman stated that even though the skies would be overcast, he did not expect it to rain. The weather system that dumped showers on Pittsburgh throughout Wednesday was now traveling up the New England coast.[13] Those who intended to attend Game Seven and took Brotzman's assessment to heart were probably shocked as they prepared to make the journey to Forbes Field. When the ballpark's bleacher gates opened at 10:00 A.M., it had already been raining for an hour in

Pittsburgh. Commissioner Landis arrived at Forbes Field just as the first group of fans began filing through the turnstiles. Landis checked the diamond and proclaimed that conditions were satisfactory enough to play a game, unless it continued to rain throughout the day. By 11:30 A.M., a steady drizzle was still falling at Forbes Field, and the skies overhead looked ominous, indicating that a heavy downpour could occur at any moment.[14]

Head groundskeeper Jack Fogarty quickly went to work preparing Forbes Field for the ultimate game. Fogarty's loyal employees immediately began to roll the base paths in order to smooth them out. Barrels of gasoline were rolled out to the skinned portion of the diamond, where their contents were dumped and lit on fire. Shivering fans cheered when the flames began to crackle on the infield dirt. Although a large tarpaulin was stretched over the infield when rain began to fall the previous afternoon, water had seeped through holes in the covering. There were puddles of water and mud between home plate and first base, and on the base path from second to third. The grounds crew hoped to fix these problems by burning off the field's moisture. Another problem arose when some of the gasoline reached the field's grass, which started to burn. Fogarty's workers were forced to use sprinkling cans of water to extinguish the various fires. The scene looked quite comical to fans in the stands, as they watched the groundskeepers frantically running around in the rain and dumping water on the sudden blazes.[15]

Mud and water were also prevalent on the paths leading from the dugouts to home plate.[16] Large sacks of sawdust were brought in and spread out in an effort to soak up excess water that could prove to be a hindrance to players on both teams.[17] The poor field conditions seemed to be more of a handicap to a team like the Pirates, a young crew noted for its blazing speed. Treacherous footing always made it tougher for a fast team than a much slower outfit. Yet, fielders from both teams would find difficulty maneuvering in the soaked grass. Hitters would not likely have problems since the batters boxes seemed to be the only dry places on Forbes Field's diamond.[18]

In spite of the poor field conditions, the perceived extra rest for Washington's older squad, and another idle afternoon for Game Seven starter Walter Johnson, assistant manager Fred Clarke felt confident that Pittsburgh would prevail in the deciding contest.

> The break in the series yesterday caused by rain will not be of more benefit to the Washington club than it will be to Pittsburgh. I don't get the dope that the Senators will be so much better when they get started again just because they had a day off.
> Our boys didn't spend the day chopping wood and they got just as much rest. As far as Walter Johnson is concerned, we all feel that we'll beat him no matter when the next game is played and how long a rest he has.
> Vic Aldridge will be getting just as much rest as Johnson. It is a good thing

that no attempt was made to play yesterday's game as it would not have been fair to either team with so much at stake. I still like the Pirates, rain or shine.[19]

An off and on drizzle fell at Forbes Field as preparations for the game continued. Outside the ballpark, scalpers were boldly grabbing passersby in an effort to unload their tickets. Prices quickly dropped as supply remained well above demand. By 12:15 P.M., the cheapest seats in the center field temporary bleachers were only one-third filled. The steady drizzle ceased at 12:30 P.M. and the sky became a little brighter as some of the dark clouds temporarily moved away. Danny Nirella's band immediately got caught up in the moment and played "It Ain't Gonna Rain No Mo'," for the Forbes Field crowd.

After having just moments earlier moved a big canvas cover to the outfield for quick access, Fogarty and his men rolled back the canvas tarp and folded it for removal from the diamond. Forbes Field's bleacher seats were now filling rapidly as the occupants of the cheaper seats lifted their spirits by singing "Sweet Adeline" and other songs. The standing room only crowd was lined up at a vacant lot near the Schenley Hotel waiting to buy tickets to the big game when the time finally arrived.[20]

When the Pirates took the field for practice at 1:00 P.M., Forbes Field's left field concrete bleachers were filled to capacity and there were few vacant seats in the center field section. The grandstand crowd had also started to push through the turnstiles, and most of the sections were filled as Pittsburgh took batting practice.

Vic Aldridge was the last Pirate player to make his way onto the field. Aldridge and Johnny Morrison both took part in early batting practice. Ray Kremer and Lee Meadows also put in some work at the plate. Bill McKechnie stated that every pitcher who was in condition to enter the final game against Washington would be used if necessary, though it was highly unlikely that Meadows would be one of those men.[21] Specialists had been working on his pitching arm since Game One over a week ago, but he did not seem to be responding to treatment; it looked as if a long rest would be the only remedy for his injured arm.[22]

The Senators took the field at 1:10 P.M. to begin their practice session. The day off seemed to do Bucky Harris' boys some good as they looked more lively than the previous afternoon. Bill McKechnie's players also seemed to be brimming with confidence as they prepared to play the biggest game of their lives.[23]

McKechnie and Harris went with standard lineups for the final game. Washington's batting order consisted of: 1. Sam Rice (CF), 2. Bucky Harris (2B), 3. Goose Goslin (LF), 4. Joe Harris (RF), 5. Joe Judge (1B), 6. Ossie Bluege (3B), 7. Roger Peckinpaugh (SS), 8. Muddy Ruel (C) and 9. Walter Johnson (P). McKechnie countered with his usual lineup of: 1. Eddie Moore (2B), 2. Max Carey (CF), 3. Hazen Cuyler (RF), 4. Clyde Barnhart (LF),

5. Pie Traynor (3B), 6. Glenn Wright (SS), 7. Stuffy McInnis (1B), 8. Earl Smith (C) and 9. Vic Aldridge (P).

Diehard baseball fans who were ecstatic that game time had finally arrived cheered on the Pirates squad using their voices, noise makers, megaphones, horns, rattlers and crickets.[24] The Pirates trotted out to take their position on Forbes Field's wet and muddy field. Vic Aldridge threw his warm-up tosses to catcher Earl Smith. Home plate umpire Barry McCormick yelled "Play Ball," and Aldridge prepared to face Sam Rice. Rice promptly drilled a single over Aldridge's head into center field. The Forbes Field crowd then cheered with approval when Clyde Barnhart hauled in Bucky Harris' long drive to left for the first out. Heavy-hitting Goose Goslin stepped up to the plate. Aldridge uncorked a wild pitch that moved Rice to second. Goslin became Washington's second runner when he drew a walk. In response, Pittsburgh's infielders walked to the mound and offered Aldridge encouragement, but the pitcher threw his second wild pitch of the inning, moving each Senators runner up 90 feet. Aldridge then walked Joe Harris to load the bases.[25]

The wet and muddy conditions were having a profound effect on Aldridge's ability to pitch. He could not properly handle the wet ball as he simultaneously slipped and slid on the mound while attempting to pitch. Aldridge's problems continued when he walked Joe Judge and forced home Rice with the game's first tally. Ossie Bluege followed with a single to left field that brought Goslin home and gave Washington a 2–0 lead. Bill McKechnie decided the time had come to remove Aldridge from the game before the situation became dire. McKechnie summoned Johnny Morrison from the bullpen to extinguish Washington's early rally.[26]

The haze at Forbes Field was so thick from the fog and rain that people in the stands had not been able to see Bluege's hit until it went over Clyde Barnhart's head.[27] Field conditions were not likely to improve as the afternoon wore on. Roger Peckinpaugh strolled to the plate with the bases loaded and one out. The Senators quickly added to their lead when umpire McCormick called Earl Smith for catcher's interference for tipping Peckinpaugh's bat. Peckinpaugh was awarded first base as Joe Harris strolled home with Washington's third run. Muddy Ruel followed and smacked an easy roller to second baseman Eddie Moore, but Judge scored and all runners were safe as Moore fumbled the grounder. Morrison finally recorded the inning's second out when he fanned Walter Johnson, who limped back to the dugout, indicating that the injury he aggravated running the bases in Game Four was still bothering him. Rice came to the plate for a second time in the frame but ended the inning when he flied out to Barnhart in left.[28]

Pittsburgh's expectations had been greatly reduced as they finally came to bat in the bottom of the first trailing 4–0. Because Johnson had allowed only one run in two World Series starts, it seemed highly unlikely that he would

13. Carey and the Pirates Overcome Johnson and the Weather 203

allow five Pirates runners to cross home plate. Eddie Moore led off the inning by attempting to drag a bunt for an infield single, but the plan was thwarted when Johnson handled the ball and threw to Judge for the first out. Max Carey then served notice that the Pirates would not go quietly as he drilled a Johnson offering to left for a double. Kiki Cuyler failed to bring home the team captain as the Flint Flash swung at three Johnson fastballs and came up empty each time. Barnhart then brought the inning to an end when he struck out, taking a vicious cut at a Johnson fastball.[29]

Morrison had success suppressing the Senators in the second inning. Bucky Harris flied out to Cuyler in right field. Goose Goslin then hit a fly ball to center that was snagged by Carey for the second out. Morrison made it an easy inning when he retired Joe Harris on a groundball to shortstop Glenn Wright.

Walter Johnson continued to look untouchable as he retired Pie Traynor on a comebacker for the first out in the bottom of the second. Wright followed Traynor by drilling a liner past Johnson that landed in center field for a base hit. Stuffy McInnis slammed another hit to the same area, moving the Pirates' shortstop to second base. As Earl Smith stepped to the plate with two runners on and one out, rain once again began to fall. Oblivious to the rain, Johnson ended any hopes of a big inning for the Pirates when he induced Smith to hit a grounder to Bucky Harris, who converted a simple double play by tagging McInnis and throwing to Judge at first base.[30]

Judge led off the top of the third inning by rapping a single that dropped in front of Max Carey in center field. Ossie Bluege was unable to move him to second base as he popped up to Eddie Moore for the first out. Roger Peckinpaugh followed and smacked a drive to Kiki Cuyler that seemed destined to drop safely, but the right fielder somehow reached the ball and made a spectacular catch as he tumbled to the ground. When Cuyler arose, he made a furious throw to first base, attempting to double up Judge. But Cuyler's lob was off the mark; Judge moved up to second when first baseman Stuffy McInnis could not handle the errant toss.[31] Fortunately, Cuyler's error following the sensational catch did nothing to deter Morrison, who retired Washington when Carey hauled in Muddy Ruel's fly ball to center field.[32]

Kiki Cuyler's catch seemed to lift his teammates' spirits as they took their turn batting in the third inning. Morrison led off by drilling a Walter Johnson offering over second base for a single. Morrison then came around to score on Eddie Moore's double off the left field wall. The Pirates cut Washington's lead in half when Carey's single past Bucky Harris drove Moore home with Pittsburgh's second tally of the day.

Washington's manager walked over to Johnson and patted him on the back as Cuyler stepped up to the plate. Cuyler moved Carey to second as he was retired on a grounder to Peckinpaugh. Carey promptly stole third base while Johnson faced Clyde Barnhart. Pittsburgh quickly made the score, 4–3, when Barnhart's single landed in front of Joe Harris in right and brought Carey home.[33]

Washington's entire infield unit walked to the mound and tried to encourage Johnson. Bucky Harris then gave Johnson another pat on the back as he prepared to face Pie Traynor. Johnson recorded the second out when Barnhart was forced at second on Traynor's grounder to Roger Peckinpaugh, and Glenn Wright ended the inning when he popped up to Bucky Harris.[34] Pittsburgh's fans cheered wildly, having just witnessed a three-run rally against the immortal Johnson.

The expectations of Forbes Field's patrons were quickly crushed by the Senators in the fourth inning. The frame started innocently enough for Johnny Morrison, as he retired Johnson on a shallow pop fly to Max Carey in center field. Sam Rice followed by lining a one-out single past Stuffy McInnis. Bucky Harris stepped to the plate and was called out on strikes by umpire Barry McCormick. Goose Goslin then kept the Senators' inning alive by rapping a single past Traynor. Rice scampered to third base while Goslin made it to second when Barnhart erroneously threw to third. Joe Harris then hit a blistering drive that went for a double when Carey fell in pursuit of the ball. Rice and Goslin both scored to give Washington a 6–3 lead. The inning finally ended when Cuyler secured Joe Judge's easy fly to right for the third out.[35]

In the bottom of the fourth, Stuffy McInnis started the stanza by singling in front of Goslin in left. Sam Rice kept the Pirates from adding a second runner when he made a spectacular shoestring catch in center, robbing Earl Smith. George Grantham batted for Morrison and gave hope to Pittsburgh fans when he slammed a Johnson pitch to deep right-center field. The cheers turned to disappointment as Harris hauled in Grantham's blast in front of the outfield fence. Eddie Moore then flied out to Goslin in left, ending the inning.[36]

Ray Kremer was called upon to pitch even though he had tossed a complete game victory only two days earlier. Bill McKechnie could not turn to Lee Meadows for two reasons. Meadows' arm was still ailing him, and the rainy weather likely would have troubled the bespectacled hurler even if he felt well. Kremer made quick work of the Senators in the fifth. Ossie Bluege was retired when Pie Traynor handled his easy grounder and threw to Stuffy McInnis. Roger Peckinpaugh grounded out to Glenn Wright. Kremer then sent Washington back to play defense when Muddy Ruel hit a liner to center that Max Carey grabbed for the inning's final out.[37]

Carey started out Pittsburgh's half of the fifth by doubling to right field for his third hit of the ballgame. Kiki Cuyler then reduced Washington's lead to 6–4 when he drove home Carey with a double of his own that landed squarely on the left field foul line. Johnson stiffened and fanned Clyde Barnhart for the first out before inducing Pie Traynor to hit a foul ball caught by Muddy

13. Carey and the Pirates Overcome Johnson and the Weather   205

Ruel in front of the Pittsburgh dugout. The Pirates' promising rally ended when Glenn Wright hit a towering pop fly that second baseman Bucky Harris handled easily in shallow right field.[38]

A steadier rain began to fall at Forbes Field during the fifth inning. As the Pirates took the field to start the sixth inning, Commissioner Landis decided that the weather had made it impossible to let the contest continue. Landis was originally reluctant to postpone the game since a huge crowd was expected; the czar had allowed Barney Dreyfuss to enjoy a huge payday. Landis now believed that it was time to protect the integrity of the World Series. Since an official game was already in the books, Landis determined that the world championship trophy should be awarded to Washington.[39]

"You're the world champions," Landis told Washington owner Clark Griffith, who was seated next to him. "I'm calling this game."

"Once you've started in the rain you've got to finish it," replied Griffith.[40]

If Pittsburgh's owner had heard this conversation, he would have protested angrily. As it stood, Dreyfuss was still confined to his apartment due to a severe cold. The point quickly became moot since Landis had a change of heart and permitted the game to proceed.

Walter Johnson led off the sixth inning by popping out to Glenn Wright at short. Sam Rice became Kremer's second victim of the frame when his grounder was easily handled by Wright, who tossed to Stuffy McInnis. Kremer set the Senators down in order when he fanned Bucky Harris, who became a strikeout victim for the second time that afternoon.[41] As the Pirate players ran off the field to take their turn at bat, the clouds suddenly opened up and dumped a heavier downpour of rain on Forbes Field.

The Pirates failed to do much against Johnson in their half of the sixth inning. McInnis popped out to Goose Goslin in shallow left for the first out. Johnson took care of Earl Smith, as Pittsburgh's catcher was retired on a fly ball to Sam Rice in center.[42] McKechnie then permitted Ray Kremer to bat for himself since the Pirates' hurler had been effective since coming on in relief of Johnny Morrison. Kremer made the last out when he fouled out to catcher Muddy Ruel.

Kremer rewarded McKechnie's faith by setting down Washington in order in the seventh inning. Goslin was retired on a comebacker that went Kremer-to-McInnis. Joe Harris recorded the second out by fouling out to Pie Traynor. The inning ended when Joe Judge flied out to Kiki Cuyler in right field.[43]

It was now so dark and murky as Washington took the field in the bottom of the seventh that players from both squads resembled ghostly figures from an English moor. The gray and dreary weather led to Pittsburgh putting a runner on base to start the seventh inning. Roger Peckinpaugh dropped Eddie Moore's pop-up when he lost the ball in the darkness. Moore pulled into second base by the time Peckinpaugh retrieved the baseball. Max Carey then followed

Veteran Max Carey starred for the Pittsburgh Pirates in Game Seven of the 1925 World Series against Walter Johnson and the Washington Senators. Carey went 4-for-5 at the plate, scored three runs, stroked two doubles and drove home two runs. Carey led all batters in the World Series with a .458 average (National Baseball Hall of Fame Library, Cooperstown, New York).

with a double along the left field line that brought Moore home and made the score, 6–5. Left fielder Goose Goslin immediately protested to the umpires that Carey's drive had landed foul. Goslin asked the arbiters to join him in the outfield so that he could show them the spot in the mud where the ball landed.[44]

The umpires called time in order to confer. After a few minutes, they turned down Washington's protest and ordered the Senators to play ball. Kiki Cuyler stepped up to the plate and sacrificed Carey to third with a beautiful bunt that Johnson fielded before firing to Bucky Harris covering at first base. Carey remained at third base when Clyde Barnhart was retired on a groundball to Harris.

It seemed that Johnson would escape the inning with Washington's lead still intact. Pie Traynor stepped to the plate and changed those expectations by launching a deep drive over the head of Joe Harris in right-center field. Carey scored the game's tying run as Traynor tore around the bases. Joe Harris finally retrieved the ball and threw a strike to second baseman Bucky Harris, the relay man. As the ball reached the infield, Traynor made the turn at third and headed home. Harris made a clean toss to Muddy Ruel, who tagged Traynor out at home.[45] Traynor was credited with a triple, but his effort fell just a few lengths short from giving Pittsburgh a one-run lead.

Pittsburgh's fans were still howling as Washington came to the plate in the eighth inning. The noise level of the crowd reached a crescendo when Ossie Bluege grounded out to Traynor for the first out of the inning. As had been the case throughout this series, emotions changed quickly when Roger Peckinpaugh gave Washington a 7–6 lead by launching a Ray Kremer pitch over the left field fence for a home run.[46]

Prior to hitting this monumental homer, Peckinpaugh had worn the Series' goat horns by committing seven errors in the field. If Walter Johnson could make the one-run lead hold up, Peckinpaugh would change from goat to hero because of one swing. In the meantime, Kremer did not let Peckinpaugh's blast bother him, as he retired Ruel on a groundball to Traynor at third. Walter Johnson then made the final out when he fouled out to Earl Smith.[47]

Throughout the afternoon, Jack Fogerty and his crew of groundskeepers had spread sawdust over wet areas around the bases and on the pitcher's mound. Still, the wet ball and insecure footing on the mound had bothered Johnson all day. Johnson had been deliberate in his delivery, taking extra time to make sure he was standing firmly on the pitching rubber. He constantly knocked mud from his spikes so that he could properly follow through with his motion.

The darkness that had descended upon Forbes Field should have helped a fastball pitcher like Johnson, but the wet conditions seemed to bother him more that Pittsburgh's pitchers. Prior to the eighth inning, Johnson went to Pittsburgh's dugout, grabbed a capful of sawdust, and took it back to the mound.[48] As Johnson stood on the hill waiting for Glenn Wright to step into the batter's box, his uniform was caked with mud and sawdust.

Wright became Johnson's first victim of the inning when he was retired on a pop foul to first baseman Joe Judge. Before facing Stuffy McInnis, Johnson called time and requested more sawdust for the mound from the groundskeepers. Once the material was spread, Johnson turned his attention to McInnis and retired him on a fly ball to Sam Rice. Washington's ace was now only four outs away from securing a second consecutive world championship for his teammates. Earl Smith strolled to the plate and found a pitch to his liking, driving a shot past Bucky Harris that landed between Rice and Joe Harris for a double. Bill McKechnie then sent the much faster Emil Yde in to run for Smith at second.[49] By letting Yde pinch run in this situation, McKechnie was also sending a message that he had no intention of using the southpaw in relief if the game progressed past nine innings.

When Carson Bigbee was announced as a pinch hitter for Ray Kremer, many in the Forbes Field crowd questioned McKechnie for turning to a player who hit only .238 during the regular season. Bigbee quickly silenced the naysayers when he connected against a Johnson offering and smacked a ball over Goose Goslin's head toward the left field screen. Yde came around to score the game's tying run, as Bigbee stood at second with a rousing double.

Those in attendance at Forbes Field could see that Johnson was tiring.[50] Washington manager Bucky Harris did not seem to agree as he left Johnson in to face Eddie Moore. Before Moore moved into the box, Pie Traynor came out with a towel, just as he had done when Bigbee pinch hit, and dried Moore's bat to improve the grip.[51] Walter Johnson tried to throw strikes to Moore, but he failed as Moore trotted to first with a walk, putting runners on first and second with two outs.[52]

Max Carey stepped up to the plate. The Pirates' captain delivered a ground ball to Roger Peckinpaugh that surely would be handled for the last out. Peckinpaugh grabbed the ball and hastily threw to Bucky Harris, who was covering at second. Peckinpaugh knew he had to hurry since the speedy Moore was bearing down on Harris. With the ball wet, Peckinpaugh failed to take perfect aim when he tossed the ball. The high throw pulled Harris off the bag. When Harris' foot landed on second base, he felt Moore's shoe on the base underneath him. Moore was safe, Peckinpaugh was charged with his eighth error of the Series, and the bases were now filled with Pirates as Hazen "Kiki" Cuyler entered the batter's box.[53]

Before Johnson began to work against Cuyler, the groundskeepers went to the mound with a rake and a bag of sawdust and attempted to fix the mound to the pitcher's specifications.[54] After performing their work, the groundskeepers left Johnson to face Cuyler. The battle between Washington's veteran hurler and Pittsburgh's young free-swinger had the makings of a classic duel. The

13. Carey and the Pirates Overcome Johnson and the Weather

count went to 2–2 on Cuyler, who then viciously fouled off several of Johnson's offerings. Cuyler then took a fastball that home plate umpire Barry McCormick called a ball. Johnson and catcher Muddy Ruel did not agree; they actually started for the Washington dugout since they believed the pitch was a strike.[55]

Cuyler did not take any chances on Johnson's next pitch. The Washington ace threw a pitch that landed in Cuyler's wheelhouse.[56] Cuyler drove the ball down the right field line into restricted territory.[57] Cuyler tore around the bases and made it all the way home as Joe Harris struggled to pick up the ball. Bigbee, Moore and Carey scored ahead of Cuyler as Pittsburgh took an apparent 11–7 lead on his triple and Harris' error. Yet, the umpires conferred and ruled that Cuyler was entitled to only a double because of Forbes Field's ground rules.[58] Harris had experienced difficulty retrieving the ball because it temporarily became stuck under the canvas tarpaulin.[59] Bill McKechnie argued with the umpires, claiming that Cuyler's hit should be ruled a home run, but the arbiters ordered Cuyler to return to second base and Carey to go back to third.[60] Walter Johnson then worked out of the inning by retiring Clyde Barnhart on a pop-up to second baseman Bucky Harris.[61] The Pirates now held a 9–7 lead as they took the field for the top of the ninth inning.

If Walter Johnson had only allowed Pittsburgh to tie the game in the eighth inning, the umpires likely would have called the game at the end of the inning and ordered a play-off the following day. It was now so dark that fielders were having extreme difficulty picking up the ball as it came off the bats of opposing players. Now that the Pirates had taken the lead in the home half of the eighth, it necessitated that Washington be given a chance to bat in the ninth regardless of how muddy and wet the field's conditions had become.

Forbes Field's press box was also in shambles due to the afternoon's lousy weather. The writers were stationed in a box right behind the catcher, with no protection from the rain. Conditions had become so bad that writers were unable to scribble notations on the wet pages of their programs.[62]

Bill McKechnie called on southpaw Red Oldham to retire Washington and bring the world championship to the Smoky City. Remarkably, Oldham was making his first appearance of the 1925 World Series. McKechnie's choices were limited since three pitchers had already been used, Yde was no longer available since pinch running for Earl Smith, and Lee Meadows was unable to go. McKechnie chose Oldham over Babe Adams and Tom Sheehan because Washington would be sending two left-handed batters to the plate in the ninth.

At 4:24 P.M. on Thursday, October 15, McKechnie gave Oldham one last piece of advice before he prepared to face the Senators.[63] "You may crossfire when ready, Oldham," instructed McKechnie to his pitcher.[64]

McKechnie also made a few other changes in the ninth inning. Carson Bigbee remained in the game and moved to left field, with Oldham placed in

Clyde Barnhart's fourth spot in the batting order. Johnny Gooch was Pittsburgh's new catcher, replacing Earl Smith. Oldham immediately went to work and fanned Sam Rice on a called third strike for the first out. After Rice was called out on strikes, he turned and argued bitterly with home plate umpire Barry McCormick. Bucky Harris then followed Rice to the plate and became the second out when he lined to second baseman Eddie Moore.[65]

The heavy-hitting Goose Goslin now stepped up to the plate, hoping to extend the game. Goslin let Oldham's first crossfire offering glide by for strike one. Goose swung mightily at Oldham's second pitch, but came up empty, missing the pitch badly. Oldham paused for a moment after receiving the throw from Gooch. He then wound up and unleashed the most important pitch of his career. Oldham's fastball caught Goslin flat-footed, as McCormick called a perfect strike for the final out of the afternoon.[66] Having pulled off one of the most amazing comebacks in the annals of the game, the Pittsburgh Pirates were now world champions.

The celebration began immediately at Forbes Field. Thousands of fans poured over the low fences onto the field and made their way toward the Pirates' dugout in order to honor the new champions. Unlikely heroes like Carson Bigbee and Red Oldham received ovations just as rousing as their counterparts who had played throughout the Series. Fans remained on the field for over an hour, celebrating Pittsburgh's victory. Some fans

Hazen "Kiki" Cuyler delivered the crucial hit that gave Pittsburgh victory in Game Seven of the 1925 World Series on October 15 at Forbes Field. With the bases loaded and two outs, Cuyler connected for a double against Walter Johnson that brought home two teammates and gave the Pirates a 9–7 lead in the eighth inning. Cuyler's heroic effort brought Pittsburgh its first world championship in 16 years (National Baseball Hall of Fame Library, Cooperstown, New York).

weaved about, doing the kind of "snake dance" that commonly followed a college football victory.[67]

At some point, almost all of the 45,000 patrons who attended the final match up between the game's two supreme teams joined in the celebration on the Forbes Field diamond. Fans celebrated by singing, dancing, and throwing cushions, hats and umbrellas into the air. Souvenir hounds began searching for pieces of memorabilia. One fan tore up the pitcher's rubber, while another came away with home plate. All three bases were also confiscated, and 300 chairs were ripped from their box seat sections by delirious fans. Danny Nirella's band entertained the raucous fans by playing music and leading a procession inside of Forbes Field. The celebration eventually made its way to the streets of Pittsburgh and lasted well past midnight. Confetti, colored paper, balloons and all sorts of noise-making devices became evident during the celebration. Automobiles, filled with fans, jammed the streets of downtown Pittsburgh and brought traffic to a halt.[68] Sirens blared, car horns honked and fans yelled as Smoky City patrons celebrated Pittsburgh's first baseball championship in 16 years.[69]

The Pirates' players made their way to the clubhouse to continue the celebration after receiving accolades from their devoted fans. Players congratulated each other and shook hands with friends through a haze of jubilation. Commissioner Landis even became involved in the celebration when he entered the room. Usually reserved, Landis grabbed the hands of those players nearest to him and offered congratulations.

Landis made one simple statement to the crowd of celebrating world champions before he departed and left in a cab.[70] "You are the greatest club that ever won a world's championship," stated baseball's commissioner, "and I want to congratulate each and every one of you upon your fine victory. It was a great game and a great Series, and you richly deserve the success that your never-say-die spirit brought you in the end."[71]

After the celebration died down in Pittsburgh's clubhouse, manager Bill McKechnie was approached by a writer. As McKechnie pulled off his mud-stained uniform and changed into street clothes, the scribe asked him what he was going to do now that the Pirates were world champions.[72]

"The first thing I'm going to do is go home and get into a clean suit of underwear," responded McKechnie, "a clean shirt and clean socks. I've been wearing what I have on now ever since we won the fifth game of the series in Washington.

"I figured it was a lucky combination, so I wouldn't change till the Series was over. And I guess my hunch was pretty good, eh? But I'm going to get into clean clothes now."[73]

Bill McKechnie was a major reason why the Pirates' young players had shown such determination when they faced daunting odds of coming back during the 1925 World Series. McKechnie steered the craft despite the claims of many experts that Pittsburgh would falter once again. Even though McKechnie was the manager of the world champions, he remained humble to the end. Now that the season was over, William Boyd McKechnie was merely concerned with going home and changing into clean clothes so that he could celebrate the achievement with family and friends in Wilkinsburg.

14

Champions of the World

For years, the Pittsburgh Pirates had underachieved due to a perceived lack of fighting spirit on the part of their players. This was no longer the case, as Bill McKechnie's 1925 Pirates showed true resilience and courage in rallying from what looked like an insurmountable deficit against Washington in the World Series. During the early games of the series, McKechnie's young team seemed to be nervous. The strain of participating on baseball's grandest stage prevented the Pirates from playing up to their ability, as they failed miserably at the plate during the Series' early contests. Once Pittsburgh's brigade of hitters caught fire, no Washington pitcher was able to counteract them. The Pirates' magnificent stand against the defending world champions allowed them to gain the admiration of fans across America.[1]

American League president Ban Johnson was one of the first people to congratulate the Pirates after they claimed victory in Game Seven of the World Series. Johnson left Pittsburgh after Game Six because of the lousy weather conditions and did not witness the final game in person. Johnson sent a message from Chicago in which he applauded Pittsburgh's victory.

The American League president also went out of his way to criticize Washington manager Bucky Harris in a telegram, principally for allowing Walter Johnson to continue on the mound in the deciding game.[2] "You put up a game fight," said Johnson. "This I admire. Lost the Series for sentimental reasons. This should never have happened in a World's Series."[3]

Ban Johnson was not the only person who was critical of the way Harris handled his pitching staff during the final game of the World Series. Harris' critics agreed with Johnson regarding the issue of sentiment. They believed that Harris was anxious to see Walter Johnson win three Series games so that he could take his rightful place among other great pitchers who had done this in the past. It was also rumored that Johnson's fellow Washington teammates wanted the Big Train to be adorned with such glory. Ban Johnson quickly elaborated on his message to Bucky Harris when pundits pressed the league president for more details.[4]

Walter Johnson never should have been permitted to continue in the box after the third inning. It was obvious to any baseball man at this stage of the game that Walter was not himself. He should have been taken out then and there. I am sure that anyone with an ounce of baseball sense will agree with me.

The American League champions were leading, 4 to 3, then and with any kind of substitute pitching could have won. The score in the innings which followed, bears out that statement. Dutch Ruether, as great a left-hander as there is in baseball, was ready to step in the breach. Ruether has had World's Series experience. There is no sound reason for his being kept out of the game. If Ruether faltered, there were other Senator pitchers ready and eager to go in. Walter Johnson, a grand, courageous fellow, was sacrificed to sentiment. That is the only possible excuse for the Senators' defeat.[5]

Bucky Harris and his players were a downcast lot as they made the trip back to Washington by train after losing the final World Series game. The Senators accepted their defeat gracefully and promised that they would be back in the thick of the American League pennant race in 1926.[6] When the Senators arrived at the Nation's Capital on the morning of October 16, they were a tired and disappointed squad. But manager Harris was in a fighting mood as he sought out baseball scribes in order to air some grievances. His belligerence was not directed at the Pirates. Harris took dead aim at Ban Johnson's comments, responding angrily to the American League president's critical remarks.[7]

> Ban Johnson's telegram is impudent and uncalled for. Johnson pitched the best ball he could, and Ban Johnson's statement is a reflection on him. I have no alibis.
>
> It is easy to point out such things after a ball game is over. Had we won I would have been a great manager. As it was I gambled and lost.
>
> The weather was terrible. The field was worse. It was dark, overcast and raining. This is ideal Walter Johnson weather. Under such conditions I knew of no greater, no brainier pitcher than Walter Johnson and I kept him there for that reason, and not sentiment.
>
> Walter Johnson is still the greatest pitcher in baseball and will continue to be such in 1926.
>
> Last year, after Johnson had twice been beaten in the Series by the Giants, I put him in at a critical moment in the final game — and he won it. I was called nervy and a great manager.
>
> President Johnson's remarks were better left unsaid.[8]

Harris' response to Ban Johnson's criticism was right on point. As Washington's manager, Harris was much more qualified to discuss his players limitations than the American League president. Harris had been reluctant to use left-handed pitchers Tom Zachary and Dutch Ruether throughout the Fall Classic because Pittsburgh's lineup was laden with right-handed batters who had crushed southpaws during the regular season. Harris' two choices in the latter moments of the seventh game boiled down to Walter Johnson and Firpo Marberry. Washington's manager believed that Johnson gave his team the best possible chance to win. Harris accepted the consequences of this decision and believed that Ban Johnson should not have second-guessed him.

From a financial standpoint, the 1925 World Series was the most successful in baseball history. The total gate receipts of $1,182,854 shattered the previous high water mark that was achieved when Washington met New York in 1924. The attendance record of 301,430 set in 1923, when the Giants and Yankees competed, remained intact as 13,600 fewer people pushed through the turnstiles during the 1925 Fall Classic.[9] Pittsburgh's percentage of the World Series money amounted to $142,650.56, while Washington's players divided the losers' share of $90,100. Each Pittsburgh player received $5,332.75 for winning the World Series while each member of the Senators' squad became $3,734.50 richer.[10] A committee of players from the Pirates squad voted to give coach Jack Onslow and secretary Sam Watters a full World Series share. Red Oldham, Fresco Thompson and George Haas were voted only a partial share of the pool money since they did not spend the entire season in Pittsburgh.[11]

There were many players who stood out as stars for both the winner and loser of the 1925 World Series. Joe Harris was the batting star for Washington, with a .440 batting average, three home runs, and six RBIs. Sam Rice (.364), Goose Goslin (.308) and Muddy Ruel (.316) performed consistently at the plate throughout the seven-game series. Bucky Harris hit only .087 at the plate, but did admirable work defensively for Washington. Despite his disappointing loss in the seventh game, Walter Johnson still put up phenomenal numbers for Washington. Johnson tossed three complete games,

Washington Senators manager Bucky Harris was criticized by American League president Ban Johnson for the way he handled his pitching staff during Game Seven of the 1925 World Series. Ban believed Harris permitted Walter Johnson to remain in the game for sentimental reasons even though Washington's star pitcher was not sharp. Harris countered by stating that Johnson was the greatest pitcher in baseball (National Baseball Hall of Fame Library, Cooperstown, New York).

won two out of three contests, and posted a sterling 2.08 ERA for the Senators. In contrast, Roger Peckinpaugh was the Series goat as he committed eight errors, many of which occurred because the Washington shortstop felt hurried by Pittsburgh's speedy runners.

Pittsburgh had a long list of notable players who performed admirably during the 1925 Fall Classic. Glenn Wright and Pie Traynor played superbly in the field. Traynor also chipped in at the plate by finishing third on the Pirates with a .346 average. Kiki Cuyler hit only .269 against the Senators, but his crucial hits secured victory for the Corsairs in both the second and seventh games. Ray Kremer (2–1, 3.00 ERA), Vic Aldridge (2–0, 4.42 ERA) and Johnny Morrison (0–0, 2.89 ERA) all did commendable work on the mound for Pittsburgh. All of these players had a hand in bringing Pittsburgh its first world championship since 1909, but none ranked as the most important contributor to the Pirates cause. This honor fell on team captain Max Carey, who gave a brilliant performance in his first World Series appearance.

Carey led all hitters from both teams with a blistering .458 average. He scored six runs, stole three bases, smacked four doubles, and was solid defensively for Pittsburgh in center field. Carey saved his best work for Game Seven, when he went 4-for-5, scored three runs and was credited with his only two RBIs of the Series. His performance was even more remarkable given that he played the last two games of the World Series while in considerable pain.[12] Carey suffered a serious injury when he collided with Bucky Harris on the base paths and was temporarily knocked out during Game Five.[13] He kept the injury a secret and continued to play in severe pain.[14]

The extent of Carey's injury did not become known until after the World Series was completed. Carey spent a week in Pittsburgh's Mercy Hospital after the Series' conclusion. Carey contracted a cold playing in the constant, drizzling downpour of Game Seven. The cold almost developed into pleurisy and might have been followed by pneumonia if Carey's doctor had not promptly admitted him to the hospital. An x-ray revealed that one of his ribs was cracked and that several ligaments had been torn loose on his right side. According to Bill McKechnie, if Game Seven had been played on October 14 as originally scheduled, Carey probably would have remained on the bench due to his rib injury. After that day's game was postponed by rain, Carey remained in bed under the constant care of his physician, determined to participate in the deciding game no matter what the cost.

McKechnie paid his popular captain a stirring tribute for his gameness.[15] "He was in agony during half of the Series," said McKechnie "but he never complained, and put everything he had into his play. I never saw a finer exhibition of genuine grit. Handicapped by illness and injury, Max made some of baseball's brightest history. He is a wonderful chap, and he proved it during the World's Series."[16]

Carey was one of the few Pirate players who planned on making Pittsburgh his home during the off-season. Members of the 1925 Pirates scattered to their homes across the country after the final game, as they were required to do so under National Commission rules.[17] Kiki Cuyler, his wife and son left for Harrisville, Michigan, by automobile around noon on October 16. Johnny Rawlings and his family departed for Los Angeles that evening. Bud Culloton began his journey to Kingston, New York, while Johnny Morrison made the trek to his homestead in Owensboro, Kentucky. Like many of his other teammates, Pie Traynor planned on taking care of affairs in the Smoky City before embarking for his home in Somerville, Massachusetts. Pittsburgh scout Joe Devine would accompany Ray Kremer and his wife on their automobile sojourn to Oakland, California.[18]

Bill McKechnie planned on remaining in the Smoky City to celebrate his team's victory for a few days before he left for a vacation to Florida on October 20. After spending some time in the sun, McKechnie intended to do some hunting before he turned his attention to the 1926 season. Before he left for Florida, McKechnie was honored at a banquet that was held by the Mifflin Avenue Methodist Episcopal Church of Wilkinsburg. J.C. Murray, president of the church's bible class, acted as the dinner's master of ceremonies. Speakers at the gathering included Reverend Judson Jefferies, the new pastor of the church. Comic entertainment was provided by Jack Thompson, while Miss Reineman and Evan Lloyd of the Carnegie Steel quartet supplied the evening's musical diversion.[19]

Like McKechnie and Carey, Eddie Moore also planned on spending the winter in Pittsburgh.[20] Moore's exploits in Game Six of the World Series earned him hero status even though he had hit only .231 for the Pirates. Moore suffered a slow start before playing better as the Series against Washington progressed. If Johnny Rawlings had not broken his ankle in September, Moore might not have been able to break into the World Series lineup.[21] Moore's biggest fan was his mother back in Baton Rouge, Louisiana. After Pittsburgh claimed victory over Washington, Mrs. Jack Larsen publicly expressed her pride in her son.[22]

"Eddie was always fond of apple pie," said Moore's mother during an interview, "and when he gets home, I am going to bake him the biggest, best, most delicious apple pie that his mother can make. As a boy Eddie always loved apple pie, and I am going to take some of the credit for myself for raising him to be the strong, strapping boy that he is."[23]

Moore's love of apple pie was not the only story associated with Pittsburgh's second baseman. The deal with San Francisco that brought Hal Rhyne and Paul Waner into the Pirates' fold potentially affected Moore. It was originally announced that Rhyne and Waner had been purchased for $100,000. A few weeks after the World Series concluded, some writers reported that the San Francisco deal involved $85,000 and three Pittsburgh players. One story stated that Carson Bigbee, Bernard Culloton and Moore were the players slated to be sent to San Francisco. This story gained traction as it was reported in newspapers throughout the country.

Barney Dreyfuss quickly rebuked the premise as he vehemently denied that these players were headed out of Pittsburgh.[24] "There is not a word of truth in the tale," said Dreyfuss. "The story is absolutely without any foundation. Not a single player on our club has ever been mentioned in any of our negotiations with the San Francisco Club for Waner and Rhyne. It is simply winter fiction."[25]

Dreyfuss then explained that the deal with San Francisco was a provisional one. The Pirates' organization had the option of paying for Waner and Rhyne with either cash, or partly in players. Both Seals players would join the Pirates on a trial basis for a full season before San Francisco received compensation. The Pirates had until December 15, 1926, to decide how they were going to pay for the two youngsters.[26]

"None of the three players named in the absurd story which is going the rounds, nor any other player on our club has ever been mentioned by the Frisco club," continued Dreyfuss. "It may develop that Frisco does not want any players at all, unless it should be a young pitcher or two, for it already has a good team, and is not in need of playing material outside of the box. After our Spring training session next year, we may turn over a young slab artist or two, but at present no players of any kind are being considered, by either club, and need not be for at least a year to come."[27]

It surprised writers such as Jesse Altenburg and J.C. Kofoed that a player like Moore who possessed so much potential was being labeled as a potential castoff after only two seasons in Pittsburgh. It was quite possible that another story that became known to the press corps had something to do with Dreyfuss possibly souring on Moore. It was reported in November that Pittsburgh management was unhappy with the behavior of one of its younger players. The player in question was not mentioned by name, but it was known that he was a prominent member of the team who was never keen on accepting advice and failed to grasp the responsibility that came with playing professional baseball. Since the World Series, this particular player had conducted himself in a manner that did not please his employer.[28] Moore's name and his practice of carousing were not mentioned in the article, but it did not take that much of a leap in judgment to ascertain that the second baseman was the source of Dreyfuss's consternation.

If Moore happened to remain on Pittsburgh's roster in 1926, there was no guarantee that he would be the team's starting second baseman. The additions of Rhyne and Waner meant that Moore and fellow infielder George Grantham would have competition for their starting positions during spring training. Besides playing the outfield, Waner had seen time at first base for San Francisco and was considered a viable option to Grantham.[29] Yet there was no chance that any changes would be made to the other half of Pittsburgh's starting infield. Glenn Wright and Pie Traynor were both young players who appeared to have 10 to 15 good seasons left in them. Many considered Wright and Traynor the greatest left-side infield combination since Jimmy Collins and Herman Long played for the Boston Beaneaters.[30]

Veteran first baseman Stuffy McInnis believed that Traynor and Wright were the best aggregation he had ever seen. "I've seen some good ones," remarked McInnis, "but this is the greatest young pair I ever saw or ever hope to see. They are two great young fellows who are not so far away from being recognized as two of the best that ever played. It's a wonderful thing to be that young and be that good with so many great years left."[31]

Talk about personnel moves and player purchases died down as baseball's off-season officially entered its first full month. Minor stories and rumors popped up from time to time. On another front, members of the Pirates finally decided that they wanted watch fobs as their personal gifts from Commissioner Kenesaw Mountain Landis for winning the World Series.[32]

A rumor also claimed that Fred Clarke was leaving the Pittsburgh organization to become part-owner and manager of the Brooklyn Robins. Clarke was on a hunting expedition near his home in Winfield, Kansas, when the story made it into print. After Pittsburgh writers wired the story to Clarke, he responded with a very terse denial.[33]

Barney Dreyfuss also seemed skeptical when he was asked about the rumor regarding Clarke. Dreyfuss said that Clarke's current obligation to the Pirates would not prevent him from pursuing an ownership stake in the Brooklyn club, if that was what he truly wanted to do. Dreyfuss believed that when spring arrived, Clarke would once again be at his post as vice-president of the Pittsburgh Pirates. After the World Series ended, it was once again reported that Clarke was part of a syndicate, including Pennsylvania Senator John P. Harris and prominent oil operator J.C. Trees, that would purchase the Pittsburgh franchise from Dreyfuss. People who knew of Dreyfuss's love and passion for the game quickly dismissed the tale as a sensational lark. Clarke had spiked the story completely when a newspaper writer approached him during the crucial championship series against Washington.[34] "I am not trying to buy the Pirates," said Clarke, "and I know that Mr. Tress, whose name has frequently been mentioned in that connection, has never made any offer for the club."[35]

Off-season honors began to pour in for Pirates players one month after their victory over Washington. Five Pittsburgh players were named to the annual all-star team selected by *The Sporting News*. Max Carey, Kiki Cuyler, Pie Traynor and Glenn Wright were named as first team all-stars while pitcher Vic Aldridge was named to the second team.[36] A few weeks later, it was announced that Cuyler finished second behind St. Louis' Rogers Hornsby for

National League MVP honors. Four more Pirates players garnered support for the award as Wright (fourth place), Traynor (eighth place), Carey (11th place) and Aldridge (21st place) received Most Valuable Player votes.[37]

While Pittsburgh players were having personal glory bestowed upon them, a local man was reaping financial reward from the Pirates' victory in the World Series. John F. Nugent claimed to hold in his possession the baseball that Cuyler smacked for the game-winning double of the final World Series game. Nugent loaned the famous ball for viewing at a New York jewelry establishment. (He later had the piece of memorabilia insured for $250 in his name.) In return for letting the jeweler exhibit the ball in his display window, Nugent received a stunning gold watch. Nugent also stated that he had numerous applications from other businesses that wished to have the ball loaned to them by its owner.[38]

As winter prepared to make its presence felt in the city of Pittsburgh, fans turned their attention to the December league meetings in New York. Many local rooters believed that trades involving the Pirates would be kept to a minimum since there were not many areas of the team that needed improvement. Prior to the meetings, there was some discussion that Brooklyn was interested in acquiring Carson Bigbee from the Pirates. It was believed that Pittsburgh sought a pitcher in return.[39]

Barney Dreyfuss, Samuel Dreyfuss, Bill McKechnie and Fred Clarke all made the trip to New York for the annual meetings. Since the Pirates were a solid team stocked with young ballplayers, not many offers came Pittsburgh's way from other teams. Managers and owners from the other seven National League clubs figured that it was useless to make Dreyfuss or McKechnie an offer unless they were willing to propose a phenomenal package.[40]

"Nobody wants to trade with the world's champions," remarked McKechnie after he returned from the meeting. "They all appear to be afraid they might further strengthen our forces by dealing with us, and I was not bothered much by offers of transfers while in New York. However, I should not worry. I've got a great ball team, and I can stand pat on it without losing any sleep."[41]

Some work was done by McKechnie and Dreyfuss in New York, even though no trades were made with National League competitors. The recent signing of Hal Rhyne made the Pittsburgh roster top heavy at the keystone sack, but the issue was alleviated when the Pirates sold Fresco Thompson outright to Buffalo of the International League. Dreyfuss also announced that Fred Clarke would be back with the team in his capacity as team vice-president and assistant manager for 1926. No official contract was signed by Clarke as the two longtime friends hammered out a deal that saw him receive an increase in pay over the 1925 season.[42] "I don't need any signed papers when dealing with Mr. Dreyfuss," said Clarke. "His word has always been as good as his bond with me."[43]

Bill McKechnie stated that he was happy to have Clarke back as his assistant on the Pittsburgh bench. Both men functioned cohesively during the 1925 season. Contrary to some published stories, Clarke at no time attempted to usurp McKechnie's authority as manager. A bizarre story that was given life during the World Series seemed to indicate that there were problems within the dugout hierarchy. It was reported that McKechnie and Clarke had a verbal confrontation during one of the Series games, which almost led to both men coming to blows. This story was vigorously denied by Clarke, and McKechnie believed the rumor was so ridiculous that he would not dignify it with a response.[44]

A few weeks after Pittsburgh's entourage returned from New York, a story was floated that McKechnie had offered catcher Earl Smith to the Philadelphia Phillies. The story contended that McKechnie desired either catcher Jimmie Wilson or fellow backstop Butch Henline from Philadelphia. When the story hit the local newspapers, McKechnie quickly denied that he had offered Smith to the Phillies.[45] Fans throughout the Smoky City were surprised that Smith's name was mentioned in connection with any potential deal. Smith was a gritty player who possessed the kind of intangibles that championship teams needed. During the World Series, his constant chatter seemed to be a major annoyance to many of Washington's players. Goose Goslin was singled out by Smith to receive the most ribbing. On more than one occasion, Smith engaged in pantomime by making the motion of trying to fly, a way of mocking Goslin.

Baseball columnist Billy Evans offered a list of the comments Smith made to Goslin during the World Series.[46]

- "Why don't you use that hook of yours instead of a bat?" chirped Smith when Goslin came to the plate after striking out in his previous at-bat. "You would make more base hits."
- "What did you slip Babe Ruth to get a place on his all-star team?"
- "If you are a star in the American League," continued Smith, "I ought to get in about five years there after I am through in the National."
- "So you are one of the few bachelors on the Washington Club. With that map of yours you are going to stay that way a long time."[47]

A man of Smith's temperament was a crucial asset for a club made up mainly of serious-minded youths who sometimes needed a comical diversion to help them deal with the pressure of a long season. Smith's clownish acts and smart remarks to opposing players relieved tension on Pittsburgh's team. Smith's strategy also served a deeper purpose, as it threw Washington's players off their game.[48]

Owner Barney Dreyfuss spent a quiet Christmas with his family before he attended to the tasks of working on the 1926 National League schedule and getting his players signed for the upcoming season.[49] Dreyfuss was prepared to pay heavily for his successful season in 1925. He set aside a large chunk of his considerable profits from the season to meet the salary demands of his players. This did not mean that Dreyfuss would be willing to give his players everything they wanted during contract negotiations. Dreyfuss always insisted on placing a value on players connected to his baseball empire. This meant that owner and player did not always agree during contract negotiations. When Kiki Cuyler came to Pittsburgh to play a few games with his professional basketball team in December, Dreyfuss and his star outfielder met to discuss contract figures. No contract was offered nor did the Flint Flash sign any document during his short stay in the Smoky City.[50]

> Often the fans are mistaken as to the value of a certain man to the team. The club owner and manager are in the best position to decide a player's real worth. A man may be a great hitter, or a great fielder, yet he may lack something which is very important in the final size-up of his worth, which ordinarily escapes the notice of the casual fan who boosts him.
>
> Moreover, it must be remembered that there is more than one salary to boost after a good year. No one man can be favored to the exclusion of all others. This is particularly true of a team of coming young players, such as Pittsburgh has at present.[51]

Other news on the Pirates' front did not involve contract negotiations. Pie Traynor came to the Smoky City so that he could enter a Pittsburgh hospital for an operation on his nose. Traynor's nose was broken when he was a child, with the problem becoming more noticeable in recent years. Once the minor operation was performed, Traynor's breathing was expected to improve substantially.[52]

Another story filtered into Pittsburgh regarding pitcher Johnny Morrison and a lawsuit. Morrison was named as a defendant in a $10,000 damage suit that was filed after C.J. Queen was fatally injured when struck by the pitcher's automobile in Owensboro, Kentucky. Morrison was being sued even though it was his brother-in-law who was driving the vehicle during the tragic accident.[53] Queen's widow was eventually awarded a judgment of $2,500.[54]

Contract news jumped back to the forefront of news in Pittsburgh when it was announced that Eddie Moore had wasted little time signing a contract for the upcoming season. Friends of the much maligned Pirates second baseman stated that Moore was not worried that Pittsburgh had purchased Hal Rhyne. Moore's self-confidence continued to be his greatest asset as he claimed that the starting job would be his when the season began. Months earlier, Moore had been rumored to be traded to San Francisco to complete the deal for Rhyne and Paul Waner. At the time, Barney Dreyfuss denied that such a move had ever been considered by Pittsburgh management. What Dreyfuss failed to mention was that Moore could not be moved without passing through waivers first, an extreme unlikelihood.[55]

Pittsburgh fans finally received the type of news they had dreaded since the closing of the previous campaign. Kiki Cuyler was officially a holdout after he returned two contracts to Dreyfuss unsigned. The word coming out of Flint, Michigan, was that Cuyler was looking for a substantial raise in salary to $10,000 a year. If this figure proved accurate, it meant that Cuyler was looking for a raise in the neighborhood of 67 percent.

Cuyler claimed that negotiations did not occur between him and Dreyfuss when the Flint Flash traveled to the Smoky City before Christmas. Cuyler believed he was doing the proper thing by remaining firm and not deviating from his original salary demands.[56] "This negotiating on contracts," said Cuyler, "is simply a part of baseball. It is just such a matter as might be engaged in between two business men when trying to put over a deal. It doesn't signify any break between me and the Pittsburgh Club."[57]

Barney Dreyfuss decided to let his son, Sam, serve as the spokesman in the matter of contracts for the 1926 season. Treasurer Sam Dreyfuss seemed to agree with Cuyler that there was no breach between player and management in this situation.[58] "The Pittsburgh Club does not care to comment on reports of holdouts in the ranks," said the younger Dreyfuss. "When the proper time comes, we will discuss such matters. No man is a holdout until he has refused to report when ordered to do so. Inasmuch as reporting time is still several weeks away, we do not consider that we have any holdouts at present."[59]

Barney Dreyfuss was not overly concerned that he did not have the signatures of star Pirates on contracts. Dreyfuss used the Golden Jubilee Dinner of the National League, which was held on February 3 in New York, as a mechanism to meet with his players face-to-face in order to reach salary agreements. Joining Pirates management in the event that officially closed out the league's year-long jubilee celebration were Max Carey, Glenn Wright, Pie Traynor, Hazen Cuyler, Vic Aldridge, Earl Smith, Clyde Barnhart, Bernard Culloton, Roy Spencer, Jewel Ens and Jack Onslow. Each member of the team took his turn visiting Pittsburgh's magnate in his room at the Waldorf Astoria Hotel. Every player seemed happy with his meeting. Dreyfuss signed all of the players who were regarded as potential holdouts by the press. Cuyler seemed to be the happiest member of the group as he quickly agreed to terms. It was believed Cuyler would receive $10,000 to play in 1926, even though a New York writer claimed he had received a 100 percent increase in salary from 1925 to $12,000 a year.[60]

One of the most important members of Pittsburgh's aggregation also agreed to terms on a new contract at the jubilee celebration. It was not announced until one week after the New York banquet that Bill McKechnie had signed to manage the Pirates in 1926. There was never any question about McKechnie coming back to pilot the team that claimed World Series glory in 1925. The terms of McKechnie's deal were not released, but he seemed thoroughly satisfied with the conditions; many in Pittsburgh reasoned that the Wilkinsburg native received a substantial raise in salary.[61]

Front Row, Left to Right: Gooch, Spencer, Culloton, Hns Cuyler, Kremer, Sheehan.
Middle Row: Smith, Haas, Oldham, Thompson, McInnis, Carey, McKechnie, Clarke, Wright, Grantham, Bigbee, Traynor.
Rear Row: Fraser, Hinchman, Onslow, Barnhart, Moore, Yde, Watters, B. Dreyfus, S. Dreyfus, Rawlings, Aldridge, Adams, Morrison, Meadows.
Bill McKechnie, Jr. Mascot.

All pieces of the Pirates' puzzle were in place as the first group of players containing pitchers and catchers embarked from Pittsburgh by train on February 21 to begin the trek to Paso Robles for spring training. This group was expected to reach California on February 25. The second squad departed Pittsburgh on February 28 and reached the coast on March 4. McKechnie planned on keeping his squad busy with training until March 19, before beginning their exhibition schedule with four games against the San Francisco Seals. Pittsburgh's whirlwind training tour was scheduled to end on April 11, when the Pirates concluded a three-game series against the Louisville Colonels.[62]

Before the Pirates began their cross-country sojourn, McKechnie and Dreyfuss made another roster move when they released George Haas outright to Atlanta of the Southern Association.[63] On another front, injuries and illness quickly became a major concern for McKechnie before any training session was even held at Paso Robles.

Stuffy McInnis showed up with a touch of stomach trouble. Eddie Moore was suffering from a bad cold. George Grantham arrived a day late because he stopped in Los Angeles to see a doctor about an old shoulder injury he suffered while playing for the Chicago Cubs. Team captain Max Carey arrived at camp a few days late due to a horrible cold he contracted while on the train to California. Carey was taken from the train in St. Louis and sent to the Deaconess Hospital.[64] A medical examination showed that Carey was threatened with the onset of pneumonia. It took several days before Carey was believed to be safe from contracting the disease. His doctor advised the Pirate veteran to wait a week before he resumed his trip to Paso Robles.[65]

The training session did not run as smoothly for Bill McKechnie as it had the previous year. Shortly after training camp began, some Pittsburgh players who took in a Saturday night dance in town returned to the team hotel at 1:30 A.M. McKechnie was waiting for them and did not mince words when he informed his guilty charges that such behavior would not be tolerated. Curfew was set for 11:30 P.M. If that rule was broken in the future, those who abused it would be punished severely. The players believed there was no harm in staying out late since the weekend should afford them additional liberties, but McKechnie reasoned that since a Sunday workout was being held, all rules and restrictions still applied.[66]

McKechnie also banned all forms of high stakes gambling during training camp. McKechnie absolutely forbade his team from dice games, while permit-

Opposite: Prior to the Golden Jubilee Dinner of the National League on February 3 in New York, Barney Dreyfuss individually met face-to-face with his players about salaries for the 1926 season. Every player who was considered a holdout by the press signed a contract. Kiki Cuyler, sitting third from the right in the front row of this 1925 Pirates team photo, saw his salary increased to somewhere between $10,000 and $12,000 a year (National Baseball Hall of Fame Library, Cooperstown, New York).

ting only card games that were classified as friendly and did not involve money.[67] Yet, Pittsburgh's players were afforded some opportunities for pleasure while they trained at Paso Robles. The entire Pirates entourage took time away from field work so that they could visit the set where the movie *Don Quixote* was being shot. Pittsburgh's players posed for photos with movie icons Douglas Fairbanks and Mary Pickford, who starred in the project.

Pittsburgh's squad was badly crippled during the spring training session. George Grantham was only able to do a little work due to an attack of neuritis. McKechnie ordered Grantham to partake in a regimen of sulfur baths to improve his condition.[68] Pie Traynor injured his ankle sliding into second base during a practice session at Paso Robles.[69] Eddie Moore suffered a sprained ankle and Stuffy McInnis received a spike wound on his instep when Kiki Cuyler injured the veteran first baseman during a camp drill.[70] Clyde Barnhart barely avoided serious injury when a Johnny Morrison pitch smacked him in the right elbow.[71]

McKechnie was concerned that Max Carey had been slow in recovering from a serious bout with the flu. Carey could not be expected to be in prime condition for opening day since he had so little practice during spring training.[72] Young Paul Waner benefited from Carey's absence as he was given ample opportunity to show off his skills. Fred Clarke quickly pronounced that Waner had star potential and resembled former Pirates great Ginger Beaumont in his batting approach.[73] As luck would have it, even Waner joined the walking wounded during Pittsburgh's final exhibition series against Louisville. Waner needed eight stitches to sew up a wound to his mouth after he was struck with a batted ball.[74]

Hard hit by injuries, Bill McKechnie's brigade opened the 1926 regular season campaign with a 7–6 loss to the St. Louis Cardinals at Sportsman's Park on April 13. Max Carey remained on the bench throughout the four-game series as Carson Bigbee, Kiki Cuyler and Clyde Barnhart patrolled Pittsburgh's outfield positions during the first three games.[75] Rookie Paul Waner made his first major league start and went hitless in the final game against St. Louis.

Carey finally made his season debut during the second game of Pittsburgh's series against Cincinnati on April 18. Carey went 0-for-4 as Pittsburgh defeated the Reds, 3–1, behind the strong pitching of Vic Aldridge.

Pittsburgh played lackluster ball throughout the season's early weeks. After St. Louis defeated Pittsburgh, 5–3, in the home opener at Forbes Field on April 22, the Pirates were entrenched in last place with a 2–7 record. Pittsburgh's team batting average stood at a pathetic .194, with no member of the Pirates' squad close to the .300 mark.[76] Cuyler (.182), Grantham (.200), Wright (.194), Traynor (.233), Barnhart (.080), Moore (.240), Smith (.261) and Carey (.063) were all struggling through the season's first nine games.

When April ended, Pittsburgh stood in seventh-place with a 7–10 record.

14. Champions of the World

The Pirates trailed the first-place Brooklyn Robins by three and a half games. Injuries continued to be a problem for McKechnie's team as the season entered the month of May. Glenn Wright saw his streak of 316 consecutive games played come to an end when he missed the final game of the first Forbes Field series against St. Louis with a spike wound to his hand.[77] Eddie Moore was finally forced to the bench with an injured ankle and replaced by rookie Hal Rhyne at second base.[78]

Two positive events did occur as the Pirates improved their fortunes in the National League race by going 16–8 in May. Off the field, George Grantham married childhood sweetheart Ruby L. Gates of Kingman, Arizona, on April 20.[79] The Pirates also signed Paul Waner's younger brother, Lloyd, to a contract after he was released from the San Francisco Seals, and then sent him to a minor league team for more seasoning.[80]

The Pirates' solid showing during the month of May pushed them up to third place in the National League standings with 23–18 record. The Pirates trailed the first-place Cincinnati Reds by four games. Even though Bill McKechnie seemed to be putting his team on track, he still faced huge problems each day. Carey was not rounding into shape, while Barnhart's play had been horrendous. Luckily, McKechnie had Waner at his disposal. The former Seals' star was placed in the starting lineup on May 8 to spell Carey, and eventually supplanted Barnhart in the outfield. Waner was the sensation of the new season as he emerged as the Pirates' best player and hit .336 during his rookie campaign. Conversely, Moore's bad luck continued as he spent a week in the hospital with influenza shortly after Rhyne replaced him as the starting second baseman.[81]

As the Pirates attempted to find their identity in 1926, McKechnie continued to look for ways to improve his club. It was reported that McKechnie was interested in adding Boston's Joe Genewich to his stable of pitchers.[82]

No matter how the campaign progressed for the Pirates, they were champions of the world for at least one season. Despite their early struggles, the Pirates did not wish to rest on their laurels and allow someone else to claim the pennant in the National League. McKechnie steered the Pirates through some difficult times during the season's early days. He believed the team was finally headed in the right direction despite a slew of injuries and early season slumps. While Pittsburgh's manager was confident that better days loomed, circumstances seemed determined to intervene.

15

The Champions' Troubles in '26

Pittsburgh's fans were given the opportunity to re-live the glorious 1925 season when the world championship banner was raised at Forbes Field on May 27, before the Pirates played their game against Chicago.[1] National League president John Heydler and Commissioner Landis attended the special ceremony that commemorated Pittsburgh's victory over Washington the previous October. Each Pirates player received an individual trophy. On behalf of the commissioner's office, Landis also presented the players with beautiful diamond-studded fobs, or medals, as they were sometimes called.[2] Optimistic fans throughout the Smoky City hoped the celebration would provide the impetus to push Pittsburgh back to the top of the National League standings.

The season continued to be difficult for certain Pirates players as summer began. Eddie Moore's name became connected with every trade rumor that involved the Pirates. The latest story claimed that Pittsburgh might strike a three-team deal that included New York and Philadelphia. Besides Moore, New York's Bill Terry and the Phillies Butch Henline were rumored to be a part of the three-way transaction.[3]

When May ended, Moore was batting an anemic .186. Moore seemed destined for bench work as the season continued. Hal Rhyne had beaten out Moore for the starting second base spot, while Clyde Barnhart and Carson Bigbee were ahead of him on the outfield depth chart that supported starters Hazen Cuyler, Max Carey and Paul Waner. Injuries and Rhyne's solid play both had a hand in Moore being relegated to the bench.

Pittsburgh's hospital list was heavy throughout the season's early months. Pitchers Ray Kremer and Vic Aldridge became the latest injury victims when each hurler experienced problems with his pitching arm. Lee Meadows was also afflicted with the same kind of sinus trouble that affected Bigbee's career.[4]

Pittsburgh's fortunes did not improve the way that local patrons hoped they would as the 1926 season progressed into June. An 11–12 record for the

15. The Champions' Troubles in '26   229

month kept Pittsburgh mired in third place, six games behind the league-leading Cincinnati Reds.

As the Pirates gallantly attempted to resuscitate their season, owner Barney Dreyfuss finalized plans for an extended vacation to Europe. During his time oversees, Pittsburgh's magnate intended to spend time in Germany, France, Switzerland and Belgium. Joining Dreyfuss on this long journey were his wife and daughter. Dreyfuss's sojourn to the continent that he once called home was expected to last until the end of the 1926 season.[5]

On June 10, Dreyfuss and his family boarded the Steamer Columbus in New York and set sail for Europe. Before Dreyfuss left the United States, his players insured the magnate that they would be leading the National League by a wide margin when he returned to America in September. Just as Dreyfuss boarded the ship, he was presented with a farewell message from his players. Every man signed the message using his given name or nickname rather than being formally signed with his full, legal moniker. This gave the farewell tribute a personal touch and showed how much the Pittsburgh players admired Dreyfuss.[6]

"Every good wish for a refreshing and comfortable voyage and a safe return to find us leading the league by a pennant-winning margin," read the players' message. "Appreciating the confidence you repose in us during your absence, we, by our personal signatures to this message, mutually pledge to each other and to you the very best that is in us to bring another pennant and world's championship to Pittsburgh. We can win, and we will."[7]

The message was not misguided, gushing sentiment on the part of Pittsburgh's players. Despite their early season problems, Bill McKechnie's players had supreme confidence that their true ability would guide them through another tough pennant race.[8] Unfortunately, injuries continued to derail Pittsburgh's dream of accomplishing this goal. Carey missed the first few games against Brooklyn during Pittsburgh's first Eastern invasion in early June. Johnny Morrison did not even make the trip with the team due to a malady that placed him on the sidelines. Moore was given a chance to reclaim his starting job at second base, but only because Hal Rhyne missed a few games due to injury.[9]

More problems awaited. While the team was in Philadelphia, McKechnie was suspended by National League president John Heydler for using offensive language when he argued with umpire Bill Klem. During their stay in New York, players who proudly wore the emblems they received as tokens of Landis' appreciation for winning the World Series were constantly misidentified as local laborers. One inquisitive merchant asked coach Jack Onslow what "boat" he was connected with, while a Pirates player was mistakenly referred to as a member of the Kokomo Fire Department.[10]

While the Pirates played the final leg of the road trip in Boston, Fred Clarke was back in New York discussing a deal with members of the Brooklyn

Robins' management team. Clarke supposedly attempted to pry either pitchers Bob McGraw or Doug McWeeny from Brooklyn for Eddie Moore. Besides Moore, Clyde Barnhart and Carson Bigbee's names were most frequently connected with trade rumors. Yet, when Clarke rejoined Pittsburgh's entourage in Boston, the Pirates' vice-president had no announcement to make regarding player transactions.[11]

The Pirates almost secured the services of a top-notch National League pitcher when they placed a waiver claim for Pete Alexander after he was released by the Chicago Cubs. New Cubs manager Joe McCarthy had tired of disciplining the great right-hander. He decided to cut Alexander loose rather than deal with his rule-breaking for an entire season. Cincinnati, St. Louis and Pittsburgh all put in claims for Alexander.[12]

On June 21, Pittsburgh defeated St. Louis by a score of 13–11 and moved into sole possession of second place in the National League. The following day, Alexander was awarded to the Cardinals since they were the lowest team in the standings that put in a claim for the pitcher. Had the Pirates lost to St. Louis the previous afternoon, Alexander would have joined Pittsburgh as the newest member of the pitching staff.[13]

Pete Alexander would have been a fine addition to Pittsburgh's staff. Lee Meadows (20–9, 3.97 ERA) and Ray Kremer (20–6, 2.61 ERA) were rocks for Bill McKechnie during the 1926 season, but the remainder of the starting rotation that supplied so much solid pitching during Pittsburgh's 1925 pennant winning season was not coming close to its potential in 1926. Vic Aldridge could not find his way and Emil Yde seemed to be damaged goods since the shellacking he took from Washington during the fourth game of the 1925 World Series. Johnny Morrison was trying his best to deal with various injuries. After consulting with his physician in July, Morrison decided that diseased tonsils were the root of his problem. He entered a Pittsburgh hospital and had the inflamed throat tissue removed.[14]

Morrison was not the only Pittsburgh player who suffered from an affliction involving his throat. Catcher Johnny Gooch could speak only in a whisper due to the fact that he had a growth on his vocal glands. It was advised that an operation would be necessary, but Gooch refused to have the procedure done during the season since it would put him on the sidelines for about two weeks.[15] Newly acquired pitcher Chester Nichols joined Pittsburgh's growing injured list immediately after arriving in the Smoky City, when a sprained ankle that he suffered pitching for New Haven made a trip to a local hospital necessary.[16] Pie Traynor's effectiveness was curtailed when he suffered a sprained ankle late in June. Glenn Wright continued to play even though he was hampered by a spike wound to his hand. Wright was finally forced to the bench as a precaution against pneumonia.[17]

Despite all of the injuries and poor performances from players like Barnhart, Carey and Moore, the Pirates found themselves in first-place at the end of July. The Pirates' 21–10 record for the month acted as a springboard, catapulting them ahead of Cincinnati and St. Louis in the National League standings. The Pirates' overall record of 55–40 was not that far off the pace that Pittsburgh had set through July in 1925. Pittsburgh found itself two games in front of second-place Cincinnati and four ahead of St. Louis.

Even though the Pirates seemed to be making a run at their second consecutive National League pennant, it was evident to followers of the team that the same camaraderie and fighting spirit that existed in 1925 was not prevalent. Tension and discord were rising to the surface, as the harmonious mood that existed during Pittsburgh's championship season became a distant memory.

A story arose claiming that Vic Aldridge and Glenn Wright had become embroiled in a bitter fist-fight. It was the scrap that supposedly forced Wright to be removed from Pittsburgh's lineup, not the concern over pneumonia that had been reported by Pirates officials. There were also rumors of other fights between players in the Pirates' clubhouse. Pittsburgh management denied that these tales had any factual basis.

Reports of all-night parties and joyrides involving Pittsburgh players once again followed on the heels of these stories about Pirates players fighting with each other. There was some truth regarding these accusations about Pittsburgh players who were not adhering to being teetotalers. Two unidentified Pirates players had indeed violated Bill McKechnie's rules of conduct. These men were seen drinking hard liquor in public and were so brash that they did not seem concerned about keeping it a secret.[18]

The need to instill discipline on McKechnie's part moved from behind the scenes and onto the diamond during a doubleheader loss at Forbes Field against the New York Giants on July 14. The Pirates were slaughtered in the first contest, 12–8, and fell to their arch rival by a score of 5–2 in the nightcap. After the two games, McKechnie announced that Eddie Moore had been fined $100 and Emil Yde $50 because of indifferent and unsatisfactory play on their part in the first game. Moore was benched for the second game and replaced by Johnny Rawlings at second base. Moore let his struggles at the plate affect the remainder of his game. During the first game of the series against New York, Moore was accused by some patrons of making no effort to field a ball that rolled past him at second base.[19]

Moore found himself firmly entrenched in manager McKechnie's doghouse. This was a bad development for a player who had fallen out of favor with owner Barney Dreyfuss the previous autumn. When Dreyfuss started to dislike a player for not attending to business in a proper way, that player usually found himself playing on a new team.[20] While Dreyfuss was in Europe, McKechnie, Fred Clarke and Sam Dreyfuss were responsible for running the Pittsburgh ball club. The temporary management hierarchy did not waste any time dealing with Moore. He was placed on waivers, with six teams from both major leagues putting in bids for his services. On July 20, Moore was awarded to the Boston Braves for the waiver price of $4,000. Moore reported to Cincinnati immediately and promptly injured an ankle in his first game with Boston.[21] The fact that the Pirates allowed Moore to walk for a paltry return of $4,000 indicated that Pittsburgh management had let personal feelings trump sound judgment because of his malcontent ways. Waiting to make a later trade that would strengthen Pittsburgh's squad would have been the more prudent move.[22]

Unfortunately, the incidents involving Moore and Yde were not isolated, as McKechnie battled to maintain discipline on his squad. Vic Aldridge was fined $50 by Pittsburgh's manager after he failed to appear on the bench during the second game of a doubleheader against Brooklyn on July 21.[23] Aldridge, who claimed he was forced to take the mound in one of the games even though he had a sore arm, did not make it out of the first inning against Brooklyn. He went to the clubhouse, changed into street clothes, and did not return to the Pirates' dugout as per team rules.[24]

While Pittsburgh fans were digesting all the fines being levied against Pirates players, another story emerged concerning a player who had run afoul of team management. Sore-armed Johnny Morrison abandoned his teammates and returned to his home in Kentucky. After a few days, McKechnie informed the pitcher that he was suspended indefinitely.

When news of the suspension reached Morrison in Owensboro, he responded with his side of the story.[25] "I just got tired of staying around Pittsburgh and not being able to do anything for the team, I came on home," claimed Morrison. "When my arm gets well I hope to be of service to the Pirates."[26]

The Morrison incident turned more bizarre with each passing day. After he was suspended by McKechnie, Morrison sent word that an x-ray examination by his doctor in Kentucky showed that his pitching arm was broken. Team officials claimed that Morrison must have broken his arm after deserting the Pirates to return home, since it was not damaged when he initially entered the hospital for his tonsil operation. They also added that Morrison was suspended without pay because he had returned to Kentucky even though he did not ask the club for permission.[27]

Morrison's claim that he was done for the season due to the injury was quickly challenged by his doctor. The Kentucky physician stated that it was Johnny's brother, Phil Morrison, who was disabled with a broken arm. Morrison was also a pitcher whose most recent assignment was with Little Rock.[28] Sensing that the charade was over, Johnny Morrison rejoined Pittsburgh after spending a few weeks in Owensboro.[29]

The situation had become so bad for the Pirates from a public relations standpoint that fans were even turning on stalwart performers who always hustled on the field and stayed clean away from it. During Pittsburgh's second Eastern invasion in late July and early August, a former Pittsburgh resident criticized the behavior of Glenn Wright and Pie Traynor during a game against Philadelphia on August 2. The Pirate fan from Haddonfield, New Jersey, voiced his concerns in a letter that appeared in *The Pittsburgh Press*. He was upset over the fact that Traynor and Wright lounged in the box seats with a couple of patrons before the game.[30] Pittsburgh fans who read this story scoffed at the ridiculous notion that two of the hardest working members of McKechnie's squad were not taking the game seriously. Diehard fans throughout the Smoky City were forced to lament a situation that involved Wright four days after the misguided fan attended the game in Philadelphia. On August 6, Wright injured his ankle while sliding into a base and was sidelined indefinitely. Wright had been playing with a bad hip, with the ankle injury occurring because he altered his slide to protect himself.[31]

The Pirates played uneven ball throughout their Eastern trip and returned home with a 10–7 record during the 18 days they spent in New York, Philadelphia and Boston. When the Pirates finally returned home to the Smoky City on August 13, they stood on top of the National League race with a 61–45 record. Second-place St. Louis stood two games behind at 61–49 while Cincinnati held down the third position, two and a half games back at 62–51. Pittsburgh fans hoped that the Pirates would now make a final push toward another pennant since they now had an extended home stand. The faithful quickly realized their optimism was unfounded, as stories decorated Pittsburgh's sport pages on August 13, indicating dissension was tearing the Pirates apart.

The Pittsburgh Press reported that a meeting involving the players, manager Bill McKechnie, vice-president Fred Clarke and treasurer Sam Dreyfuss was scheduled for that afternoon, when the Pirates reached the city after being marooned in New York the previous night because of flooding.[32] The clubhouse meeting came on the heels of a vote that was taken by Pittsburgh's players over whether assistant manager Clarke should be asked to leave the bench. The vote favored Clarke by a tally of 18 to 6. It was announced that veterans Max Carey, Carson Bigbee and Babe Adams were three of the players who cast votes against Clarke.[33] When pundits dug a little deeper into the details of this incident, it was revealed that Carey was one of the ringleaders of what was being referred to as a mutiny.

Carey explained the course of events surrounding the vote over the phone to writer Ralph S. Davis.[34]

> I feel that a statement is due myself and the other veteran members of the team, who have only its best interests at heart.
>
> Anything that we did was done because we wanted to see the club win. After we lost that doubleheader in Boston, McKechnie suggested that a meeting be

held to discuss the welfare of the club. A time was set for the session, but about a half hour before it was to be held, McKechnie called it off.

Later Clarke came to the clubhouse, and said he would not appear again on the bench if he was not wanted. The next day a vote was taken by the players as to whether he should be asked to retire. That is all there is to it.

But I feel that Manager McKechnie should make a statement, setting forth my part and that of the other players in the matter. We simply wanted to get results.

No team can thrive under two managers. That is not said with any special reference to Fred Clarke, for he and I are good friends, but it is general baseball proposition that holds true on any club. There were conditions existing on our club which were losing games for us, and it was primarily with a view of getting better results that we jumped at McKechnie's suggestion to hold a meeting and try to iron out our difficulties, regardless of what they might be.[35]

Information obtained the previous evening stated that Carey, Bigbee and Adams were charged with being the perpetrators in the movement to have Clarke removed from the dugout. Clarke actually did leave the bench during the series in Brooklyn when he became aware of the players' mutinous intentions. McKechnie was shocked when the veteran players informed him of their intentions. Pittsburgh's manager immediately called Clarke into conference so that they could discuss the matter. Clarke asked McKechnie what he should do, but Bill did not give an immediate response, preferring to think the matter over carefully. McKechnie issued a statement of his own when the Pirates returned home after their excursion through the east.[36]

"I don't know what I will do yet," said McKechnie. "I want to protect the best interests of the club alone. I am interested in winning another pennant for Pittsburgh, and I am going to be governed accordingly. Whatever I may have to say will be said after full consideration has been given to every point."[37]

A writer then asked McKechnie about the extent of Clarke's authority regarding the Pittsburgh club. "He is supreme," McKechnie replied. "He is the president of the club right now. Mr. Dreyfuss gave him full authority when he left for Europe."

"Does his authority extend over you?" another writer asked.

"I would say that it does," answered Pittsburgh's manager. "But I want to make it strong that Fred has never exercised it, so far as I am concerned. He has been fine with me, and we are the closest and best of friends. We have never had a word of difference. He has never tried to dictate to me. I have managed the club according to my own ideas, although, of course, Fred and I have conferred daily."[38]

McKechnie, Clarke and Sam Dreyfuss held a meeting of their own at Forbes Field's club offices on the morning of August 13. Loud talk could be heard behind the closed doors, but people who stood nearby were unable to ascertain what was being said. On a number of occasions, Clarke's raised voice was heard screaming, "I want...," but exactly what he was referring to could not be determined. Clarke even refused to leave the meeting when he was asked to do so. After the conference, Clarke was quoted as saying that the ringleaders of the mutiny should be punished. On the night of August 12, Clarke had also met with Carey, Bigbee and Adams in his hotel room. Clarke explained to the players why he sat on the bench. He stated that it was not for the purpose of criticizing them or interfering with McKechnie running the baseball team. Clarke then asked the mutineers to speak honestly, but their response never became part of the public record.[39]

The reason behind the players' revolt did become public as more information surrounding team disharmony became known. It seemed that the player vote that asked for Clarke to leave the bench came out of an event that occurred while the team was playing a doubleheader against Boston on August 7. Clarke sat on the bench for the first game and watched the Braves' Johnny Wertz shut out Pittsburgh, 2–0. Clarke intended to leave before the second game started so that he could board a train to New York and arrive ahead of the team for the next series against Brooklyn. When he stood up from the bench to leave, Clarke approached manager McKechnie and offered a suggestion that ended up having negative reverberations throughout the organization.[40]

"Better get some one out there to play centerfield," said Clarke. "Max is having a hard time of it."

"I haven't got anybody," McKechnie replied.

"Put somebody out there, even if it is a pitcher," suggested Clarke as he left the dugout.[41]

Carey did not hear the derogatory comments. Teammates who were nearby when Clarke made the statements relayed the conversation to Pittsburgh's team captain. Veteran players Carey, Adams and Bigbee decided to hold a meeting so that Clarke's behavior could be discussed.[42] After the story came out, many in the press believed this was not the first time Carey had been approached regarding Clarke's critical comments and his presence on the bench.[43]

Pittsburgh players held their meeting once the team reached New York. Three unidentified players voted with Carey, Bigbee and Adams to have Clarke removed from the dugout. When reporters questioned every man on the team other than the instigators as to whether they voted to have Clarke leave the bench, all players denied they had cast a vote against Pittsburgh's vice-president.[44]

Pittsburgh management acted swiftly after the players met with Clarke, McKechnie and Sam Dreyfuss during a meeting at Forbes Field on August 13. Clarke, who demanded that the mutineers be punished, came out on top of the power struggle between players and management. Treasurer Dreyfuss addressed the media that evening and announced that Adams and Bigbee had been released unconditionally. Carey would be suspended indefinitely until waivers could be secured on the veteran outfielder. Pie Traynor was also named to replace Carey as Pittsburgh's captain.

Dreyfuss read a prepared statement that explained the decision to cut loose Pittsburgh's three longest-tenured players.[45]

> I have been chosen to talk to you about a most serious matter, and I assure you that I am not at all tickled over the task, which is certainly a rough one, and naturally I do not like to have to tell it to you. Bill McKechnie and myself both felt that the attack made upon Fred Clarke was totally unnecessary and unwarranted, and a step which could cause only trouble. It is entirely beyond me how a group of men could, after giving thought to a matter of that kind, go through with the proposition. Surely, they must have foreseen the trouble it was certain to cause the team and the management, as well as the baseball public.
>
> It is something that we think must be stopped at the source, and stopped quickly. We have engaged or hired our players to play ball as well as to give their very best services both on and off the field.
>
> Clarke, McKechnie and myself are paid to run the ball club, each having his respective duties to perform, whatever they might happen to cover.[46]

After Dreyfuss related the information surrounding the disciplined players, he concluded by stating that the team's expectations had not changed due to this unfortunate incident. "Manager McKechnie and myself," continued Dreyfuss, "both firmly believe that if those players who have been loyal to their fellow players and employers will continue to bear down every day, the team will finish on top, where it belongs."[47]

Sam Dreyfuss's feelings were likely genuine when he stated that he was not pleased with handling this particular task. His father had always handled such matters, but Barney Dreyfuss was not on hand since he was vacationing in Europe. Fans throughout the Smoky City were also not pleased over the dismissal of three of the most honorable players who had ever worn a Pirates uniform. They

On August 13, 1926, Babe Adams and Carson Bigbee were released and Max Carey was waived after the three veteran players initiated a vote to have Fred Clarke removed from Pittsburgh's bench. Adams, who debuted in 1909 when Clarke managed the Pirates, was Pittsburgh's longest tenured player before his release (National Baseball Hall of Fame Library, Cooperstown, New York).

were stunned that a man of integrity such as Max Carey would be treated in such a manner. Last fall, Carey had been hailed as the driving force behind Pittsburgh's victory in the World Series. During a banquet that honored McKechnie after Pittsburgh's triumph, Carey showed the depth of his honorable and righteous demeanor when he explained who was responsible for the World Series victory.[48] "I have always believed in prayer and divine guidance," said Carey, "and I am inclined to give God Almighty a lot of credit for our victory."[49]

After Sam Dreyfuss read his prepared statement to the press, Pittsburgh's players filed out of the room as if they attended a funeral. They realized that Dreyfuss had acted upon the wishes of Fred Clarke by dismissing the three, battle-tested veterans. There was also little doubt in their minds that manager McKechnie was subservient to Clarke. McKechnie looked devastated as he left the room after Dreyfuss's verdict regarding Carey, Bigbee and Adams became known to the public.[50] Fans quickly sided with the three players in the matter and placed the blame for their dismissal at the feet of Clarke and McKechnie. They felt Clarke had let his pride grow out of control and that McKechnie did not properly handle the situation. One writer claimed that Clarke and Barney Dreyfuss were the ones who should shoulder the blame for the entire matter.

Writer John B. Sheridan stated that Dreyfuss put McKechnie in an impossible situation when he brought Clarke back as an assistant to the manager in 1925. Sheridan believed Pittsburgh would have won the National League pennant without Clarke's presence in the dugout. He also felt that McKechnie should have tendered his resignation when Dreyfuss appointed Clarke to assist him in the dugout. As far as the recent events involving team mutiny, Sheridan claimed that Clarke spoke in a loud voice when he made his derogatory comments about Carey so that other players would hear him. He also believed that Carey, Bigbee and Adams were badly mistreated in this instance. Sheridan reasoned the matter would have been handled differently if Barney Dreyfuss was still in Pittsburgh. Sheridan concluded by stating that Clarke had won out in the end and that McKechnie agreed with him so that he would not lose his job.[51]

Pittsburgh fans loyal to Carey, Bigbee and Adams continued to show their support for the maligned players. As the days passed, even more fans began to side with the three released players. *The Pittsburgh Press* received numerous letters to the editor that lashed out at Pittsburgh management. Some fans even suggested that games at Forbes Field should be boycotted until the three players were permitted to rejoin the team. One old-time fan who signed his letter — "A Northside Man"— even took shots at Clarke for how he mishandled players during his tenure as Pittsburgh's manager in the past.[52]

> Mr. Dear Sir — I desire to commend you for the stand you have taken in the present baseball squabble. I am one of the large concourse of fans who believes that Carey, Adams and Bigbee are being made the "goats" in this unfortunate situation.
>
> Noting the disposition of "certain" Pittsburgh sports writers to give Fred Clarke credit for making Carey the star player that he is, I would like to ask Mr. Clarke why he failed to make stars of Marty O'Toole or Bill Abstein in their respective positions?[53]

Carey and his fellow banished players did not plan on letting Pittsburgh management have the final say in this matter. Carey took his case to Commissioner Landis on behalf of the three players. Landis told Carey that he could not take action on the matter and instead referred him to National League president John Heydler. Carey went directly to Heydler's office after he talked to Landis.[54] Heydler agreed to hear Carey's case in Pittsburgh. Heydler traveled to the Smoky City and held hearings at the William Penn Hotel and at Forbes Field. Carey wanted an audience with the National League president for the purpose of clearing his name and the names of Bigbee and Adams.

After the proceedings that involved the three players, along with Clarke, McKechnie, Sam Dreyfuss and Sam Watters, Heydler issued his findings. On August 18, Heydler released a statement in which he said that even though the three players acted with mistaken zeal, their behavior was neither insubordinate nor malicious. Heydler also backed Pittsburgh management's decision to release the players since it was within their right to make any personnel moves that they wished.

During the hearing, Clarke made an interesting statement to Carey about why he was permitted to sit on the Pirates bench.[55] "I did not want to sit on the bench in the first place," stated Clarke, "I was ordered to sit there by Mr. Dreyfuss, the club owner. I was also asked to sit there by Manager McKechnie. I am hired to sit there by the club owner, just the same as you are hired by that same club owner to play center field. I am sitting there for the good of the club. I will be glad to leave that bench any time it is thought by the owner that it is for the good of the club."[56]

On the same day that Heydler issued his ruling, Sam Dreyfuss announced that Carey had been awarded to Brooklyn via waivers.[57] Pittsburgh management hoped that the team could now concentrate on playing baseball since, from their perspective, the matter involving the three players was now closed. Yet, Sam Dreyfuss did not understand that the heart of the Pirates had been torn away. The three players were not putting up big numbers in 1926, but they were still revered by their teammates.

Even though Pittsburgh was clinging to first-place over St. Louis when Heydler made his announcement on August 18, the season remained in jeopardy. The Pirates struggled throughout the season's final six weeks, as they could post nothing better than a 22–23 record. As a result, there would be no National League pennant for the Pirates in 1926; they finished in third place with an 84–69 record, four and a half games behind first-place St. Louis.

As the Pirates play continued to deteriorate through late August and September, talk in Pittsburgh centered around the situation involving Adams, Bigbee and Carey, which was now referred to as the "ABC Affair" by members of the press. Opinions continued to be expressed about as the Pirates struggled to overcome a turbulent season ruined by injuries and dissension. A former Pittsburgh player gave an odd opinion regarding the blowup. Former Pirate pitcher Wilbur Cooper felt vindicated that the team's true troublemakers were finally exposed.[58]

"I notice in the newspapers about the big shake-up of the Pirates," wrote Cooper to a Pittsburgh friend, "and am glad that the people of Pittsburgh have finally found out the real ones, though I have always been the one blamed. I really feel that this is one of the biggest triumphs I ever had in baseball. They have finally brought to light what I foretold them at a meeting a few years back — the real cause."[59]

Fans who read this letter in print wondered about Cooper's statement. Cooper had never been considered a troublemaker, and the three dismissed Pirates never caused problems in the past. Other fans pondered when they would finally hear from the most important member of the Pirates' organization. Owner Barney Dreyfuss had not been heard from since leaving for his European vacation. There were a number of fans who believed that Dreyfuss had ordered his son to dismiss Pittsburgh's three mutinous players, but this was not the case.

Dreyfuss finally released a statement on August 22 from Paris three days before he boarded the Columbus to begin his return trip back to the United States.[60]

> I am a sentimental fellow, and therefore I feel deeply the departure of these players, but sentiment has no place in baseball. The fans insist on a winning team and won't tolerate a loser. I thoroughly approve of anything done by McKechnie and my son, who offered to handle my affairs in order to permit me to have a vacation. They did not consult me. I got only a brief telegram from my son saying the releases were necessary. I saw the details in an American newspaper in Paris.
>
> Carey's departure by the waiver route means writing a loss of $96,000 in the club's books. I could have sold him for that price last year. For 16 years Carey was a member of the Pirates and certainly he was the club's most valuable player last season. But there is room on a club for only one manager. Therefore, sentiment was brushed aside. Adams had been with me 20 years and could have stayed longer. I was considering making him a pitching coach to keep him on the payroll.
>
> When I left Pittsburgh, in June, there was no inkling of dissension. I don't yet

know the ground-floor reasons for the trouble, but when trouble breaks out in mid-season, especially when a club is leading the league, it is necessary for a manager to act quickly and efficiently.[61]

Dreyfuss arrived back in Pittsburgh on August 31 after arriving in New York hours earlier via boat. Pittsburgh's owner immediately went to his office at Forbes Field and immersed himself in club business. Dreyfuss elaborated on the statement he made in Paris for a reporter that searched out the magnate upon his return.[62]

> Whatever Sam, Bill and Fred did stands. I could not do anything even if I wanted to and I do not want to do anything. I put Clarke, my son and McKechnie in charge when I went away and told them then that I didn't want to know what was going on while I was away.
>
> Before I went abroad I met the players and the other officers of the club in Brooklyn. I told them my plans for direction of the club while I was away, and asked them if they had any suggestions. Nobody said anything, so I took it for granted everybody was satisfied. I don't fully understand the flare-up yet.[63]

The writer then told Dreyfuss that Carey, Adams and Bigbee had expressed the kindliest of feelings toward him.[64] "Why shouldn't they?" replied Dreyfuss. "I have always treated them well, and I don't see how they could feel otherwise than kindly toward me."[65]

Writers were not the only people who reached out to Dreyfuss after he returned from Europe. Max Carey, Carson Bigbee and Babe Adams wasted no time requesting an audience with Pittsburgh's owner. The three players met with Dreyfuss and discussed the unfortunate event that occurred while he was away. Carey gave out a statement on September 1, in which he stated that Dreyfuss received the trio cordially and that the entire conversation between the four men was friendly. Carey explained that the players wanted to speak with Dreyfuss so that they could assure him they never conspired to do harm to the Pittsburgh baseball club or anyone connected with it. After the summit, Dreyfuss made no formal statement to the press and stated that he would have nothing to say until he conferred with his son, Clarke, and McKechnie in person about the incident.[66]

Dreyfuss never granted an interview or issued any statements to members of Pittsburgh's press corps after he talked to his management team. In the middle of September, Dreyfuss did permit New York sports writer Frank Wallace to interview him. This came on the heels of Dreyfuss informing a writer from *The Pittsburgh Press* that he did not believe in fighting his battles through the newspapers and therefore would make no comments about team dissension in 1926.[67] Perhaps Pittsburgh's owner turned to an out-of-town scribe to report his point of view surrounding the ABC Affair since he sensed that local writers were supportive of Carey, Bigbee and Adams' plight. Wallace began the interview by stating that many fans across the country believed the recent mutiny had caused the players to fight among themselves, which in turn killed Pittsburgh's pennant hopes.[68]

"That affair did the team good," replied Dreyfuss. "And people are likely to say anything. Our trouble was that Wright was unable to play for seven weeks."[69]

Wallace then dug up every unfavorable rumor that surrounded the Pittsburgh team, but Dreyfuss shot each one down in quick fashion. When Wallace claimed that Kiki Cuyler was the only player who occupied a training table at Paso Robles in the spring, Dreyfuss stated that he was there and did not witness such malingering by his players. Dreyfuss made the claim even though he did not actually accompany Pittsburgh's squad during its 1926 spring training trip to California. Wallace then asked Dreyfuss if there was a problem on the team with players divided over religion. Dreyfuss responded by saying that he never hired a man for his religion. The New York writer then asked about Max Carey being jealous of Cuyler and wanting to get rid of him for the last three years. Wallace also claimed that Cuyler wished to be traded to another team. Dreyfuss answered by stating that Carey never approached him about any jealousy and that he had not heard anything about Cuyler's desire to be traded.[70]

When the conversation turned to Dreyfuss's meeting with the three admonished players, the owner's response contradicted what Carey had said after the four gentlemen met. Dreyfuss's remarks indicated that the three players had not been received in a kind and sympathetic manner, as had been previously reported.[71] "You'll wait until your beards grow long before I exonerate you, or even listen to you," Dreyfuss claimed he told the three players during their meeting.

"They pulled a boner by not waiting until I came back before they did anything," continued Dreyfuss. "They made a mistake, and they know it now. Whatever happened during my absence was handled by the men I left in charge, I never even asked my son Sam about his side of it.

"Carey fell down this year," concluded Pittsburgh's owner. "His sickness was his own fault. I wired him and wrote him to stay in the hospital and get better, but he came to camp prematurely."[72]

Dreyfuss's opinion of Carey did not seem to mesh with how his fellow National League players and Pittsburgh fans felt about the star outfielder. A rumor indicating how much Carey was revered by opposing players contended that rival pitchers were grooving balls for him so that he could record a solid batting average in Brooklyn for the remainder of the campaign.[73] It was believed the players' brotherhood was angry over the way Carey had been treated by Pittsburgh management. When Carey returned to Forbes Field as a Brooklyn Robin for the first time, fans lustily cheered for the former Pirate player each time he stepped up to the plate.[74]

The strong showing of affection did not go unnoticed on Carey's behalf.

"When a lot of them came to me after that last game I played here with the Robins," said Carey, "and with tears running down their cheeks, expressed their regret over my going, it was almost more than I could stand. It was a demonstration I had never expected to witness. A fellow could hardly go wrong when he knows he has people like that pulling for him."[75]

Carey, Bigbee and Adams showed goodwill by waiting until Pittsburgh's season ended before they explained what had led to festering dissension on the ball club. It was their contention that a less than harmonious attitude had existed for a long time. They claimed the trouble started after the World Series money was divided among the players the previous October. Bill McKechnie had appointed a committee of players to decide how the money should be split. Initially, the committee did not vote Fred Clarke a share since he already owned stock in the Pirates. Carey did not participate in the proposition, but after the vote was conducted, he made an appeal on Clarke's behalf. During a second ballot by the committee, it was determined by a margin of one vote that Clarke would receive $1,000.[76]

The three players further claimed that when Clarke became aware of how this process played out, he sent his check with a letter to McKechnie. In the letter, Clarke explained that the money should be given to McKechnie, who could put it to better use. Clarke only accepted the $1,000 bonus after Barney Dreyfuss urged him to do so. Carey, Bigbee and Adams pointed to this event as proof harmony and dissension existed before 1926. They also referred to an incident involving Eddie Moore that backed their claim that Clarke's presence on Pittsburgh's bench was causing turbulence and annoyance. On more than one occasion, Moore had demanded that Clarke "get off the bench" after the team vice-president was critical of his play. Clarke responded with a statement of his own in which he declared that he never interfered with McKechnie managing the squad. Clarke also denied that any player ever demanded that he leave Pittsburgh's dugout.[77]

It was highly unlikely that Moore offered a proxy vote to remove Clarke from the bench when Pittsburgh's players held their August ballot in a New York hotel. This meant that three players voted against Clarke, along with Carey, Bigbee and Adams. It was never revealed which three members of the Pittsburgh organization voted in unison with their disciplined counterparts. After his release, Adams stated that he did not even know the identity of *one* of the players.[78] Chester L. Smith of the *Pittsburgh-Gazette Times* speculated that George Grantham and Kiki Cuyler may have been two of the other players who voted against Clarke. Those two players, along with Moore, supposedly did not like Clarke or his methods. Grantham even went to Bigbee after the players' revolt and said that he would be willing to tell the world about his role in the insurrection and accept whatever punishment came his way. Bigbee urged Grantham to remain quiet since he was still a young man with a long career in front of him. Bigbee felt enough damage had already been done.[79]

Many followers throughout Pittsburgh reasoned that the vote count against Clarke would have been higher if some players did not become nervous when the time came to take action.[80] As was the case since he assumed control of the Pittsburgh franchise, Barney Dreyfuss had the final word regarding the fallout from the ABC Affair. On September 25, 1926, first baseman Stuffy McInnis was given his unconditional release. This move was expected for several weeks, since it was believed McInnis had leaked the news about a player vote against Clarke to the newspapers. McInnis did this after Bill McKechnie told his players that anyone who divulged their meeting to the press would be released.[81]

McKechnie quickly followed McInnis out the door when Dreyfuss announced that he would not manage the Pirates in 1927. After conducting a meeting with McKechnie on October 12, Dreyfuss handed the manager his release. When Dreyfuss alerted the press of his decision, his only statement was a one-line comment he made to McKechnie during their conference.[82]

"ABC Affair" mutineer Carson Bigbee advised George Grantham to remain quiet about his role in the vote to remove Fred Clarke from Pittsburgh's dugout. Bigbee reasoned that Grantham should not throw his baseball career away since he was a young man with a bright future ahead of him (National Baseball Hall of Fame Library, Cooperstown, New York).

"The people of Pittsburgh want a change and we must give it to them," declared Dreyfuss.[83]

The fans of Pittsburgh continued to receive the change they wanted when Fred Clarke mailed his resignation as vice-president and director to Dreyfuss in late October.[84] Pittsburgh's board of club directors met and immediately accepted Clarke's resignation. The club also announced that arrangements were being made to repurchase the small amount of stock that Clarke previously held.[85] Dreyfuss then signed Donie Bush to a one-year contract as a replacement for McKechnie.[86]

During the off-season, Hazen Cuyler's name was mentioned numerous times in relation to trade rumors involving other clubs.[87] Cuyler remained with the squad for the 1927 season, but insubordination became a key element once again when Pittsburgh's star outfielder clashed with Bush.

The Pittsburgh Pirates failed to repeat as world champions in 1926 because stubborn pride and apathy destroyed the harmonious attitude that existed during the glorious season of 1925. For most of Pittsburgh's players, 1925 represented the only time they were connected to a team crowned world champions of baseball. These men had battled gallantly against difficult odds in 1925, but could not overcome petty differences during the 1926 season.

After being fired by Barney Dreyfuss, McKechnie was philosophical about the events that ended his tenure as Pittsburgh's manager. "He treated me fine all the time I worked for him and I haven't a word of complaint to utter," said McKechnie in discussing Dreyfuss. "I realize that many of the fans had turned against me, and that I was being criticized as a result of the dissension which broke out in the club during the past season. My only comment is that I always did my best."[88]

Shortstop Glenn Wright survived as the last living member of the 1925 Pittsburgh Pirates; he passed away on April 6, 1984. Two years prior to Wright's death, he responded to a letter from a fan named "Mark" in 1982. Mark asked Wright a variety of questions involving his playing career. Wright told the fan that Grover Cleveland Alexander was the best pitcher he had ever faced, even though Pete did not possess the best stuff. Glenn also wrote that Wilbert Robinson was his favorite manager, while Bill McKechnie was the best manager he had ever played for during his career. In closing, Wright told Mark about the favorite moment of his baseball career.

"My biggest thrill was standing at attention while the band played our National Anthem before the first game of the '25 World Series."

Appendix A:
1925 Pittsburgh Pirates Statistics

Batting Statistics — Team Batting Average .307

	G	AB	R	H	2B	3B	HR	RBI	BB	SO	SB	CS	AVG	SLG
Kiki Cuyler	153	617	144	220	43	26	18	102	58	56	41	13	.357	.598
Glenn Wright	153	614	97	189	32	10	18	121	31	32	3	7	.308	.480
Pie Traynor	150	591	114	189	39	14	6	106	52	19	15	9	.320	.464
Eddie Moore	142	547	106	163	29	8	6	77	73	26	19	7	.298	.413
Max Carey	133	542	109	186	39	13	5	44	66	19	46	11	.343	.491
Clyde Barnhart	142	539	85	175	32	11	4	114	59	25	9	5	.325	.447
George Grantham	114	359	74	117	24	6	8	52	50	29	14	4	.326	.493
Earl Smith	109	329	34	103	22	3	8	64	31	13	4	1	.313	.471
Johnny Gooch	79	215	24	64	8	4	0	30	20	16	1	0	.298	.372
Stuffy McInnis	59	155	19	57	10	4	0	24	17	1	1	1	.368	.484
Carson Bigbee	66	126	31	30	7	0	0	8	7	8	2	2	.238	.294
Johnny Rawlings	36	110	17	31	7	0	2	13	8	8	0	1	.282	.400
Lee Meadows	35	97	10	17	3	0	1	7	7	21	0	0	.175	.237
Emil Yde	47	89	11	17	4	1	0	11	2	13	1	1	.191	.258
Vic Aldridge	30	86	3	20	0	0	1	10	0	4	0	0	.233	.267
Johnny Morrison	44	73	4	13	0	2	0	8	1	17	0	0	.178	.233
Ray Kremer	40	71	9	14	5	1	0	7	5	25	0	0	.197	.296
Al Niehaus	17	64	7	14	8	0	0	7	1	5	0	0	.219	.344
Fresco Thompson	14	37	4	9	2	1	0	8	4	1	2	1	.243	.351
Babe Adams	33	31	3	7	1	0	0	1	3	6	0	0	.226	.258
Roy Spencer	14	28	1	6	1	0	0	2	1	3	1	0	.214	.250
Tom Sheehan	24	20	0	3	0	0	0	1	1	6	0	0	.150	.150
Red Oldham	11	18	2	6	0	1	0	1	2	4	0	0	.333	.444
Jewel Ens	3	5	2	1	0	0	1	2	0	1	0	0	.200	.800
Mule Haas	4	3	1	0	0	0	0	0	0	1	0	0	.000	.000

	G	AB	R	H	2B	3B	HR	RBI	BB	SO	SB	CS	AVG	SLG
Bud Culloton	9	3	0	0	0	0	0	0	0	3	0	0	.000	.000
Don Songer	8	2	0	0	0	0	0	0	0	0	0	0	.000	.000
Lou Koupal	7	1	1	0	0	0	0	0	0	1	0	0	.000	.000

Pitching Statistics — Team ERA 3.87

	W	L	ERA	G	GS	CG	SV	IP	H	R	ER	HR	BB	SO
Lee Meadows	19	10	3.67	35	31	20	1	255	272	128	104	11	67	87
Ray Kremer	17	8	3.69	40	27	14	2	214	232	106	88	19	47	62
Vic Aldridge	15	7	3.63	30	26	14	0	213	218	99	86	15	74	88
Johnny Morrison	17	14	3.88	44	26	10	4	211	245	113	91	12	60	60
Emil Yde	17	9	4.13	33	28	13	0	207	254	125	95	11	75	41
Babe Adams	6	5	5.42	33	10	3	3	101	129	67	61	7	17	18
Tom Sheehan	1	1	2.67	23	0	0	2	57	63	25	17	2	13	13
Red Oldham	3	2	3.91	11	4	3	1	53	66	27	23	2	18	10
Bud Culloton	0	1	2.57	9	1	0	0	21	19	8	6	1	1	3
Don Songer	0	1	2.31	8	0	0	0	11	14	7	3	0	8	4
Lou Koupal	0	0	9.00	6	0	0	0	9	14	10	9	1	7	0

Appendix B:
1925 World Series Box Scores

• GAME ONE •

Wednesday, October 7, 1925, at Forbes Field
Washington Senators 4 — Pittsburgh Pirates 1

WASHINGTON	AB	R	H	RBI	PITTSBURGH	AB	R	H	RBI
Rice cf, rf	4	0	2	2	Moore 2b	4	0	0	0
Harris, B. 2b	3	0	0	0	Carey cf	2	0	0	0
Goslin lf	4	1	1	0	Cuyler rf	4	0	1	0
Judge 1b	3	0	0	0	Barnhart lf	4	0	1	0
Harris, J. rf	4	2	2	1	Traynor 3b	4	1	2	1
McNeely cf	0	0	0	0	Wright ss	4	0	0	0
Bluege 3b	4	1	2	1	Grantham 1b	3	0	0	0
Peckinpaugh ss	4	0	1	0	Smith c	3	0	1	0
Ruel c	3	0	0	0	Bigbee pr	0	0	0	0
Johnson p	3	0	0	0	Gooch c	0	0	0	0
TOTALS	32	4	8	4	Meadows p	1	0	0	0
					McInnis ph	1	0	0	0
					Morrison p	0	0	0	0
					TOTALS	30	1	5	1

WASHINGTON	TIP	H	R	ER	BB	SO	PITTSBURGH	TIP	H	R	ER	BB	SO
Johnson W (1–0)	9.0	5	1	1	1	10	Meadows L (0–1)	8.0	6	3	3	0	4
TOTALS	9.0	5	1	1	1	10	Morrison	1.0	2	1	1	0	1
							TOTALS	9.0	8	4	4	0	5

WASHINGTON 0 1 0 0 2 0 0 0 1 - 4 8 1
PITTSBURGH 0 0 0 0 1 0 0 0 0 - 1 5 0

E–Peckinpaugh (1). DP–Washington 1, Pittsburgh 1. HR–Washington J Harris (1, 2nd inning off Meadows 0 on, 1 out), Pittsburgh Traynor (1, 5th inning off Johnson 0 on, 0 out). SH–Judge (1, off Morrison). HBP–B Harris (1, by Meadows); Carey 2 (2, by Johnson 2). SB–Grantham (1, 2nd base off Johnson/Ruel); Bigbee (1, 2nd base off Johnson/Ruel). CS–Carey (1, 2nd base by Johnson/Ruel). HBP–Johnson 2 (2, Carey 2); Meadows (1, B Harris). U–HP–Cy Rigler (NL), 1B–Brick Owens (AL), 2B–Barry McCormick (NL), 3B–George Moriarty (AL). T–1:57. A–41,723.

• Game Two •

Thursday, October 8, 1925, at Forbes Field
Washington Senators 2 — Pittsburgh Pirates 3

WASHINGTON	AB	R	H	RBI	PITTSBURGH	AB	R	H	RBI
Rice cf	5	0	2	0	Moore 2b	4	1	0	0
Harris, B. 2b	3	0	0	0	Carey cf	4	0	2	0
Goslin lf	4	0	0	0	Cuyler rf	3	1	1	2
Judge 1b	4	1	1	1	Barnhart lf	4	0	1	0
Harris, J. rf	3	0	2	0	Traynor 3b	3	0	0	0
McNeely pr	0	1	0	0	Wright ss	4	1	2	1
Bluege 3b	2	0	0	0	Grantham 1b	4	0	0	0
Myer pr, 3b	1	0	1	0	Smith c	3	0	1	0
Peckinpaugh ss	3	0	1	0	Aldridge p	3	0	0	0
Ruel c	3	0	1	0	TOTALS	32	3	7	3
Veach ph	0	0	0	1					
Coveleski p	2	0	0	0					
Ruether ph	1	0	0	0					
TOTALS	31	2	8	2					

WASHINGTON	TIP	H	R	ER	BB	SO	PITTSBURGH	TIP	H	R	ER	BB	SO
Coveleski L (0–1)	8.0	7	3	2	1	3	Aldridge W (1–0)	9.0	8	2	2	2	4
TOTALS	8.0	7	3	2	1	3	TOTALS	9.0	8	2	2	2	4

WASHINGTON	0	1	0	0	0	0	0	0	1	-	2	8	2
PITTSBURGH	0	0	0	1	0	0	0	2		-	3	7	0

E–Peckinpaugh 2 (3). PB–Ruel (1). HR–Washington Judge (1, 2nd inning off Aldridge 0 on, 0 out), Pittsburgh Wright (1, 4th inning off Coveleski 0 on, 2 out); Cuyler (1, 8th inning off Coveleski 1 on, 1 out). SH–Coveleski (1, off Aldridge); B Harris (1, off Aldridge); Cuyler (1, off Coveleski). SF–Veach (1, off Aldridge). HBP–Bluege (1, by Aldridge). CS–J Harris (1, 2nd base by Aldridge/Smith); Myer (1, 2nd base by Aldridge/Smith). BK–Aldridge (1). HBP–Aldridge (1, Bluege). U–HP–Brick Owens (AL), 1B–Barry McCormick (NL), 2B–George Moriarty (AL), 3B–Cy Rigler (NL). T–2:04. A–43,364.

• GAME THREE •

Saturday, October 10, 1925, at Griffith Stadium
Pittsburgh Pirates 3 — Washington Senators 4

PITTSBURGH	AB	R	H	RBI	WASHINGTON	AB	R	H	RBI
Moore 2b	3	0	1	0	Rice cf, rf	5	1	2	0
Carey cf	4	0	2	0	Harris, B. 2b	3	1	1	0
Cuyler rf	4	1	1	0	Goslin lf	4	1	2	1
Barnhart lf	5	0	1	1	Judge 1b	3	0	1	2
Traynor 3b	4	1	1	0	Harris, J. rf	4	0	2	1
Wright ss	3	1	0	1	Marberry p	0	0	0	0
Grantham 1b	4	0	0	0	Myer 3b	3	0	0	0
Smith c	3	0	1	0	Peckinpaugh ss	4	0	1	0
Kremer p	3	0	1	1	Ruel c	3	0	1	0
Bigbee ph	1	0	0	0	Ferguson p	2	0	0	0
TOTALS	34	3	8	3	Leibold ph	0	0	0	0
					McNeely pr, cf	0	1	0	0
					TOTALS	31	4	10	4

PITTSBURGH	TIP	H	R	ER	BB	SO	WASHINGTON	TIP	H	R	ER	BB	SO
Kremer L (0–1)	8.0	10	4	4	3	5	Ferguson W (1–0)	7.0	6	3	2	4	5
TOTALS	8.0	10	4	4	3	5	Marberry SV (1)	2.0	2	0	0	0	2
							TOTALS	9.0	8	3	2	4	7

PITTSBURGH 0 1 0 1 0 1 0 0 0 – 3 8 2
WASHINGTON 0 0 1 0 0 1 2 0 – 4 10 1

E–Carey (1), Wright (1), Peckinpaugh (4). DP–Pittsburgh 1, Washington 1. PB–Smith (1). 2B–Pittsburgh Cuyler (1, off Ferguson); Carey (1, off Ferguson), Washington Judge (1, off Kremer). 3B–Pittsburgh Traynor (1, off Ferguson). HR–Washington Goslin (1, 6th inning off Kremer 0 on, 0 out). SF–Wright (1, off Ferguson); Judge (1, off Kremer). HBP–Carey (3, by Ferguson); Cuyler (1, by Marberry). IBB–Smith (1, by Ferguson). SH–B Harris (2, off Kremer); Marberry (1, off Kremer). CS–Peckinpaugh (1, 2nd base by Kremer/Smith). HBP–Ferguson (1, Carey); Marberry (1, Cuyler). IBB–Ferguson (1, Smith). U-HP–Barry McCormick (NL), 1B–George Moriarty (AL), 2B–Cy Rigler (NL), 3B–Brick Owens (AL). T–2:10. A–36,495.

• GAME FOUR •

Sunday, October 11, 1925, at Griffith Stadium
Pittsburgh Pirates 0 — Washington Senators 4

PITTSBURGH	AB	R	H	RBI	WASHINGTON	AB	R	H	RBI
Moore 2b	4	0	1	0	Rice cf	5	1	2	0
Carey cf	3	0	1	0	Harris, B. 2b	3	1	1	0

PITTSBURGH	AB	R	H	RBI	WASHINGTON	AB	R	H	RBI
Cuyler rf	4	0	0	0	Goslin lf	3	1	2	3
Barnhart lf	3	0	0	0	Harris, J. rf	4	1	1	1
Traynor 3b	4	0	2	0	Judge 1b	3	0	0	0
Wright ss	4	0	0	0	Peckinpaugh ss	4	0	1	0
Grantham 1b	3	0	2	0	Ruel c	3	0	3	0
Gooch c	3	0	0	0	Myer 3b	4	0	1	0
Yde p	1	0	0	0	Johnson p	4	0	1	0
Morrison p	1	0	0	0	TOTALS	33	4	12	4
Bigbee ph	1	0	0	0					
Adams p	0	0	0	0					
TOTALS	31	0	6	0					

PITTSBURGH	TIP	H	R	ER	BB	SO	WASHINGTON	TIP	H	R	ER	BB	SO
Yde L (0–1)	2.1	5	4	3	3	1	Johnson W (2–0)	9.0	6	0	0	2	2
Morrison	4.2	5	0	0	1	4	TOTALS	9.0	6	0	0	2	2
Adams	1.0	2	0	0	0	0							
TOTALS	8.0	12	4	3	4	5							

PITTSBURGH	0	0	0	0	0	0	0	0	-	0	6	1
WASHINGTON	0	0	4	0	0	0	0	0	-	4	12	0

E–Wright (2). DP–Pittsburgh 1, Washington 2. 2B–Washington Ruel (1, off Adams). HR–Washington Goslin (2, 3rd inning off Yde 2 on, 1 out); J Harris (2, 3rd inning off Yde 0 on, 1 out). SB–Carey (1, 2nd base off Johnson/Ruel); Peckinpaugh (1, 2nd base off Morrison/Gooch). CS–Judge (1, 2nd base by Morrison/Gooch). U-HP–George Moriarty (AL), 1B–Cy Rigler (NL), 2B–Brick Owens (AL), 3B–Barry McCormick (NL). T–2:00. A–38,701.

• GAME FIVE •

Monday, October 12, 1925, at Griffith Stadium
Pittsburgh Pirates 6 — Washington Senators 3

PITTSBURGH	AB	R	H	RBI	WASHINGTON	AB	R	H	RBI
Moore 2b	4	1	1	0	Rice cf	5	1	2	1
Carey cf	4	2	2	0	Harris, B. 2b	3	0	0	0
Cuyler rf	4	1	2	1	Goslin lf	4	0	1	1
Barnhart lf	4	1	2	2	Judge 1b	3	0	0	0
Traynor 3b	3	0	1	1	Harris, J. rf	3	1	2	1
Wright ss	5	1	2	1	Peckinpaugh ss	3	0	0	0
McInnis 1b	5	0	1	1	Ruel c	3	0	1	0
Smith c	3	0	2	0	Bluege 3b	4	0	1	0
Aldridge p	4	0	0	0	Coveleski p	1	0	0	0
TOTALS	36	6	13	6	Ballou p	0	0	0	0

1925 World Series Box Scores

WASHINGTON	AB	R	H	RBI
Leibold ph	1	1	1	0
Zachary p	0	0	0	0
Marberry p	0	0	0	0
Adams ph	1	0	0	0
TOTALS	31	3	8	3

PITTSBURGH	TIP	H	R	ER	BB	SO	WASHINGTON	TIP	H	R	ER	BB	SO
Aldridge W (2-0)	9.0	8	3	3	4	5	Coveleski L (0-2)	6.1	9	4	4	4	0
TOTALS	9.0	8	3	3	4	5	Ballou	0.2	0	0	0	0	1
							Zachary	1.2	3	2	2	1	0
							Marberry	0.1	1	0	0	0	0
							TOTALS	9.0	13	6	6	5	1

```
PITTSBURGH   0 0 2 0 0 0 2 1 1 - 6 13 0
WASHINGTON   1 0 0 1 0 0 1 0 0 - 3  8 1
```

E-Peckinpaugh (5). DP-Pittsburgh 1, Washington 2. 2B-Pittsburgh Wright (1, off Zachary), Washington Goslin (1, off Aldridge); Bluege (1, off Aldridge); Leibold (1, off Aldridge). HR-Washington J Harris (3, 4th inning off Aldridge 0 on, 0 out). SH-Smith (1, off Zachary); B Harris 2 (4, off Aldridge 2); Peckinpaugh (1, off Aldridge). SF-Traynor (1, off Coveleski). SB-Carey (2, 2nd base off Coveleski/Ruel); Barnhart (1, 2nd base off Coveleski/Ruel). CS-J Harris (2, 3rd base by Aldridge/Smith). U-HP-Cy Rigler (NL), 1B-Brick Owens (AL), 2B-Barry McCormick (NL), 3B-George Moriarty (AL). T-2:26. A-35,899.

• GAME SIX •

Tuesday, October 13, 1925, at Forbes Field
Washington Senators 2 — Pittsburgh Pirates 3

WASHINGTON	AB	R	H	RBI	PITTSBURGH	AB	R	H	RBI
Rice cf	4	0	0	0	Moore 2b	3	2	2	1
Harris, B. 2b	3	0	0	0	Carey cf	2	1	0	0
Veach ph	1	0	0	0	Cuyler rf	3	0	0	0
Ballou p	0	0	0	0	Barnhart lf	3	0	1	1
Goslin lf	3	1	1	1	Traynor 3b	4	0	2	1
Harris, J. rf	4	0	1	0	Wright ss	3	0	0	0
Judge 1b	4	0	1	0	McInnis 1b	4	0	1	0
Bluege 3b	4	1	1	0	Smith c	4	0	1	0
Peckinpaugh ss	3	0	1	1	Kremer p	3	0	0	0
Severeid c	3	0	1	0	TOTALS	29	3	7	3
McNeely pr	0	0	0	0					
Adams 2b	0	0	0	0					
Ferguson p	2	0	0	0					

WASHINGTON	AB	R	H	RBI
Leibold ph	1	0	0	0
Ruel c	0	0	0	0
TOTALS	32	2	6	2

WASHINGTON	IP	H	R	ER	BB	SO	PITTSBURGH	IP	H	R	ER	BB	SO
Ferguson L (1–1)	7.0	7	3	3	2	6	Kremer W (1–1)	9.0	6	2	2	1	3
Ballou	1.0	0	0	0	1	0	TOTALS	9.0	6	2	2	1	3
TOTALS	8.0	7	3	3	3	6							

WASHINGTON 1 1 0 0 0 0 0 0 - 2 6 2
PITTSBURGH 0 0 2 0 1 0 0 0 - 3 7 1

E–Peckinpaugh (6), Severeid (1), Kremer (1). DP–Washington 1. 2B–Washington Peckinpaugh (1, off Kremer); J Harris (1, off Kremer), Pittsburgh Barnhart (1, off Ferguson). HR–Washington Goslin (3, 1st inning off Kremer 0 on, 2 out), Pittsburgh Moore (1, 5th inning off Ferguson 0 on, 0 out). SH–Carey 2 (2, off Ferguson 2); Cuyler (2, off Ferguson). SB–McNeely (1, 2nd base off Kremer/Smith); Traynor (1, 2nd base off Ferguson/Severeid). U–HP–Brick Owens (AL), 1B–Barry McCormick (NL), 2B–George Moriarty (AL), 3B–Cy Rigler (NL). T–1:57. A–43,810.

• GAME SEVEN •

Thursday, October 15, 1925, at Forbes Field
Washington Senators 7 — Pittsburgh Pirates 9

WASHINGTON	AB	R	H	RBI	PITTSBURGH	AB	R	H	RBI
Rice cf	5	2	2	0	Moore 2b	4	3	1	1
Harris, B. 2b	5	0	0	0	Carey cf	5	3	4	2
Goslin lf	4	2	1	0	Cuyler rf	4	0	2	3
Harris, J. rf	3	1	1	2	Barnhart lf	5	0	1	1
Judge 1b	3	1	1	1	Oldham p	0	0	0	0
Bluege 3b	4	0	1	1	Traynor 3b	4	0	1	1
Peckinpaugh ss	3	1	1	2	Wright ss	4	0	1	0
Ruel c	4	0	0	1	McInnis 1b	4	0	2	0
Johnson p	4	0	0	0	Smith c	4	0	1	0
TOTALS	35	7	7	7	Yde pr	0	1	0	0
					Gooch c	0	0	0	0
					Aldridge p	0	0	0	0
					Morrison p	1	1	1	0
					Grantham ph	1	0	0	0
					Kremer p	1	0	0	0
					Bigbee ph, lf	1	1	1	1
					TOTALS	38	9	15	9

WASHINGTON	IP	H	R	ER	BB	SO	PITTSBURGH	IP	H	R	ER	BB	SO
Johnson L (2–1)	8.0	15	9	5	1	3	Aldridge	0.1	2	4	4	3	0
TOTALS	8.0	15	9	5	1	3	Morrison	3.2	4	2	2	0	2
							Kremer W (2–1)	4.0	1	1	1	0	1
							Oldham SV (1)	1.0	0	0	0	0	2
							TOTALS	9.0	7	7	7	3	5

WASHINGTON	4	0	0	2	0	0	0	1	0	–	7	7 2
PITTSBURGH	0	0	3	0	1	0	2	3		–	9	15 3

E–Peckinpaugh 2 (8), Moore (1), Cuyler (1), Smith (1). DP–Washington 1. 2B–Washington J Harris (2, off Morrison), Pittsburgh Carey 3 (4, off Johnson 3); Moore (1, off Johnson); Cuyler 2 (3, off Johnson 2); Smith (1, off Johnson); Bigbee (1, off Johnson). 3B–Pittsburgh Traynor (2, off Johnson). HR–Washington Peckinpaugh (1, 8th inning off Kremer 0 on, 1 out). SH–Cuyler (3, off Johnson). SB–Carey (3, 3rd base off Johnson/Ruel). WP–Aldridge 2 (2). U–HP–Barry McCormick (NL), 1B–George Moriarty (AL), 2B–Cy Rigler (NL), 3B–Brick Owens (AL). T–2:31. A–42,856.

Appendix C: 1925 World Series Statistics

• 1925 WORLD SERIES BATTING STATISTICS •

Washington Senators — Team Batting Average .262

	G	AB	R	H	2B	3B	HR	RBI	BB	SO	SB	CS	AVG	SLG
Spencer Adams	2	1	0	0	0	0	0	0	0	0	0	0	.000	.000
Win Ballou	2	0	0	0	0	0	0	0	0	0	0	0	.000	.000
Ossie Bluege	5	18	2	5	1	0	0	2	0	4	0	0	.278	.333
Stan Coveleski	2	3	0	0	0	0	0	0	1	2	0	0	.000	.000
Alex Ferguson	2	4	0	0	0	0	0	0	0	3	0	0	.000	.000
Goose Goslin	7	26	6	8	1	0	3	6	3	3	0	0	.308	.692
Bucky Harris	7	23	2	2	0	0	0	0	1	3	0	0	.087	.087
Joe Harris	7	25	5	11	2	0	3	6	3	4	0	2	.440	.880
Walter Johnson	3	11	0	1	0	0	0	0	0	3	0	0	.091	.091
Joe Judge	7	23	2	4	1	0	1	4	3	2	0	1	.174	.348
Nemo Leibold	3	2	1	1	1	0	0	0	1	0	0	0	.500	1.000
Firpo Marberry	2	0	0	0	0	0	0	0	0	0	0	0	.000	.000
Earl McNeely	4	0	2	0	0	0	0	0	0	0	1	0	.000	.000
Buddy Myer	3	8	0	2	0	0	0	0	1	2	0	1	.250	.250
Roger Peckinpaugh	7	24	1	6	1	0	1	3	1	2	1	1	.250	.417
Sam Rice	7	33	5	12	0	0	0	3	0	1	0	0	.364	.364
Muddy Ruel	7	19	0	6	1	0	0	1	3	2	0	0	.316	.368
Dutch Ruether	1	1	0	0	0	0	0	0	1	0	0	0	.000	.000
Hank Severeid	1	3	0	1	0	0	0	0	0	0	0	0	.333	.333
Bobby Veach	2	1	0	0	0	0	0	1	0	0	0	0	.000	.000
Tom Zachary	1	0	0	0	0	0	0	0	0	0	0	0	.000	.000

Pittsburgh Pirates — Team Batting Average .265

	G	AB	R	H	2B	3B	HR	RBI	BB	SO	SB	CS	AVG	SLG
Babe Adams	1	0	0	0	0	0	0	0	0	0	0	0	.000	.000
Vic Aldridge	3	7	0	0	0	0	0	0	0	0	0	0	.000	.000
Clyde Barnhart	7	28	1	7	1	0	0	5	3	5	1	0	.250	.286
Carson Bigbee	4	3	1	1	1	0	0	1	0	0	1	0	.333	.667
Max Carey	7	24	6	11	4	0	0	2	2	3	3	1	.458	.625
Kiki Cuyler	7	26	3	7	3	0	1	6	1	4	0	0	.269	.500
Johnny Gooch	3	3	0	0	0	0	0	0	0	0	0	0	.000	.000
George Grantham	5	15	0	2	0	0	0	0	0	3	1	0	.133	.133
Ray Kremer	3	7	0	1	0	0	0	1	0	5	0	0	.143	.143
Stuffy McInnis	4	14	0	4	0	0	0	1	0	2	0	0	.286	.286
Lee Meadows	1	1	0	0	0	0	0	0	1	1	0	0	.000	.000
Eddie Moore	7	26	7	6	1	0	1	2	5	2	0	0	.231	.385
Johnny Morrison	3	2	1	1	0	0	0	0	0	0	0	0	.500	.500
Red Oldham	1	0	0	0	0	0	0	0	0	0	0	0	.000	.000
Earl Smith	6	20	0	7	1	0	0	0	1	2	0	0	.350	.400
Pie Traynor	7	26	2	9	0	2	1	4	3	1	1	0	.346	.615
Glenn Wright	7	27	3	5	1	0	1	3	1	4	0	0	.185	.333
Emil Yde	2	1	1	0	0	0	0	0	0	0	0	0	.000	.000

• 1925 WORLD SERIES PITCHING STATISTICS •

Washington Senators — Team ERA 2.85

	G	GS	CG	SV	TIP	H	HR	R	ER	BB	SO	W	L	ERA
Win Ballou	2	0	0	0	1.2	0	0	0	0	1	1	0	0	0.00
Stan Coveleski	2	2	1	0	14.1	16	2	7	6	5	3	0	2	3.77
Alex Ferguson	2	2	0	0	14.0	13	1	6	5	6	11	1	1	3.21
Walter Johnson	3	3	3	0	26.0	26	1	10	6	4	15	2	1	2.08
Firpo Marberry	2	0	0	1	2.1	3	0	0	0	0	2	0	0	0.00
Tom Zachary	1	0	0	0	1.2	3	0	2	2	1	0	0	0	10.80

Pittsburgh Pirates — Team ERA 3.69

	G	GS	CG	SV	TIP	H	HR	R	ER	BB	SO	W	L	ERA
Babe Adams	1	0	0	0	1.0	2	0	0	0	0	0	0	0	0.00
Vic Aldridge	3	3	2	0	18.1	18	2	9	9	9	9	2	0	4.42
Ray Kremer	3	2	2	0	21.0	17	3	7	7	4	9	2	1	3.00
Lee Meadows	1	1	0	0	8.0	6	1	3	3	0	4	0	1	3.38
Johnny Morrison	3	0	0	0	9.1	11	0	3	3	1	7	0	0	2.89
Red Oldham	1	0	0	1	1.0	0	0	0	0	0	2	0	0	0.00
Emil Yde	1	1	0	0	2.1	5	2	4	3	3	1	0	1	11.57

Chapter Notes

Chapter 1

1. Frederick G. Lieb, *The Pittsburgh Pirates 1948*. (Reprint, Carbondale, IL: Southern Illinois University Press, 2003), page 191.
2. Lieb, *The Pittsburgh Pirates*, page 193.
3. *Ibid.*
4. *Ibid.*
5. *Ibid.*
6. Lieb, *The Pittsburgh Pirates*, page 192.
7. Lieb, *The Pittsburgh Pirates*, page 193.
8. Ralph S. Davis, "Win Them at Home and Fans Come Out: That's Experience of Pittsburgh Club So Far This Season," *The Sporting News*, June 7, 1923, page 3.
9. Ralph S. Davis, "Slight Changes to Make Pirates Win: One Hoped For to Come Through Trade of Maranville," *The Sporting News*, January 3, 1924, page 3.
10. Ralph S. Davis, "Pittsburgh Divides into Rival Camps: Some Are for Maranville and Some Against Him," *The Sporting News*, January 24, 1924, page 3.
11. *Ibid.*
12. *Ibid.*
13. Ralph S. Davis, "Barney Tells Them How Much He'll Pay: Contracts Being Sent Out to Men on Pittsburgh Roster," *The Sporting News*, January 10, 1924, page 3.
14. Ralph S. Davis, "Pirate Squad Cut Before Going West: Dreyfuss and McKechnie Start to Lop Off Recruits," *The Sporting News*, January 31, 1924, page 3.
15. Ralph S. Davis, "Two Minor Buys Are Pittsburgh Balkers: Wright and Kremer Asking Part of Purchase Price," *The Sporting News*, February 14, 1924, page 3.
16. Ralph S. Davis, "Pirates Leave Cold of the East Behind: First Party on Its Way Toward California Camp," *The Sporting News*, February 28, 1924, page 2.
17. Ralph S. Davis, "Pirates Get Good Weather at Camp: Pittsburgh Team Finds California Ideal for Training," *The Sporting News*, March 13, 1924, page 2.
18. Ralph S. Davis, "Pirates Are Busy at Paso Robles: Grimm and Cooper Satisfied, Join Rest of Team," *The Sporting News*, March 6, 1924, page 3.
19. *Ibid.*
20. *Ibid.*
21. *Ibid.*
22. *Ibid.*
23. *Ibid.*
24. Ralph S. Davis, "Pirates Go in Air, So Does McKechnie: Manager Issues Drastic Order After Plane Incident," *The Sporting News*, March 20, 1924, page 3.
25. Davis, "Pirates Get Good Weather at Camp: Pittsburgh Team Finds California Ideal for Training," page 2.
26. Ralph S. Davis, "Pirates Have Lost but One Day's Work: Paso Robles Conditions Could Not Have Been Better," *The Sporting News*, March 27, 1924, page 3.
27. Davis, "Pirates Are Busy at Paso Robles: Grimm and Cooper Satisfied, Join Rest of Team," page 3.
28. Davis, "Pirates Have Lost but One Day's Work: Paso Robles Conditions Could Not Have Been Better," page 3.
29. *Ibid.*
30. Ralph S. Davis, "Bucs Get Acid Test First Three Weeks: Pirates Face Red Pitching Eight Times in That Period," *The Sporting News*, April 17, 1924, page 3.
31. *Ibid.*
32. *Ibid.*
33. Ralph S. Davis, "Pirates Due to Get Morning Practice!: McKechnie Not Pleased with Way Team Has Been Going," *The Sporting News*, May 1, 1924, page 5.

34. Ralph S. Davis, "Pirates Could Use Several Kremers: One Recruit Who Has Cheering Effect Upon McKechnie," *The Sporting News*, May 15, 1924, page 3.
35. Ralph S. Davis, "Pirates Kick About Umpire's Retorts: Davis Says Players Believe Bad Example Is Thus Set," *The Sporting News*, May 22, 1924, page 3.
36. Ralph S. Davis, "McKechnie Rumors Nailed by Dreyfuss: Club Owner Fully Satisfied with Manager's Efforts," *The Sporting News*, May 29, 1924, page 2.
37. *Ibid.*
38. Davis, "Pirates Could Use Several Kremers: One Recruit Who Has Cheering Effect Upon McKechnie," page 3.
39. *Ibid.*
40. Davis, "Pirates Kick about Umpire's Retorts: Davis Says Players Believe Bad Example Is Thus Set," page 3.
41. *Ibid.*
42. Ralph S. Davis, "McKechnie Spurred to Drastic Action: Traynor and Bigbee Benched in Effort to Bring Out Punch," *The Sporting News*, June 26, 1924, page 3.
43. L.H. Wollen, "Pie May Have to Remain on Pirate Bench: Moore's Work Sensational," *The Pittsburgh Press*, June 24, 1924, page 28.
44. Ralph S. Davis, "Jekyll-Hyde Role Held by Pittsburgh: Good One Day and Bad Next Has Been Team Rule," *The Sporting News*, July 10, 1924, page 3.
45. Davis, "McKechnie Spurred to Drastic Action: Traynor and Bigbee Benched in Effort to Bring Out Punch," page 3.
46. Davis, "Jekyll-Hyde Role Held by Pittsburgh: Good One Day and Bad Next Has Been Team Rule," page 3.
47. Ralph S. Davis, "Recruits Credited for Pirates' Climb: Cuyler, Kremer, Moore, Yde and Stone Real Heroes," *The Sporting News*, July 3, 1924, page 3.
48. Ralph Davis, "Sport Chat: Emil Yde Likes the Majors," *The Pittsburgh Press*, August 5, 1924, page 22.
49. Ralph S. Davis, "Bucs Show to Best Advantage of Year: Cuyler Has Had Much to Do with Success of Pirates," *The Sporting News*, July 24, 1924, page 2.
50. Ralph Davis, "Sport Chat: Pirates to Aid Recruiting," *The Pittsburgh Press*, July 16, 1924, page 24.
51. Ralph S. Davis, "Pirates Beginning to Say It with Hits: Cuyler Continues to be Leading Spirit with Stick," *The Sporting News*, August 7, 1924, page 1.
52. *Ibid.*

53. Ralph S. Davis, "Bucs Not Conceding Pennant to McGraw: McKechnie's Speedsters Make Great Record on Road," *The Sporting News*, August 14, 1924, page 1.
54. Ralph Davis, "Sport Chat: Cuyler on Stealing Bases," *The Pittsburgh Press*, August 25, 1924, page 18.
55. Ralph Davis, "Sport Chat: Hazen Cuyler, Hero," *The Pittsburgh Press*, August 18, 1924, page 18.
56. *Ibid.*
57. Ralph S. Davis, "Giants Practically Sure of Another Flag: McGraw Set for Record," *The Pittsburgh Press*, July 27, 1924, page 2.
58. Ralph S. Davis, "Mad Scramble Continues in National Race: Three Clubs in Running," *The Pittsburgh Press*, August 24, 1924, page 2.
59. Ralph S. Davis, "Ex-Members Spoil Bucs' Calculations: Vance and Grimes Pittsburghers Once Upon a Time," *The Sporting News*, August 28, 1924, page 3.
60. Ralph S. Davis, "Spineless Bucs Dig Their Own Graves: Team Lacks Proper Mental Poise to Win Championship," *The Sporting News*, October 2, 1924, page 1.
61. *Ibid.*
62. Ralph Davis, "Sport Chat: A Tip to John McGraw," *The Pittsburgh Press*, August 15, 1924, page 24.
63. L.H. Wollen, "Barney Dreyfuss and McGraw Lock Horns Again: Local Mogul on Warpath," *The Pittsburgh Press*, September 23, 1924, page 26.
64. Gotham, "Ghosts of Bribe Scandal Fail to Effect Playing of Games: Experience Proves Big Asset to McGraw," *The Sporting News*, October 9, 1924, page 1.
65. Paul W. White, "McGraw Takes Fling at Dreyfuss," *The Pittsburgh Press*, October 3, 1924, page 1.
66. Ralph S. Davis, "But for Recruits Where'd Bucs Be? Yde, Kremer, Wright, Cuyler and Moore have been Life-Savers," *The Sporting News*, September 25, 1924, page 2.

Chapter 2

1. "Gives National Late Thrill: Manager Bill McKechnie," *The Sporting News*, August 14, 1924, page 1.
2. *Ibid.*
3. *Ibid.*
4. *Ibid.*
5. "Capt'n Bold of Pirate Hold: Max Carey," *The Sporting News*, September 10, 1925, page 1.

6. Frederick G. Lieb, *The Pittsburgh Pirates 1948*. (Reprint, Carbondale, IL: Southern Illinois University Press, 2003), page 159.
7. *Ibid.*
8. *Ibid.*
9. Lieb, *The Pittsburgh Pirates*, page 175.
10. "Youth that Serves Itself: Third Baseman Pie Traynor," *The Sporting News*, September 24, 1925, page 5.
11. *Ibid.*
12. *Ibid.*
13. *Ibid.*
14. *Ibid.*
15. Ralph Davis, "Sport Chat: Says Pirate Pitcher Is Whole Battery," *The Pittsburgh Press*, May 13, 1924, page 32.
16. "Pittsburgh's Young Catching Reliance: Johnny Gooch," *The Sporting News*, July 3, 1924, page 2.
17. *Ibid.*
18. John J. Ward, "The Third Member of the Pirates Great Outfield," *Baseball Magazine*, November, 1925, page 547.
19. *Ibid.*
20. *Ibid.*
21. *Ibid.*
22. "Pirates' Great Young Hitter: Outfielder Hazen Cuyler," *The Sporting News*, August 21, 1924, page 1.
23. *Ibid.*
24. *Ibid.*
25. *Ibid.*
26. John J. Ward, "Has Pittsburgh Found a Worthy Successor to Hans Wagner?," *Baseball Magazine*, November, 1925, page 538.
27. *Ibid.*
28. *Ibid.*
29. *Ibid.*
30. "Hops into the Rabbit's Shoes: Second Baseman Eddie Moore," *The Sporting News*, November 27, 1924, page 1.
31. "Pirates' Reliable Recruit Southpaw: Emil Yde," *The Sporting News*, July 24, 1924, page 2.
32. "Pirates' New Mound Ace: Wiz Kremer," *The Sporting News*, June 5, 1924, page 1.
33. *Ibid.*
34. "He's Seeing Pirates Through: Pitcher Lee Meadows," *The Sporting News*, July 30, 1925, page 1.
35. *Ibid.*
36. *Ibid.*
37. Ralph S. Davis, "But for Recruits Where'd Bucs Be?: Yde, Kremer, Wright, Cuyler and Moore Have Been Life-Savers," *The Sporting News*, September 25, 1924, page 2.
38. *Ibid.*
39. *Ibid.*
40. *Ibid.*
41. *Ibid.*
42. Ralph S. Davis, "Anyway, Big Swap Satisfies Barney: Some Fans Are Inclined to Think Owner of Bucs Got Stung," *The Sporting News*, November 6, 1924, page 1.
43. *Ibid.*
44. *Ibid.*
45. *Ibid.*
46. *Ibid.*
47. "Jiggers! Bucky, the Teacher: Pitcher Vic Aldridge," *The Sporting News*, October 1, 1925, page 1.
48. *Ibid.*
49. Ralph S. Davis, "Buccaneers' View Is, Let 'Em Rant: Trading Niehaus for Bottomley Just Idle Talk," *The Sporting News*, November 13, 1924, page 5.
50. *Ibid.*

Chapter 3

1. Ralph S. Davis, "McKechnie Hears Shouting of Mob: Dreyfuss Says He's Satisfied with Bill's Work, However," *The Sporting News*, October 9, 1924, page 1.
2. *Ibid.*
3. Ralph S. Davis, "No, Landis Wasn't at Barney's Party: Another Engagement Keeps Judge Away from Testimonial," *The Sporting News*, October 30, 1924, page 1.
4. Ralph S. Davis, "Landis Refuses to Talk to Dreyfuss: Exciting Incident Occurs When They Meet in Washington," *The Sporting News*, October 16, 1924, page 1.
5. *Ibid.*
6. *Ibid.*
7. *Ibid.*
8. *Ibid.*
9. "Dreyfuss Says Inquiry Should Go Much Deeper," *The Sporting News*, October 9, 1924, page 2.
10. Ralph S. Davis, "Mr. Yde Gets What His Boss Couldn't: Ah Yes! It Was an Interview with Commissioner Landis," *The Sporting News*, October 23, 1924, page 3.
11. *Ibid.*
12. *Ibid.*
13. *Ibid.*
14. Ralph Davis, "Sport Chat: Yde Gets Big Salary," *The Pittsburgh Press*, October 15, 1924, page 26.
15. Davis, "Mr. Yde Gets What His Boss Couldn't: Ah Yes! It Was an Interview with Commissioner Landis," page 3.
16. Gotham, "Ghosts of Bribe Scandal Fail to Effect Playing of Games: Experience Proves

Big Asset to McGraw," *The Sporting News*, October 9, 1924, page 1.
17. *Ibid.*
18. Ralph Davis, "Sport Chat: Dreyfuss Going to Coast Early," *The Pittsburgh Press*, January 16, 1925, page 33.
19. *Ibid.*
20. Ralph Davis, "Sport Chat: Tipping Off the Pirate Owner," *The Pittsburgh Press*, October 9, 1924, page 31.
21. *Ibid.*
22. *Ibid.*
23. Davis, "McKechnie Hears Shouting of Mob: Dreyfuss Says He's Satisfied with Bill's Work, However," page 1.
24. Ralph S. Davis, "Holdout Season Drawing Near: Contracts to Be Sent Soon to Athletes," *The Pittsburgh Press,* January 4, 1925, page 2.
25. *Ibid.*
26. Ralph S. Davis, "No, Landis Wasn't at Barney's Party: Another Engagement Keeps Judge Away from Testimonial," *The Sporting News*, October 30, 1924, page 1.
27. "Hops into the Rabbit's Shoes: Second Baseman Eddie Moore," *The Sporting News*, November 27, 1924, page 1.
28. Ralph S. Davis, "Pirates All Set, Is View of Owner: Dreyfuss Satisfied That Team Is Stronger Than in 1924," *The Sporting News*, December 11, 1924, page 2.
29. *Ibid.*
30. "Who Wouldn't be Ambitious: Second Baseman Chick Thompson," *The Sporting News*, February 26, 1925, page 1.
31. Davis, "Pirates All Set, Is View of Owner: Dreyfuss Satisfied That Team Is Stronger Than in 1924," page 2.
32. *Ibid.*
33. *Ibid.*
34. Ralph S. Davis, "Big League Moguls will Confer: No More Corsair Trades Pending," *The Pittsburgh Press*, December 7, 1924, page 3.
35. L.H. Wollen, "Deal with Cards Is Possibility," *The Pittsburgh Press*, December 9, 1924, page 33.
36. Davis, "Landis Refuses to Talk to Dreyfuss: Exciting Incident Occurs When They Meet in Washington," page 1.
37. Ralph S. Davis, "Schmidt's Salary Works Against Him: Catcher Released by Pittsburgh was $12,000-a-Year Man," *The Sporting News*, December 25, 1924, page 1.
38. *Ibid.*
39. *Ibid.*
40. "Business Is Good, Burch Will Agree: Pitcher Louis Koupal," *The Sporting News*, December 25, 1924, page 2.

41. Ralph S. Davis, "It's Dreyfuss Time in Schedule Time: Pittsburgh Owner Now at Work on Program for 1925," *The Sporting News*, January 1, 1925, page 2.
42. Ralph S. Davis, "McKechnie Figures Infield Will Shine: Pittsburgh Chief Plans on Using Moore at Second Base," *The Sporting News*, January 22, 1925, page 2.
43. *Ibid.*
44. Ralph S. Davis, "Heydler Is Sure of Re-Election: No Movement Against Him," *The Pittsburgh Press*, November 30, 1924, page 6.
45. *Ibid.*
46. Davis, "It's Dreyfuss Time in Schedule Time: Pittsburgh Owner Now at Work on Program for 1925," page 2.
47. "Caught on the Fly," *The Sporting News*, January 8, 1925, page 8.
48. "Coldest Weather of Winter Grips Allegheny County," *The Pittsburgh Press*, January 28, 1925, page 1.
49. Ralph S. Davis, "Looks Like Barney Is Harboring Hunch: Anyway, He Will Be Able to Handle World's Series Crowd," *The Sporting News*, February 5, 1925, page 2.
50. *Ibid.*
51. *Ibid.*
52. Ralph S. Davis, "And Dreyfuss Did It All by Himself: Pirates Will Spend More for Rail Fare Than Any Other Club," *The Sporting News*, February 12, 1925, page 2.
53. *Ibid.*
54. Ralph S. Davis, "Fine! Says Barney of Purchase Divvy: Plan to Give Players Part of Sale Price Gets Dreyfuss' Vote," *The Sporting News*, November 20, 1924, page 1.
55. Davis, "And Dreyfuss Did It All by Himself: Pirates Will Spend More for Rail Fare Than Any Other Club," page 2.
56. *Ibid.*
57. Ralph S. Davis, "Pittsburgh Heads West Next Week: First Work-Out at Paso Robles Will Be Staged March 2," *The Sporting News*, February 19, 1925, page 2.
58. *Ibid.*
59. Lou Wollen, "Corsairs Near End of Journey: Grantham to Report Today," *The Pittsburgh Press*, February 27, 1925, page 36.
60. Ralph S. Davis, "Proving an Owner Can Hold Out, Too: That Is What Dreyfuss Plans to Do in Aldridge's Case," *The Sporting News*, March 5, 1925, page 1.
61. *Ibid.*
62. *Ibid.*
63. Ralph S. Davis, "Long Arid Stretch Ahead for Pirates: Bill McKechnie Puts Every Man on Water Wagon," *The Sporting News*, March 12, 1925, page 1.

64. Lou Wollen, "McKechnie Lays Down Law to Team: New Policy Decided On," *The Pittsburgh Press*, March 2, 1925, page 20.
65. *Ibid.*
66. "Caught on the Fly," *The Sporting News*, January 15, 1925, page 8.
67. Davis, "McKechnie Figures Infield will Shine: Pittsburgh Chief Plans on Using Moore at Second Base," page 2.
68. Lou Wollen, "Wright Not in Best of Health: Glenn Must Take it Easy," *The Pittsburgh Press*, March 3, 1925, page 24.
69. *Ibid.*
70. Ralph S. Davis, "Niehaus Shapes Up Okeh for Pirates: Youngster Not Under-Estimating What's Expected of Him," *The Sporting News*, March 19, 1925, page 2.
71. Lou Wollen, "Pirates Prepare for Outside Contests: Morrison to Be Lost for Time," *The Pittsburgh Press*, March 13, 1925, page 38.
72. *Ibid.*
73. Lou Wollen, "Pirates Engage Outside Teams: Regular Lineup Is Unchanged," *The Pittsburgh Press*, March 14, 1925, page 11.
74. Davis, "Niehaus Shapes Up Okeh for Pirates: Youngster Not Under-Estimating What's Expected of Him," page 2.
75. Ralph S, Davis, "Bucs Break Camp and Hit the Road: Team Will Be Kept on Jump Now Until Season Opens," *The Sporting News*, March 26, 1925, page 1.
76. "Training Camp Notes," *The Sporting News*, March 26, 1925, page 8.
77. Ralph S. Davis, "Pittsburgh Trying to Smoke Out Vic: Aldridge Found to Be Missing Link in Pirate Machine," *The Sporting News*, April 9, 1925, page 2.
78. Lou Wollen, "Pirates Meet Little Rock Today: Yde or Kremer to Work in Opener," *The Pittsburgh Press*, April 10, 1925, page 38.
79. Lou Wollen, "Niehaus' Injury May Cause Big Shift: Rawlings Tried at Old Position," *The Pittsburgh Press*, April 11, 1925, page 13.
80. Lou Wollen, "Pirate Lineup for Opening Day Uncertain: Infield Places Are Undecided," *The Pittsburgh Press*, April 13, 1925, page 25.
81. "Training Camp Notes," *The Sporting News*, April 2, 1925, page 8.
82. Davis, "Pittsburgh Trying to Smoke Out Vic: Aldridge Found to be Missing Link in Pirate Machine," page 2.
83. "National League Standing on Tuesday Morning," *The Sporting News*, April 23, 1925, page 7.

Chapter 4

1. "Scribbled by the Scribes," *The Sporting News*, March 26, 1925, page 4.
2. "Training Camp Notes," *The Sporting News*, March 26, 1925, page 8.
3. Lou Wollen, "Regular Pirate Lineup to Play in Opener: Lee Meadows May Be Mound Choice," *The Pittsburgh Press*, April 14, 1925, page 26.
4. Lou Wollen, "Lee Meadows Will Oppose Cubs Today: Pirate Lineup to Be the Same," *The Pittsburgh Press*, April 15, 1925, page 26.
5. *Ibid.*
6. "National League Standing on Tuesday Morning," *The Sporting News*, April 23, 1925, page 7.
7. *Ibid.*
8. Ralph S. Davis, "Impotent Flinging Heads Pirates Ills: Team Naturally Gets Away Under Heavy Handicap," *The Sporting News*, April 23, 1925, page 3.
9. Lou Wollen, "Pirates Now Strive for an Even Break: Morrison on Mound Today," *The Pittsburgh Press*, April 16, 1925, page 38.
10. "Rain May Halt Pirate-Red Game: Park Is Soggy After Downpour," *The Pittsburgh Press*, April 18, 1925, page 11.
11. Lou Wollen, "Buccos Badly Beaten," *The Pittsburgh Press*, April 19, 1925, page 1.
12. *Ibid.*
13. "Ebbets, Baseball Magnate, Dies: Brooklyn Club Head Expires in N.Y. Hotel," *The Pittsburgh Press*, April 18, 1925, page 1.
14. "Caught on the Fly," *The Sporting News*, April 30, 1925, page 9.
15. "National League Standing on Tuesday Morning," *The Sporting News*, April 23, 1925, page 7.
16. Lou Wollen, "Buccaneers Home After Two Long Months: Believe Losing Streak Broken," *The Pittsburgh Press*, April 21, 1925, page 30.
17. *Ibid.*
18. Ralph S. Davis, "Pirate Followers Haven't Lost Hope: Fans Believe Team Has Ability and Will Come Through," *The Sporting News*, April 30, 1925, page 3.
19. Lou Wollen, "Stage Set for Forbes Field Opener Today: Corsairs and Cubs Grapple," *The Pittsburgh Press*, April 22, 1925, page 29.
20. *Ibid.*
21. "Caught on the Fly," *The Sporting News*, April 30, 1925, page 9.
22. Wollen, "Stage Set for Forbes Field Opener Today: Corsairs and Cubs Grapple," page 29.

23. "Baseball Gossip of the Major Leagues," *The Pittsburgh Press*, April 23, 1925, page 34.
24. Lou Wollen, "Ray Kremer to Try for Third Straight Pirate Victory: Bucs Encouraged by Fine Showing," *The Pittsburgh Press*, April 23, 1925, page 34.
25. *Ibid.*
26. Davis, "Pirate Followers Haven't Lost Hope: Fans Believe Team Has Ability and Will Come Through," page 3.
27. Lou Wollen, "Lee Meadows Opposes Chicago in Last Game of Series: Pirates Travel to St. Louis Tonight," *The Pittsburgh Press*, April 25, 1925, page 9.
28. *Ibid.*
29. Lou Wollen, "Homers Defeat Buccos," *The Pittsburgh Press*, April 26, 1925, page 16.
30. *Ibid.*
31. Davis, "Pirate Followers Haven't Lost Hope: Fans Believe Team Has Ability and Will Come Through," page 3.
32. "National League Standing on Tuesday Morning," *The Sporting News*, April 30, 1925, page 9.
33. "St. Louis Club Is in Batting Slump," *The Pittsburgh Press*, April 28, 1925, page 26.
34. "Pirates Will Wind Up Series at St. Louis This Afternoon: Ray Kremer May Face Cardinals," *The Pittsburgh Press*, April 29, 1925, page 28.
35. "National League Standing on Tuesday Morning," *The Sporting News*, May 7, 1925, page 9.
36. "Baseball By-Plays," *The Sporting News*, May 14, 1925, page 4.
37. *Ibid.*
38. "National League Standing on Tuesday Morning," *The Sporting News*, May 7, 1925, page 9.
39. "National League Standing on Tuesday Morning," *The Sporting News*, May 14, 1925, page 9.
40. Lou Wollen, "Buccaneers and Cardinals Clash After Idle Period: Eastern Invasion Opens Tomorrow," *The Pittsburgh Press*, May 7, 1925, page 28.
41. Ralph S. Davis, "Pirates' Big Test Impending in East: Team Gives Evidence of Reaching Stride Expected of it," *The Sporting News*, May 7, 1925, page 2.
42. "Only Five Players Did It Before Him: Shortstop Glenn Wright," *The Sporting News*, May 14, 1925, page 2.
43. "Sullen Pirate Crew Starts Eastern Trip: Open Series with Phillies Today," *The Pittsburgh Press*, May 8, 1925, page 38.
44. Lou Wollen, "Injuries Increase Woes of Corsairs: Poor Pitching Is Holding Team Back," *The Pittsburgh Press*, May 9, 1925, page 9.
45. *Ibid.*
46. Lou Wollen, "Pirates Defeat Quakers," *The Pittsburgh Press*, May 10, 1925, page 1.
47. Wollen, "Pirates Defeat Quakers," page 2.
48. *Ibid.*
49. "National League Standing on Tuesday Morning," *The Sporting News*, May 14, 1925, page 9.
50. Lou Wollen, "Corsairs Expect Better Luck: Club Morale Is Improved," *The Pittsburgh Press*, May 11, 1925, page 24.
51. *Ibid.*
52. Lou Wollen, "McKechnie to Bench Al Niehaus: Grantham to Cover First," *The Pittsburgh Press*, May 13, 1925, page 28.
53. *Ibid.*
54. *Ibid.*
55. Ralph S. Davis, "Waste of Energy, Is Pirate Batting: Eight Members of Team Hitting More Than .300 Mark," *The Sporting News*, May 21, 1925, page 2.
56. Lou Wollen, "Songer May Face Braves Today: New Infield Looks Good," *The Pittsburgh Press*, May 14, 1925, page 34.
57. "Baseball Gossip of the Major Leagues," *The Pittsburgh Press*, May 14, 1925, page 34.
58. Wollen, "Songer May Face Braves Today: New Infield Looks Good," page 34.
59. Lou Wollen, *The Pittsburgh Press*, May 15, 1925, "Rain Prevents Third Game of Corsair-Brave Series: Earl Smith Is Set Down by Heydler," *The Pittsburgh Press*, May 15, 1925, page 38.
60. *Ibid.*

Chapter 5

1. Lou Wollen, "Rain Prevents Third Game of Corsair-Brave Series: Earl Smith Is Set Down by Heydler," *The Pittsburgh Press*, May 15, 1925, page 38.
2. Ralph S. Davis, "Waste of Energy, is Pirate Batting: Eight Members of Team Hitting More Than .300 Mark," *The Sporting News*, May 21, 1925, page 2.
3. Lou Wollen, "Hearing of Earl Smith Is Postponed: Missouri Veteran to Pitch," *The Pittsburgh Press*, May 16, 1925, page 9.
4. Wollen, "Rain Prevents Third Game of Corsair-Brave Series: Earl Smith Is Set Down by Heydler," page 38.
5. Lou Wollen, "Bucs Hope to Resume Winning Streak: Morrison to Face Robins," *The Pittsburgh Press*, May 19, 1925, page 26.

6. *Ibid.*
7. Lou Wollen, "Buccaneers After Even Break: Meet Giants on Thursday," *The Pittsburgh Press*, May 20, 1925, page 29.
8. *Ibid.*
9. Davis, "Waste of Energy, Is Pirate Batting: Eight Members of Team Hitting More than .300 Mark," page 2.
10. Lou Wollen "Pirates Open New York Series: Lee Meadows Will Twirl," *The Pittsburgh Press*, May 21, 1925, page 30.
11. *Ibid.*
12. Lou Wollen, "Buccos Out to Even Up New York Series: Lee Meadows Will Pitch," *The Pittsburgh Press*, May 22, 1925, page 38.
13. *Ibid.*
14. Lou Wollen "Pirates Hope to End Journey in Blaze of Glory: Take Next Two Corsairs' Slogan," *The Pittsburgh Press*, May 23, 1925, page 9.
15. *Ibid.*
16. *Ibid.*
17. Lou Wollen, "Giants Beat Buccaneers 10–1: Yde Driven from Mound," *The Pittsburgh Press*, May 24, 1925, page 1.
18. *Ibid.*
19. Lou Wollen, "Pirates Open Long Home Stay with Cubs: Ready to Make a Firm Stand," *The Pittsburgh Press*, May 25, 1925, page 20.
20. Wollen, "Pirates Hope to End Journey in Blaze of Glory: Take Next Two Corsairs' Slogan," page 9.
21. Wollen, "Pirates Open Long Home Stay with Cubs: Ready to Make a Firm Stand," page 20.
22. Ralph S. Davis, "Heavy Hitting Puts Bucs on Their Feet: Team Greatly Improves Standing During Road Jaunt," *The Sporting News*, May 28, 1925, page 2.
23. *Ibid.*
24. Lou Wollen, "Pirates and Cubs Clash in Second Contest of Series Today: Cooper Is Due to Pitch for Bruins," *The Pittsburgh Press*, May 26, 1925, page 30.
25. *Ibid.*
26. *Ibid.*
27. "Bucs, Outhit, Beat Cubs in Second Game," *The Pittsburgh Press*, May 27, 1925, page 28.
28. *Ibid.*
29. "National League Standing on Tuesday Morning," *The Sporting News*, June 4, 1925, page 9.
30. *Ibid.*
31. Ralph S. Davis, "Wherein McKechnie Grants Cubs Point: Stuffy McInnis Is Signed to Take Niehaus' Place at First," *The Sporting News*, June 4, 1925, page 1.
32. *Ibid.*
33. *Ibid.*
34. Lou Wollen, "Buccaneers Twice Defeat St. Louis Cardinals: Great Crowd Sees Afternoon Clash," *The Pittsburgh Press*, May 31, 1925, page 18.
35. *Ibid.*
36. *Ibid.*
37. Wollen, "Buccaneers Twice Defeat St. Louis Cardinals: Great Crowd Sees Afternoon Clash," page 17.
38. "Pirates Play Exhibition Game at South Bend, Ind. Today: Corsairs Return Home Thursday," *The Pittsburgh Press*, June 2, 1925, page 26.
39. "Vic Aldridge to Face Cubs in Last Game of Series at Chicago: Cooper Ready to Work for Bruins," *The Pittsburgh Press*, June 1, 1925, page 18.
40. Lou Wollen, "Bucs Play Another Exhibition," *The Pittsburgh Press*, June 3, 1925, page 32.
41. "Record Heat Wave Continues: 93 May be High Mark of Day Says Brotzman," *The Pittsburgh Press*, June 3, 1925, page 1.
42. "Intense Heat Closes Schools: 95 Degrees May be Day's Record Says Forecaster," *The Pittsburgh Press*, June 4, 1925, page 1.
43. Wollen, "Bucs Play Another Exhibition," page 32.
44. Lou Wollen, "Pirates Open Stand Against East Today," *The Pittsburgh Press*, June 4, 1925, page 35.
45. Davis, "Wherein McKechnie Grants Cubs Point: Stuffy McInnis Is Signed to Take Niehaus' Place at First," page 1.
46. Wollen, "Pirates Open Stand Against East Today," page 35.
47. "Baseball Gossip of the Major Leagues," *The Pittsburgh Press*, June 5, 1925, page 38.
48. Lou Wollen, "Pirates Press Dodgers in Battle for Runner-Up Place: Only Half Game Separates Clubs," *The Pittsburgh Press*, June 5, 1925, page 38.
49. "National League Standing on Tuesday Morning," *The Sporting News*, June 11, 1925, page 7.
50. Ralph S. Davis, "Pirates of 1901 Beaten by 1925 Bucs: Veterans Are Given Ovation," *The Pittsburgh Press*, June 7, 1925, page 2.
51. Lou Wollen, "Old-Timers Game Feature of Golden Jubilee Program: Bucs Meet Phils in Last Contest," *The Pittsburgh Press*, June 6, 1925, page 11.
52. Davis, "Pirates of 1901 Beaten by 1925 Bucs: Veterans Are Given Ovation," page 2.
53. *Ibid.*
54. *Ibid.*

Notes — Chapter 6

55. Davis, "Pirates of 1901 Beaten by 1925 Bucs: Veterans Are Given Ovation," page 1.
56. Lou Wollen, "Pirates Trounce Phils, 9 to 3: Quakers Hurlers Are Wild," *The Pittsburgh Press*, June 7, 1925, page 2.
57. *Ibid.*
58. Wollen, "Old-Timers Game Feature of Golden Jubilee Program: Bucs Meet Phils in Last Contest," page 11.
59. "National League Standing on Tuesday Morning," *The Sporting News*, June 18, 1925, page 7.
60. *Ibid.*
61. Lou Wollen, "Pirates Tackle Giants in Series Opener: League Leaders Under Handicap," *The Pittsburgh Press,* June 12, 1925, page 38.

Chapter 6

1. Lou Wollen, "Pirates Tackle Giants in Series Opener: League Leaders Under Handicap," *The Pittsburgh Press*, June 12, 1925, page 38.
2. Lou Wollen, "Huge Crowd Sees Second Clash Between Corsairs and Giants: Pirates Move Up in Pennant Race," *The Pittsburgh Press*, June 13, 1925, page 9.
3. *Ibid.*
4. Lou Wollen, "Buccaneers Again Defeat New York Giants, 6 to 4: Corsairs Win Out in Seventh," *The Pittsburgh Press*, June 14, 1925, page 2.
5. *Ibid.*
6. "Baseball Gossip of the Major Leagues," *The Pittsburgh Press*, June 14, 1925, page 2.
7. Ralph S. Davis, "Clarke Goes Back with His Old Team: Former Manager to Serve as an Assistant to Dreyfuss," *The Sporting News*, June 18, 1925, page 3.
8. "Clarke Returns to Buccaneers," *The Pittsburgh Press*, June 13, 1925, page 9.
9. *Ibid.*
10. Davis, "Clarke Goes Back with His Old Team: Former Manager to Serve as an Assistant to Dreyfuss," page 3.
11. "Clarke Returns to Buccaneers," page 9.
12. "National League Standing on Tuesday Morning," *The Sporting News*, June 18, 1925, page 7.
13. Lou Wollen, "Clean Sweep Over League Leaders Aim of Buccaneers: Giants Play Last Game Here Today," *The Pittsburgh Press*, June 16, 1925, page 26.
14. Ralph S. Davis, "There's Something to Those Pirates: They Have Beaten Back Gamely and Are Dangerous," *The Sporting News*, June 25, 1925, page 1.
15. *Ibid.*
16. *Ibid.*
17. Davis, "Clarke Goes Back with His Old Team: Former Manager to Serve as an Assistant to Dreyfuss," page 3.
18. "National League Standing on Tuesday Morning," *The Sporting News*, June 25, 1925, page 7.
19. *Ibid.*
20. Lou Wollen, "Buccaneers to Look at Dazzy Vance in Second Game of Series: Pirates Closing Gap to Pinnacle," *The Pittsburgh Press*, June 18, 1825, page 26.
21. "National League Standing on Tuesday Morning," *The Sporting News*, June 25, 1925, page 7.
22. "Pirates Rally in Seventh and Down Dodgers," *The Pittsburgh Press*, June 20, 1925, page 9.
23. Lou Wollen, "Buccaneers Overwhelm Brooklyn Robins, 21 to 5: Superbas Trounced," *The Pittsburgh Press*, June 21, 1925, page 1.
24. *Ibid.*
25. Ralph Davis, "Sport Chat: Max Carey to Get Watch," *The Pittsburgh Press*, June 19, 1925, page 35.
26. Ralph Davis, "Sport Chat: Homewood and the Grays," *The Pittsburgh Press*, June 22, 1925, page 20.
27. "Koupal, Young Bucco Hurler, Is Released," *The Pittsburgh Press*, June 21, 1925, page 2.
28. "National League Standing on Tuesday Morning," *The Sporting News*, June 25, 1925, page 7.
29. "Chance Offered Buccaneers to Overtake Giants: Oppose Cards in Two Games," *The Pittsburgh Press*, June 23, 1925, page 28.
30. "Buccaneers Strive Again to Shake Giants Off Top: Twin Bill Carded in St. Louis Today," *The Pittsburgh Press*, June 24, 1925, page 26.
31. "Pirates Wind Up Series in St. Louis: Meadows to Face Cards," *The Pittsburgh Press*, June 25, 1925, page 27.
32. Lou Wollen, "Pirates Home for Series with Redlegs: Buccos Trample Heals of Giants," *The Pittsburgh Press*, June 26, 1925, page 35.
33. "Pirates Wind Up Series in St. Louis: Meadows to Face Cards," page 27.
34. Lou Wollen, "Twin Bill Today Closes Pirate Home Stay: Buccos on Road Again Tomorrow," *The Pittsburgh Press*, June 27, 1925, page 9.
35. Ralph S. Davis, "Properly Pitched, Ball

Isn't So Wild: But Ralph Davis Thinks Owners Are Panicky about it," *The Sporting News*, July 9, 1925, page 1.
 36. *Ibid.*
 37. "National League Standing on Tuesday Morning," *The Sporting News*, July 2, 1925, page 7.
 38. "Corsairs Beat Reds and Take Lead in Chase," *The Pittsburgh Press*, June 30, 1925, page 24.
 39. "Bucs Limited to Three Hits, Lose to Cubs," *The Pittsburgh Press*, July 1, 1925, page 24.
 40. "Pirates Wind Up Series with Cubs at Chicago Today: Ray Kremer to Hurl for Bucs," *The Pittsburgh Press*, July 1, 1925, page 24.
 41. Lou Wollen, "Series with Reds Opens at Forbes Field: Three Buccaneers Slightly Injured," *The Pittsburgh Press*, July 2, 1925, page 26.
 42. "His Job Is to Keep Boat from Leaking: Fred Clarke," *The Sporting News*, July 2, 1925, page 4.
 43. "National League Standing on Tuesday Morning," *The Sporting News*, July 9, 1925, page 7.
 44. Lou Wollen, "Pirates Win Twice Over Red Rivals: Gain Ground in Mad Race for Pennant," *The Pittsburgh Press*, July 5, 1925, page 1.
 45. *Ibid.*
 46. *Ibid.*
 47. *Ibid.*
 48. "National League Standing on Tuesday Morning," *The Sporting News*, July 9, 1925, page 7.
 49. "Pirates Down Senators in Exhibition," *The Pittsburgh Press*, July 7, 1925, page 26.
 50. "Pirates' Games in East to Be Shown on Moose Score Board," *The Pittsburgh Press*, July 6, 1925, page 20.
 51. Ralph S. Davis, "Spirit of Pirates Best in Long Time: Aggressiveness and Harmony Go Arm-in-Arm This Year," *The Sporting News*, July 16, 1925, page 3.
 52. Lou Wollen, "Travel-Worn Buccaneers Meet New Yorkers in Double-Header at Polo Grounds: Two Defeats Mean a Drop," *The Pittsburgh Press*, July 8, 1925, page 22.
 53. Davis, "Spirit of Pirates Best in Long Time: Aggressiveness and Harmony Go Arm-in-Arm This Year," page 3.
 54. Wollen, "Travel-Worn Buccaneers Meet New Yorkers in Double-Header at Polo Grounds: Two Defeats Mean a Drop," page 22.
 55. Lou Wollen, "Pirates and Giants Play Bargain Matinee Today: Yde and Morrison Picked as Hurlers," *The Pittsburgh Press*, July 9, 1925, page 23.
 56. Ralph S. Davis, "Lively Bucs Helping Make Ball Livelier: What Chance Has Pitcher Against Pirates' Batting?" *The Sporting News*, July 2, 1925, page 3.
 57. Davis, "Properly Pitched, Ball Isn't So Wild: But Ralph Davis Thinks Owners Are Panicky About It," page 1.
 58. "Babe Adams Says Balls Are Just Like Modern Flappers," *The Pittsburgh Press*, July 10, 1925, page 28.
 59. *Ibid.*

Chapter 7

 1. "Storm Causes Heavy Damage: Cellars Flooded; Traffic Tied Up," *The Pittsburgh Press*, July 10, 1925, page 1.
 2. Ralph S. Davis, "Spirit of Pirates Best in Long Time: Aggressiveness and Harmony Go Arm-in-Arm This Year," *The Sporting News*, July 16, 1925, page 3.
 3. *Ibid.*
 4. "National League Standing on Tuesday Morning," *The Sporting News*, July 16, 1925, page 7.
 5. *Ibid.*
 6. "Ninth Inning Rally Brings Buc Victory," *The Pittsburgh Press*, July 14, 1925, page 24.
 7. "Pirate Revenge Pleases," *The Pittsburgh Press*, July 15, 1925, page 24.
 8. *Ibid.*
 9. *Ibid.*
 10. "Baseball Gossip of the Major Leagues," *The Pittsburgh Press*, July 16, 1925, page 28.
 11. Lou Wollen, "Pirates' Margin Over New York Rivals Dwindles: Lead at Stake in Today's Contest," *The Pittsburgh Press*, July 16, 1925, page 28.
 12. "National League Standing on Tuesday Morning," *The Sporting News*, July 23, 1925, page 7.
 13. Lou Wollen, "Pirates Win, Then Lose to Boston: Gain Ground in Flag Race," *The Pittsburgh Press*, July 19, 1925, page 1.
 14. Wollen, "Pirates Win, Then Lose to Boston: Gain Ground in Flag Race," pages 1–2.
 15. Wollen, "Pirates Win, Then Lose to Boston: Gain Ground in Flag Race," page 2.
 16. "Smith Hearing Is Postponed," *The Pittsburgh Press*, July 19, 1925, page 1.
 17. "Pirates Win Hard Tussle from Orioles," *The Pittsburgh Press*, July 20, 1925, page 16.

18. Ralph S. Davis, "Ten Pirates Still Batting Over .300: And Pitching has been Showing Some Improvement," *The Sporting News*, July 23, 1925, page 1.
19. "National League Standing on Tuesday Morning," *The Sporting News*, July 23, 1925, page 7.
20. Ralph Davis, "Sport Chat: A Word from Bucky Harris," *The Pittsburgh Press*, July 21, 1925, page 24.
21. *Ibid*.
22. *Ibid*.
23. "National League Standing on Tuesday Morning," *The Sporting News*, July 30, 1925, page 7.
24. "Pirates Rally in Last Frame to Beat Cards," *The Pittsburgh Press*, July 24, 1925, page 28.
25. Davis, "Ten Pirates Still Batting Over .300: And Pitching Has Been Showing Some Improvement," page 1.
26. Lou Wollen, "Pirates Lose to Cardinals, 7 to 3: Mails Allows but Three Hits," *The Pittsburgh Press*, July 26, 1925, page 1.
27. Lou Wollen, "Buccaneers Seek to Continue Victorious Dash: Braves Opponent in Third Struggle," *The Pittsburgh Press*, July 29, 1925, page 26.
28. Ralph S. Davis, "Bucs Try to Prove They Are Fighters: Gooch and Cuyler Tangle When One Resents Criticism," *The Sporting News*, August 6, 1925, page 1.
29. *Ibid*.
30. "National League Standing on Tuesday Morning," *The Sporting News*, July 30, 1925, page 7.
31. Davis, "Bucs Try to Prove They Are Fighters: Gooch and Cuyler Tangle When One Resents Criticism," page 1.
32. "Pirates Rally in Fifth Inning and Win Again," *The Pittsburgh Press*, July 29, 1925, page 26.
33. Lou Wollen, "Pirates Lead in Pennant Chase Shrinks Again: Quakers Open Series Today," *The Pittsburgh Press*, July 31, 1925, page 29.
34. "National League Standing on Tuesday Morning," *The Sporting News*, August 6, 1925, page 7.
35. Lou Wollen, "Buccaneers Knocked Out of National League Lead: Drop Two to Phils," *The Pittsburgh Press*, August 2, 1925, page 1.
36. *Ibid*.
37. *Ibid*.
38. Wollen, "Buccaneers Knocked Out of National League Lead: Drop Two to Phils," page 2.
39. *Ibid*.
40. Lou Wollen, "Quakers Conclude Stay at Forbes Field Today: Corsairs Must Face Mitchell," *The Pittsburgh Press*, August 4, 1925, page 24.
41. Lou Wollen, "Pirates and Phillies Clash in Another Twin Bill: Grantham May be Used in Left," *The Pittsburgh Press*, August 3, 1925, page 20.
42. "National League Standing on Tuesday Morning," *The Sporting News*, August 6, 1925, page 7.
43. Ralph Davis, "Sport Chat: Speaking for McKechnie," *The Pittsburgh Press*, August 7, 1925, page 24.
44. *Ibid*.
45. Lou Wollen, "Vance and Kremer Battle in Series Opener: Corsairs and Robins Clash," *The Pittsburgh Press*, August 6, 1925, page 24.
46. "Vance Beaten Again by Bucs in First Game," *The Pittsburgh Press*, August 7, 1925, page 24.
47. "National League Standing on Tuesday Morning," *The Sporting News*, August 13, 1925, page 7.
48. *Ibid*.
49. Ralph S. Davis, "They'll Not Fool Barney This Time: Head of Pittsburgh Club Rejects All Series Reservations," *The Sporting News*, August 20, 1925, page 1.

Chapter 8

1. Ralph Davis, "Sport Chat: Baseball and Mud," *The Pittsburgh Press*, August 11, 1925, page 24.
2. "Giants Defeat Buccaneers in Series Opener," *The Pittsburgh Press*, August 11, 1925, page 24.
3. *Ibid*.
4. Lou Wollen, "Pirates and Giants Clash in Second Game: Kremer Likely to Work Today," *The Pittsburgh Press*, August 11, 1925, page 24.
5. *Ibid*.
6. "National League Standing on Tuesday Morning," *The Sporting News*, August 20, 1925, page 7.
7. "Kelly's Error Helps Bucs to Defeat Giants," *The Pittsburgh Press*, August 12, 1925, page 22.
8. *Ibid*.
9. "Pirates Score Early, Defeat Giants Again," *The Pittsburgh Press*, August 13, 1925, page 26.
10. *Ibid*.
11. *Ibid*.
12. "National League Standing on Tuesday

Morning," *The Sporting News*, August 20, 1925, page 7.
13. *Ibid.*
14. Ralph S. Davis, "They'll Not Fool Barney This Time: Head of Pittsburgh Club Rejects All Series Reservations," *The Sporting News*, August 20, 1925, page 1.
15. "National League Standing on Tuesday Morning," *The Sporting News*, August 20, 1925, page 7.
16. *Ibid.*
17. Davis, "They'll Not Fool Barney This Time: Head of Pittsburgh Club Rejects All Series Reservations," page 1.
18. *Ibid.*
19. "National League Standing on Tuesday Morning," *The Sporting News*, August 20, 1925, page 7.
20. *Ibid.*
21. Lou Wollen, "Buccaneers Leave for East after Exhibition Contest: Pirates Oppose Mackmen Today," *The Pittsburgh Press*, August 17, 1925, page 17.
22. Lou Wollen, "Absence of Carey Is Felt," *The Pittsburgh Press*, August 19, 1925, page 22.
23. *Ibid.*
24. Ralph Davis, "Sport Chat: Says Moore Is Weak," *The Pittsburgh Press*, August 19, 1925, page 22.
25. *Ibid.*
26. "Pirates Lace Dazzy Vance but Go Down," *The Pittsburgh Press*, August 20, 1925, page 22.
27. Lou Wollen, "Pirate Pitching Staff has Collapsed: Hurlers Unable to Last Full Game," *The Pittsburgh Press*, August 20, 1925, page 22.
28. "National League Standing on Tuesday Morning," *The Sporting News*, August 27, 1925, page 7.
29. Lou Wollen, "Monster Crowd at Polo Grounds Today: Gotham Wild Over Important Games," *The Pittsburgh Press*, August 22, 1925, page 9.
30. Ralph S. Davis, "Nothing Wrong with Backbone of Pirates, John McGraw Finds: Bucs Play Title Ball at Polo Grounds," *The Sporting News*, August 27, 1925, page 1.
31. Lou Wollen, "Pirates Twice Defeat New York: Fifty Thousand See Big Triumph," *The Pittsburgh Press*, August 23, 1925, page 1.
32. *Ibid.*
33. "National League Standing on Tuesday Morning," *The Sporting News*, August 27, 1925, page 7.
34. "Pirates in Even Break with Giants," *The Pittsburgh Press*, August 24, 1925, page 17.
35. Ralph S. Davis, "Fans Everywhere Pull for Pirates: Corsair Triumph Would Be Popular," *The Pittsburgh Press*, August 23, 1925, page 2.
36. "National League Standing on Tuesday Morning," *The Sporting News*, August 27, 1925, page 7.
37. "National League Standing on Tuesday Morning," *The Sporting News*, September 3, 1925, page 7.
38. *Ibid.*
39. "National League Batting," *The Sporting News*, September 3, 1925, page 7.
40. "National League Standings on Tuesday Morning," *The Sporting News*, September 3, 1925.
41. *Ibid.*
42. *Ibid.*
43. Lou Wollen, "Pirates Twice Trounce Phillies: Quaker Hurlers Are Badly Mauled," *The Pittsburgh Press*, August 30, 1925, page 1.
44. *Ibid.*
45. "National League Standing on Tuesday Morning," *The Sporting News*, September 3, 1925, page 7.
46. Ralph S. Davis, "Up Go Cross-Bones, Here Come Pirates: McKechnie's Men Will Soon be Pillaging Series Coin Chest," *The Sporting News*, September 3, 1925, page 1.
47. "National League Standing on Tuesday Morning," *The Sporting News*, September 10, 1925, page 7.
48. Ralph S. Davis, "Ouch! Maybe Bill's Got a Cracked Lip: McKechnie Gets a Laugh Out of Latest Chicago Reaction," *The Sporting News*, September 10, 1925, page 1.
49. *Ibid.*
50. "National League Standing on Tuesday Morning," *The Sporting News*, September 10, 1925, page 7.
51. *Ibid.*
52. Davis, "Ouch! Maybe Bill's Got a Cracked Lip: McKechnie Gets a Laugh Out of Latest Chicago Reaction," page 1.
53. "National League Standing on Tuesday Morning," *The Sporting News*, September 10, 1925, page 7.

Chapter 9

1. "National League Standing on Tuesday Morning," *The Sporting News*, September 17, 1925, page 7.
2. Lou Wollen, "Pirates and Cubs Clash for Last Time This Season: Kremer Likely to Face Bruins," *The Pittsburgh Press*, September 9, 1925, page 26.
3. "National League Standing on Tuesday

Notes — Chapter 9

Morning," *The Sporting News*, September 10, 1925, page 7.
  4. "National League Standing on Tuesday Morning," *The Sporting News*, September 17, 1925, page 7.
  5. *Ibid.*
  6. *Ibid.*
  7. *Ibid.*
  8. *Ibid.*
  9. *Ibid.*
  10. "National League Standing on Tuesday Morning," *The Sporting News*, September 10, 1925, page 7.
  11. John J. Ward, "Has Pittsburgh Found a Worthy Successor to Hans Wagner," *Baseball Magazine*, November 1925, page 538.
  12. "National League Standing on Tuesday Morning," *The Sporting News*, September 17, 1925, page 7.
  13. "National League Standing on Tuesday Morning," *The Sporting News*, September 24, 1925, page 9.
  14. "Pirates Take Dodgers Over in Two Games," *The Pittsburgh Press*, September 17, 1925, page 24.
  15. Lou Wollen, "Yde or Aldridge to Face Braves in Second Game: Corsairs Draw Closer to Flag," *The Pittsburgh Press*, September 18, 1925, page 32.
  16. Ralph Davis, "Sport Chat: An Unspoiled Hero," *The Pittsburgh Press*, September 24, 1925, page 30.
  17. "A Word on the Proper Batting Stance," *Baseball Magazine*, November 1925, page 542.
  18. Lou Wollen, "Aldridge to Face Braves in Last Game of Series: Phils Here on Monday," *The Pittsburgh Press*, September 19, 1925, page 9.
  19. *Ibid.*
  20. Lou Wollen, "Pirates Make Clean Sweep of Series with Braves: Wright Wins Hard Battle," *The Pittsburgh Press*, September 20, 1925, page 2.
  21. "National League Standing on Tuesday Morning," *The Sporting News*, September 24, 1925, page 9.
  22. Lou Wollen, "Buccaneers May Cinch Pennant Today: Phils Make Last Appearance Here," *The Pittsburgh Press*, September 23, 1925, page 26.
  23. "Pirates Clinch Pennant; Take Ninth in a Row," *The Pittsburgh Press*, September 24, 1925, page 30.
  24. "Pirate Victory Popular," *The Pittsburgh Press*, September 24, 1925, page 30.
  25. *Ibid.*
  26. *Ibid.*
  27. *Ibid.*
  28. Ralph S. Davis, "It's Cash-in-Hand Affair with Barney: Persons Who Failed to Certify Checks, Out of Luck," *The Sporting News*, September 24, 1925, page 1.
  29. "National League Standing on Tuesday Morning," *The Sporting News*, September 17, 1925, page 7.
  30. Davis, "It's Cash-in-Hand Affair with Barney: Persons Who Failed to Certify Checks, Out of Luck," page 1.
  31. "Early Reserved Seat Sell-Outs at Washington and Pittsburgh," *The Sporting News*, September 24, 1925, page 3.
  32. *Ibid.*
  33. "C. of C. to Entertain," *The Pittsburgh Press*, September 24, 1925, page 30.
  34. "William 'Bill' McKechnie, First Citizen of Wilkinsburg, Manager New League Champs, Modest Pal to All Friends," *The Pittsburgh Press*, September 25, 1925, page 1.
  35. *Ibid.*
  36. *Ibid.*
  37. *Ibid.*
  38. "William 'Bill' McKechnie, First Citizen of Wilkinsburg, Manager New League Champs, Modest Pal to All Friends," page 8.
  39. "Today's Pirate-Giant Game Called Off: Double Bill on Saturday," *The Pittsburgh Press*, September 25, 1925, page 38.
  40. *Ibid.*
  41. Ralph S. Davis, "Pirates Best Team Ever, Says Clarke: Beats Anything Pittsburgh Had in Four Other Flag Years," *The Sporting News*, October 8, 1925, page 1.
  42. "Corsairs Take Short Contest from Redlegs," *The Pittsburgh Press*, September 28, 1925, page 24.
  43. Lou Wollen, "Pirates Loaf Four Days before Next League Game: Light Workouts Carded for Bucs," *The Pittsburgh Press*, September 28, 1925, page 24.
  44. *Ibid.*
  45. *Ibid.*
  46. "National League Standing on Tuesday Morning," *The Sporting News*, October 8, 1925, page 7.
  47. Davis, "Pirates Best Team Ever, Says Clarke: Beats Anything Pittsburgh Had in Four Other Flag Years," page 1.
  48. *Ibid.*
  49. "Do the Pirates of 1925 Outrank the Pirates of 1909?" *Baseball Magazine*, December 1925, page 303.
  50. *Ibid.*
  51. Ralph S. Davis, "Pirates Welcome Chance to Relax: Everything in Shape for First Games in Pittsburgh," *The Sporting News*, October 1, 1925, page 1.

52. *Ibid.*
53. "McKechnie to Use Six Hurlers in Games with Redlegs: Pilot Priming Men for Test," *The Pittsburgh Press*, October 3, 1925, page 9.
54. "Wet Grounds Force Bucs and Redlegs into Idleness: Corsairs Take Brisk Workout," *The Pittsburgh Press*, October 4, 1925, page 1.
55. "Most Valuable Player Honor Bestowed on Roger Peckinpaugh," *The Sporting News*, October 1, 1925, page 2.
56. "Baseball Writers Concede Pirates Slight Advantage in World's Series," *The Sporting News*, October 1, 1925, page 3.
57. *Ibid.*

Chapter 10

1. "Booze Sleuths on Guard Here," *The Pittsburgh Press*, October 7, 1925, page 1.
2. "Bleacher Seats and Standing Room Only to Be Placed on Sale," *The Pittsburgh Press*, October 4, 1925, page 2.
3. "Baseball Frenzy Grips Pittsburgh: Populace Excited as Buccos and Nats Meet in First Game," *The Pittsburgh Press*, October 7, 1925, page 2.
4. *Ibid.*
5. *Ibid.*
6. "Bleacher Seats and Standing Room Only to Be Placed on Sale," page 2.
7. "Baseball Frenzy Grips Pittsburgh: Populace Excited as Buccos and Nats Meet in First Game," page 2.
8. "Hungry Fans Mill About Park Gates," *The Pittsburgh Press*, October 7, 1925, page 26.
9. "Fair but Cold, Prediction of Weatherman," *The Pittsburgh Press*, October 7, 1925, page 1.
10. "Pirates and Senators Clash in First Game: Fans of Nation Respond as Fall Classic Opens," *The Pittsburgh Press*, October 7, 1925, page 1.
11. "Pirates and Senators Clash in First Game: Fans of Nation Respond as Fall Classic Opens," page 2.
12. *Ibid.*
13. "Nats' Twirler Fans Ten Bucs in Winning First Contest: Gossip of First Game," *The Sporting News*, October 15, 1925, page 3.
14. "Baseball Frenzy Grips Pittsburgh: Populace Excited as Buccos and Nats Meet in First Game," page 2.
15. "Nats' Twirler Fans Ten Bucs in Winning First Contest: Gossip of First Game," *The Sporting News*, October 15, 1925, page 3.
16. *Ibid.*
17. "Nats' Twirler Fans Ten Bucs in Winning First Contest: First Game in Detail," *The Sporting News*, October 15, 1925, page 3.
18. *Ibid.*
19. "Nats' Twirler Fans Ten Bucs in Winning First Contest: Gossip of First Game," *The Sporting News*, October 15, 1925, page 3.
20. "Nats' Twirler Fans Ten Bucs in Winning First Contest: First Game in Detail," *The Sporting News*, October 15, 1925, page 3.
21. *Ibid.*
22. *Ibid.*
23. "Nats' Twirler Fans Ten Bucs in Winning First Contest: Gossip of First Game," *The Sporting News*, October 15, 1925, page 3.
24. "Nats' Twirler Fans Ten Bucs in Winning First Contest: First Game in Detail," *The Sporting News*, October 15, 1925, page 3
25. *Ibid.*
26. *Ibid.*
27. *Ibid.*
28. *Ibid.*
29. *Ibid.*
30. *Ibid.*
31. " Nats' Twirler Fans Ten Bucs in Winning First Contest: Gossip of First Game," *The Sporting News*, October 15, 1925, page 3.
32. "Nats' Twirler Fans Ten Bucs in Winning First Contest: First Game in Detail," *The Sporting News*, October 15, 1925, page 3.
33. *Ibid.*
34. *Ibid.*
35. "Nats' Twirler Fans Ten Bucs in Winning First Contest: Gossip of First Game," *The Sporting News*, October 15, 1925, page 3.
36. "Nats' Twirler Fans Ten Bucs in Winning First Contest: First Game in Detail," *The Sporting News*, October 15, 1925, page 3.
37. "Standing on Tuesday Morning: World's Series Data," *The Sporting News*, October 15, 1925, page 3.
38. Ralph S. Davis, "Still Major Parks Aren't Big Enough: Dreyfuss Could Have Used Five Times Forbes' Capacity," *The Sporting News*, October 15, 1925, page 2.
39. Ralph S. Davis, "Pirates and Senators Clash in Second Game of World's Series: Crowds on Hand Early for Bleacher Seats," *The Pittsburgh Press*, October 8, 1925, page 1.
40. *Ibid.*
41. "Death of Christy Mathewson Removes Noted Figure of Game," *The Sporting News*, October 15, 1925, page 2.
42. *Ibid.*
43. *Ibid.*
44. *Ibid.*
45. "Cuyler's Homer Following Peck's Error

Decides Second: Second Game in Detail," *The Sporting News*, October 15, 1925, page 3.
46. *Ibid.*
47. *Ibid.*
48. *Ibid.*
49. *Ibid.*
50. *Ibid.*
51. "Cuyler's Homer Following Peck's Error Decides Second: Gossip of Second Game," *The Sporting News*, October 15, 1925, page 3.
52. "Cuyler's Homer Following Peck's Error Decides Second: Second Game in Detail," *The Sporting News*, October 15, 1925, page 3.
53. *Ibid.*
54. *Ibid.*
55. "Cuyler's Homer Following Peck's Error Decides Second: Gossip of Second Game," *The Sporting News*, October 15, 1925, page 3.
56. "Cuyler's Homer Following Peck's Error Decides Second: Second Game in Detail," *The Sporting News*, October 15, 1925, page 3.
57. *Ibid.*
58. *Ibid.*
59. *Ibid.*
60. *Ibid.*
61. *Ibid.*
62. *Ibid.*
63. "Cuyler's Homer Following Peck's Error Decides Second: Gossip of Second Game," *The Sporting News*, October 15, 1925, page 3.
64. "Cuyler's Homer Following Peck's Error Decides Second: Second Game in Detail," *The Sporting News*, October 15, 1925, page 3.
65. *Ibid.*
66. *Ibid.*
67. "Standing on Tuesday Morning: World's Series Data," page 3.
68. "Rising from Distillery Clerk to Big League Magnate, Pirate Owner Is Sportsman Who Takes Gambling Chance," *The Pittsburgh Press*, September 26, 1925, page 1.
69. *Ibid.*
70. Henry L. Farrell, "Third World's Series Game Postponed: Showers Prevent Today's Contest," *The Pittsburgh Press*, October 9, 1925, page 8.

Chapter 11

1. Henry L. Farrell, "Third World's Series Game Postponed: Showers Prevent Today's Contest," *The Pittsburgh Press*, October 9, 1925, page 8.
2. *Ibid.*
3. "Third World's Series Game Postponed: Showers Prevent Today's Contest," page 1.
4. *Ibid.*
5. *Ibid.*
6. Ralph Davis, "Sport Chat: Who Got the Break?" *The Pittsburgh Press*, October 10, 1925, page 9.
7. *Ibid.*
8. Ralph Davis, "Sport Chat: Grantham Holds Up His End," *The Pittsburgh Press*, October 9, 1925, page 38.
9. Ralph S. Davis, "Shivering Fans Watch Third Series Game: Wintry Breeze Sweeping Capital Stadium," *The Pittsburgh Press*, October 10, 1925, page 2.
10. Davis, "Shivering Fans Watch Third Series Game: Wintry Breeze Sweeping Capital Stadium," page 1.
11. Ralph S. Davis, "Pirates Meet President and have a Big Day—Everywhere Except in Baseball Arena," *The Pittsburgh Press*, October 11, 1925, page 1.
12. *Ibid.*
13. *Ibid.*
14. Ralph S. Davis, "Senators Beat Pirates: Johnson and Yde Slated to Pitch," *The Pittsburgh Press*, October 11, 1925, page 1.
15. Davis, "Shivering Fans Watch Third Series Game: Wintry Breeze Sweeping Capital Stadium," page 2.
16. Davis, "Pirates Meet President and have a Big Day—Everywhere Except in Baseball Arena," page 1.
17. "Marberry's Relief Work Features Third Contest: Third Game in Detail," *The Sporting News*, October 15, 1925, page 5.
18. *Ibid.*
19. *Ibid.*
20. *Ibid.*
21. *Ibid.*
22. *Ibid.*
23. *Ibid.*
24. *Ibid.*
25. "Marberry's Relief Work Features Third Contest: Gossip of Third Game," *The Sporting News*, October 15, 1925, page 5.
26. "Marberry's Relief Work Features Third Contest: Third Game in Detail," *The Sporting News*, October 15, 1925, page 5.
27. *Ibid.*
28. *Ibid.*
29. *Ibid.*
30. "Marberry's Relief Work Features Third Contest: Gossip of Third Game," *The Sporting News*, October 15, 1925, page 5.
31. "Marberry's Relief Work Features Third Contest: Third Game in Detail," *The Sporting News*, October 15, 1925, page 5.
32. "Marberry's Relief Work Features Third Contest: Gossip of Third Game," *The Sporting News*, October 15, 1925, page 5.

33. "Marberry's Relief Work Features Third Contest: Third Game in Detail," *The Sporting News*, October 15, 1925, page 5.
34. *Ibid.*
35. "Marberry's Relief Work Features Third Contest: Gossip of Third Game," *The Sporting News*, October 15, 1925, page 5.
36. "Marberry's Relief Work Features Third Contest: Third Game in Detail," *The Sporting News*, October 15, 1925, page 5.
37. *Ibid.*
38. *Ibid.*
39. "Marberry's Relief Work Features Third Contest: Gossip of Third Game," *The Sporting News*, October 15, 1925, page 5.
40. "Marberry's Relief Work Features Third Contest: Third Game in Detail," *The Sporting News*, October 15, 1925, page 5.
41. Paul W. Eaton, "Usual Calm Marks Senators in Series: Harris, in Fact, Takes Classic as He Would Any Games," *The Sporting News*, October 8, 1925, page 1.
42. "Standing on Tuesday Morning: World's Series Data," *The Sporting News*, October 15, 1925, page 3.
43. "Landis Refuses to Consider Protest: Fans Say Rice Did Not Get Smith's Long Fly," *The Pittsburgh Press*, October 11, 1925, page 1.
44. Ralph S. Davis, "No Protest to Be Made by Pirates," *The Pittsburgh Press*, October 11, 1925, page 1.
45. *Ibid.*
46. Ralph S. Davis, "President Prevented a Protest," *The Pittsburgh Press*, October 12, 1925, page 24.
47. *Ibid.*
48. Davis, "No Protest to Be Made by Pirates," page 1.
49. *Ibid.*
50. Davis, "President Prevented a Protest," page 24.
51. *Ibid.*
52. "Barney Again Puzzles Bucs, Scoring Shutout in Fourth: Gossip of Fourth Game," *The Sporting News*, October 15, 1925, page 5.
53. "Barney Again Puzzles Bucs, Scoring Shutout in Fourth: Fourth Game in Detail," *The Sporting News*, October 15, 1925, page 5.
54. *Ibid.*
55. *Ibid.*
56. *Ibid.*
57. "Barney Again Puzzles Bucs, Scoring Shutout in Fourth," *The Sporting News*, October 15, 1925, page 5.
58. "Barney Again Puzzles Bucs, Scoring Shutout in Fourth: Fourth Game in Detail," *The Sporting News*, October 15, 1925, page 5.
59. "Barney Again Puzzles Bucs, Scoring Shutout in Fourth: Gossip of Fourth Game," *The Sporting News*, October 15, 1925, page 5.
60. "Barney Again Puzzles Bucs, Scoring Shutout in Fourth: Fourth Game in Detail," *The Sporting News*, October 15, 1925, page 5.
61. *Ibid.*
62. *Ibid.*
63. *Ibid.*
64. *Ibid.*
65. *Ibid.*
66. *Ibid.*
67. *Ibid.*
68. "Barney Again Puzzles Bucs, Scoring Shutout in Fourth: Gossip of Fourth Game," *The Sporting News*, October 15, 1925, page 5.
69. *Ibid.*
70. "Barney Again Puzzles Bucs, Scoring Shutout in Fourth: Fourth Game in Detail," *The Sporting News*, October 15, 1925, page 5.
71. "Barney Again Puzzles Bucs, Scoring Shutout in Fourth: Gossip of Fourth Game," *The Sporting News*, October 15, 1925, page 5.
72. "Barney Again Puzzles Bucs, Scoring Shutout in Fourth: Fourth Game in Detail," *The Sporting News*, October 15, 1925, page 5.
73. "Barney Again Puzzles Bucs, Scoring Shutout in Fourth: Gossip of Fourth Game," *The Sporting News*, October 15, 1925, page 5.
74. "Barney Again Puzzles Bucs, Scoring Shutout in Fourth: Fourth Game in Detail," *The Sporting News*, October 15, 1925, page 5.
75. *Ibid.*
76. "Barney Again Puzzles Bucs, Scoring Shutout in Fourth: Gossip of Fourth Game," *The Sporting News*, October 15, 1925, page 5.
77. "Standing on Tuesday Morning: World's Series Data," page 3.

Chapter 12

1. Ralph Davis, "Sport Chat: Pirates Not Down Hearted," *The Pittsburgh Press*, October 12, 1925, page 24.
2. *Ibid.*
3. Ralph Davis, "Sport Chat: Clarke Also Hopeful," *The Pittsburgh Press*, October 12, 1925, page 24.
4. *Ibid.*
5. *Ibid.*
6. Ralph Davis, "Sport Chat: Carey to Stay with Pirates," *The Pittsburgh Press*, October 12, 1925, page 24.
7. *Ibid.*
8. "Griffith Denies Tale of Sale of Two Stars," *The Pittsburgh Press*, October 12, 1925, page 24.

9. *Ibid.*
10. Ralph S. Davis, "Aldridge Pitches Fifth Game: Pirates Battle Against Big Odds," *The Pittsburgh Press*, October 12, 1925, page 1.
11. *Ibid.*
12. Frederick G. Lieb, *The Pittsburgh Pirates, 1948*. (Reprint, Carbondale, IL: Southern Illinois University Press, 2003), page 213.
13. *Ibid.*
14. "Pirates Wreck Senators' Staff in Fifth Contest: Fifth Game in Detail," *The Sporting News*, October 15, 1925, page 5.
15. *Ibid.*
16. "Pirates Wreck Senators' Staff in Fifth Contest: Gossip of Fifth Game," *The Sporting News*, October 15, 1925, page 6.
17. "Pirates Wreck Senators' Staff in Fifth Contest: Fifth Game in Detail," *The Sporting News*, October 15, 1925, page 5.
18. "Pirates Wreck Senators' Staff in Fifth Contest: Gossip of Fifth Game," *The Sporting News*, October 15, 1925, page 6.
19. "Pirates Wreck Senators' Staff in Fifth Contest: Fifth Game in Detail," *The Sporting News*, October 15, 1925, page 5.
20. *Ibid.*
21. "Pirates Wreck Senators' Staff in Fifth Contest: Gossip of Fifth Game," *The Sporting News*, October 15, 1925, page 6.
22. "Pirates Wreck Senators' Staff in Fifth Contest: Fifth Game in Detail," *The Sporting News*, October 15, 1925, page 5.
23. *Ibid.*
24. *Ibid.*
25. *Ibid.*
26. "Pirates Wreck Senators' Staff in Fifth Contest: Gossip of Fifth Game," *The Sporting News*, October 15, 1925, page 6.
27. *Ibid.*
28. "Pirates Wreck Senators' Staff in Fifth Contest: Fifth Game in Detail," *The Sporting News*, October 15, 1925, page 5.
29. "Pirates Wreck Senators' Staff in Fifth Contest: Gossip of Fifth Game," *The Sporting News*, October 15, 1925, page 6.
30. "Pirates Wreck Senators' Staff in Fifth Contest: Fifth Game in Detail," *The Sporting News*, October 15, 1925, pages 5.
31. "Pirates Wreck Senators' Staff in Fifth Contest: Fifth Game in Detail," *The Sporting News*, October 15, 1925, pages 5–6.
32. "Pirates Wreck Senators' Staff in Fifth Contest: Fifth Game in Detail," *The Sporting News*, October 15, 1925, page 6.
33. *Ibid.*
34. *Ibid.*
35. *Ibid.*
36. *Ibid.*
37. *Ibid.*
38. *Ibid.*
39. Ralph Davis, "Sport Chat: A New Lease on Life," *The Pittsburgh Press*, October 13, 1925, page 30.
40. *Ibid.*
41. "Pirates Wreck Senators Staff in Fifth Contest: Gossip of Fifth Game," *The Sporting News*, October 15, 1925, page 6.
42. Davis, "Aldridge Pitches Fifth Game: Pirates Battle Against Big Odds," page 2.
43. Ralph S. Davis, "Glenn Wright, Pirate Shortstop, Wins High Praise for Stellar Work in World's Series," *The Pittsburgh Press*, October 13, 1925, page 1.
44. Frank Getty, "McInnis Was Big Factor," *The Pittsburgh Press*, October 13, 1925, page 30.
45. Ralph Davis, "Sport Chat: Autograph Hunters Busy," *The Pittsburgh Press*, October 13, 1925, page 30.
46. *Ibid.*
47. "Apprehensive but Hopeful, Fans Crowd Way into Forbes Field for Crucial Battle," *The Pittsburgh Press*, October 13, 1925, page 1.
48. Ralph S. Davis, "Pirates Out to Win: McKechnie Will Use Oldham Tomorrow if Game Is Played," *The Pittsburgh Press*, October 13, 1925, page 1.
49. Davis, "Pirates Out to Win: McKechnie Will Use Oldham Tomorrow if Game Is Played," page 2.
50. Ralph Davis, "Sport Chat: Game Little Eddie Moore," *The Pittsburgh Press*, October 14, 1925, page 24.
51. Hans Wagner, "Eddie Moore Cried, but Not from Pain," *The Pittsburgh Press*, October 14, 1925, page 25.
52. *Ibid.*
53. "Eddie Moore's Home Run Decides Sixth Contest: Gossip of Sixth Game," *The Sporting News*, October 22, 1925, page 3.
54. "Eddie Moore's Home Run Decides Sixth Contest: Sixth Game in Detail," *The Sporting News*, October 22, 1925, page 3.
55. Joe Vila, "Blood Runs White in Pittsburgh Fans: Show Very Poor Sportsmanship Toward Sammy Rice." *The Sporting News*, October 22, 1925, page 1.
56. "Eddie Moore's Home Run Decides Sixth Contest: Sixth Game in Detail," *The Sporting News*, October 22, 1925, page 3.
57. Davis, "Sport Chat: Game Little Eddie Moore," page 24.
58. "Eddie Moore's Home Run Decides Sixth Contest: Sixth Game in Detail," *The Sporting News*, October 22, 1925, page 3.
59. *Ibid.*

60. *Ibid.*
61. "Eddie Moore's Home Run Decides Sixth Contest: Gossip of Sixth Game," *The Sporting News*, October 22, 1925, page 3.
62. "Eddie Moore's Home Run Decides Sixth Contest: Sixth Game in Detail," *The Sporting News*, October 22, 1925, page 3.
63. *Ibid.*
64. Paul W. Eaton, "Griffs Vision Jinx in Player Awards: Most Valuable Title Anything but Good for Peck," *The Sporting News*, October 22, 1925, page 1.
65. "Eddie Moore's Home Run Decides Sixth Contest: Sixth Game in Detail," *The Sporting News*, October 22, 1925, page 3.
66. *Ibid.*
67. *Ibid.*
68. Davis, "Sport Chat: Game Little Eddie Moore," page 24.
69. "Eddie Moore's Home Run Decides Sixth Contest: Sixth Game in Detail," *The Sporting News*, October 22, 1925, page 3.
70. *Ibid.*
71. "Eddie Moore's Home Run Decides Sixth Contest: Gossip of Sixth Game," *The Sporting News*, October 22, 1925, page 3.
72. "Eddie Moore's Home Run Decides Sixth Contest: Sixth Game in Detail," *The Sporting News*, October 22, 1925, page 3.
73. *Ibid.*
74. *Ibid.*
75. *Ibid.*
76. *Ibid.*
77. "Eddie Moore's Home Run Decides Sixth Contest: Gossip of Sixth Game," *The Sporting News*, October 22, 1925, page 3.
78. "Eddie Moore's Home Run Decides Sixth Contest: Sixth Game in Detail," *The Sporting News*, October 22, 1925, page 3.
79. *Ibid.*

Chapter 13

1. Ralph S. Davis, "Pirates Out to Win: McKechnie Will Use Oldham Tomorrow if Game Is Played," *The Pittsburgh Press*, October 13, 1925, page 1.
2. "Scribbled by the Scribes," *The Sporting News*, October 29, 1925, page 4.
3. *Ibid.*
4. "Series Experting Blow to Player-Writer Fad: Two Washington Men Apologize for Remarks About Umpire," *The Sporting News*, October 22, 1925, page 3.
5. Ralph Davis, "Sport Chat: Player Purchase Confirmed," *The Pittsburgh Press*, October 14, 1925, page 24.
6. "Enthusiastic Fans Anxiously Await Start of Final Game: Crowds Rush Gates Hours before Time Set for Start of Concluding Title Battle," *The Pittsburgh Press*, October 14, 1925, page 1.
7. Ralph S. Davis, "Play Final World's Series Game: Johnson Is Slated to Oppose Locals Despite Short Rest," *The Pittsburgh Press*, October 14, 1925.
8. *Ibid.*
9. *Ibid.*
10. Ralph Davis, "Sport Chat: Why Did Landis Delay?" *The Pittsburgh Press*, October 15, 1925, page 30.
11. Ralph Davis, "Sport Chat: Bill Changed His Mind," *The Pittsburgh Press*, October 15, 1925, page 30.
12. "Bucs Can't Lose Now; Even Butler Black Cat Fails as Jinx," *The Pittsburgh Press*, October 15, 1925, page 1.
13. "Cloudy, No Rain — Brotzman," *The Pittsburgh Press*, October 15, 1925, page 1.
14. Ralph S. Davis, "Burn Gasoline to Dry Forbes Field: Fans Slow Arriving for Deciding Game of World's Series," *The Pittsburgh Press*, October 15, 1925, page 1.
15. *Ibid.*
16. *Ibid.*
17. Davis, "Burn Gasoline to Dry Forbes Field: Fans Slow Arriving for Deciding Game of World's Series," page 6.
18. Davis, "Burn Gasoline to Dry Forbes Field: Fans Slow Arriving for Deciding Game of World's Series," page 1.
19. "Clarke Still Sure Pirates Will Win," *The Pittsburgh Press*, October 15, 1925, page 30.
20. Davis, "Burn Gasoline to Dry Forbes Field: Fans Slow Arriving for Deciding Game of World's Series," page 6.
21. *Ibid.*
22. Ralph Davis, "Sport Chat: It's Tough on Meadows," *The Pittsburgh Press*, October 15, 1925, page 30.
23. Davis, "Burn Gasoline to Dry Forbes Field: Fans Slow Arriving for Deciding Game of World's Series," page 6.
24. Ralph Davis, "Sport Chat: An Enthusiastic Crowd," *The Pittsburgh Press*, October 15, 1925, page 30.
25. "Johnson, Poor Mudder, Batted Hard in Final: Seventh Game in Detail," *The Sporting News*, October 22, 1925, page 6.
26. *Ibid.*
27. *Ibid.*
28. *Ibid.*
29. *Ibid.*
30. *Ibid.*
31. *Ibid.*

32. *Ibid.*
33. *Ibid.*
34. *Ibid.*
35. *Ibid.*
36. *Ibid.*
37. *Ibid.*
38. *Ibid.*
39. Jeff Carroll, *Sam Rice: A Biography of the Washington Senators Hall of Famer.* (Jefferson, NC: McFarland, 2008), page 139.
40. *Ibid.*
41. "Johnson, Poor Mudder, Batted Hard in Final: Seventh Game in Detail," *The Sporting News*, October 22, 1925, page 6.
42. *Ibid.*
43. *Ibid.*
44. *Ibid.*
45. *Ibid.*
46. *Ibid.*
47. *Ibid.*
48. "Johnson, Poor Mudder, Batted Hard in Final: Gossip of Seventh Game," *The Sporting News*, October 22, 1925, page 6.
49. "Johnson, Poor Mudder, Batted Hard in Final: Seventh Game in Detail," *The Sporting News*, October 22, 1925, page 6.
50. Ralph S. Davis, "Sport Chat: Never a Game Like It," *The Pittsburgh Press*, October 16, 1925, page 38.
51. Ralph S. Davis, "Sport Chat: The Exuberant Mr. Traynor," *The Pittsburgh Press*, October 16, 1925, page 38.
52. Davis, "Sport Chat: Never a Game Like It," page 38.
53. *Ibid.*
54. "Johnson, Poor Mudder, Batted Hard in Final: Seventh Game in Detail," *The Sporting News*, October 22, 1925, page 6.
55. Carroll, *Sam Rice: A Biography of the Washington Senators Hall of Famer* (Jefferson, NC: McFarland, 2008), page 140.
56. *Ibid.*
57. Davis, "Sport Chat: Never a Game Like It," page 38.
58. "Johnson, Poor Mudder, Batted Hard in Final: Seventh Game in Detail," *The Sporting News*, October 22, 1925, page 6.
59. Carroll, *Sam Rice: A Biography of the Washington Senators Hall of Famer* (Jefferson, NC: McFarland, 2008), page 140.
60. Frederick G. Lieb, *The Pittsburgh Pirates, 1948.* (Reprint, Carbondale, IL: Southern Illinois University Press, 2003), page 218.
61. "Johnson, Poor Mudder, Batted Hard in Final: Seventh Game in Detail," *The Sporting News*, October 22, 1925, page 6.
62. "Johnson, Poor Mudder, Batted Hard in Final: Gossip of Seventh Game," *The Sporting News*, October 22, 1925, page 6.
63. Ralph Davis, "Sport Chat: Famous World Series Sayings," *The Pittsburgh Press*, October 20, 1925, page 32.
64. *Ibid.*
65. "Johnson, Poor Mudder, Batted Hard in Final: Seventh Game in Detail," *The Sporting News*, October 22, 1925, page 6.
66. Davis, "Sport Chat: Never a Game Like It," page 38.
67. "Johnson, Poor Mudder, Batted Hard in Final: Gossip of Seventh Game," page 6.
68. Ralph S. Davis, "Sweet Part of Pirate Victory Is Answer to Lack of Courage: Made Gamest Fight in Series History," *The Sporting News*, October 22, 1925, page 1.
69. "Roar of Victory, Din of Celebration Encompass City as Tribute Is Paid to Greatest Ball Club in World," *The Pittsburgh Press*, October 16, 1925, page 1.
70. Lou Wollen, "Gameness Won World's Title for Pirates: Uphill Struggle Brings Success," *The Pittsburgh Press*, October 16, 1925, page 38.
71. *Ibid.*
72. "McKechnie Would Not Change Shirt, Sox or Underwear Till Pirates Had Won," *The Pittsburgh Press*, October 16, 1925, page 1.
73. *Ibid.*

Chapter 14

1. Ralph S. Davis, "Sweet Part of Pirate Victory Is Answer to Lack of Courage: Made Gamest Fight in Series History," *The Sporting News*, October 22, 1925, page 1.
2. "Pittsburgh Makes Great Fight to Wrest World's Series Title," *The Sporting News*, October 22, 1925, page 3.
3. *Ibid.*
4. *Ibid.*
5. *Ibid.*
6. "Johnson, Poor Mudder, Batted Hard in Final: Gossip of Seventh Game," *The Sporting News*, October 22, 1925, page 6.
7. "Ban Johnson Draws Bucky Harris' Wrath," *The Pittsburgh Press*, October 16, 1925, page 38.
8. "Pittsburgh Makes Great Fight to Wrest World's Series Title," page 3.
9. *Ibid.*
10. John B. Sheridan, "Back of the Home Plate," *The Sporting News*, November 5, 1925, page 4.
11. "Caught on the Fly," *The Sporting News*, October 22, 1925, page 6.

12. Ralph S. Davis, "Pirates Look Good for Years to Come: Team has been Built Up Around Ideal Young Athletes," *The Sporting News*, October 29, 1925, page 1.
13. Ralph S. Davis, "Winter Fiction, Says Dreyfuss of Report on Moore and Bigbee: Club Has Year to Pay for Rhyne, Waner," *The Sporting News*, November 5, 1925, page 1.
14. Davis, "Pirates Look Good for Years to Come: Team Has Been Built Up Around Ideal Young Athletes," page 1.
15. Davis, "Winter Fiction, Says Dreyfuss of Report on Moore and Bigbee: Club Has Year to Pay for Rhyne, Waner," page 1.
16. *Ibid.*
17. "Johnson, Poor Mudder, Batted Hard in Final: Gossip of Seventh Game," *The Sporting News*, October 22, 1925, page 6.
18. Lou Wollen, "Exodus of World's Champs Begins: Bucs Leave for Homes," *The Pittsburgh Press*, October 17, 1925, page 9.
19. Ralph Davis, "Sport Chat: Churchmen Dine McKechnie," *The Pittsburgh Press*, October 20, 1925, page 32.
20. Wollen, "Exodus of World's Champs Begins: Bucs Leave for Homes," page 9.
21. Davis, "Pirates Look Good for Years to Come: Team Has Been Built Up Around Ideal Young Athletes," page 1.
22. Ralph Davis, "Sport Chat: Moore Likes Apple Pie," *The Pittsburgh Press*, October 28, 1925, page 26.
23. *Ibid.*
24. Davis, "Winter Fiction, Says Dreyfuss of Report on Moore and Bigbee: Club Has Year to Pay for Rhyne, Waner," page 1.
25. *Ibid.*
26. *Ibid.*
27. *Ibid.*
28. Ralph S. Davis, "Clarke Not Likely to Desert Pirates: Veteran Denies That He Is After Interest in Robins," *The Sporting News*, November 12, 1925, page 1.
29. Ralph S. Davis, "Dreyfuss Leaves Door Trifle Ajar: Satisfied with Team, but Might Talk a Little Trade," *The Sporting News*, December 3, 1925, page 1.
30. "Scribbled by the Scribes," *The Sporting News*, November 12, 1925, page 4.
31. *Ibid.*
32. "Caught on the Fly," *The Sporting News*, November 5, 1925, page 8.
33. Davis, "Clarke Not Likely to Desert Pirates: Veteran Denies He Is After Interest in Robins," page 1.
34. *Ibid.*
35. *Ibid.*
36. "Big League Writers Select All-Star Team for The Sporting News," *The Sporting News*, November 19, 1925, page 3.
37. "Hornsby, National's Prize Star, Has Averaged .397 for Six Years," *The Sporting News*, December 10, 1925, page 3.
38. "Caught on the Fly," *The Sporting News*, December 10, 1925, page 8.
39. Ralph S. Davis, "Pittsburgh Cheers Our All-Star Team: Selection of Four Pirate Players Makes Decided Hit," *The Sporting News*, November 26, 1925, page 2.
40. Ralph S. Davis, "Clarke to Return as McKechnie's Aid: Announcement Belies Reported Rift Over Management," *The Sporting News*, December 17, 1925, page 1.
41. *Ibid.*
42. *Ibid.*
43. *Ibid.*
44. *Ibid.*
45. Ralph S. Davis, "Neighborly Stuff from Philadelphia: But Earl Smith Is Likely to Stay with Barney Dreyfuss," *The Sporting News*, December 31, 1925, page 1.
46. Billy Evans, "According to Billy Evans," *The Sporting News*, December 3, 1925, page 4.
47. *Ibid.*
48. Davis, "Neighborly Stuff from Philadelphia: But Earl Smith Is Likely to Stay with Barney Dreyfuss," *The Sporting News*, December 3, page 1.
49. *Ibid.*
50. Ralph S. Davis, "Pennant Pleasures Generally Run High: So Barney Dreyfuss Is Prepared to Do Some Spending," *The Sporting News*, January 7, 1926, page 1.
51. Ralph S. Davis, "Financiers Begin to Do Their Stuff: Writing Arms Out of Shape When It Comes to Signing," *The Sporting News*, January 21, 1926, page 5.
52. Ralph S. Davis. "Figures Emphasize Power of Pirates: Four Members of Team Drove in 443 Runs Between Them," *The Sporting News*, January 14, 1926, page 2.
53. "Caught on the Fly," *The Sporting News*, January 7, 1926, page 8.
54. "Caught on the Fly," *The Sporting News*, March 4, 1926, page 8.
55. Ralph S. Davis, "National Schedule O.K.'d by Dreyfuss: Slight Extension of Closing Day Believed Solution," *The Sporting News*, January 28, 1926, page 3.
56. Ralph S. Davis, "Cuyler Is Hep to Business Methods: Pittsburgh's Star Twice Returns Contract Proffered Him," *The Sporting News*, February 4, 1926, page 5.
57. *Ibid.*
58. *Ibid.*
59. *Ibid.*

60. Ralph S. Davis, "B. Dreyfuss Holds Jubilee of His Own: Gets Pittsburgh Stars in Festive Mood, Then Signs 'Em," *The Sporting News*, February 11, 1926, page 1.
61. Ralph S. Davis, "Dreyfuss also Has a Satisfied Pilot: Bill McKechnie Said to Have Been Handsomely Rewarded," *The Sporting News*, February 18, 1926, page 5.
62. Davis, "Pennant Pleasures Generally Run High: So Barney Dreyfuss Is Prepared to Do Some Spending," page 1.
63. Ralph S. Davis, "Dreyfuss and McKechnie Can Laugh Matters Off Nowadays: All but Two of Pirates Answer Muster," *The Sporting News*, February 25, 1926, page 1.
64. Ralph S. Davis, "Carey Still Hears from Injured Ribs: New Pneumonia Threat Laid to Collision in Series," *The Sporting News*, March 11, 1926, page 1.
65. "Caught on the Fly," *The Sporting News*, March 11, 1926, page 8.
66. Ralph S. Davis, "Fred Clarke Puts His Seal on Waner: Recruit Takes Veteran Back to Days of Ginger Beaumont," *The Sporting News*, March 18, 1926, page 2.
67. *Ibid.*
68. *Ibid.*
69. "Training Camp Notes," *The Sporting News*, March 18, 1926, page 8.
70. "Training Camp Notes," *The Sporting News*, March 25, 1926, page 8.
71. "Training Camp Notes," *The Sporting News*, April 1, 1926, page 8.
72. Ralph S. Davis, "Pirates Get Test from Very Start: After Opening with Cardinals, Reds Are Encountered," *The Sporting News*, April 15, 1926, page 1.
73. Davis, "Fred Clarke Puts His Seal on Waner: Recruit Takes Veteran Back to Days of Ginger Beaumont," page 2.
74. "Training Camp Notes," *The Sporting News*, April 15, 1926, page 8.
75. Ralph S. Davis, "Usual Slow Start for Pirate Champs: Pitching Reaches High Standard, but Punch Isn't There," *The Sporting News*, April 22, 1926, page 3.
76. Ralph S. Davis, "Pirates Get Their Directions Mixed: World's Champs Try to Go North by Heading for South," *The Sporting News*, April 29, 1926, page 1.
77. "National League Standing on Tuesday Morning," *The Sporting News*, April 29, 1926, page 9.
78. Ralph S. Davis, "Pirate Bats Begin to Say Something: And When They Speak Up, It Is More Than a Whisper," *The Sporting News*, May 6, 1926, page 3.
79. "National League Standing on Tuesday Morning," *The Sporting News*, April 29, 1926, page 9.
80. "National League Standing on Tuesday Morning," *The Sporting News*, May 6, 1926, page 7.
81. Ralph S. Davis, "Fans Wait for Bucs to Begin Real Drive: Batting Shows Signs of Coming into Own with Bang," *The Sporting News*, May 20, 1926, page 1.
82. "Bucs Likely to Get Genewich in Trade," *The Sporting News*, May 13, 1926, page 1.

Chapter 15

1. "National League Standing on Tuesday Morning," *The Sporting News*, June 3, 1926, page 3.
2. Ralph S. Davis, "Pirate-Giant Trade? Never, So They Say: Pittsburgh Magnate Still Bears Feelings Against McGraw," *The Sporting News*, June 3, 1926, page 1.
3. *Ibid.*
4. *Ibid.*
5. "Caught on the Fly," *The Sporting News*, June 10, 1926, page 10.
6. Ralph S. Davis, "Dreyfuss Goes on His Way Rejoicing: Pirates' Bon Voyage to Their Boss Carries Fine Sentiment," *The Sporting News*, June 17, 1926, page 1.
7. *Ibid.*
8. *Ibid.*
9. *Ibid.*
10. "National League Standing on Tuesday Morning," *The Sporting News*, June 17, 1926, page 7.
11. Ralph S. Davis, "Fate of Pirates in Hands of Pitchers: Youngsters Must Come Through to Aid Wobbling Vets," *The Sporting News*, June 24, 1926, page 3.
12. Ralph S. Davis, "Pirates Feel Sure Worst Is Now Over: Bucs Have Rid Schedule of Most of Games in West," *The Sporting News*, July 1, 1926, page 3.
13. *Ibid.*
14. Ralph S. Davis, "McKechnie's Luck Is No Luck at All: Pirates Simply Can't Place Full Strength on Field," *The Sporting News*, July 15, 1926, page 3.
15. "National League Standing on Tuesday Morning," *The Sporting News*, July 8, 1926, page 7.
16. Davis, "McKechnie's Luck Is No Luck at All: Pirates Simply Can't Place Full Strength on Field," page 3.
17. Ralph S. Davis, "All Isn't So Well in Pirate Menage: Truth Is, Some of 'Em Have Been Cutting Up a Little," *The Sporting News*, July 8, 1926, page 1.

18. *Ibid.*
19. Ralph S. Davis, "They'll Be Careful Now, if Not Serious: But Why Must Big Leaguers Be Driven and Disciplined?" *The Sporting News*, July 22, 1926, page 1.
20. *Ibid.*
21. Ralph S. Davis, "McKechnie Wields an Iron Fist to Restore Champions to Order: Rigid Disciplinary Rule Being Followed," *The Sporting News*, July 29, 1926, page 1.
22. Lou Wollen, "Playing the Game with the Pirates," *The Pittsburgh Press*, July 21, 1926, page 26.
23. Davis, "McKechnie Wields an Iron Fist to Restore Champions to Order: Rigid Disciplinary Rule Being Followed," page 1.
24. "National League Standing on Tuesday Morning," *The Sporting News*, July 29, 1926, page 7.
25. Davis, "McKechnie Wields an Iron Fist to Restore Champions to Order: Rigid Disciplinary Rule Being Followed," page 1.
26. *Ibid.*
27. Ralph S. Davis, "Bucs Now Bearing More Serious Mien: Begin to Realize Flag Will Not Be Brought to Them," *The Sporting News*, August 5, 1926, page 1.
28. "National League Standing on Tuesday Morning," *The Sporting News*, August 12, 1926, page 7.
29. "National League Standing on Tuesday Morning," *The Sporting News*, August 19, 1926, page 7.
30. Ralph Davis, "Ralph Davis Says: A Pittsburgh Fan's Kick," *The Pittsburgh Press*, August 7, 1926, page 11.
31. "National League Standing on Tuesday Morning," *The Sporting News*, August 12, 1926, page 7.
32. Ralph S. Davis, "Showdown Near in Pirate Controversy: No Team Can Serve Two Managers, Says Captain Max Carey," *The Pittsburgh Press*, August 13, 1926, page 1.
33. Ralph S. Davis, "Guillotine Quickly Puts Down Pirate Anti-Clarke Rebellion: Carey's Head Falls with Two Other Vets," *The Sporting News*, August 19, 1926, page 1.
34. Davis, "Showdown Near in Pirate Controversy: No Team Can Serve Two Managers, Says Captain Max Carey," page 1.
35. *Ibid.*
36. *Ibid.*
37. *Ibid.*
38. *Ibid.*
39. *Ibid.*
40. "Carey Wages Fight in Rebellion Ouster," *The Sporting News*, August 19, 1926, page 1.
41. *Ibid.*
42. *Ibid.*
43. "Scribbled by Scribes," *The Sporting News*, August 19, 1926, page 4.
44. "Carey Wages Fight in Rebellion Ouster," page 1.
45. Davis, "Guillotine Quickly Puts Down Pirate Anti-Clarke Rebellion: Carey's Head Falls with the Two Other Vets," page 1.
46. *Ibid.*
47. *Ibid.*
48. "Carey and Adams Outstanding Figures in Baseball World," *The Pittsburgh Press*, August 13, 1926, page 1.
49. *Ibid.*
50. Ralph S. Davis, "Carey, Bigbee and Adams Expected to Tell Real Story," *The Pittsburgh Press*, August 14, 1926, page 2.
51. John B. Sheridan, "Back of the Home Plate," *The Sporting News*, August 26, 1926, page 4.
52. "What Pirate Fans Think of McKechnie, Clarke, Carey, Bigbee and Adams: Views Differ about Merits of Disputants," *The Pittsburgh Press*, August 18, 1926, page 8.
53. *Ibid.*
54. Ralph S. Davis, "Landis Tells Carey to See Heydler: Judge Passes Buck When Max Protests Pirate Dismissals," *The Pittsburgh Press*, August 16, 1926, page 1.
55. "Heydler's Statement," *The Pittsburgh Press*, August 18, 1926, page 25.
56. *Ibid.*
57. "Carey Awarded to Brooklyn: Former Pirate Uncertain of Future Course," *The Pittsburgh Press*, August 18, 1926, page 1.
58. "National League Standing on Tuesday Morning," *The Sporting News*, August 26, 1926, page 7.
59. *Ibid.*
60. "No Sentiment in Baseball — President Dreyfuss: Approves Dismissal of Trio of Veterans," *The Pittsburgh Press*, August 22, 1926, page 1.
61. *Ibid.*
62. "Dreyfuss Will Not Reopen Case of Dismissed Players: Action Stands Says President; Will See Men if They Wish," *The Pittsburgh Press*, August 31, 1926, page 1.
63. *Ibid.*
64. *Ibid.*
65. *Ibid.*
66. "Dreyfuss Has No Statement," *The Pittsburgh Press*, September 1, 1926, page 14.
67. Ralph Davis, "Ralph Davis Says: Mr. Barney Dreyfuss Grants an Interview," *The Pittsburgh Press*, September 14, 1926, page 28.
68. *Ibid.*
69. *Ibid.*

Notes — Chapter 15

70. *Ibid.*
71. *Ibid.*
72. *Ibid.*
73. Ralph S. Davis, "Clatter of Bones Haunts Pittsburgh: Fans Simply Will Not Let Up on Dismissal Incident," *The Sporting News*, September 9, 1926, page 1.
74. Ralph S. Davis, "Carey May Be Gone, but Not His Friends: Buc-Robin Series Turns Out to Be Demonstration for Max," *The Sporting News*, September 2, 1926, page 3.
75. Ralph S. Davis, "Downfall of World's Champions Ball Season's Greatest Shock: Pirates Were Expected to Maintain High Standing for Several More Seasons," *The Pittsburgh Press*, September 12, 1926, page 2.
76. Ralph S. Davis, "Murder Will Out, Even with Pirates: Misplaced Zeal Trio Does Some Talking for Press," *The Sporting News*, October 7, 1926, page 1.
77. *Ibid.*
78. Ralph Davis, "Ralph Davis Says: The Passing of Stuffy McInnis," *The Pittsburgh Press*, September 27, 1926, page 22.
79. "Scribbled by Scribes," *The Sporting News*, October 7, 1926, page 4.
80. Ralph Davis, "Ralph Davis Says: Does Fred Clarke Get the Credit," *The Pittsburgh Press*, September 2, 1926, page 28.
81. Davis, "Murder Will Out, Even with Pirates: Misplaced Zeal Trio Does Some Talking for Press," page 1.
82. "McKechnie Let Out as Manager," *The Sporting News*, October 21, 1926, page 1.
83. *Ibid.*
84. "New Pirate Manager Assured Free Rein as Fred Clarke Quits: Fans Win Fight for One-Man Leadership," *The Pittsburgh Press*, October 27, 1926, page 26.
85. Ralph S. Davis, "Dreyfuss Figures His House in Order: Resignation of Clarke Comes with Bush's Signing," *The Sporting News*, November 4, 1926, page 1.
86. "Manager Bush to Come Shortly for Conference with New Employer: Is Promised Free Hand by Dreyfuss," *The Pittsburgh Press*, October 26, 1926, page 32.
87. Ralph S. Davis, "Donie Bush at Work on Personal Staff: Release of Onslow First Move in Reorganization of Coaches," *The Sporting News*, November 25, 1926, page 7.
88. Ralph S. Davis, "Donie Bush Named to Pacify Pirates: McKechnie's Successor has Fine Record in Indianapolis " *The Sporting News*, October 28, 1926, page 1.

Bibliography

Books

Carroll, Jeff. *Sam Rice: A Biography of the Washington Senators Hall of Famer.* Jefferson, NC: McFarland, 2008.
Finoli, David, and Bill Ranier. *The Pittsburgh Pirates Encyclopedia.* Champaign, IL: Sports Publishing, 2003.
Lieb, Frederick G. *The Pittsburgh Pirates 1948.* Reprint. Carbondale: Southern Illinois University Press, 2003.
McCollister, John. *Bucs: The Story of the Pittsburgh Pirates.* Lenexa, Kansas: Addax Publishing, 1998.
Parker, Clifton Blue. *Big and Little Poison: Paul and Lloyd Waner, Baseball Brothers.* Jefferson, NC: McFarland, 2003.
Segar, Charles, ed. *75th Anniversary of the National League.* New York: Jay, 1951.

Newspapers and Periodicals

Baseball Magazine
Boston Telegram
Brooklyn Daily Eagle
The Chicago American
Chicago Daily News
Chicago Herald and Examiner
Cincinnati Post
Cleveland-Plain Dealer
Detroit News
New York Evening Post
New York Sun
Philadelphia Evening Bulletin
Philadelphia Inquirer
Philadelphia Record
Pittsburgh Chronicle-Telegraph
Pittsburgh Gazette-Times
Pittsburgh Post
The Pittsburgh Press
St. Louis Post
St. Louis Star
The Sporting News
Washington Post

Statistical Sources

www.baseball-reference.com
www.thebaseballcube.com
www.retrosheet.org

The Pittsburgh Press
The Sporting News

Informational Web Sites

www.baseball-reference.com
www.paperofrecord.com
www.sabr.org
www.worldvitalrecords.com

Index

Numbers in ***bold italics*** indicate pages with photographs.

Abbaticchio, Ed 83
Abstein, Bill 238
Adams, Charles "Babe" 12–13, 15, 24–25, 52, 57, 60, 61–62, 64, 68, 72, 74, 78, 83–85, 89, 91–94, 97, 99, 101, 105, 107–109, 113, 115–116, 120, 125, 127, 130, 135, 141, 143, 153, 177, 199, 209, 233–235, ***236***, 237–240, 242
Adams, Sparky 56, 96, 109, 133
Adams, Spencer 141, 185, 193
Aldridge, Vic "Schoolmaster" 11, 35–36, 38, 48–49, ***52***, 54, 60–61, 64, 67, 72, 75–77, 80, 84, 86, 93–94, 96, 99, 102, 104–105, 109, 111, 113, 116, 120, 122, 124–125, 127–131, 134, 136, 138, 141, 143, 147, 151, 157–158, 160–163, 165, 181–185, ***186***, 187, 196, 199, 201–202, 216, 219–220, 223, 226, 228, 230–232
Alexander, Grover Cleveland "Pete" 37, 55, 60, 80, 96, 133, 230, 244
Altenburg, Jesse 218
Altrock, Nick 151, 157, 188, 198
Amundsen, Roald 2
Arkle, Ralph 150
Asham, R.J. 172
Atlanta Crackers 30, 225
Augusta Tygers 34

Baird, Frederick C. 149
Baker, William F. 8
Baker Bowl 74, 108, 127
Ballou, Win 141, 184, 193
Baltimore Orioles 106
Bancroft, Dave 69, 106, 136
Barnes, Jesse 33, 85, 110, 138
Barnes, Virgil 18, 86, 90, 120, 124–125
Barnhart, Clyde "Pooch" 8, 12, 15, 28–29, 36, 42, 48, 53, 58–62, 66–69, 72–75, 77, 79–81, ***82***, 88–89, 91–96, 98–100,

103–107, 109–113, 116, 118, 121–128, 133–137, 141, 143, 147, 151–155, 158, 160–162, 167–170, 172, 174–176, 178–179, 181–185, 189–192, 201–204, 207, 209–210, 223, 226–228, 230
Barrett, Bob 60
Bay City Wolves 29
Beaumont, Clarence "Ginger" 47, 81, 83, 226
Becker, W.H. 147
Bell, Les 64, 135
Benton, Larry 105, 111, 127
Benton, Rube 63, 95
Bezdek, Hugo 5
Biemiller, Harry 98
Bigbee, Carson "Skeeter" 8, 12, 14, 25–26, 29, 36, 42, 44, 53, 55, 57–58, 66, 72, 75, 81, 84, 106, 112, 122, 124–125, 130, 132–133, 138, 141, 154, 171, 177, 208–210, 218, 220, 226, 228, 230, 233–235, 237–240, 242, ***243***
Birmingham Barons 26–28, 34, 121
Blake, Sheriff 56–57, 77, 80
Bloom, Congressman Sol 40
Bluege, Ossie 140–141, 151–155, 158, 160–161, 164–165, 167, 173, 181–185, 188–193, 201–204, 207
Bohne, Sammy 58
Boston Americans 5, 166
Boston Beaneaters 219
Boston Braves 16, 23, 33, 64, 68–70, 72, 78, 84–85, 105–107, 109–111, 116, 126–127, 129, 135–138, 143, 157, 227, 232, 235
Boston Red Sox 180
Bottomley, Jim 44, 64, 93, 134
Bradenton Growers 36
Bransfield, Kitty 47, 83
Braves Field 70, 126–127
Bressler, Rube 98

279

Brett, Herbert 103
Brooklyn Robins 3, 16, 18–20, 57–58, 72–74, 84, 90–92, 103–104, 108, 114–116, 122–124, 129, 135–136, 219–220, 227, 229–230, 235, 238, 241–242
Brooks, Mandy 132–133
Brotzman, W.S. 81, 150, 199
Brown, Eddie 123
Brown, Warren W. 148
Bryan, William Jennings 2
Buffalo Bisons 220
Burch, Barney 45
Burke, Congressman James F. 166
Burke, Jimmy 83
Burns, George 67
Burns, Robert L. 45
Burrus, Dick 69, 106, 111
Burton, William 123
Bush, Donie 243–244
Bush, Guy 132
Butler, Art 23

Calhoun, John C. 13
Callahan, Jimmy 5, 24
Camp, Walter 2
Campbell, Congressman Guy 180
Cantillon, Joe 23
Canton Watchmakers 23
Cantrell, Guy 136
Carey, Max "Scoops" 8, 12, 17, 20, 24, 36, 50, 53, 55, 57–62, 64–66, 68, 72–74, 77–80, 82, 84–86, **87**, 88–96, 98, 100, 104, 106, 108–109, 111–112, 114–116, 118, 120–122, 130, 132–134, 137–139, 141, 143, 146–147, 150–155, 158, 160–163, 165, 167–172, 174, 176–177, 179–185, 189–193, 196–197, 201, 203–205, **206**, 207–209, 216–217, 219–220, 223, 225–229, 231, 233–235, 237–242
Carlson, Hal 65, 84, 113, 129
Caveney, Ike 98
Cedar Rapids Rabbits 31
Chance, Frank 16
Charleston Pals 29
Chattanooga Lookouts 36
Chesbro, Jack 47, 84
Chicago Cardinals 2
Chicago Cubs 13, 15, 18, 34–38, 42–43, 45, 49, 52, 54–61, 73, 76–78, 80, 95–96, 98–99, 102–103, 109, 130–134, 136, 138, 180, 225, 228, 230
Chicago White Sox 5, 172
Chief Yellow Horse 6–7
Cincinnati Reds 13, 23, 33, 44, 48, 57–58, 62, 78, 94–96, 98, 111, 116–117, 121–122, 129, 143, 146–147, 226–227, 229–231, 233
Clarke, Annette 83

Clarke, Fred 5, 23–24, 42, 47, 61–62, 81, 83, 88–89, 95–96, **97**, 104, 110, 113, 137, 145, 149, 151, 166, 171, 179, 184–185, 189, 200, 219–221, 229–231, 233–237, 240, 242–243
Clarke, Helen 83
Clarke, Muriel 83
Clemente, Roberto 2
Cleveland Indians 140
Cobb, Ty 2, 5, 25, 34, 41, 118, 145, 151
Collins, Jimmy 145, 218
Concordia College 24–25
Concordia Missouri Lutheran Seminary 92
Coolidge, Pres. Calvin 166–167, 180, 187
Cooney, Jimmy 64
Cooney, Johnny 106, 111
Cooper, Wilbur 8–10, 13, 21, 32, 35–36, 42, 45, 54, 56, 73, 102, 132, 239
Couch, Johnny 113, 128
Coveleski, Stan 140–141, 147, 157–158, 160–165, 181–185
Cox, Dick 91
Critz, Hughie 57, 98, 121
Cronin, Joe 84
Cubs Park 55
Culloton, Bernard "Bud" 51–52, 57, 65, 75, 97, 99, 106, 113, 141, 147, 157, 217–218, 223
Cuyler, Hazen "Kiki" 3, 8, 12, 14, 16, 17, 20–21, 29, 33–34, 36, 42, 53, 55–56, 58–64, 66–69, 72, 74, 77–82, 84–96, 98–99, 104–106, 108–111, 115–116, 118, 120–125, 127–129, 132–138, **139**, 141, 145, 147, 151–155, 158, 160–163, 165–171, 174, 176–177, 179, 181–185, 187, 189–192, 201, 203–205, 207–209, **210**, 216–217, 219–220, 222–223, 226, 228, 241–243

Daubert, Jake 44
Davis, Harry 149
Davis, Secretary of Labor James J. 180
Davis, Ralph S. 45, 148, 165, 233
Day, Pea Ridge 79
Dean, Wayland 75, 118, 126
Decatur, Art 112, 127
Des Moines Demons 118, 121
Detroit Tigers 2, 5, 22, 24, 34, 118, 162
Devine, Joe 197, 217
Dickerman, Leo 78, 94, 134
Dobbs, Johnny 36
Dolan, Cozy 19–20, 38–40, 50
Donohue, Pete 57, 63, 94, 97–98, 121, 129
Dougher, Louis 146
Dreyfuss, Barney 1, 3, 5–10, 12–13, 18–23, 26, 29–31, 33–36, 38–44, 46–49, 52, 58–59, 73, 78–83, 85–86, 88–89, 92, 94–96, 107, 112–113, 116–118, 121, 126, 129, 140–141, 149, 155, 163, 166, 173, 193, 198,

Index 281

205, 218–223, 225, 229, 231, 234, 236–244
Dreyfuss, Samuel "Sammy" 3, 43, 59, 83, 95, 166, 197, 220, 223, 231, 233–238, 240–241
Duncan, Pat 27
Duncan, Rosetta 144, 151
Duncan, Viviana 144
Dunn, Jack 106
Dunn, Lt. W.A. 16
Durham Bulls 32
Dyer, Eddie 79

Eaton, Paul W. 148
Eaton, W.F. 147
Ebbets, Charles H. 57–59
Ebbets, Charles H., Jr. 58
Ebbets, Genevieve 58
Ebbets Field 19, 104, 122–123
Edwards, Henry P. 148
Ehrhardt, Rube 91, 115, 136
Eichleay, J.P. 83
Ely, Fred "Bones" 13
Enid Harvesters 34
Ens, Jewel 10–11, 43, 56, 58, 141, 198, 223
Erie Sailors 36
Evans, Billy 187, 221
Evers, Johnny 16
Exposition Park 18

Fairbanks, Douglas 226
Farrell, Eddie 89
Felix, Gus 106, 127, 137
Ferguson, Alex 141, 167–170, 189–192, 197
Fitzsimmons, Freddie 120, 125, 143
Flack, Max 93
Fogarty, Jack 200–201, 207
Fonseca, Lew 66, 82, 112–113, 128
Forbes Field 2, 13, 15–19, 25, 29, 37, 46–47, 58–60, 63–64, 66, 76, 79–84, 88, 90–92, 94, 98–99, 108, 110–118, 120, 126, 129–132, 134–136, 141–143, 146, 149–153, 155, 157–158, 162–163, 187–191, 193, 197–202, 204–205, 207–211, 226–228, 231, 234, 237–238, 240–241
Ford, Hod 103
Fordham University 51
Fournier, Jack 103–104
Fraser, Chick 33–34, 45
Freigau, Howard 133
Friberg, Bernie 112–113
Frisch, Frankie 17–20, 86, 120, 125–126
Fuchs, Judge Emil 16

Gates, Ruby L. 227
Gautreau, Doc 106, 126
Gehrig, Lou 2
Genewich, Joe 105, 227

Gibson, George 5–7, 22–24, 131
Glazner, Whitey 32
Gooch, Johnny 8, 15, 27–29, 53, 57, 66–67, 72, 79, 85, 95, 100, 103–106, **110**, 111–112, 118, 121, 123–126, 128, 130, 141, 147, 154, 173–177, 210, 230
Goslin, Goose 140–141, 147, 151–154, 158, 160–162, 167–170, 172–176, 178, 180–185, 187, 189–193, 196, 201–205, 207–208, 210, 215, 221
Gould, James M. 146–147
Gowdy, Hank 33, 88
Graham, Skinny 85
Grant, Aggie 25
Grantham, George "Boots" 35–36, 38, 42, 53–55, **56**, 61, 66, 68, 72–73, 75, 77–79, 81, 84–87, 89–96, 100, 102, 104, 107, 109, 112–113, 115–116, 118, 122, 125, 127–129, 131, 133, 136, 141, 147, 151–154, 158, 160–162, 165, 167–170, 174–179, 181, 204, 218–219, 225–227, 242
Greene, Nelson 91–92
Greene, Sam 148
Greenfield, Kent 99, 120, 125
Griffith, Clark 180, 185
Griffith, Tommy 77
Griffith Stadium 141, 163–164, 166, 169, 172, 180–181, 183, 185
Grimes, Burleigh 91, 115, 123
Grimm, Charlie 6–7, 9, 16, 35–36, 42, 45, 51, 54, 60, 73, 78, 80, 96
Groh, Heinie 18–19, 89
Gruber, John H. 146

Haas, George "Mule" 34, 53, 121, 141, 215, 225
Haines, Jesse 62, 78, 93, 108, 134
Hake, Dan 148
Hallahan, Bill 64
Hargrave, Bubbles 98
Harper, George 65, 67, 81–82, 107, 128, 139
Harris, Dave 110
Harris, Joe 141, 147, 151–155, 158, 160–163, 167–171, 173–177, 181–183, 187–189, 191–193, 196, 201–202, 204–205, 207–209, 215
Harris, Sen. John P. 95, 219
Harris, Stanley "Bucky" 107, 140–141, 147, 149–155, 158, 160–162, 167–170, 172–178, 181–185, 187–193, 196, 198, 201–205, 207–210, 213–214, **215**, 216
Hart, Bob 108, 115
Hartley, Grover 125
Hartnett, Gabby 55–57, 60–61, 80, 99
Hawks, Chicken 84
Heathcote, Cliff 56, 60, 77, 99
Hendricks, Jack 36
Henline, Butch 112–113, 221, 228

Herrmann, Garry 151
Heydler, John 8, 13, 19–20, 70, 72, 81, 83, 90, 115, 140–141, 151, 228–229, 238
Hollocher, Charlie 11
Holmes, Thomas 148
Homestead Grays 92
Hood, Abie 105
Hornsby, Rogers 17, 64, 78–79, 93, 108, 130, 219
Hoyt, Waite 33
Hubbell, Bill 92, 104, 122
Huber, Clarence 107, 112, 128
Huntzinger, Walt 90

Independence Producers 30
Indianapolis Hoosiers 23
Indianapolis Indians 36

Jackson, Travis 86, 117, 120
Jacksonville Indians 36
Jahn, Art 99, 133
Jeanes, Tex 141
Jefferies, Rev. Judson 217
Jennings, Hughie 86
Johnson, Ban 20, 40, 141, 151, 213–215
Johnson, Walter 140–141, 147, 150–155, 157, 164–165, 167, 173–176, *177*, 178–179, 187, 195–196, 198–205, 207–209, 213–215
Johnstown Johnnies 84
Jones, Percy 77
Judge, Joe 140–141, 147, 151–155, 158, 160–162, 167–170, 173–178, 181–185, 189, 191–193, 201–205, 208, 217

Kansas City Blues 8, 24, 30, 92, 123
Kaufmann, Tony 59, 95, 109, 132, 134
Kelly, Billy 33
Kelly, George 20, 75, 88–90, 100, 118, 120
Killefer, Bill 11, 35, 54, 78, 102
Kimmick, Wally 128
Kiner, Ralph 147
Klem, Bill 90, 229
Kline, Robert 150
Knight, Jack 81, 84, 139
Knox, Cliff 16, 33
Kofoed, J.C. 218
Koupal, Louis "Lou" 44–45, 51–52, 57, 60, 65, 72, 75, 92
Kremer, Ray "Whiz" 8–9, 12–13, 20–21, 29, *31*, 33, 52, 56–57, 60–61, 65, 67–68, 74, 76–78, 80, 82, 85, 91, 93–94, 96, 99, 104–105, 107, 109, 112, 114, 118, 121, 123, 126–127, 129, 132, 134–136, 138, 141, 143, 147, 167–172, 189–193, 195, 201, 204–205, 207–208, 216, 228, 230

Land, Grover 43
Landis, Commissioner Kenesaw 19–20, 38–40, 42, 81, 83, 141, 143, 151, 164, 172, 197–200, 205, 211, 219, 228, 238
Larsen, Mrs. Jack 217
Lazzeri, Tony 2
Leach, Freddie 113, 128
Leach, Tommy 47, 81, 83
Leever, Sam 47
Leibold, Nemo 141, 170, 183–184, 192
Lewis, Sgt. Ralph 172
Lewis, Walter J. 70, 133
Lindstrom, Fred 19, 75, 86
Little Rock Travelers 46, 51, 232
Lloyd, Evan 217
Loftus, Dick 92
Long, Herman 219
Los Angeles Angels 46, 51
Louisville Colonels 24, 225
Luce, Frank 8

Mack, Connie 16, 94, 107, 122, 157
Mackey, Gordon 148
Magee, May. William 61
Mails, Duster 108, 135
Mann, Les 126
Maranville, Walter "Rabbit" 6–8, *11*, 16, 30, 33, 35, 37, 42, 45, 51, 54, 61, 73, 96, 102–103, 109, 131
Marberry, Fred "Firpo" 140–141, 147, 161, 168–172, 182–183, 185, 214
Marriott, William 85
Martineck, Mike 84
Mathewson, Christy 23, 157, 166
Mazeroski, Bill 2
McAuley, Ike 77
McCarthy, Alex 25
McCarthy, Joe 230
McCormick, Barry 90, 151, 166–167, 169, 202, 204, 209–210
McCreery, Tom 42, 47, 83
McGraw, Bob 230
McGraw, John 6, 16, 18–20, 22, 32–33, 39, 53, 76, 86, 90, 116–117, 124–126, 136, 151, 180–181
McInnis, Stuffy 78, 82, 92–95, 98, 106, 110–113, 121–122, 125–126, 130–132, 134, 136, 141, 147, 150, 154, 181–185, 187, 189, 191–193, 202–205, 208, 219, 225–226, 243
McKechnie, Beatrice 142
McKechnie, Beryl 142
McKechnie, Bill 6–11, 13–15, 17–18, 20–25, 29, 32–33, 35–39, 42–58, 61–68, 70, 72–86, 88–90, 92–96, *97*, 98–102, 104–107, 109–118, 121–124, 127–129, 131–134, 136, 138, 140, 142–143, *144*, 145–146, 149–152, 154, 157–158, 160–161, 164–176, 178–182, 185, 187–189, 191, 193, 195–196, 198–199, 201–202, 204–205, 208–209,

211–213, 216–217, 220–221, 223, 225–227, 229, 231–240, 242–244
McKechnie, Jimmy 142
McKechnie, William "Billy," Jr. 142, *144*, 150, 166
McLaughlin, Peter 69, 115
McNeely, Earl 19, 141, 155, 162, 170–173, 192
McQuillan Hugh 18, 74, 88
McWeeny, Doug 230
Meadows, Lee "Specs" 15, 18, 32, 52, 56, 58, 60, 63, 65–68, 72, 74–75, 77–78, 81, 85, 88, 91, 93–95, 98, *103*, 105, 107, 109–112, 117–118, 121, 123–124, 126, 128, 130, 132, 134, 136, 138, 141, 146–147, 151–155, 157, 196, 201, 204, 209, 228, 230
Memphis Chickasaws 36, 46
Meusel, Irish 19, 75, 88, 117, 120
Minneapolis Millers 23
Miss Reineman 217
Mitchell, Clarence 66, 82, 107, 113
Montague, Eddie 84
Moore, Eddie 8, 12, 14, 20, 29–30, 33, 42–43, 51–53, 55, 57, 58–68, 74, 77–80, 84–86, 88–89, 91–95, 98–100, 105–107, 110–112, 114–116, 118, 121–124, 126–130, *131*, 136, 138, 141, 147, 151–154, 158, 160–163, 167–169, 171, 173–177, 179, 181–184, 188–193, *194*, 195, 197, 201–205, 207–210, 217–218, 222, 225–232, 242
Moran, Charlie 108, 117, 137
Moriarty, George 151, 169, 177, 190, 197
Morrison, Johnny 27, 29, 32, 38, 50–52, 56–57, 59, 61–63, 66, 69, 74, 76–77, 79, 82, 85, 89, 93–95, 97, 100, 105–106, 108–113, 115–116, 118, *119*, 122, 125, 129–130, 134–135, 138, 141, 143, 147, 154, 174–175, 177, 196, 199, 201–205, 216–217, 222, 226, 229–230, 232
Morrison, Phil 232
Murray, Billy 83
Murray, J.C. 217
Myer, Buddy 141, 161–162, 167–170, 173–177

Nashville Volunteers 28–29
Nehf, Art 18, 90
Nelly, Harry 197
Nesbit, Harrison 83
New York Giants 1, 6, 16–23, 32–33, 40, 53, 69, 74–76, 80, 84–90, 95–96, 98–100, 102, 105, 107–109, 114, 116–118, 120–122, 124–127, 129, 132, 134–136, 138–143, 147, 164, 180, 214–215, 228, 231
New York Yankees 6, 167, 215
Newark Peppers 23
Nichols, Chester 230
Niehaus, Al 35–36, 38, 42, 44–45, 51–54, 56, 59, 61–62, 64, 66–68, 77–78, 84, 111

Nirella, Danny 59, 151, 198, 200, 211
Northern Arizona University 36
Notre Dame University 80
Nugent, John F. 220

Oakland Oaks 32
O'Connell, Jimmy 18–20, 38–40, 50
O'Connor, Jack 47
O'Connor, Leslie 83
O'Day, Hank 117, 120
O'Farrell, Bob 94
Ogden, Jack 33
Oklahoma City Indians 31, 34, 46, 92
Oldham, John "Red" 118, 121, 123, 125, 131–132, 134, 136, 141, 143, 161, 168–169, 196, 198–199, 209–210, 215
Omaha Buffaloes 30, 34, 36, 42–43, 45
O'Neal, Skinny 128
O'Neil, Mickey 137
Onslow, Jack 43, 146, 215, 223, 229
Osborne, Tiny 91, 104, 136
O'Toole, Marty 238
Owens, Brick 151, 158, 169, 192

Packard, Dr. N. 157
Padgett, Ernie 64
Peckinpaugh, Roger 140–141, 147, 151–155, 158, 160–162, 167–171, 173–177, 180–184, 187, 189–192, 196–197, 201–205, 207–208, 216
Petty, Jesse 91–92
Pfeffer, Jeff 44
Pfirman, Cy 115
Philadelphia Athletics 107, 122, 132, 140–141, 147, 157
Philadelphia Phillies 8, 16, 20, 32–33, 39, 47, 50, 65–68, 80–84, 96, 107–108, 111–113, 116, 127–129, 135, 138–140, 221, 228, 233
Phillippe, Deacon 42, 47, 83–84, 199
Pickford, Mary 226
Pierce, Ray 128–129
Pinchot, Gov. Gifford 151
Pinelli, Babe 58, 98
Pitt Stadium 155
Pittenger, Clark 103
Pittsburgh Pirates 1–2, 5–6, 8–14, 16–20, 22, 23–35, 37–40, 42–70, 72–118, 120–155, 157–158, 160–176, 178–185, 187–193, 195–205, 207–223, *224*, 225–244
Pittsfield Hillies 34
Pollard, Charley 199
Polo Grounds 18–19, 74, 76, 85, 99, 121, 124–125
Portland Beavers 36
Portsmouth Truckers 26
Pottsville (PA) Maroons 2
Pratt, Al 83

284   Index

Pulliam, Harry C. 107
Putnam, George A. 197

Queen, C.J. 222
Quigley, Ernie 117

Rawlings, Johnny 32–33, 44, 53, 66, 68, 85–88, 95, 122–128, 130–131, 141, 150, 217, 231
Redland Field 13, 57, 146
Reese, John "Bonesetter" 12–13, 172
Reinhart, Art 130, 135
Rhem, Flint 62, 92–93
Rhyne, Harold "Hal" 197, 217–218, 220, 222, 227–229
Rice, Sam 140–141, 147, 151–155, 158, 160–163, 167–170, *171*, 172–178, 181–185, 187, 189–192, 201–202, 204–205, 208, 210, 215
Richmond Colts 43
Rickey, Branch 2
Rigler, Cy 69, 151, 169, 171–172, 189
Ring, Jimmy 8, 67, 107, 112, 139
Ritchey, Claude 47, 83, 178
Rixey, Eppa 58, 98, 122
Robert, Harry C. 147
Robinson, Wilbert 92, 244
Rochester Hustlers 33
Roush, Edd 23, 57, 63, 94, 121
Ruel, Muddy 19, 140–141, 147, 151–154, 158, 160–162, 168–169, 171–178, 182–183, 189, 193, 197, 201–205, 207, 209, 215
Ruether, Dutch 140–141, 147, 158, 162, 183, 189, 214
Runyan, Damon 187
Russell, Allen 141
Ruth, Babe 2, 5, 41, 151, 175
Ryan, Rosy 105

Sacramento-Mission Wolves 31
St. Louis Browns 140
St. Louis Cardinals 5, 24, 32, 44, 61–64, 66, 77–79, 92–94, 108–109, 116, 129–130, 134–136, 139, 219, 226–227, 230–231, 233, 238–239
St. Paul Saints 23
St. Petersburg Saints 30
Sand, Heinie 20, 39, 50, 65–66, 82, 113
San Francisco Seals 46, 51, 197, 217–218, 222, 225, 227
Schacht, Al 151, 157, 188, 198
Schmidt, Walter 9, 15, 34, 44–45
Scopes, John Thomas 2
Scott, Everett 141
Scott, Jack 74, 89–90, 117, 125, 143
Severeid, Hank 141, 189–192
Sheehan, Tom 78, 80, 85, 94, 96, 99–100, 109, 111, 113, 116, 120, 127, 130, 134–135, 140–141, 150, 169, 209

Sherdel, Bill 93, 129
Sheridan, John B. 237
Shinners, Ralph 64
Siemer, Oscar 106, 111
Smith, Bob 126–127
Smith, Chester L. 242
Smith, Earl "Oil" 16, 33, 44, 53, 55–56, 59–60, 62, 64–67, 69–70, *71*, 72–73, 77, 79, 86, 91–93, 95–96, 105–106, 112–114, 116, 118, 128–129, 136–137, 141, 143, 147, 151–154, 158, 160–162, 167–173, 179, 181–185, 189–193, 202–205, 207–210, 221, 223, 226
Smith, Jack 93
Snyder, Frank 89
Songer, Don 34, 51–52, 57, 60, 65, 72, 92
Sothoron, Alan 79
South Bend Bronchos 25
Southworth, Billy 88, 90, 117
Spencer, Roy 34, 45, 53, 109, 115, 141, 223
Sportsman's Park 92, 134, 226
Stargell, Willie 2, 147
Statz, Jigger 57, 60
Steinfeldt, Harry 16
Stock, Milt 92, 104
Stockton, J. Roy 147
Stone, Arnold 42
Stowe, Harriet Beecher 144
Stuart, Johnny 14, 92–93
Swope, Tom 147

Tacoma Tigers 25, 36
Talladega Tigers 28
Tannehill, Jesse 47, 84
Tate, Bennie 141
Taylor, Zack 103–104
Terry, Bill 74–75, 86, 88, 90, 118, 120, 228
Thompson, Jack 217
Thompson, Lafayette "Fresco" 42–43, 51, 53, 123, 130–132, 141, 215, 220
Tierney, James "Cotton" 6, 32, 123
Tinker, Joe 16
Toledo Iron Men 33
Torporcer, George "Specs" 93
Traynor, Harold "Pie" 8, 14–16, *26*, 27–29, 39, 50, 53, 55–56, 58–59, 61–62, 66–68, 72–75, 78–80, 82, 84–85, 88–89, 91–92, 94–96, 98–100, 103–105, 108–113, 115–116, 118, 120, 122–131, 133–134, 136–139, 141, 143, 145, 147, 151–155, *156*, 158, 160–162, 167–172, 174–179, 181–185, 187, 190–193, 196, 202–205, 207–208, 216–217, 219–220, 222–223, 226, 230, 233, 235
Trees, J.C. 95, 219

University of Missouri 30
University of Oregon 25

University of Pennsylvania 89
University of Pittsburgh 155

Vance, Dazzy 18, 72, 91, 104, 114, 123
Vancouver Beavers 31
Veach, Bobby 141, 162, 183, 193
Veeck, William "Bill" 35, 102
Vernon Tigers 46, 51
Victoria Bees 33
Vila, Joe 147

Wagner, Honus 2, 14, 42, 47, 83–84, 113, 137, 145, 151, 188
Walker, Curt 57
Wallace, Frank 240–241
Waner, Lloyd 227
Waner, Paul 197, 217–218, 222, 226–228
Ward, Joe 147
Warner, George 103
Warwick, Bill 135
Washington and Jefferson University 23
Washington Senators 2, 19–20, 40, 98–99, 107, 122, 132, 140–141, 145–155, 157–158, 160–185, 187–193, 195–198, 200–205, 207–209, 213–216, 219, 221, 228, 230
Watson, Mule 33
Watters, Sam 59, 166, 215, 238
Weis, Arthur "Butch" 96
Welsh, Jimmy 106, 126–127, 138
Welsh, Regis M. 147
Wertz, Johnny 235
Wheat, Zack 17, 74, 103–104, 124

Wheeler, Eddie 25
Wheeling Stogies 23
Whitted, George "Possum" 6
Williamsport Billies 34
Wilson, Hack 74–75
Wilson, Jimmie 84, 112, 221
Wisner, Jack 126
Wright, Glenn "Buckshot" 8–9, 12–14, 16–17, 20–21, 29–30, 33, 50, 53, 55–64, **65**, 66–68, 72–75, 77–80, 84, 86, 90–96, 98, 100, 104–106, 108–112, 115, 113, 120, 125, 127–129, 132–135, 137–141, 145, 147, 151–155, 158, **159**, 160–163, 165, 167–171, 174–179, 181–185, 187, 189–193, 196, 202–205, 208, 216, 219–220, 223, 226–227, 230–231, 233, 241, 244
Wrightstone, Russ 82, 113, 129

Yde, Emil 8, 12, 15–16, **20**, 21, 29, 31–34, 36, 39–40, 52, 55, 58, 60, 63–64, 68, 72, 75–76, 79, 84–85, 90, 93, 95, 98, 100, 104–106, 108–109, 111, 113, 115, 118, 120, 122, 126–128, 130, 133, 135, 140–141, 147, 158, 160–161, 173–175, 179, 196, 208–209, 230–232
Young, Cy 157
Young, Frank H. 148
Youngs, Ross 20, 75, 88, 117–118, 120, 125

Zachary, Tom 140–141, 147, 182–185, 214
Zimmer, Chief 47, 81, 83

www.ingramcontent.com/pod-product-compliance
Ingram Content Group UK Ltd.
Pitfield, Milton Keynes, MK11 3LW, UK
UKHW041928140426
5217IPUK00014B/366